YACOV Y. HAIMES
Risk Modeling, Assessment, and Manage

DENNIS M. BUEDE
The Engineering Design of Systems: Mod

ANDREW P. SAGE and JAMES E. ARMSTR
Introduction to Systems Engineering

WILLIAM B. ROUSE
Essential Challenges of Strategic Management

YEFIM FASSER and DONALD BRETTNER
Management for Quality in High-Technology Enterprises

THOMAS B. SHERIDAN
Humans and Automation: System Design and Research Issues

ALEXANDER KOSSIAKOFF and WILLIAM N. SWEET
Systems Engineering Principles and Practice

HAROLD R. BOOHER
Handbook of Human Systems Integration

JEFFREY T. POLLOCK AND RALPH HODGSON
Adaptive Information: Improving Business Through Semantic Interoperability, Grid Computing, and Enterprise Integration

ALAN L. PORTER AND SCOTT W. CUNNINGHAM
Tech Mining: Exploiting New Technologies for Competitive Advantage

REX BROWN
Rational Choice and Judgment: Decision Analysis for the Decider

WILLIAM B. ROUSE AND KENNETH R. BOFF (editors)
Organizational Simulation

HOWARD EISNER
Managing Complex Systems: Thinking Outside the Box

STEVE BELL
Lean Enterprise Systems: Using IT for Continuous Improvement

J. JERRY KAUFMAN AND ROY WOODHEAD
Stimulating Innovation in Products and Services: With Function Analysis and Mapping

WILLIAM B. ROUSE
Enterprise Tranformation: Understanding and Enabling Fundamental Change

JOHN E. GIBSON, WILLIAM T. SCHERER, AND WILLAM F. GIBSON
How to Do Systems Analysis

WILLIAM F. CHRISTOPHER
Holistic Management: Managing What Matters for Company Success

WILLIAM B. ROUSE
People and Organizations: Explorations of Human-Centered Design

HOW TO DO SYSTEMS ANALYSIS

THE WILEY BICENTENNIAL–KNOWLEDGE FOR GENERATIONS

$\mathcal{E}$ach generation has its unique needs and aspirations. When Charles Wiley first opened his small printing shop in lower Manhattan in 1807, it was a generation of boundless potential searching for an identity. And we were there, helping to define a new American literary tradition. Over half a century later, in the midst of the Second Industrial Revolution, it was a generation focused on building the future. Once again, we were there, supplying the critical scientific, technical, and engineering knowledge that helped frame the world. Throughout the 20th Century, and into the new millennium, nations began to reach out beyond their own borders and a new international community was born. Wiley was there, expanding its operations around the world to enable a global exchange of ideas, opinions, and know-how.

For 200 years, Wiley has been an integral part of each generation's journey, enabling the flow of information and understanding necessary to meet their needs and fulfill their aspirations. Today, bold new technologies are changing the way we live and learn. Wiley will be there, providing you the must-have knowledge you need to imagine new worlds, new possibilities, and new opportunities.

Generations come and go, but you can always count on Wiley to provide you the knowledge you need, when and where you need it!

WILLIAM J. PESCE
PRESIDENT AND CHIEF EXECUTIVE OFFICER

PETER BOOTH WILEY
CHAIRMAN OF THE BOARD

HOW TO DO SYSTEMS ANALYSIS

JOHN E. GIBSON
WILLIAM T. SCHERER
School of Engineering and Applied Science
Department of Systems and Information Engineering
University of Virginia

WILLIAM F. GIBSON

BICENTENNIAL
1807
WILEY
2007
BICENTENNIAL

Wiley-Interscience
A JOHN WILEY & SONS, INC., PUBLICATION

For general information on our other products and services or for technical support, please contact our
Customer Care Department within the United States at (800) 762–2974, outside the United States at
(317) 572–3993 or fax (317) 572–4002.

Wiley also publishes its books in a variety of electronic formats. Some content that appears in print may
not be available in electronic formats. For more information about Wiley products, visit our web site at
www.wiley.com.

Library of Congress Cataloging-in-Publication Data:

Gibson, John E.
How to do systems analysis / by John E. Gibson, William T. Scherer, and William F. Gibson.
        p. cm.
    Includes index.
    ISBN 978-0-470-00765-5 (cloth)
    1. System analysis.   I. Scherer, William T.   II. Title.
    T57.6.G543 2007
    658.4′032 – dc22

                                                          2006033568

Printed in the United States of America.

10 9 8 7 6 5 4 3 2

Contents

Preface

There is significant front matter in this book, but as I hope we make it clear in the text, the contextual integrity is critical! Following this introduction are a personal note from me, a note from Jack's son, Will Gibson, a perspective of a former student of Jack and me, Scott Ferber, and, finally, Jack's original preface.

The unique approach in this book is to motivate systems thinking, or as we like to say: "See the world with new eyes—that of a systems thinker." Throughout the book are examples, from the past and from today's pressing issues, which illustrate these concepts, along with case studies to give the reader exposure to the practice of systems analysis and systems engineering. The resulting book is appropriate for numerous fields and professionals that need input from systems engineering, including anyone working in the analysis of complex systems, such as in business consulting, health care, telecommunications, and so on.

I believe that the present books in the area of Systems Analysis and Systems Engineering are excellent; however, many fail to emphasize the art of systems problem solving (systems analysis) by focusing instead on operations research methods (mathematical models such as linear programming) or on the formal Systems Engineering processes (as stressed by INCOSE: The International Council on Systems Engineering). This book focuses on systems analysis, broadly defined also to include problem formulation and interpretation of proposed alternatives in terms of the value systems of stakeholders. Therefore, this book is a *complement*, not a substitute, to the other "traditional" books when teaching systems engineering and systems analysis. However, the nature of problem-solving discussed in this book is appropriate to a wide range of systems analyses. Thus the book can be used as a stand-alone book for teaching the analysis of systems.

Numerous other books describe the processes of systems engineering, including systems engineering handbooks developed by NASA, DOD, Boeing, and so on.

Currently, there is also considerable discussion on the concept of system-of-systems (S.O.S.)—that is, systems that are of significant complexity and order that they require methodologies beyond the classic systems methodologies that are all basically derivatives of MIL-499B, a classic systems engineering military standard. The emphasis of this book, however, is not on the formal process of systems engineering eloquently described in the footnoted books, but on the systems analysis component and the associated thought processes.

The design of this book is such that it can be used at different educational levels. Undergraduates, for example, focus on the basic problem-solving ideas, and the expected depth in their analyses and cases would be significantly less than expected from graduate students. How the book is used—that is, as a primary text or supplemental/complementary text—also depends on the student level. My experiences in using the draft at both levels has shown that experienced students (such as our Accelerated Master's Degrees students—working professionals in an executive format degree program) clearly understand (from their experiences) the issues addressed in the book and can relate the material directly to their work experiences, especially from what I call the systemic perspective; thus, for them the book is a required and a primary source. Undergraduates, typically without the benefit of significant work experience, see the value in a general problem-solving method that applies to many situations, with more focus on the systematic aspects of the material. For them we use the book as supplemental.

Fundamentally, I see two worlds typical in systems engineering (both are necessary!):

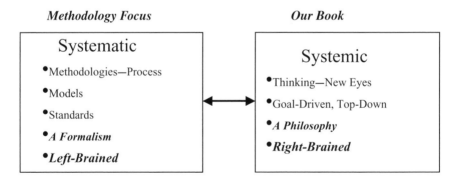

By systemic, we mean affecting the entire system or holistic.* By systematic, we mean a formal step-by-step process (in the most direct form, computer code is an

---

* A wide-reaching term, designating views in which the individual elements of a system are determined by their relations to all other elements of that system. Being highly relational, holistic theories do not see the sum of the parts as adding up to the whole. In addition to the individual parts of a system, there are "emergent," or "arising," properties that add to or transform the individual parts. As such, holistic theories claim that no element of a system can exist apart from the system in which it is a part. Holistic theories can be found in philosophical, religious, social, or scientific doctrines. [*source*: Public Broadcasting Systems.]

example). This book makes a unique contribution by addressing the right-hand side, the systemic side. An analogy could be made to the left-brain (logical; often engineers) and right-brain (artistic) thinkers. The book focuses on problem definition, which is in my opinion a very difficult part of the systems process and an often neglected (or failed) part in practice (and books).

So, we have *How to Do Systems Analysis*. This book is not intended to be an instructional guide to systems engineering (such as practiced in industry or government), but a book that engages one in beginning or enhancing their journey toward becoming a systems thinker—a requisite skill for systems engineers and all problem solvers. *Trends come and go, but quality Systems Analysis thinking abides.* Throughout the book are pointers and references to excellent books and articles that provide detailed techniques, research, and think pieces on the disparate aspects of systems analysis. I have deliberately left much of Jack's original material alone. I feel strongly that there is considerable wisdom in these words and that this wisdom is timeless. Unfortunately, systems thinking and good systems engineering remain elusive, as evidenced by the recent (summer 2006) experiences with the Big Dig in Boston. Many of Jack's examples and experiences, some dating to the 1950s, add considerable insight into the realm of systems thinking. I have been using draft parts of this book since taking over Jack's graduate course, *Introduction to Systems Engineering*, in 1992. The material has uniformly received excellent reviews from students for its unique perspective on problem solving in all types of domains. It is particularly relevant for students with some professional experience who appreciate its practical and accessible concepts.

How would I read this book? Top-down of course. I would start with reading Chapter 10 completely, followed by Chapter 1, then reading the first several pages of Chapters 2–9. Next would be Chapters 2–4. Finally, the remaining portions of Chapters 5–9. For undergraduate students, Chapters 2–4 form the core concepts of a general systems analysis methodology. Chapter 10 is in effect an executive summary of systems analysis and can basically stand on its own.

I encourage you engage in and enjoy the material.

WILLIAM T. SCHERER

Charlottesville, Virginia
March 2007

A Personal Note from William T. Scherer

He stormed into the room, a large man with a commanding presence with a shock of white hair—the Dean of The School of Engineering and Applied Science at The University of Virginia. Twenty or so of us—all undergraduate transfer students—sat-up at attention and dare not speak while the Dean greeted us, told us we were joining a select group of students, and then gave us a strong challenge and charge to be the best. That was my first meeting with Jack in 1978 as a third-year (junior) transfer student to the new Department of Systems Engineering at UVa. My second meeting did not go as well. Ten of us (rising fourth years) had been selected to a summer research program and were called by the Dean to attend an early morning meeting during the summer program. Unfortunately, being undergraduates and students, the morning hours were not our best or favorite. None of the 10 students made it to the meeting with the Dean. Following an informative letter, a second meeting was arranged and the attendance was perfect. Our lecture from the Dean on being a professional, an adult, responsible, and so on, was, to say the least, not in the current collaborative style of lecturing that many of us employ. My third interaction was not even as good as the second. During my graduate studies I started a course with Jack on *Management for Engineers*, and in the second class I challenged Jack on the lack of exact specifications in the homework assignment and the rampant ambiguity. I was informed, in a fairly rigorous Type A manner, about my being a typical bottom-up engineer who was incapable of handling the inherent ambiguity in any real-world, open-ended problem, a skill required in systems engineering. After a brief but spirited conversation, I was invited to leave the class. That was 1981 and I had begun my systems training through some hard lessons. By the late 1980s I was a colleague of Jack's in the Systems Department, and, more importantly, I had finally figured it out and was beginning to think like a systems engineer. For the last several years of Jack's life I was able to share numerous conversations with him and also work on several projects with his consulting business.

Through these interactions I began the continuing, but never-ending, journey toward being a systemic thinker. Most enjoyable, since my office was next to his, was when he would storm in with a new idea or a frustration over some mind-numbing, anti-systems activity going on at the University or elsewhere. My varied interactions with Jack contributed significantly to my growth as a "systems" professional.

WILLIAM T. SCHERER

Charlottesville, Virginia
March 2007

A Personal Note from William F. Gibson

At the time of his death in August 1991, my father was completing *How to Do Systems Analysis*. He was looking forward to using this text in his undergraduate- and graduate-level classes in the Systems Engineering Department at the University of Virginia. He was doing what he enjoyed most—-imparting his insight and knowledge to a group of inquisitive minds.

Jack Gibson spent his life as a student and an educator. He was a student of life; for an engineer, he was unparalleled in his voracious quest for information about those disciplines not normally associated with "hard sciences." He was an educator; he chose a career that was not as rewarding in a monetary sense (although he provided well for his family). No, my dad's rewards were paid in the responsiveness that he saw in the eyes of his students, fellow academicians, and clients, to new ideas. Jack constantly challenged people to do better, to think more deeply, and to articulate more clearly.

How to Do Systems Analysis is the last of Jack's "nontraditional" engineering education texts. He recognized that the end product of a university classroom is to educate students in the engineering disciplines so that they could get a job upon graduation. He wanted their course material to be relevant; he wanted examples to be topical. Those students learned that the business world is nonlinear, has no "correct answers," and is filled with managers who make tremendous demands with deadlines that are impossible to meet. This book is designed to reinforce that perspective.

I enjoyed editing the last 10 of my father's books. I used to spend my spare time in college and graduate school correcting syntax and grammar. When I finally started working, I began to understand the concepts that Jack tried to communicate to students; I was able to provide salient examples that Jack used in his books. This text is more special, however. This is the last one. Perhaps I delayed in completing this one because it was the last opportunity that Jack was able to use to speak to me.

I hope that you can share in his insights, learn from his experiences, and apply the lessons to your own benefit.

I need to thank a number of people who either assisted in the production of this text or kept driving me to complete it. First are Jack's colleagues and students. Among the former are Drs. Julia Pet-Edwards and Manuel Rossetti and Maj. Richard Metro, for their continuing interest and desire in the subject matter and requests to use the textbook at their universities. Especially among the latter is Jennifer Tyler, who was my dad's last graduate assistant. Jennifer helped tremendously, in 1992 and 1993, in my revisions to the text.

Finally, are my wife, Hilary Wechsler Gibson, and my Dad. They never had the chance to meet; I know that they would have enjoyed each other immensely. Hilary kept pushing me to my desk, so I would complete this work. To my Dad, all I can say is "Thank you." As with all his previous books, I know that my Dad would dedicate the book to his wife, my mom. So, this book is dedicated . . . To Nancy.

WILLIAM F. GIBSON

New York, New York
March 2007

A Personal Note from Scott F. Ferber

How to Do Systems Analysis = *How to Solve Problems.* I attended the University of Virginia to study Systems Engineering under Jack Gibson and Bill Scherer so that I could learn how to solve problems, any type of problem. Their program was unique in that it focused on problem-solving for all disciplines rather than one discipline.

This book epitomizes the philosophy that attracted me to their department. Whenever confronted with a challenge, I apply the exact approach as outlined in this book. *How to Do Systems Analysis* has guided me through countless academic, business, and personal opportunities since I took Jack's class based on this book in 1990. For example, I am applying the Systems methodology today on a multitude of issues, ranging from career moves to planning my 4-year-old son's birthday party.

To learn how to solve problems is to learn how to do systems analysis. Everyone can benefit from improved problem-solving; hence, this book is for people from all disciplines and all walks of life. Thank you Jack, Will, and Bill for bringing to fruition the greatest insights I have ever learned. I promise not to forget what you taught me, to always use it, and to use it for good.

SCOTT F. FERBER

Original Preface from Jack Gibson

There appear to be three generic points of view one may take in writing a textbook. These are . . . the *problem-centered* viewpoint, the *technique-centered* viewpoint, and the *reader-centered* viewpoint. Of course, it is also possible to write a book with no consistent point of view at all, one probably need not add. The problem-centered view is not common in general texts but is an acceptable approach for advanced texts on focused, narrow topics. My text *Designing the New City*, Wiley, 1977, was written from this perspective. However, if the author has an introductory, general purpose in mind, this approach leads to difficulties. In such a situation, problem-centering usually leads to a book of recipes. That is, the author is led to saying for a series of instances, "given this problem, here is how to handle it." One becomes bogged down in specifics, and it is difficult to achieve a general perspective of the topic. This is a severe limitation in itself, and, furthermore, it is unappealing to the academic mind.

The technique-centered approach is more common in basic introductory texts. Generally speaking, technique-centered texts typically provide a chapter or two of introduction and then launch into a survey of the main topics and techniques in the field. It is assumed that the reader will be able to select the appropriate tools to solve his or her specific problem. If one is faced with a problem similar to the type of problems used to illustrate the technique under discussion in the text, this is a good approach. But what it gains in general perspective and an overall viewpoint, it may lose in usefulness in applicability. The technique-centered approach seems to be popular with academics, since we generally have a mind bent that seeks general understanding and we are less interested in problem-solving and specifics. I have written several texts with this perspective, among them being *Introduction to Engineering Design*, Holt, Rinehart & Winston, 1968, and *Nonlinear Automatic Control*, McGraw-Hill, 1963.

The reader-centered point of view has initial appeal as a guide to the perplexed, but in practice it sometimes descends to pontification and anecdotal generalities—that is, retailing of old and possibly irrelevant personal "war stories." This approach assumes a common starting point for its readers, and, as in the present text, this starting point is usually an assumption of a reader's unfamiliarity with the topic. *Scientific American* magazine practices this approach in a masterly way. The first paragraph or two of each of its articles is couched at a simple, obvious level and then acceleration is smooth and gradual.

For better or worse, the reader-centered approach is the one taken in this text. I will assume you are a systems analyst faced with a problem situation. We will go through a step-by-step approach to the application of the systems approach to the situation, using techniques as the need arises. We will not focus on the details of the analytic techniques to be used; it is assumed that you will learn the details of these (mostly mathematical) techniques elsewhere. From the present text, I hope you will learn just what "systems analysis" (SA) is and what the "systems approach" means. You will see from examining the cases, which are based on actual practice, how the need for mathematical techniques develops and how to apply them. Moreover, I hope that you will develop a sense of the pitfalls and difficulties in practicing SA. This is a tall order, especially for readers without professional work experience.

Unless you are able to provide a "reality check" from your own work experience, you may be tempted to accept the suggestions herein for analyzing problems as simple and obvious. In reality they are neither, but unlike advanced mathematics, which is obviously difficult going in, SA appears almost trivial on first observation. We will discuss this trap as we go on.

JACK GIBSON

Ivy, Virginia
January 1991

Acknowledgments

Many people have contributed to this book, but first and foremost is John Egan Gibson, one of the most intelligent and insightful people I have met and a true systems thinker. Many graduate students and faculty have provided insights and wisdom for the book. Drew Talarico provided considerable assistance in editing, fact checking, formatting, and proofreading. Finally, I'd like to acknowledge the considerable support and love from my wife, Amy, and my "Goddess Trio" of daughters: Kendall, Merritt, and Linden.

W.T.S.

This book is the culmination of the work of many individuals. The primary is John Egan Gibson. Over the years, I continue to be pleasantly surprised by the comments I receive from his students, colleagues, clients, and friends. His seminal ideas and insights continue to provide the framework by which individuals and groups analyze problems. Many of Jack's former graduate students, and faculty members provided valuable comments and perspectives on this work. Additionally, during my many hours at my computer and on the phone, when I was editing and managing the process of getting this text into print, I could not have completed my work without the help of two very important people. This book would not be in your hands without the love and support of my wife, Hilary Wechsler Gibson, and our son Teddy.

W.F.G.

Chapter **1**

Introduction

sys·tem (sĭs′təm) *n.*

1. A group of interacting, interrelated, or interdependent elements forming a complex whole.
2. A functionally related group of elements, especially:
   a. The human body regarded as a functional physiological unit.
   b. An organism as a whole, especially with regard to its vital processes or functions.
   c. A group of physiologically or anatomically complementary organs or parts: *the nervous system; the skeletal system.*
   d. A group of interacting mechanical or electrical components.
   e. A network of structures and channels, as for communication, travel, or distribution.
   f. A network of related computer software, hardware, and data transmission devices.
3. An organized set of interrelated ideas or principles.
4. A social, economic, or political organizational form.
5. A naturally occurring group of objects or phenomena: *the solar system.*
6. A set of objects or phenomena grouped together for classification or analysis.
7. A condition of harmonious, orderly interaction.

8. An organized and coordinated method; a procedure.
9. The prevailing social order; the establishment. Used with: *You can't beat the system.*

[Late Latin systēma, systēmat-, from Greek sustēma, from sunistanai, to combine : sun-, syn- + histanai, set up, establish.]
Source: Answers.com: American Heritage

> In the systems approach, concentration is on the analysis and design of the whole, as distinct from . . . the components or parts . . . The systems approach relates the technology to the need, the social to the technological aspects; it starts by insisting on a clear understanding of exactly what the problem is and the goal that should dominate the solution and lead to the criteria for evaluating alternative avenues . . . The systems approach is the application of logic and common sense on a sophisticated technological basis . . . It provides for simulation and modeling so as to make possible predicting the performance before the entire system is brought into being. And it makes feasible the selection of the best approach from the many alternatives.
>
> Simon Ramo, *Cure for Chaos*, pp. 11, 12

1.1 WHAT IS A SYSTEM?

A system is a set of elements so interconnected as to aid in driving toward a defined goal. There are three operative parts to this short definition. First is the existence of a set of elements—that is, a group of objects with some characteristics in common. All the passengers who have flown in a Boeing 777 or all the books written on systems engineering form a set, but mere membership in a definable set is not sufficient to form a system according to our definition. Second, the objects must be interconnected or influence one another. The members of a football team then would qualify as a system because each individual's performance influences the other members.

Finally, the interconnected elements must have been formed to achieve some defined goal or objective. A random collection of people or things, even if they are in close proximity and thus influence each other in some sense, would not for this reason form a meaningful system. A football team meets this third condition of purposefulness, because it seeks a common goal. While these three components of our working definition fit within American Heritage's definitions, we should note that we are restricting our attention to "goal-directed" or purposeful systems, and thus our use of the term is narrower than a layman's intuition might indicate.[1]

It must be possible to estimate how well a system is doing in its drive toward the goal, or how closely one design option or another approaches the ideal—that is, more or less closely achieves the goal. We call this measure of progress or achievement the *Index of Performance (IP)* (alternatively, *Measures of Effectiveness [MOE], Performance Measures [PM], etc.*). Proper choice of an Index of Performance is crucial in successful system design. A measurable and meaningful measure of performance is simple enough in concept, although one sometimes has difficulty in conveying its importance to a client. It may be complex in practice, however, to establish an index that is both measurable and meaningful. The temptation is to count what can be counted if what really matters seems indefinable. Much justifiable criticism has been directed at system analysts in this regard. (Hoos, 1972). The Index of Performance concept is discussed in detail in Section 2.3.

Our definition of a system permits components, or the entire system in fact, to be of living form. The complexity of biological systems and social systems is such that complete mathematical descriptions are difficult, or impossible, with our present state of knowledge. We must content ourselves in such a situation with statistical or qualitative descriptions of the influence of elements one on another, rather than complete analytic and explicit functional relationships. This presents obvious objective obstacles, as well as more subtle subjective difficulties. It requires maturity by the system team members to work across disciplinary boundaries toward a common goal when their disciplinary methodologies are different not only in detail but in kind.

From these efforts at definition, we are forced to conclude that the words "system," "subsystem," and "parameter" do not have an objective meaning, independent of context. The electric utility of a region, for example, could be a system, or a subsystem, or could establish the value of a parameter depending on the observer's point of view of the situation. An engineer for the Detroit Edison Company could think of his electric utility as a system. Yet, he would readily admit that it is a subsystem in the Michigan Electric Coordinated System (MECS), which in turn is connected to the power pool covering the northeastern portion of the United States and eastern Canada. On the other hand, the city planner can ignore the system aspect of Detroit Edison and think of it merely supplying energy at a certain dollar cost. This is so if it is reasonable for him to assume that electricity can be provided in any reasonable amount to any point within the region. In this sense, the cost of electricity is a regional parameter. The massive Northeast U.S. power failure in 2003, along with the resulting repercussions directly affecting over 50 million people, clearly illustrates the regional nature of these systems.

That the function of an object and its relationship to neighboring objects depends on the observer's viewpoint must not be considered unusual. Koestler, for example, argues persuasively that this is true for <u>all</u> organisms as well as social organizations. For these units, which we have called "systems," he coins the term "holon."

But "wholes" and "parts" in this absolute sense just do not exist anywhere, either in the domain of living organisms or of social organizations. What we find are intermediate structures or a series of levels in an ascending order of complexity: sub-wholes which display, according to the way you look at them, some of the characteristics commonly attributed to wholes and some of the characteristics commonly attributed to parts.... The members of a hierarchy, like the Roman god Janus, all have two faces looking in opposite directions: the face turned toward the subordinate levels is that of a self-contained whole; the face turned upward toward the apex, that of a dependent part. One is the face of the master, the other the face of the servant. This "Janus effect" is a fundamental characteristic of sub-wholes in all types of hierarchies. [Koestler, 1971]

1.2 TERMINOLOGY CONFUSION

Because one is often introduced to system analysis in a specific context, it may be confusing subsequently to find the method used in an entirely different context. Engineering students, for example, may follow a "systems" curriculum that specializes in automatic control, communications theory, computer science, information retrieval, and so on, and which entirely excludes general system planning and policy-oriented questions. (Brown and Scherer, 2000). Students of management may think of fiscal control or ERP (Enterprise Resource Planning) "systems" when they use the phrase "system analysis." We have sewage systems, social systems, and horse players' systems. Perhaps Koestler was wise to avoid the word "system" entirely, but then again, he only renamed the problem. Here is an example of a dual use of the word "system" that resulted in initial confusion by members of a government advisory panel.

A panel of engineers was requested by the federal government to establish the future research and development needs in the field of high-speed ground transportation (HSGT) (U. S. Department of Commerce, 1967; Herbert, 1968). The panel originally conceived the study in the categories shown in Figure 1.1. It soon became apparent, however, to the "system" subpanel that a number of the tasks, which they had been asked to consider, fell into the category we will call "general system planning." Such items as subsystem interaction, reliability, and system management are included in this category. Yet what about communications and control, the question of a single, overall centralized control computer system versus many individual machines, or the reporting of the position and velocity of individual vehicles? Just as surely, these are more specific "systems." Thus, the final report of the HSGT panel was organized as shown in Figure 1.2. This is a more functional arrangement, and it helped the panel to produce a less confusing and thus more useful report.

Thus far we have discussed the difference between the general or "comprehensive" system viewpoint we take in this text, i.e., the specific problem at issue, plus all of the

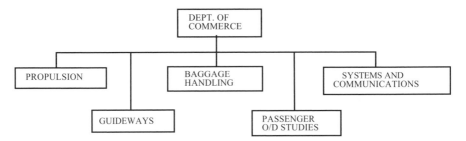

FIGURE 1.1 The original HSGT study concept. The Department of Commerce wished to assemble a study team to establish the concept of high-speed ground transportation (HSGT) on a conceptually correct basis. Originally, it felt that the study should have the five units shown above. However, when the team of experts assembled, they discovered that there existed considerable confusion as to the meaning of the "systems and communications" unit.

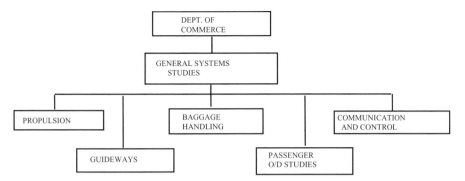

FIGURE 1.2 The final HSGT report formulation. Here we see the general systems aspect of the problem broken out and placed in the overall coordinating position. Now the term "communication and control system" is less ambiguous.

interactions and impacts of the specific issue with its setting, including policy issues and a more localized, exclusively technological "control system" point of view. There are at least three additional semantic difficulties to be discussed.

Later in the chapter, we indicate that *Operations Research* (OR) may be considered an immediate precursor of systems analysis. Thus one may fairly inquire as to exactly the difference between the two. In Section 1.8, we will see that Smith argues that when RAND added an explicit policy component to OR studies, a new synthesis was achieved. Thus for us, system analysis equals an analytic OR study, plus a policy analysis.

Symbolically, then, Smith might say

$$SA = OR + PA$$

In other words, in modern usage, SA is a more general design philosophy than is OR, and it exhibits marks that are readily observable to an outside inquirer. See Section 1.3 for further discussion on this matter.

Finally, one may ask if SA differs from "system design" and/or "system engineering." In a precise technical sense, "analysis" is defined as taking apart into constituent elements, while "design" generally means "synthesis" or combining elements into a functional new whole. Unfortunately for all of us interested in precise terminology, the common use of "system analysis" in the literature almost always includes not merely an "analytic" phase, but also the development or recommendations for the solution or amelioration of the problem at hand—that is, "design" or synthesis. Following this usage, we include in the term "SA" that wider sense of synthesis.

What of the term "systems engineering?" In the older and narrower usage, "engineering" includes analysis and synthesis, but it is restricted to the design and operation of physical devices, that is, hardware design. However, in the broader and more modern sense, systems engineering (SE) includes all of the matters we include within the term systems analysis (SA). Thus for us in this text

$$SE = SA$$

Numerous books describe the process of systems engineering,[2] including systems engineering handbooks developed by NASA, DOD, Boeing, and so on. Currently, there is also considerable discussion on the concept of system-of-systems (S.O.S.)—that is, systems that are of significant complexity and order that they require methodologies beyond the classic systems methodologies that are all basically derivatives of MIL-499B.[3] The emphasis of this book, however, is not on the formal process of systems engineering eloquently described in the footnoted books (and the synonym of the word system: "Method"), but on the systems analysis component as described above and the associated thought processes.

1.3   SYSTEMS ANALYSIS EQUALS OPERATIONS RESEARCH PLUS POLICY ANALYSIS

We will see in a later section of this chapter that the RAND approach to systems analysis began with operations research and added a policy analysis component. We subscribe to that approach in this text. Of course, defining a term using two other ill-defined terms doesn't help very much. So we should feel obliged to define OR and PA. Fortunately a number of students of the field have defined OR and Table 1.1 gives a collection of these definitions.

TABLE 1.1. Some Typical Definitions of Operations Research

"OR is simply the application of scientific method (i.e., quantitative, analytic thinking with empiric checking) to the problems of an executive authority."

—Waddington

"OR is the application of scientific ideas and methods to improve the efficiency of an industrial process, an organization or, in the most general of senses, the working of any part of society."

—Frend, et al.

"OR is a scientific method of providing executive departments with a quantitative basis for decisions regarding operations under their control."

—Goodover

"OR in world government emphasizes the study of complex structures. It is the stress on model building which distinguishes OR from other management services."

—Ward

"OR is the application of mathematical techniques to problems of organization with the objective of optimizing the performance of the system."

—Wardle

"OR is by definition the scientific study of the process and methods of work in the field, office, or on the bench, to the extent that it does succeed in discovering ways of improvement."

—Singh

"OR is an experimental and applied science devoted to observing, understanding, and predicting the behavior of purposeful non-machine systems."

Op. Res., Vol. 19–3, No. 71, p. 1135

We notice the frequent occurrence of terms such as "scientific" and "mathematical" in these definitions; also there is the use of "optimization" and the emphasis on the concept of a "client." The term "client" itself does not appear, but synonyms such as "executive authority," "organization," "society," and so on, do. Thus, while the details differ among these definitions, a common basis emerges. We could go on with this definitional exercise to discover the typical analytic techniques of OR, such as linear programming, queuing theory, optimization techniques, simulation methods, and so on.

"Policy analysis" is a little more difficult to limit. But, if we note how RAND came to include the policy analysis aspect, matters become clearer. RAND knew from working with the military mind that it is hierarchal, a primary attribute of a Tayloristic value set. Taylorism, as we shall see, includes a rigid separation of "thinking" by managers from "doing" by workers. Thus, the U.S. Air Force, RAND's original sole sponsor, tended to come to it with orders to do a certain analysis. When RAND analysts asked "why," they were rebuffed. But as we will see, the Tayloristic mind set is not suitable for creative analysis of new issues. The System Analyst must know the goals of the issue in order to conduct an analysis properly. In the Air Force's view, this took RAND out of the realm of OR into management's territory, Policy Analysis. So RAND simply included policy analysis in its definition of what it did and that helped matters somewhat.

1.4 ATTRIBUTES OF LARGE-SCALE SYSTEMS

In this text we will concentrate on a particular aspect of the field called large-scale systems. How does a large-scale system differ from a non-large-scale system? Almost certainly there is a policy component to the issue under consideration. Generally, a large-scale problem is not merely one containing many components, although that can occur. The usage has become common to differentiate between (a) the low-order, well-defined physical system to which almost all of the mathematical theory of operations research is directed and (b) larger, more complex issues with a policy component. By "policy component," we generally mean that the goals of the system and the index of performance are subject to the personal standards and judgment of the client. The typical large-scale system will have many of the following attributes:

> Policy Component. In addition to the physical infrastructure, or the so-called "engineering component," a large-scale system often contains a social or "policy" component whose effectiveness must be evaluated by its accord with general social, governmental, or other high-order judgments, rather than by simple economic efficiency.
>
> High Order. A large-scale system (LSS), or "General System," will usually have a large number of discernible subsystems or parts. These parts can be quite different from one another and may be interconnected in complex ways. Some of the elements of the large-scale system may include living elements as linkages. In addition, social, economic, political, environmental, and technological considerations will often be involved.

Complex to Describe. Because of the large number and variety of its elements, the LSS is often difficult to describe analytically or to model precisely via dynamic computer simulation.

Lengthy Installation. Because of the cost and effort needed for its installation, the LSS may take a number of years to construct and install. Thus special care is needed with respect to graceful phasing-in of the new system and phasing-out of the old system that it replaces.

Unique. Often the LSS will be unique in its overall concept. Thus special care must be given to careful preliminary design and complete analysis. The designer will not be able to correct design errors in early models later in the production run, if only one is to be built.

Prior Complete Testing Impractical. Because of the size and cost of the LSS, it may be impractical to construct a test prototype prior to installation of the operating system, or even to assemble the complete system off-site for preliminary testing. We are thinking here of complete subway systems, and so on.

One could cite an almost endless list of LSS, of which the following are a few examples:

- The "Big Dig" transportation project in Boston
- The information technology infrastructure for the Department of Homeland Security
- President Reagan's "Star Wars" initiative in the 1980s
- The Manned Mars Mission (considered in a later chapter)
- The complete water supply for a large city (or any infrastructure component)
- The integrated Highway/Rail/Air/River transportation system for a developing nation such as Colombia, funded by the World Bank in the 1960s
- The long-range business plan for a complex international corporation such as Royal Dutch Shell in the months before the 1970s OPEC oil crisis
- The New Orleans flood containment system (levees, pumps, drainage, staff, policies, etc., or the flood evacuation process)
- The U.S. Social Security System

1.5 INTELLIGENT TRANSPORTATION SYSTEMS (ITS): AN EXAMPLE OF A LARGE-SCALE SYSTEM

ITS systems involve the use of disparate technology to improve, typically without capacity increases, the performance of a transportation system. The preliminary analysis, design, and installation of an ITS is complex and lengthy. The system is of high order. It may involve numerous subsystems, from transit rail to freeways to arterial signal systems. Some of the elements may be analyzed in exact detail—for example, individual intersection signals and the associated control computers. Other elements may submit to statistical analysis; passenger origin/demand studies are an example. Design data are typically necessary from disparate sources, such as U.S. Census origin/destination data and local traffic management centers. Financial estimates of system operation will be less precise, but still well within the bounds of approximate analysis. But other elements upon which the success of the system rests seem to be beyond analytic description.

For example, *the demographics* of the urban region may change dramatically in 30 years. A recent study shows that, within a period of five years, one-half of the families in a typical American community have changed their place of residence (He and Schachter, 2003). Housing prices, which dramatically affect traffic congestion and have major ITS implications, have been soaring in the 2000s and also doubling in a five-year timeframe; however, a bubble burst is predicted by many (Anonymous, 2005a). Thus, if the return on investment of several ITS technologies is calculated on the basis of a 30-year operating life, one must extrapolate over six half-lives of the demographic base that the system is designed to serve—a rather risky process.

Political questions are even more difficult with which to grapple than demographic. For example, the so-called U.S. "Highway Trust Fund" is a special-purpose federal gasoline tax with a limited set of permissible uses. Currently, funds can be returned to the states to reimburse approved state highway construction and reconstruction based on a complicated allocation formula. Will the trust fund allocation process be broadened to include ITS type of improvements? This is a political question, but one that will have a greater impact on the benefit–cost studies than almost any technological factor. Another example is photo-red, where camera systems can be installed to detect and issue tickets to vehicles that run red lights (Anonymous, 2005b). Systems can be operated by local or state governments, or they can be operated by local entities via a profit sharing formula. Evaluation of such systems has proved their capability in terms of technology, accident reductions, and economic viability; however, considerable political opposition has limited their deployment in the United States, where the opposition is based on claims of invasion of privacy. Regions have been turning off effective and proven photo-red cameras, against the wishes of police agencies, for political reasons (Stockwell, 2005).

Sociological factors are most difficult of all to predict. What will be an acceptable level of urban pollution produced by a transportation system? What is an acceptable level of delay on the highways? What will be the performance requirements placed by federal dictate on the next generation of individual vehicles and transit vehicles? What safety needs, real and perceived, must be met by ITS technology in the future? What about questions of "ambience" and "user-friendliness?"

All of the above factors also contribute to the complexity of description of the system as well. For example, it is not easy to define "the city" or region for which one is analyzing the transportation needs. Should the Metropolitan Planning Organization (MPO) definition or the Standard Metropolitan Statistical Area (SMSA) definition be used? There are over 30 definitions of the word "city" in current use (Gibson,1977), and federal regulations require that, to qualify for federal matching funds, a regional approach must be taken in the analysis rather than a parochial one limited to political boundaries.

The typical urban transportation system takes a long time to install. The Bay Area Rapid Transit (BART) system in San Francisco–Oakland took over a decade to design and construct, while the District of Columbia Metro subway has been in planning and construction even longer. Detroit has discussed and planned its subway for over 35 years, and as yet not a spade of earth has been moved. Some of the links of the interstate highway system initiated under Eisenhower are as yet untouched after 50 years. In the meantime, the existing transport networks must continue to function, and indeed many of the elements of the existing transport system must continue to function even after the new system is installed. Recently opened after 18 years of planning and construction and almost $15 billion in costs, the Big Dig is the largest civil works project in history.

Each ITS system is unique. Certainly, many of the individual components are identical to those used in other systems, and indeed commonality with other systems is highly to be desired. Doubtless also, much of the design and construction experience obtained from earlier work should be transferable. But the particular combination of elements and the interconnections among subsystems will be unlike those faced elsewhere.

Some engineers are uninterested in issues of public policy, and they may choose their careers to be able to focus on the design of physical objects and to avoid "people problems." One might imagine such focused individuals designing traction drives and electronic controls for subways, but one cannot long escape from the real world. Many of the initial problems faced by BART were due to selection of inexperienced contractors who used untried and untested techniques. When certain BART engineers warned against this, they were fired, and eventually BART authorities were required by law to pay damages to these courageous, "whistle-blowing" professionals.

Finally, it is patently impractical to set up a complete ITS somewhere for a lengthy test period, prior to installing it in its final location. This means that components and subsystems must be carefully field-tested prior to final installation. It further means that extraordinary care must be given to the system aspect as opposed to the component aspect of the analysis. Time spent on computer simulation of the operation of the system in the preliminary design phase, long before bending metal, will more than repay itself, for example. Such a computer simulation should be specifically designed to test system performance aspects.

For example, it is possible to mock up on computers interface systems and system controls. Then various conditions could be entered into the simulated system, without the user's knowledge, to test his and the system's response. It should also be possible to vary vehicle volumes, passenger loadings, route choices, station locations, and so on, on the simulated system to test the response to off-design-center operating conditions. The analyst should be able to demonstrate that as off-design-center conditions become more and more pronounced, the system undergoes graceful degradation, as opposed to sudden and catastrophic collapse. Yet rarely, if ever, is such a comprehensive simulation study actually conducted in practice that actually involves the human–computer interface (HCI).

For example, suppose a rapid transit system is to be controlled by a central control computer that is programmed to dispatch units in accordance with historical traffic variations. Suppose a main artery near the city center is cut off in a sudden emergency. What will the central computer do? Or suppose the central computer itself fails. Does the whole system halt in a catastrophic collapse? The alternative to "catastrophic collapse" is "graceful degradation." If control degenerates to separate sector computers and then back to the individual units operated by hand, at reduced speed in the face of a major emergency, performance of the system has gracefully degraded.

It is apparent that ITS are often constructed and operated with little or no thought given to overall policy questions such as those we have just raised. It also seems likely that traditionally trained transportation designers and operators would ignore or resist policy-oriented analyses if they were made. Should this surprise or dismay the system analyst? Not at all. It is the normal state of affairs, *even though we know that these problems will occur*!

In Chapter 6 of Smith's book on RAND (Smith, 1966), he gives an excellent description of a pivotal study done by RAND on the location of bases of the Strategic Air Command (SAC) of the U.S. Air Force. This was one of the earliest studies anywhere in which a clear policy-oriented approach was adopted. This approach heavily influenced RAND's subsequent development of a "strategic sense" and may be viewed as the progenitor of the modern policy-oriented system study. A. J. Wohlstetter, the task leader, was faced with precisely the same problems in beginning this analysis and then persuading the Air Force decision makers to accept and act on the conclusions of the study as the analyst of a mass transit system or any other large-scale system would face in working with real-world decision makers. Smith's text, and especially Chapter 6, should be required reading for all analysts of large-scale systems.

1.6 SYSTEMS INTEGRATION

We have pointed out that confusion exists as to the meaning of the term "systems analysis." This confusion has been partially resolved by coining a new phrase "systems integration." *Systems integration* is a logical, objective procedure for applying in an efficient, timely manner new and/or expanded performance requirements to the design, procurement, installation, and operation of an operational configuration consisting of distinct modules (or subsystems), each of which may embody inherent constraints or limitations.

This definition of SI contains a number of key terms. "Logical, objective procedure" means that the process is defendable to external critics and that all of the steps have an audit trail built in. "Efficient and timely" imply that the process will not be unduly burdened with delays and bureaucratic procedures that increase cost to the client and delay deployment of the system. "Design, procurement, installation, and operation" indicates that the SI process will be employed throughout the entire process. It further implies that life-cycle costing will be considered and that retro-fits, extension of system capability, and the like will be built-in. The concept of "distinct modules" with inherent limits or constraints is central to the concept of SI. Systems Integration would be unnecessary if the entire configuration to be deployed were a stand-alone device without intimate connections with other devices previously deployed or to be deployed under a later procurement, and if the device were designed and constructed *de novo* by a single party with complete design responsibility. No such animal exists in the modern world, of course, and thus the ubiquitous necessity for SI.

At a tactical level, SI is involved with ensuring that specific hardware components will fit together smoothly in a configuration. Indeed at this level, SI is often referred to as "configuration management." But at a broader, more strategic level, SI is concerned with interpreting overall performance needs of a sponsor into technical performance specifications and then the creation of a full options field from which to select those option profiles that best meet the client's needs.

A number of pitfalls exist in the process. Among them are the following:

- Failure to provide a clear audit trail through the SI process.
- Breaks or discontinuities in the SI process caused by intuitive leaps from a general requirements level to a specific hardware configuration, without objective development of the steps in the process.
- Failure to assess completely the full range of client requirements including operation of the proposed system over the full time horizon required.
- Failure to evaluate full life-cycle costing.
- Failure to provide in advance for maintenance and periodic upgrades and retrofits during the system life cycle.

As we continue with our detailed discussion of the phases of systems analysis, we will see that this new term "systems integration" is synonymous. Over the last two decades, the term "system architecting" has also become prevalent. Defined as "the art and science of designing and building systems," it follows the same analogy as systems integration; once again, *for our purposes*, we will use the term interchangeably with systems analysis (Rechtin and Maier, 1997).

1.7   WHAT MAKES A "SYSTEMS ANALYSIS" DIFFERENT?

Almost the whole of the remainder of this text will be devoted to the systems analysis (SA) methodology and how to perform an SA. But, before we begin, we wonder if this notion of system analysis is merely a mental discipline or a training regime through which we put ourselves, or if, on the other hand, there are distinctive marks or attributes that an external observer could use to detect that SA has been used. Even if it were only a mental discipline, SA could be valuable. For example, "Zen" is said to help warriors and athletes, even though it is "only" a mental attitude. We will argue that the SA methodology is more than just an attitude, however.

Even if there are external marks to SA, these marks might be of no functional value. For example, the marks might be only cosmetic, as when special jargon (of which we have a considerable amount) is used. However, we will argue that the marks of SA are more than cosmetic. There are recognizable characteristics in a well-done SA that enable an external observer to recognize it as such. Not every SA will display all of these marks, but the fewer that are evident, the further the analysis diverges from a paradigmatic system study. The following distinguishing eight marks define a systems study.

1. The "Top-Down" Nature of the Study. The well-done system analysis starts with an analysis of the general goals of the effort and proceeds to the specific. This is a reversal of the approach often advocated in engineering design. The reader will find a comparison of the "top-down" approach and the "bottom-up" incremental approach in Chapters 2 and 3. These two design philosophies are sometimes considered antithetical, but this not so. One does not choose one or the other in a systems analysis. In SA, top-down alternates with bottom-up, in an iterative manner.

2. A Goal-Centered Approach. The goal-oriented approach contrasts with the step-by-step or chronological or "laundry-list" approach. A system analysis starts by determining the situation or condition after the system under design is complete and operating successfully and works backward from there to determine the specifications of the intermediate links. This approach is discussed in detail in Section 2.2.

3. Rational, Objective Basis for Analysis. Rationality and objectivity are hallmarks of the scientific method and in engineering design. By "rational" we mean based on carefully gathered evidence weighed and analyzed using a logical procedure, and by "objective" we mean fair, balanced, unbiased, and free from personal whim. These features are not common in the political arena. Lawyers, for example, are not constrained by these criteria. A legal brief will include all of the arguments for a given position, even if some of the arguments are self-contradictory. The reader of such a brief is expected to pick any of the arguments that are pleasing, provided only that support for the advocate's position is obtained.

4. An Analytic/Quantitative Component plus a Policy Component. Operations research (OR, or equivalently management science, decision analytics, etc.) is a major component of SA, as we will see. OR contributes the analytic, quantitative component to systems analysis. The addition of the policy component makes SA unique. See Section 1.3.

5. A Generalized Problem, which Includes the Problem Setting. The word "generalize" here means to expand or broaden the scope of, as opposed to the alternate meaning of "generalizing from the particular to a broader class." A properly done SA always includes a consideration of the problem environment. It includes consideration of all of the stakeholders, non-users as well as users. By "generalized problem" we mean a core of mathematical quantification and analysis, plus the addition of human factors considerations and the policy component where indicated, all in the context within which the issue at hand is embedded, and specifically including the client on whose behalf the analysis is being conducted. See Section 3.2 for a more complete explanation of the rationale for "generalizing" the problem.

6. Optimization, often through Analytical Modeling and Simulation. Identification of the critical parameters of the problem and calculation of their optimum setting to maximize the index of performance is a basic characteristic in SA. Often this

iteration and optimization is best accomplished by use of computer simulation. See Section 5.10.

7. Explicit Analysis of the Operative Values Assumed, and Declaration of the Analyst's Biases or Interests. Effective handling of the policy component in an SA requires that the operative value system be analyzed. This is the so-called "axiological component" of the analysis.

8. Problem/Client Orientation rather than Technique or Abstract Orientation. SA is client-oriented not technique-oriented. Maslow (1969) makes the importance of this distinction abundantly clear. Neither OR studies nor SA are conducted for their intrinsic value or the entertainment of the analysts.

This listing isn't designed to justify or explain these marks of SA. The remainder of the text is designed to do that. Here we merely wish to point out the unique characteristics of the SA approach, so that the reader can be alert for them as they occur in the text. Whether SA is effective and where it should be applied will also be made clear (one hopes!) in the remaining chapters.

1.8 DISTANT ROOTS OF SYSTEMS ANALYSIS

Frederick Winslow Taylor is among the earliest of the zealots in the cult of industrial efficiency, and by his somewhat extreme stands he made himself a favorite target, beginning in his lifetime and continuing to the present. As Ellul (1964,1973) points out, Taylor viewed "the shop" as a totally autonomous entity. He had no concern for the purpose to which the product produced would be put or for the external goals of the shop workers. Only efficient production mattered. This analytic suboptimization approach is still common, but it lacks contextual integrity. One should read Taylor's own words to get the flavor (Taylor, 1911).

Taylor is the exemplar of what McGregor (1960) labeled "Theory X" management style. Taylor viewed workers as objects rather than as individuals, but he should not be viewed as deliberately ignoring the human content of work. That is a concept developed only many years after Taylor's death. While one might expect opposition to Taylor's new method by many workers, we are surprised that Taylor failed to be acclaimed widely by managers. Copley (1923) makes clear in his laudatory biography that Taylor had considerable difficulty in winning converts among employers. His undivided allegiance to pure efficiency drove away many of those whose profits he would have served. Only an inherited income allowed him to continue his crusade.

One may note with interest that the military services were early converts to Taylorism. In 1907, there were efforts to apply Taylor's methods at the Brooklyn Navy Yard. The military were also among the first to use operations research in World War II. In the conventional wisdom, the military mind is not often credited as a flexible or innovating instrument, yet the fact remains it led the way in scientific management and operations research. Why?

Taylor's invention of time and motion study, the efficient design of the workplace, development of optimized tools (from shovels to cutting steel), work scheduling, and incentive pay for workers allowed him to demonstrate spectacular increases in productivity where his methods were introduced. However, his dogmatism, arrogance, and unwillingness to persuade or explain, his demands for absolute loyalty from his associates, his efforts to stamp out heretical variations of his methods, his need for complete control, and his obsessive dedication to work make him a suitable subject for retrospective psychoanalysis. He appears to have had a well-developed martyr complex and to have viewed his work as a calling of supreme importance, so much so that he dedicated his life, his fortune, and ultimately his health to the cause.

Taylorism, or "scientific management" as he wished it to be called, made steady progress before World War II and became better known as industrial engineering and industrial management. The importance of increasing productivity was a lesson successfully taught by Taylor, and as less fanatic persons with broader and more humane concerns became involved and as the disciplined resistance of organized labor began to be felt, the worst excesses of early Taylorism in the American factory were trimmed away. Nevertheless, even today one carries a clipboard and stopwatch out onto a machine shop floor at one's own risk. Taylorism was probably appropriate for the educational and social maturity of workers 100 years ago, but it is widely felt to be inappropriate and retrograde today. The Tayloristic mind set continues to be ubiquitous among American engineering educators.

1.9 IMMEDIATE PRECURSORS TO SYSTEMS ANALYSIS

The period immediately prior to World War II in Great Britain, circa 1937–1940, saw the development of what was called "operational research"; later, in the United States, this was called "operations research" (OR). When the threat of Hitler was real, but before massive involvement by Great Britain, it became apparent to Churchill and his close advisors that only by deploying its severely limited forces in the most efficient manner could England hope to survive. Radar had been developed and the Spitfire was in production, but the number of operational units was severely limited.

Because of the traditional close connection of government leaders and the universities in Britain, Churchill felt comfortable in turning to a family friend who was professor of physics at Cambridge, Professor Lindemann (later Lord Cherwell). Lindemann drew Sir Henry Tizard, Sir Watson-Watt, and other academics into aiding the war effort (Birkenhead, 1962). Mathematicians and physicists were asked how best to deploy available weaponry in military operations.

This was new. Scientists were accustomed to being called upon to develop new weapons, but the matter of organizing their use lies at the heart of military science, it would seem. It is hard to see how a more conventional mind than Churchill's would have conceived such audacity. Statistical analysis groups were set up and controlled experiments were run (Morse, 1970). Bombing patterns were modified, and ocean convoy procedures were changed as a result of these studies. Because of the academic background of the early OR practitioners, a great deal of elegant and useful mathematics came into play: statistical analysis, queueing theory, probability theory, and so forth. See Chapter 1 of D. J. White's *Operational Research* for examples of typical military OR problems of the period (White, 1985).

New mathematics such as linear programming, dynamic programming, game theory, and decision analysis were later developed. OR began to influence industrial engineering and management after the war and crept into industrial practice. Because of the interesting theory involved, OR found a home in university curricula soon after the War. Courses were offered at Hull University by Swann; soon afterward, 1958–1959, the first graduate-degree program in OR was offered at Birmingham (D.J. White, personal communication).

Another, separate contribution of scientists and engineers in World War II was the development of the techniques of automatic control. As weapons became faster, larger, and more powerful, it became increasingly less practical to operate them by hand. The aerodynamic pressures on the control surfaces of large, high-speed bombers grew so great that mechanical boosters were necessary. Multiple machine guns mounted in these bombers were so heavy that gunners could not move them unaided. The gun turrets of naval warships had to be stabilized against ocean-wave motion if the guns were to be effective. Late in the war, automatic navigation systems for aircraft and ships, as well as ways of allowing radar automatically to direct weapons fire, were sought.

For these and other applications, design engineers first thought that simple mechanical and hydraulic boosters could be used to substitute for the muscles of humans. But in many cases when the boosters were added, the mechanisms failed to operate as expected. Sometimes the units did not work at all and in other cases the units went into wild, uncontrollable oscillations before destroying themselves. Many potentially valuable devices were rendered useless by these mysterious failures. For months it appeared that a fundamental limitation dictated by unknown laws of nature was at work.

Help came from an unexpected source. For a number of years, telephone engineers at the Bell Laboratories had been attempting to understand the oscillations set up in electronic amplifiers needed for long-distance telephony. Beginning with H. S. Black's investigations on the theory of negative feedback (Black, 1934) and culminating in the classic work of Bode (Bode, 1945), the theoretical principles for analyzing and stabilizing feedback systems were laid bare. Workers at Bell Labs and at General Electric Laboratories reduced the theoretical principles to practice. Dramatic stories can be told of the stabilization of the B-29 bomber fire control system and of the Navy gyroscopically controlled gun laying systems, after unstable devices were in production and being installed on operational units. The best overall documentation of this wartime effort remains Volume 25 of the Radiation Laboratory series (James et al., 1947).

From this beginning, the theory of feedback has been developed to include complex systems with many interacting elements and with humans as integral parts of various loops. Following the war, as analog computers became widespread in university and industrial research laboratories, feedback automatic-control theorists and others developed an intense interest in the concept and practice of dynamic computer simulation models of whole industrial processes, cities, and, some say, the world. See Sections 5.10–5.16.

One further precursor of system analysis remains to be mentioned . . . econometrics. John Maynard Keynes was a seminal figure in economics in the period between World Wars I and II (Harrod, 1951). He early conceived that by manipulating and controlling certain parameters of a nation's economy, one could influence almost all other segments of the nation's economic life. When one proposes to influence the economy of a nation, much more is needed than merely qualitative descriptions of the processes involved. Keynes played a leading role in beginning the conversion of economics from a qualitative, descriptive art into a quantitative science that continues today. Keynes influenced the transition to quantitative economics or econometrics, not only by his prolific writing, but also by playing an active role in the British government. He was also fortunate in attracting several brilliant and prolific individuals to become early followers, among them P. A. Samuelson (Stiglitz, 1966).

In 1941 Leontief published his classic work on input–output models, which is still widely used (Leontief, 1941). The Leontief economic model of a nation is a static representation. It provides within itself no predictive capability, although, of course, a series of such static descriptions can be used as a basis for extrapolation. Yet the immense expense of collecting even these static coefficients for a model of the United States that is sufficiently disaggregated to be of value is staggering. Even with the resources of the U.S. Government, data for 1967 were not published until 1974 (U.S. Department of Commerce, 1974)! Despite these difficulties, econometricians have pushed forward into dynamic modeling of the nation's economy. Among the leaders of this more recent effort was Lawrence Klein and his Wharton model (Klein, 1950; Klein and Goldberger, 1955; Anonymous, 1975). With increased use of advanced statistical techniques, dynamic modeling, and so on, econometrics and operations research now began to find common ground (Teil et al., 1965).

Industrial management, operations research, automatic control system design, and econometrics appear to the systems analyst as precursors to his generalized discipline. Yet active practitioners of each of these specialties might resent the implication that they are somehow being superseded by a new group of generalists. Thus we need to remind ourselves that it is all in one's point of view. Perhaps we system analysts ought to acknowledge our "parent disciplines" rather than calling them precursors.

1.10   DEVELOPMENT OF SYSTEMS ANALYSIS AS A DISTINCT DISCIPLINE: THE INFLUENCE OF RAND

Operations research emerged from World War II as a new and exciting approach to the organization of large-scale groups to accomplish specific goals. But why limit OR to the operational deployment of men and machines? Why not use it as well for discovering what new devices and processes are needed to meet defined goals? The need for a rational, objective process of analysis of all factors is especially relevant in the development of large weapons systems such as guided missile systems and in private industry in such complex undertakings as long-distance telephone networks and airline operations. The name "operations research," always rather confining, seems inappropriate for this newer, broader mission, which includes operations as only one portion of the cycle of bringing a new device into being and using it efficiently. Terms such as "system analysis," "system design," "systems engineering," and the "system approach" began to be more commonly used.

When many diverse parts of a large-scale system must be designed so as to work together in a harmonious whole, and especially when it is difficult or impractical to test the parts in advance of final assembly, a systematic approach is almost mandatory. The U.S. Air Force and AT&T were among the first organizations to recognize this. The Air Force set up a system command to study the overall problem of bringing the intercontinental ballistic missile into the U.S. defense arsenal, and in 1948 it sponsored the formation of the RAND Corporation (Smith, 1966). RAND's charter was to develop and apply the system approach to a wide range of Air Force problems. RAND's independence allowed it the necessary freedom to develop the skills needed for solving large, long-range problems without day-to-day interference and diversion of personnel to meet tactical emergencies. Later it was recognized that these new system skills being developed by RAND were of general applicability.

The Air Force supported RAND as an external contractor and it enjoyed rather wide freedoms. RAND paid excellent salaries, provided pleasant working conditions in a nonmilitary atmosphere, and addressed challenging problems of its own selection from a shopping list proposed by the Air Force. One of the difficulties of professional life in a think tank such as Arthur D. Little, SRI, Calspan, Battelle, and so on, is the need continually to "sell one's time." This can lead to compromises in the kind of work undertaken and the quality of the results (Dickson, 1971). RAND was free of this concern.

RAND was a prime mover in the development of such theory as linear programming, decision theory, dynamic programming, Monte Carlo simulation, game theory, and PPBS (Planning and Performance Budgeting System). Its counsels were sought at the highest strategic levels. A young systems professional at RAND could influence the course of world events, a heady experience. Smith, in his well-done book, credits RAND with the original development of policy-oriented system analysis. RAND began its work as a project office in Douglas Aircraft Company, doing standard operations research tasks for the Air Force.

> In the early years. . . RAND studies tended to be engineering efforts or else analyses of rather low-level problems akin to what operations researchers did in World War II. The studies were elaborately mathematical in nature and showed little concern for integrating a number of complex variables, some qualitative in nature, into a broad context of some future 'system' whose contours and implications in terms of military effectiveness can only be dimly foreseen.
>
> [Smith, 1966, p. 103]

Gradually, however, RAND personnel began to develop what Smith calls "a strategic sense."

> Something of a revolution took place in the 1950s which transformed the typical RAND systems analysis from a narrowly technical product into a novel application of numerous professional skills to a broad policy problem.
>
> [Smith, 1966, p. 104]

While the proportion of broad-scale policy analysts at RAND never exceeded 15% of the professional staff at any one time, Smith argues that this policy flavor, or "strategic sense," is what set RAND's system studies apart from the more traditional, narrowly technical OR studies done by other organizations of the period, and which in effect created the wholly new area of policy science (Smith, 1966, p. 105).

In the 1960s, the influence of RAND began to wane. Competing organizations such as SDC, MITRE, and ANSER were spun off from RAND, but none were given as long a leash. The Viet Nam war was divisive for RAND. Daniel Ellsberg of the "Pentagon Papers" fame was a former RAND employee. Air Force support was cut back, and RAND sought and received permission to seek funding from other sources. This was a period of great social ferment, and when Mayor Lindsay invited RAND to set itself up in New York City and to apply system techniques to the organization of snow removal and garbage collection, RAND obliged. However, RAND/NYC found that urban problems are more complex than aerospace system problems (Szanton, 1972).

Urban goals are often left obscure on principle, RAND/NYC discovered to its befuddlement. The client is ill-defined, and lethargy, the *status quo*, and discrete incrementalism are the rule in urban bureaucracies. RAND/NYC funding stopped in 1973. The RAND/NYC experience seems to teach several things. Certainly, RAND's system approach to social problems was superior to the earlier and equally well-intentioned State of California effort to enlist aerospace contractors to address pressing public issues at the state level (Gibson, 1977, pp. 59–91). Yet there remained much of the naïve, ingenuous, academic, abstract flavor in the RAND/NYC studies and little of the experienced, realistic, slightly cynical, but still hopeful veteran. Perhaps the RAND/NYC program needed fewer fresh Ph.D. Eagle Scouts and more Kojaks.

RAND alumni moved into positions of influence throughout the Defense Department and into universities, carrying with them linear programming, queuing theory, dynamic programming, decision analysis, benefit–cost analysis, and the whole analytic tool kit now so familiar in operations research. RAND also helped define the general steps to be taken in a system analysis, including explicit development of goals and quantitative indices of performance, the development of alternative scenarios, trade-off studies, and the like.

Opposition came from simple inertia and reluctance to change. Other opposition to the "systems approach" was and is generated by the behavior of system analysts themselves. If one goes into an existing organization with an arrogant attitude of superiority, one is not likely to gain the cooperation of the old timers. There is also informed opposition to inflated claims of incompetent charlatans posing as skilled professionals. And finally there is opposition from those who understand quite clearly that an objective, careful analysis of the current situation is likely to uncover the existence of sloppy, comfortable or self-serving behavior and require a change of ways. Stockfisch (1970) provides an anecdotal description of some of these sources of opposition to the installation of the system approach.

Other laboratories in the United States were also developing and utilizing the new tools in addition to RAND; of course, the Willow Run Research Center of the University of Michigan is among them. Out of Willow Run came the first comprehensive text on the design of large-scale systems, Goode and Machol (1957). Five years later, Hall's classic text (Hall, 1962) appeared, based on his work at Bell Labs. Hall introduced for the first time a comprehensive, integrated general methodology for the analysis and synthesis of large-scale systems.

HISTORICAL CASE STUDY: IIASA (A)

By the early 1970s, excessive claims and subsequent failures had generated a critical reassessment of the system approach. Prominent among SA critics is Hoos (1972). Hoos does not attempt to be objective but rather adopts an adversarial position. Nevertheless, several of Hoos' arguments are well-taken. One of these has to do with the choice of an optimizing criterion. Hoos charges that analysts often pick a criterion for optimization simply because it is easy to measure rather than because it truly measures the desired goals.

Hoos concentrates on the mistakes made by some of those former aerospace system analysts who turned to social system design when the aerospace industry took a downturn in the 1960s, and one must admit that she was offered a number of ripe targets. She missed one major target in particular, however. Robert MacNamara is a prototypical system analyst in the RAND tradition, and he forced PPBS on the Defense Department when he was Secretary under JFK and LBJ. It was this PPBS style that developed the justly infamous body-count criterion in Viet Nam. Some of these same problematic metrics still continue to exist in the 2003 (and on) war in Iraq.

Former aerospace persons do not have a monopoly on creating system errors, however. Computer simulations in particular and urban system studies in general have attracted the ire of Brewer (1973). Brewer documents the selling of computer simulation studies for the cities of San Francisco and Pittsburgh by two different system teams in the 1960s. Neither simulation worked, and Brewer's analysis shows why.

A current model of a large-scale systems organization, and one on which it may still be necessary to reserve judgment after almost 35 years of wandering, is the International Institute of Applied System Analysis (IIASA) (Anonymous, 1972). Founded in 1972 as an element in East–West political "detente," and with a prominent scholar and RAND alumnus as director, IIASA was supported by the United States, the Soviet Union, and about a dozen other nations. Austria refurbished Schloss Laxenburg, a former Habsburg hunting lodge on the outskirts of Vienna, and invited IIASA to occupy it. Located near Baden and the Vienna Woods and restored to its original Baroque grandeur, the Schloss provides a sumptuous, almost decadent atmosphere within which system analysts their wonders to work.

A defender of the founding director points out that it is a miracle that IIASA exists at all. It was clearly to be an instrument of international diplomacy and a gesture toward detente, yet, in practice, IIASA analysts were buffered from political interference, for which the founding director may deserve credit. A good, if not distinguished, professional staff was assembled and individuals were encouraged to go about self-chosen tasks at Louis XIV desks, surrounded by purple velvet walls embossed with gold fleur-de-lis, and multilingual secretaries were employed; coffee and cakes were served *mit schlag*, by uniformed staff, in the courtyard or on the terrace. A corps of para-professional assistants substituted for graduate students; computers, a library, and free chauffeured limo service to and from downtown Vienna were available.

A management system analysis, of the sort invented at RAND, would have un-covered a number of organizational problems faced by IIASA. Here are several such issues that were evident but unsolved during IIASA's first decade.

1. <u>Absence of Goals Structure</u>. IIASA had no discernible goals structure. By "discernible" one means evident from a close reading of the available IIASA literature, including its rather large number of glossy publicity pieces, or from personal conversations with IIASA professionals and administrators of the period, or as revealed in seminars and lectures given by IIASA officials, some videotaped and widely distributed.

Problems for study appear to have been accepted or rejected on the basis of the personal whim of individual professional staff members. Some important problems were chosen for study by IIASA individuals and groups. However, this choice appears to have been based on personal interest.

2. <u>Absence of System Approach</u>. Despite its name, IIASA did not practice any definable system approach. Many of the professional staff vigorously denied that any such thing as a "systems methodology" exists. This produced certain tensions between IIASA personnel and the systems community.

3. <u>Absence of Systemic Management Structure</u>. Admittedly, to gather professionals from over a dozen nations with as many languages and social backgrounds and to expect immediate consensus is unreasonable. Yet the IIASA professionals do (i.e., should, if properly recruited) share a common background of interest in system analysis. They are volunteers who should understand the need for collegial cooperation. Thus a minimal sense of order should have been relatively easy to achieve.

Yet three years after it opened its doors, IIASA management had permitted more than 10 major study areas to be established. Because there were 70 professionals, only half of whom were in residence at IIASA, the average group could expect to have only about three resident professionals working on a problem. A competent manager should understand that this is hardly sufficient to make an international impact.

The allocation of resources was overbalanced toward technical support personnel and under-allocated toward library and database resources. Short-term professional appointments appeared to have been the rule; furthermore, the comings and goings, while adding a pleasant sense of excitement and a little-needed excuse for another party, interfered with sustained work on important problems. A short-term visitor, no matter how distinguished, working on his own problem added nothing to the solution of IIASA-selected problems and indeed could and did interfere with their solution by requiring attention and resources and by distracting those few professionals who had been persuaded to give up work on their own problem to work on a team problem.

Study topics were often unwisely chosen. A project on the causes of Austrian highway fatalities stumbled because the professional responsible finished his tour of duty and left IIASA before the data could be assembled and shipped to the Schloss. Often the nominal group leader absented himself in body or spirit. Some group leaders were away from the Schloss for months at a time, and other leaders apparently felt no responsibility for coordinating the direction of their group. More than one group "leader" simply appropriated group resources to apply to his own problem and his own publications.

All of these problems are perfectly simple to forestall or to correct, given a reasonable management structure. Most developed simply from inexperience in the predominantly young professional staff, who generally were on their first independent professional assignment.

4. Failure to Internalize Appropriate Goals. IIASA saw itself as something of an international political football. Whether this is true or false, in fact, is irrelevant to the following argument. But, as a matter of fact, some outside observers would argue that IIASA has been remarkably free of outside interference. What some naïve young IIASA professionals interpreted as interference seems to some external observers to have been a minimum of concern by donor nations as to how their tax dollars are spent.

One could argue that the professional staff members at IIASA had not internalized an acceptable professional goals structure. When some of these people were asked by a visitor if they would explain the overall professional goals at IIASA, they replied that they are unable to do so, but added that the question seemed irrelevant because each individual was interested only in "doing my own thing."

When one visitor asked if this refusal to generate an appropriate goals structure might not interfere with continued funding, he was told, "Don't be silly, two million dollars a year (the initial U.S. contribution) is a cheap price to pay for East–West detente." This is a "let them eat cake" response that lacks all contextual integrity. It indicates a cynicism that saps a commitment to acceptable professional goals. It is clear that this attitude was dangerous for IIASA, but even more so for young professionals who expected to have a successful career elsewhere.

5. Failure to Build Constituencies. Several natural constituencies exist for IIASA. Unfortunately, none of these were cultivated. IIASA publications policy was confused and was addressed toward unfocused and conventional academic clienteles, not necessarily a part of the natural system constituency. What are some examples of natural constituencies? The most obvious is satisfied clients. If IIASA could produce applied system studies, which are declared effective by users, this would provide important rationale for continued support.

A second natural constituency is the international body of system practitioners in industry, government, and universities. If these individuals could be persuaded to view IIASA as the paradigmatic systems institute, it would be a mark of public esteem and recognition. If, in addition, IIASA were to demonstrate ideal methodologies and excellent performance in practice, it would act to raise and unify standards of system practice worldwide.

By failing to perform so as to attract the support of these natural professional constituencies, IIASA will be forced into the role of international political whore in order to solicit funds for reasons not related to its professional performance. Thus to view itself as a political football was not only to cripple its own resolve, but also to produce a self-fulfilling prophecy.

As econometricians and other social scientists became interested in the concepts and the utility of feedback theory and computer simulation following World War II, they extended the ideas, without proof, to fields that ranged far afield from the design of engineering systems, or so-called "hard systems." The attempts to apply these tools and concepts to "soft system" design, urban systems, governmental systems and social systems in general have not proven as successful as they have been in the design of electromechanical and aerospace systems. The terms "hard systems" and "soft systems" are used in the literature analogously to the conventional terms "hard science," i.e., rigorously quantitative such as mathematics, physics, and chemistry, and "soft science," i.e., nonquantitative such as psychology, and sociology.

Soft systems are those in which people and their sociology play a major role. We have not learned to describe actions of societies with simple linear differential equations, but systems of such equations describe the electromechanical world quite nicely. Some politicians said in the 1970s:

> "If we can put a man on the moon, why can't we cure poverty in our cities?"

One answer is:

> "Because the mathematics and physical laws that govern space flight have nothing whatever to do with poverty in the cities and other urban affairs."

But urban systems and other soft systems have an undeniable fascination, and we system analysts, instead of turning our backs, have attempted to do what we can (Gibson, 1977). We can see that the RAND effort to add a policy orientation to its OR work began to lead us into the "soft" system arena. However, the RAND policy orientation generally entered, prior to its NYC misadventures at least, only into the interpretation of the results or the constraints on the problem, not into the essential core of the analysis. RAND did not recognize this distinction, however, until it was too late.

The differences and similarities between "hard" and "soft" systems have attracted the attention of a wide range of thinkers (Tominson and Kiss, 1984), and progress is being made in ameliorating the difficulties. When we think about it, perhaps the distinction between hard and soft is one that latter-day analysts developed for their own convenience. After all, operations research originated in people-oriented problems in

World War II. We drew away from these people-oriented or client-oriented problems to suit our own analytic convenience.

Where is systems analysis today? Ubiquitous. All industries and government agencies have people engaged in the practice of systems analysis. Such people may work under varied titles—operations analyst, systems analyst, "manager," systems architect, systems engineer, business analyst, operations specialist, and so on; the list goes on and on.[4] In the course of the following chapters we give approaches, insights, and examples beneficial to anyone engaged in the design and analysis of systems.

EXERCISES

1.1 The World Bank made a major intervention during the period 1950–1962 into the economy of Colombia by lending it an amount almost equal to 20% of its annual GNP to reconstruct its national transportation system. However, this intervention had important and unforeseen cross-impacts. Read Haefele (1969) on the matter for class discussion. This seems to be an exemplar of some of the dangers inherent in broad-scale social planning for third-world nations without careful controls and detailed analysis by local experts.

1.2 Review the discussion concerning the Washington Metro Rail expansion discussed for Northern Virginia, which would expand Metro through Tyson's Corner to Dulles Airport. Discuss the complexities associated with this proposal and the likely issues that must be addressed in order for a successful system modification.

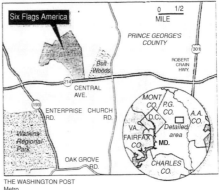

THE WASHINGTON POST
Metro
Traffic Stalls Six Flags Fun for Many
Jackie Spinner
Washington Post Staff Writer

FIGURE 1.3 Ted's fax.

Copyright 1999, The Washington Post Co. Reprinted with Permission.

Traffic overwhelmed the main highway serving the new **Six Flags** America amusement park in Prince George's County yesterday as the number of parkgoers grew so large that parking lots ran out of room and frustrated families began leaving their cars on shoulders and nearby grassy areas.

The four-lane Route 214—one of the main arteries through the central part of the county—was clogged for hours between St. Michael's Drive and Church Road, angering visitors as well as residents trying to run weekend errands.

Weekend congestion has been an off-and-on problem since the old Adventure World park reopened May 8 with the new **Six Flags** brand name and a $40 million expansion.

Park officials acknowledged that they have been overwhelmed by the record-setting number of visitors who have flocked to the revamped park. Officials had expected 7,000 people on opening day, when 21,000 turned out.

Visitors have raved about the new attractions based on Warner Bros. and DC Comics characters. Crowds started arriving yesterday a half-hour before the park opened at 10:30 a.m. By 4:15 p.m., parking had run out and gates to the lots were closed, forcing customers to begin looking for space on the shoulders and grass along Route 214—which in turn caused problems for police, who said the practice was illegal.

"It was a mess. It's terrible," said Steven Kiefner, of Baltimore, who found a spot near a church a half-mile from the park.

There are 5,000 parking spaces at the amusement park, and attendants squeezed hundreds of other cars onto the site wherever they could find space. Park officials said they are considering converting an employee lot into customer parking, among other options.

"The system temporarily broke down," said John Mulcahy, marketing director for **Six Flags** America. "It's growing pains. It's a matter of working with other agencies to get a handle on it."

The congestion yesterday afternoon confounded park and police officials, who had believed that the problem had been resolved a week ago when the timing of the traffic signal at the park entrance was changed to allow more cars during each cycle to make the left-hand turn from eastbound Route 214. Traffic was not nearly as bad last weekend as it was on opening day.

But the backups returned yesterday—particularly for those attempting the left-hand turn.

Mulcahy said the slowdowns intensified when parking attendants failed to open additional lots to accommodate a surge in traffic about noon. Cars were squeezed together under trees and on grassy hills. Even some of the overflow lots were full an hour after the park opened.

Maryland State Police Sgt. Michael Hawkins said officers were sent to the scene to monitor the situation and to help determine whether other traffic signals along Route 214 will have to be adjusted.

"They have only one entrance there, and that can't happen for an amusement park this size. They are going to have to add an extra entrance or widen 214. It's just not working," Hawkins said.

Karen Wright, an Upper Marlboro resident, could not believe the traffic jam that awaited her on 214, also called Central Avenue, when she left the Giant Food supermarket in Mitchellville Plaza about 1 p.m.

"Without **Six Flags**, it was bad enough," she said. Now, "it's outrageous."

Katherine Isaac, a District resident, got out of the traffic to fill her car with gas at a Mobil station at Enterprise Road. She was on her way to see her son play baseball. She was already an hour late and did not expect to make it there before the end of the game.

"It's ridiculous that I have to sit in this traffic," she said.

Greg Waul avoided the gridlock by navigating the back roads from his home in Bowie to the barbershop at the Mitchellville Plaza. He said the traffic on Central Avenue was worse yesterday than what it is during a normal rush hour.

"This is bad, especially for a Saturday," he said. "You don't expect this on a weekend. I guess **Six Flags** is doing all of this. It wasn't like this when it was Adventure World."

CASE STUDY: FUN AT SIX FLAGS?

May 1999. Ted returned from his yearly retreat week deep in the woods (without his cell phone) to find urgent messages in his e-mail, voice mail, and mailbox—there had been some problems at the amusement park over the weekend. His boss, Mary, requested a meeting in her office @ 9:00 AM. Given that it was 8:15 AM, Ted had less than one hour to prepare some thoughts.

Recalling that his college roommate, Bill, was a senior consultant with IQC (*I*nternational *Q*uality *C*onsultants), Ted decided to get some quick help with the problem. He phoned Bill, and to his surprise, Bill actually answered the phone. Unfortunately for Ted, Bill answered the phone from a base camp on Mt. Everest where he was beginning his month-long climb (Bill was one of the several subscribers to Iridium and was, therefore, reachable anywhere in the world). Bill told Ted that he could fax any information he had to one of his top young people, Lisa, who would send him back some thoughts in the next 30–45 minutes. Ted thanked Bill and wished him luck on his climb, and as he was hanging up he wondered what the odds were that Bill would survive the climb and he began working through the probabilities . . . .

Lisa received Ted's fax (a brief newspaper article—shown in Figure 1.3) and Bill's request to help as she was settling down to get an early jump on an RFP that was due next week. So much for the RFP—she had at most 45 minutes to put something together and get it to Ted.

HISTORICAL CASE STUDY: IIASA (B)[5]

Glenn Perrier, a consultant for Crystal Banditz, was sitting in his office early one Spring morning in 1985, soon after he had joined the firm, looking out over the Potomac at the White House. His boss, Tom McNeil, walked in and remarked with a smile: "Glenn, I have an assignment that I think is just right for you. I got a call this morning from Tony Sarducci over at the Department of Energy and he wants us to take a look at the International Institute of Applied Systems Analysis (IIASA)."[5]

Glenn took his feet off the desk and responded, "I've never heard of IIASA, Tom. What's it all about, and what's it got to do with DOE?"

"IIASA is an international organization located near Vienna, Austria, that performs large-scale systems studies. It has been funded by the Soviets, ourselves, the Brits, the Germans, Canadians, etc. Anyway, the American Academy of Arts and Sciences took over the role as the American Member of IIASA after the Reagan Administration decided that the National Science Foundation wouldn't be allowed to continue to pay the $2.3 million in annual dues. The Academy is a private organization and is currently supporting its membership in IIASA by getting contributions from individual private foundations. It recently proposed that Federal agencies such as the Department of Energy be allowed to contribute to IIASA if they wish."

"So where do we come in?"

"IIASA hired a new Director, Thomas Lee, in October of last year who seems to be a decent manager. He is an old GE type and was a student of Harold Chestnut, a well-known system engineer. Tony wants us to check him out to see if he has things moving in the right direction over there. Tony's afraid his boss might be premature in contributing DOE money to IIASA. In order to protect his boss, and himself, he has agreed to let us charge a few hours to our standing work order with DOE to check it out. I'll need to tell him something by next week."

"Is that going to be enough time for us?"

"There may not be enough time for us, but that's all the time you have."

Tom started to walk out when Glenn shot to his feet and said with some dismay, "Wait a minute, Tom, I'm new here, and I have no idea of what you want. I need some guidance."

Tom stood thinking for a moment and obviously he was somewhat annoyed at the need to spoon-feed Glenn. Then he seemed to say to himself, "O.K., just this once.

"Well, Glenn, this is a systems house and we expect our professionals to be able to work on their own. We don't have the time or inclination to keep you under a tight leash. I suppose that the first thing you should do is to find out something of the background of IIASA. I seem to remember that it was a product of detente and that some guy from Harvard was the first director. Tony gave me the copy of the IIASA house organ I just gave you. It has an article by Lee in it (Lee, 1984).

I'll expect a 20-minute presentation by you in my office next Thursday afternoon. It won't be formal, but I will need some explicit points to give to Tony, and I'll need some recommendations for him as well."

Questions on IIASA (B)

1. Precisely what is the problem at IIASA?
2. Who has the problem?
3. Why did IIASA get into trouble?
4. What does Lee intend to do about it?
5. What will be the internal impacts of Lee's initiatives?
6. What will be the external impacts of Lee's initiatives?
7. Are there general lessons to be learned from the IIASA experience?

References for IIASA (B)

Anonymous (1981). U.S. announces pullout from IIASA in Vienna. *Science*, Dec. 11. p. 1222.

Walsh, J. (1982). Lack of reciprocity prompts IIASA cutoff. *Science*, Apr 2.

Anonymous (1982). British join U.S. in IIASA pullout. *Science*, Sept. 10. p. 987.

Lee, T. H. (1984). Director's corner. *OPTIONS*, newsletter of the International Institute of Applied Systems Analysis, Laxenburg, Austria.

Holden, C. (1984). IIASA wins support. *Science*, Oct. 12. p. 150.

NOTES

1. Some definitions of a system do not require goal-directed behavior, especially some from General Systems Theory; see Flood and Carson (1993).

2. See, for example, Buede (2000), Blanchard (2004), Sage and Armstrong (2000), Sage (1992), Daellenbach (1994), and Blanchard and Fabrycky (1998).

3. Military standard MIL-STD-499B, never formally released, was designed to address systems engineering as a whole. The prior standard that was released, MIL-STD-499A, focused on the management function of systems engineering. See Honour (1998).

4. See the International Council on Systems Engineering (INCOSE; www.incose.org) for an extensive collection of publications on systems engineering, standards, and so on, and current working groups and information on issues such as SE certification.

5. This case does not necessarily illustrate either good or bad management and is meant solely to provide a basis for classroom discussion. The inclusion of DOE in the case and the existence of Crystal Banditz Inc. are totally apocryphal.

Chapter 2

Six Major Phases of Systems Analysis

2.1 THE SYSTEMS ANALYSIS METHOD: SIX MAJOR PHASES

The six major phases of a properly conducted system study are the following:

1. Determine goals of system.
2. Establish criteria for ranking alternative candidates.
3. Develop alternative solutions.
4. Rank alternative candidates.
5. Iterate.
6. Action.

2.1.1 Determine Goals

The performance requirements of a proposed system are often unclear to the client. Thus this problem definition phase is particularly critical to the ultimate success of the project. It may seem unlikely to the novice systems analyst that a client would not understand his own problem, but such is often the case. The fact that the client cannot define his own problem is particularly exasperating to a theorist who has been taught that one cannot handle a problem until it is completely defined. In practice, the converse is true. *The systems analyst must expect to engage in a dialogue with his client to arrive at a suitable statement of a large-scale system problem.* Your sponsor

How to Do Systems Analysis. By John E. Gibson, William T. Scherer, and William F. Gibson
Copyright © 2007 John Wiley & Sons, Inc.

cannot present you with a well-defined problem for analysis. Rather, you must expect to define the problem properly yourself. To ask the sponsor to define his problem is to ask him to assume an important part of the systems analysis task and to complete for himself what is perhaps the most important and difficult phase in the entire process. We do not advise this.

Perhaps an analogy to the patient–physician relationship will clarify matters. Most of the time, although not always, the patient knows he is sick. He has a list of symptoms, although he has no way of telling which ones are critical and which ones are not. He does not know what questions to ask, or data to gather, or treatment to apply. The physician would be quite unwise to permit the patient to diagnose his own disease and prescribe his own cure. Likewise, the lawyer would not let his client dictate how his case is to be tried. The same is generally true in large-scale systems analysis.

A good example of the difficulty in extracting the real crux of a societal problem is the Appalachian program initiated by the President's Appalachian Commission Report of 1964 and funded by the Appalachian Regional Development Act of 1965. It would seem, on its face, that the problem in Appalachia is poverty and rural isolation, yet Rothblatt (1971) points out that it took two years for the states within the Appalachian planning region to discover and articulate their planning goals. In the meantime, over 450 million dollars were expended on activities that were not necessarily integrated into the overall goals and plans as finally approved.

Subject-area specialists who join a system team are especially likely to attempt to avoid the task of problem definition by referring to authority (i.e., the client) or by suggesting that other specialists be added to the team to address each new aspect of the overall problem as it becomes evident. These tactics are attempts to avoid the issue rather than handling it properly and therefore are unacceptable. Indeed the generalization process implicit in goal determination becomes so threatening to some technique-fixated specialists that they are unable to participate effectively and must withdraw from the team.

2.1.2   Establish Criteria for Ranking Alternative Candidates

While developing realistic goals for the system has been called the most difficult phase of a system's study, it is also true that developing an index of performance (IP), with which to judge the performance of a system may be considered the most controversial. The term "goal" refers to the client's objective, while the term "index of performance" refers to the measurement of the relative success in achieving the goal. In the simple case, the goal is to maximize a specific IP. Critics of the systems approach, such as Hoos, emphasize the great temptation to choose, as a criterion for the system, a physical parameter that is easily measured even if it is not meaningful. And there is no doubt about the difficulty of choosing meaningful indices for complex large-scale systems, which have major policy components.

An effort to represent a complex system by an index of performance seems analogous to attempting to represent reality with a measuring stick. In the most general sense, the task seems futile. Yet those interested in the performance of a system will be forced to choose <u>some</u> pragmatic success measure. The system method makes this choice explicit, objective, and, hopefully, more meaningful. Often, through careful discussions with an informed client, factors initially expressed as "goals" may be reinterpreted as bounds, limits, or constraints, thus simplifying the optimization process.

All too often, without the guidance of an experienced policy analyst, goals for a project are chosen for which there exists no agreed-upon index of performance. This happened, for example, in President Eisenhower's Commission on National Goals, as we will see, and in the Fitch paper on Goals for Urban America discussed below. At best, unmeasurable goals are meaningless platitudes, and, at worst, they can lead to serious dissension, wasted resources, and ultimate failure of the project. In numerous domains the authors have heard "it's a great system, but too complex to measure the actual performance . . . ". In recent years, this has been seen extensively in information technology systems like data warehousing and Enterprise Resource Planning (ERP) systems, where up to hundreds of millions of dollars have been spent with no proper IPs. Bottom line: If it's not measurable (as described in Chapter 4), it's not worth doing. Period.

Critics sometimes argue that the problem of choosing meaningful indices of performance for complex large-scale systems is different in kind from the problem in simple mechanical systems in which an index of performance is supposedly easy to design and to apply. In this presumption, such critics are quite wrong. It is not easy to agree on a single, meaningful criterion for <u>any</u> realistic system. For example, we can testify from personal experience that the arguments against subjecting straightforward, linear automatic control systems to standard specifications engendered the same kind of intense emotional opposition when first proposed as does the concept of a performance index from critics of large-scale systems analysis, and for some of the same reasons (Gibson et al., 1961). Not only was it argued that a meaningful criterion would be difficult to construct, but designers also resisted what they viewed as an attempt to restrict their design freedom.

Engineers and politicians are alike in one respect. Each would prefer to be able to choose his own judgment criterion *after the fact*, so as to place his creation in the best possible light.

2.1.3 Develop Alternative Solutions

While the principle of developing alternative scenarios seems simple enough, there are pitfalls. It is interesting to note that, while the client often has great difficulty with goal development and with the selection of an index of performance, it is the analyst who often resists the development of alternative scenarios.

Simple, existing <u>technological</u> alternatives may be obvious, but one must also include functional and long-term structural alternatives. For example, in an urban transportation system, one would certainly include as modal alternatives the auto, taxis, subways, pedestrian walkways, and buses. But a new subway for a major city could cost more than a billion dollars and 10 years to construct. BART in San Francisco cost over $1.6 billion (original estimate $1.0 billion) before it was finished. The Washington, D.C., subway cost over $4.7 billion (original estimate $2.5 billion), and it has been under construction since 1969. A single extension, such as the Washington Metro E-Route, which opened in 1999, cost over $600 million. And the "Big Dig" in Boston is in a class of its own.[1]

Long-term <u>functional</u> alternatives for such massive undertakings should not be ignored. For example, will the video-phone or internet conferencing take the place of much business travel? Ten years from now, will it be common for white-collar employees to work at home, in front of a computer terminal, instead of going to the office? Some of us already do this. Will citizens insist on retaining the right to use their personal auto even if they are forced to pay the full cost of bringing it into the Central Business District ("CBD") or edge city? Consider the cases of London and Singapore, which added entry fees into their CBDs. In London there is considerable complaining, but people still enter in large numbers, while in Singapore only buses and taxis are typically found in the CBD. Thus, in the case of London, the tariff is too low to achieve the goal of traffic reduction; however, if the goal is revenue generation, they may be successful.[2]

As a functional alternative, one might ask, Will the dispersal of urban work places render the concentrated CBD obsolete? These and other long-term questions make the typical transportation analyst nervous. It is natural to wish to restrict oneself to specific, tactical engineering designs. Yet, shouldn't long-range and somewhat speculative options be presented to the urban decision maker? Perhaps the decision maker will not wish to consider them in detail, but the analyst ought to have first-order costs and benefits at hand, if only to put the more conventional options in better perspective.

2.1.4 Rank Alternatives

The indices of performance and constraints are next applied to the list of candidates and a rank ordering of their acceptability is developed. At this point, a number of additional concerns, which are not normally listed as performance constraints, must be considered. Here are some examples of nonperformance concerns:

- *Effect on Nonusers.* Questions such as noise insult and pollution resultant from implementation of large-scale systems come to mind but more generally the analyst must ask, Does a particular candidate solution result in a differential disadvantage to some stakeholders? A classic, ubiquitous example is noise generated by airports: Numerous non-users are impacted by the noise generated, and the result has been countless lawsuits, protests, policies, and so on, to address the issues.
- *Effect of Incremental Introduction.* Many large-scale systems are so large that they must be introduced piecemeal. This can provide opportunities as well as disadvantages. A candidate solution that is critically dependent on complete installation before performance begins is very vulnerable. Introduction of e-commerce

and data warehousing into a large corporation are examples of this potential pitfall, and such systems have suffered from the difficulty in determining indices of performance.

- *Impact on Existing System.* It is rare for an important system to be considered *de novo*. Usually there is an existing solution in place which is unsatisfactory in important ways, or the study would not be authorized. But the cost of totally replacing the existing solution could be high. An analysis that ignores such situations lacks contextual integrity. The replacement of Stapleton International Airport in Denver with the Denver International Airport (DIA) is an example of this high cost and the impact on the airport support services that are integral to the successful operation of the facility.

- *Sensitivity of IP to Parameter Variation.* Often a pseudo-optimal candidate appears that suffers significantly if certain of its parameters or constraints are revised slightly. Such a candidate lacks robustness and should not be recommended. Consider a transportation system solution that assumes a certain price and availability of oil as a critical parameter. Given the extended timeframe to implement significant transportation solutions, this could radically alter the viability of the solution and needs to be studied carefully as part of the systems analysis.

- *Ratification Procedures.* The technical person sometimes imagines that one can fight free of political pressures and select the "best" system in a vacuum. This has probably never been true, and most rational men know it.[3] Indeed, one could argue that democracy demands a public ratification procedure. The attempt of the Department of Commerce to persuade the U. S. Congress to support R&D in the housing industry, the CITP program discussed below, is an object lesson of the failure of a system analyst to consider ratification proceedings.

One might say to each of the example concerns given above, "But, I can take care of that." Of course this is true. But it misses the point. We aren't presenting a definitive checklist of nonperformance concerns here. We are saying that concerns other than the idealized performance of the idealized system must also be considered.

2.1.5   Iterate

After obtaining a group of prime candidates, one can initiate a more careful analysis of the reduced group. A more precise definition of the problem should also be developed for the next iteration. One cannot expect to have a full appreciation of a meaningful systems problem *a priori*. An attempt to do general systems planning on a straight-through basis (i.e., without iteration) will generally delay project initiation, will result in premature loss of options, will waste money and time on portions of the problem later found to be irrelevant, will reduce the probability of selecting the optimum candidate, and will sometimes cause outright failure of the effort.

In a well-conducted systems study, one expects to see a smooth and orderly narrowing and deepening of the analysis. A study that does not begin broadly enough, or that fails to deepen in intensity of analysis as weak candidates are rejected, or that abruptly leaps from a general level to an extremely specific solution is suspect. In our consulting practices, we've seen numerous examples of failure to accomplish this process of careful iteration and focusing in a professional manner and its consequences.

We were called in to help diagnose and treat a crisis with which our client was unexpectedly confronted. Not long before, our client was awarded a very large contract to upgrade and re-engineer the software and hardware of an extraordinarily large logistics supply system. As the prime contractor of the system, our client's organization had systems integration responsibility in addition to procurement responsibilities. But well into the initial phase of the work, the sponsor raised serious objections to the systems integration aspect of the process. Hundreds of millions of dollars were at stake.

It appeared to us that our client had written an outstanding response to the initial proposal. Our evidence for this conclusion is that it won the competition against tough odds. It also seemed that our client was doing excellent day-by-day work on the software reengineering. The problem was that, in the first few months after winning the competition, our client had not developed a clear and precise narrative of the systems integration process to be followed. A systems integration plan should proceed from the general scope of the successful response to the RFP through several levels of increasing detail to show how the systems integration and procurement will be accomplished within the goals and constraints imposed by the sponsor.

Clients are almost always short-term oriented and press prematurely for detailed responses to detailed interrogatories. This case was no exception. When pressed by the sponsor, our client had leaped from the general, overall specifications to one specific implementation plan which it presented to the sponsor. But some sponsor personnel who opposed this specific implementation made life distinctly uncomfortable for our client for a week or so by exploiting this gap in the systems integration process.

A common question concerning iteration is, How many times should we iterate? The iteration should focus in smoothly to an optimum result. Each iteration clarifies and refines the solution but costs time and money. One stops when the additional cost of one more iteration exceeds the probable benefit of the additional clarification. More will be said on the suggested timescale of these iterations in the chapter on managing the systems team (Chapter 8).

2.1.6   Action

The point of a systems study is to achieve the client's goal, not merely to deliver a final report. The final report represents only an intermediate milepost. The final report must thus have an action orientation. This is difficult to achieve if the systems team considers the report as its final goal. Much to be preferred is the team that internalizes the client's goal and whose report in effect says, "here is *our* problem and here is how *we* will move forward together to solve it." This action orientation should include a step-by-step, organized procedure for achieving the goals outlined in the report. This step-by-step process is called the *transition scenario*. See Section 7.3.

2.2   THE GOAL-CENTERED OR TOP-DOWN APPROACH

Systems analysis takes a problem-centered or *goal-centered* approach rather than a *technologically centered* approach. Other, less-than-optimal planning methods include approaches centered on political expediency, incrementalism, tradition, and so on. Another possible trap is the step-by-step, or *chronological*, approach. The goal-centered approach begins, in a sense, with what appears to be a completely backward way of going at things. Instead of starting at the beginning, one starts at the end.

What could be more logical than starting at the beginning of the problem and making a list of steps to be taken in chronological order to complete it? This chronological or so-called "laundry list" approach contains several major difficulties, however:

- Unless the goal is precisely known, the step-by-step approach may waste effort in developing task segments which turn out not to be needed (See the Manned Mars Mission case study below).
- Without a set end-point for each subtask, these subtasks may be elaborated upon to an unnecessary degree, thus wasting resources.
- Without a known end-point, the specification of a vital subtask may be underestimated, thus setting up a performance deficiency.

In Figures 2.1 and 2.2, we portray the goal-centered approach in contrast to the step-by-step approach in a specific systems study of a proposed NASA Manned Mars

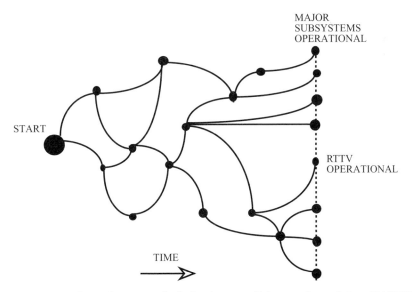

FIGURE 2.1 A schematic portrayal of all subsystem linkages of a real-time TV (RTTV) system for a Manned Mars Mission (MMM). This is a hypothetical portrayal of the myriad of systems linkages that must go together to make the MMM successful. However, our team has been asked to examine the feasibility of only the RTTV system. Note how easily the RTTV feasibility study could be sidetracked if the system team took the chronological approach to the problem.

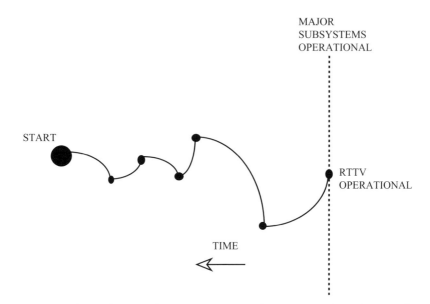

FIGURE 2.2 The goal-oriented or "inverse-temporal" approach. If, on the other hand, the RTTV feasibility study starts with the assumption that the system is operational, and works backward link by link establishing performance requirements for each subsystem in order, analysis goes more expeditiously.

Mission (MMM). The entire MMM study was a paper study and thus hypothetical in a sense, but was done in sufficient detail as to uncover as many practical design problems as possible, in order to develop timely solutions.

One systems team was assigned to analyze the concept of a Real-Time Television Link (RTTV) between Earth and the spacecraft. The critical aspect of such a link is the bit-rate or bandwidth; for example, current technically feasible low bit-rates may not allow for many real-time activities, including the potential detection of life on Mars. In order to analyze the performance of the RTTV concept, one needs to establish (a) the performance specifications of the TV link and (b) the characteristics of the various interfaces with other subsystems of the spacecraft. One approach to this analysis task would be to take a "chronological" approach. In such a step-by-step (also called "incremental," or "logical") approach, one is blocked from defining accurate performance specifications for the TV link until design specifications for all other links have been established. This impediment arises because it is difficult to predict, before the overall system design is complete, while other subsystems will impact the performance of the TV link.

On the other hand, the goal-centered approach of the analysis to the TV link begins with the final element and moves backward through the chain, setting detailed specifications for each link as the process unfolds. Only those links on whose performance the TV link is seen to depend need be considered. The output requirements for the immediate predecessor links to any given link in the TV chain can be established, given the performance requirements placed on the RTTV. Immediate predecessors are defined as those subsystems directly connected to and supporting the performance of the TV link. Thus the goal-centered approach appears to provide the advantage of simplicity compared with alternate methods more commonly utilized. Nevertheless, the goal-centered approach is so strange to planners not familiar with systems analysis that it often provides a major conceptual stumbling block for them.

One somewhat simplistic, albeit accurate, way to consider this method of grappling with a problem is to consider a puzzle book of children's mazes. As a child goes through the book and the mazes become more complex and convoluted, one will note that the inventive child may well start at the end-point and work backwards to the origin. Sometimes we, the older, "wiser" consultants can learn potential solutions to seemingly intractable problems from the practices of those not distracted by the more formal "ways things are done around here."

The state of computer software design 15 or 20 years ago provides an illustration of some of the disadvantages of the chronological approach to system design. Undisciplined first-generation computer-software programmers, "spaghetti twirlers," thought in terms of starting a software project by "writing code." These were programmers for whom flow charting and program structuring in advance were too much trouble. As a result, they almost inevitably produced code with many intertwinings, using "GO TO" statements. When the flow chart was finally completed, after the fact, it often looked like the proverbial bowl of spaghetti. This "bottom-up" approach has now been replaced almost entirely by the more sophisticated and disciplined "top-down" approach of structured and object-oriented programming. We advocate precisely this top-down approach in the process of system analysis. Consider how Apple Computers are designed. Steve Jobs, the CEO, articulates what the end result of a specific computer model should be and its capabilities. From that top-down information (goals/capabilities), the engineers and programmers work backwards to develop the design schema that the manufacturers use.[4]

Conventional engineering design, however, often continues to utilize an exclusively "bottom-up" approach. That is, in conventional engineering analysis, one assumes the *status quo* and proceeds by step-by-step increments to a given, externally defined, technological goal. There seems little doubt that this is indeed an excellent methodology if the *status quo* is unchanging, the goals are clear, and the problem is familiar (see Table 2.1). Unfortunately, this incremental approach, if applied in isolation, has been found expensive and fallible in new and unfamiliar design environments.

A "top-down" approach inverts the problem. There, one starts with the normative situation, or "preferred future," that one desires to create. In 1991, we had an opportunity to assist as a consultant in a top-down determination of a strategic plan for R&D in a national multimodal transportation network. The issue could be defined as, "What should be the condition of the national transport infrastructure in, say, 25 years, and what new R&D will be needed to get there?" Based on a simple consensus of the desired future, one next identifies important long-term transport issues and filters them through existing and needed R&D capabilities and technology to produce the R&D strategic plan. This four-phase concept is illustrated in Figure 2.3.

TABLE 2.1. Top-Down and Bottom-Up Planning Compared

Top-Down Planning

Attributes
• Moves from the general to the specific
• Based on goals and objectives

Strengths
• Based on the general assumptions and trends of the planning environment
• Identifies changes in the planning environment and adjusts to them

Weaknesses
• Can lose focus and objectivity if not executed properly
• Does not provide sufficient detail for effective action on short-range issues

Bottom-Up Planning

Attributes
• Based on current conditions
• Employs current technology plus minor extrapolations
• Employs an incremental, step-by-step approach

Strengths
• Lends itself to immediate evaluation of cost effectiveness
• Consistent with conventional engineering design methodology

Weaknesses
• Tends to focus vision on short-term problems
• Produces ever-decreasing incremental improvements
• Locks-in current technology and operational structure

One might be tempted to believe that the first step shown in Figure 2.3 is the most difficult, but this is not so. It would present a daunting prospect, it is true, if one means to require a completely articulated set of national goals from which to derive deductively the objectives for a national transport R&D program. This is so because

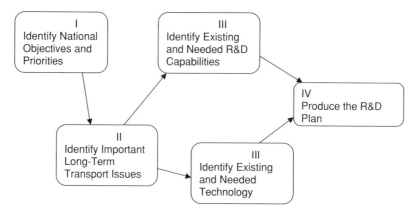

FIGURE 2.3 The four steps in strategic planning of national transport research and development.

in no Western nation does such an agreed-upon value structure exist. In fact, one can argue that in a democracy it could not exist. Fortunately, however, no such complete articulation is needed. Even the barest minimum consensus on the existing *status quo* and a few agreed-upon extrapolations will be sufficient.

What might one expect to gain by substituting a top-down R&D planning environment for a more conventional engineering bottom-up approach? Table 2.1 should provide a clue. In a bottom-up environment, one would expect to find short-term, narrowly focused, single-mode projects with little concern given to broader, national concerns. The individual projects would be narrowly technological "hardware" in focus with very specific, short-term goals. In the case at hand, these projects were of very high quality and accomplished in a completely professional manner, but the individual project managers could not be expected to have decades-long national goals in mind while accomplishing them. The danger is that the national environment is in a rather rapid process of change, and this short-term hardware approach could be viewed as producing good answers to increasingly less important problems.

Newly important issues such as the changes needed in aircraft traffic control and the location of airports to accommodate the move to the hub-and-spoke network might be overlooked. Multimodal research might not receive sufficient emphasis, and those specific topics of vital importance because of special national geographic factors might be neglected in this conventional bottom-up environment.

Top-down analysis corrects the errors of the bottom-up approach; however, when employed alone, it creates its own problems. Top-down analysis in isolation has an ethereal, unworldly appearance that seems to say, "stop the world, while I cogitate on developing a plan for the best of all possible worlds." Unfortunately, the world won't stop. Aircraft crash and burn in today's world while we wait for nonflammable materials and the perfect air traffic control system. Citizens die on today's highways in today's autos, and pollution is a fact in today's environment.

The preferred procedure, it seems clear, is to alternate between top-down and bottom-up in an iterative fashion. This is not to say, however, that equal time and effort need to be given to both. The addition of a long-range top-down viewpoint to an existing short-range, bottom-up planning cycle can be done quite economically and will thus tend to produce disproportionate gains in effectiveness and credibility. It is difficult to assign proportions to the effort required in the two modes in the abstract, but 20% top-down and 80% bottom-up seems a not unreasonable rough estimate.

Even if one accepts the concept of the top-down design approach in principle, and even if one agrees with the need to alternate between top-down and bottom-up planning, there remains the question of precisely how one bridges the chasm between (a) the ideal future condition produced by top-down analysis and (b) the "here and now." The first step in closing this gap is to prepare a "descriptive scenario" and a "normative scenario." We will discuss these two planning techniques in more detail in Sections 3.3 and 3.4, respectively, but a brief definition will suffice here. The *descriptive scenario*, "DS," is a narrative that describes the *status quo*, the "here and now," and is obtained by means of a bottom-up analysis of the existing condition.

The *normative scenario*, "NS," is a narrative that describes the problem environment when the ideal system (which has not yet been designed in detail) is in place and operating successfully.

Each of these scenarios is a careful, complete, quantitative portrayal of the condition of the issue, at the current time and the completion date, respectively. We do not ignore reality in the normative scenario, but we do assume that the critical issues that have been identified in the course of the SA have been properly resolved. This is called a "base-line" normative scenario. A separate analysis will be made of the critical assumptions in this base-line scenario and potential variances or "critical incidents" will be addressed (see Section 3.4).

Given the descriptive and normative scenarios, the next step is to construct a "transition scenario" that describes how to get from "here" (DS) to "there" (NS). The transition scenario is a practical, step-by-step planning document and includes as its fundamental component, the *critical path* of events and actions needed to accomplish the transition. This critical path includes interim mileposts that help to measure progress. We recommend that the transition scenario be constructed in reverse temporal order, that is, working backward from the goal, as described in Figure 2.2. The transition scenario is the heart of the final report. It constitutes the work product or "deliverable" of the SA (see Section 7.3).

2.3 THE INDEX OF PERFORMANCE CONCEPT

Perhaps the most basic and fundamental concept in the system approach is that an objective index of performance (IP), be established with which to measure the quality of operation of a system. The IP, at minimum, consists of a set of separate indices for each of the several separate objectives of the system, but ideally it is an overall utility measure in a multiple-objective optimization process. This is an idea that has been taken over from operations research and refined in recent years. Credit for creating this bold concept must go to the early developers of OR. The audacity of the notion is somewhat dimmed now by several decades of familiarity, but in the 1950s the IP concept seemed truly revolutionary.

The usual reaction of a decision-maker who considers for the first time the concept of an objective index of performance for a large-scale system or organization takes one of two modalities. The first, and perhaps the most common, response is that the idea is trivial. "Why waste time on something so obvious?" one may be asked. Everyone knows that the object of the army is to kill the enemy, the object of the navy is to keep open the sea lanes, the object of a business is to make money, and so on. Consider the war in Iraq (2003 and on), where the United States is engaged in numerous cities in the country after an initial invasion. Discussions with returning commanders indicated that in the initial years units were to be measured by engagements with, and kills of, insurgents. Several commanders on-site realized that if the goal is long-term stability and recovery, such measures might not be achieving these goals. Different measures, including those such as the number of patrols led by Iraqi troops, might be directly traceable to the goals of stability and recovery.

But if one persists in pressing the matter by asking precisely *how* the navy, for example, will do its "obvious" job, with planes, or destroyers, or subs, or aircraft carriers, or battleships, or precisely which lines of business will optimize the rate of return, one is met with the second modal response. The "expert" responds that it would be too complex and too time-consuming to attempt to reduce the involved and sensitive plans of a complex organization to a single equation written on a scrap of paper. The "expert" may go on to say that this (any) organization is made up of hundreds (thousands) of people with millions (billions) of dollars invested in capital equipment, and its leadership has taken years (decades) to grasp the intricacies of the interplay of the organization with those it serves and those with which it competes. It is inconceivable that the "expert" should attempt to explain all of this to a "system analyst," much less that the analyst could grasp it even if it were explained. So the analyst is bounced from one extreme to the other. Either the index of performance concept is trivial or it is impractically complex.

Let us consider an example of an organization with an apparent relatively simple index of performance and use the very real involutions we will discover, to indicate just how complex the establishment is of a meaningful index of performance. Take a typical, large, publicly held corporation. It would not be difficult to quote from one corporate charter after another to the effect that the goal of the enterprise is to return to the stockholders a "fair return" on their investment by engaging in the manufacture and/or distribution and/or sales of a particular line of products and/or services. Consider the automobile business, for example, and General Motors in particular.

Traditionally (i.e., prior to 1975), GM's return on investment was higher than other American auto manufacturers, and its share of the U.S. auto market was about 50%. Its gross revenues were larger than the gross national product of all but a half dozen of the largest nations in the world. Is General Motors' goal to increase its return on investment? Or to increase its market share? Or what? Perhaps we should ask the Chairman of the GM Board of Directors? Or perhaps objective outside observers would be better able to interpret corporate behavior?

There seems to be agreement among experienced business observers that, prior to 1975, GM's corporate goal was to maintain its traditionally high return on investment, *without* increasing its share of the U.S. market. The corporation would not have been content to lose control of any important share of its market, of course, but it was even more concerned that it not increase that share. GM corporate strategists of that period were convinced that if GM increased substantially its share of the American automobile market, it would be subjected to anti-trust action by the U.S. Attorney General (*Wall Street Journal*, 1967, 1970; Ludvissen, 1972). The late Senator Phil Hart, of Michigan ironically enough, was a strong proponent of GM breakup.

There are *pro* and *con* arguments about the desirability of this dismantling, but we aren't concerned with them here. The point is that GM deliberately held back from increasing its share of the market by regulating its own prices. By virtue of its size and resultant economies of scale and its widely admired management skills, it was able to maintain corporate pride and competitiveness, while maximizing profits without seeking to increase its market share. However, at the beginning of the 1976 model year, under the spur of increased foreign competition, GM let it be known that it was taking off all wraps. It announced that it intended to maximize sales.

John Kenneth Galbraith, on the other hand, argues in his *New Industrial State* that to maximize profits is not truly the index of performance of the modern American corporation (Galbraith, 1967). He interprets the 25 years of market restraint by GM quite differently than we have done above. He argues that in almost all important industrial segments, the marketplace is dominated by a few large firms, which, by their size, control the market.

Galbraith goes on to argue that American auto companies can make the buyer accept whatever they wish to produce, simply by not offering any alternatives. This does not require explicit collusion between the leaders, Galbraith says, because they are all subject to the same market environment, and the corporate executives have the same individual self-interests. Thus they will come to the same conclusions about their optimum policy without collusion. And of course one cannot deny that in autos, steel, electric manufacturing, and a number of other basic industries, a few market giants do dominate. More conventional economists argue that Galbraith ignores customer resistance, the possibility of product substitution, foreign competition, and so on, in his concept of market control, but this debate is not our concern here.

Galbraith maintains that American industrial executives use this market control, the "technostructure," so as to maintain and improve their personal job security and income, while ignoring both their customers' interest and return to the investor:

> ...the technostructure is protecting something more important than its profits— something indeed which profits themselves protect. That is its autonomy.
>
> [Galbraith, 1967, p. 173]

The way in which the technostructure ensures its survival is clear, according to Galbraith:

> Once the safety of the technostructure is insured [sic] by a minimum level of earnings, there is then a measure of choice as to goals. Nothing is so compelling as the need to survive. However, there is little doubt as to how, overwhelmingly, this choice is exercised: it is to achieve the greatest possible rate of corporate growth as measured in sales.
>
> [Galbraith, 1967, p. 174]

This means more jobs with more responsibility for the technostructure and more promotions and more compensation. To the critic who claims that Galbraith has merely rediscovered the wheel and the principle of self-interest in the capitalistic system, he replies not so. Galbraith argues that to maximize growth does not necessarily result in maximizing profits in either the short- or long-run.

We have suggested at least the following four possible goals for a large corporation:

1. Maintain a given share of market while maximizing (long-term) return on investment (announced GM policy prior to 1975).
2. Maximize sales (announced GM corporate policy, *circa* 1975).

3. Maximize (short-term) profits (Wall St. investors' goal).
4. Maximize market control (J. K. Galbraith thesis).

But there are other possible goals, as U.S. corporations discover when they cross national boundaries. Corporate practice can, and does, become an instrument of national policy. Extractive industries such as oil, copper, iron, and so on, are obvious examples, but we will stick with automobiles. One is perhaps not surprised to learn that, for an auto company to do business in a given country, it may be forced to locate a portion of its manufacturing within the nation. One could view this as a constraint, however, and not a change in corporate goal. But what of Renault and other companies partially owned by governments? Renault in France, Singapore Air, and the Post Office Service in the United States are semi-autonomous corporations and examples of organizations which have found that none of the goals mentioned above apply to them.

In 1975, Renault's top management was not convinced that its auto business would continue to remain profitable (*Business Week*, 1975). Thus, what to do to improve profitability? Diversify? Cut unprofitable activities in the auto divisions? Yes and no. A top Renault official declared:

> We know that we would make more profit from good money management and from banking agreements than from selling cars. But as our mission is to employ 200,000 people in France, we will have to find the money in other fields to keep the automobile business going.

Here is a new goal! Make money if possible, but even if you lose money, *"... employ 200,000 people in France."* Quite obviously, there will be decision points at which full employment and return on investment are diametrically opposed.

We have gone on at some length in this example to illustrate that even in the apparently simplest of cases, such as a well-established, for-profit business firm with a single generic product line, the index of performance is not obvious. How much more so is this true in a social system.

However, in a smaller-scale business operations environment, the problem of establishing good indices of performance is equally difficult. Consider the case of a financial institution's collections call center that we were helping our client improve operations via a systems analysis. Of critical importance to such a center is the ability of operators to generate revenue via the in-bound phone channel. IPs for the operators, therefore, drive the success of the call center. The metric driving the performance of the call center when we arrived was Right Party Connects (RPCs—getting the right person on the phone to talk) and Promises to Pay (PTP—an account agreeing to make some payment on debt). Unfortunately, both of these metrics are easy to game and do not necessarily correlate with the client's goal of revenue generation. As a result, the call center was losing money and on the verge of being shut down. A more appropriate metric in this case might be the actual dollars generated per hour by an operator.

In the following chapters we will emphasize how the system analyst goes about interacting with the client to establish jointly the index of performance. Often this interactive process can only be accomplished by the client as he observes the impact of different performance indices on candidate solutions. We give an example of this interaction between the two phases of a system study in the Woodward Avenue subway case discussed in the following section.

2.4 DEVELOPING ALTERNATIVE SCENARIOS

It may fairly be asked:

> "Why should we invent artificial alternatives once we know one good solution? Why not spend the design team's time (and the client's money) on further developing this one solution?"

Before the reader proceeds, we hope he or she will formulate a response to this inquiry.

Perhaps your response is, *"That's right. I agree."* And of course, on occasion, this is the best procedure. But we must ask, "How do you know that you have the 'right' solution?" Obviously, any particular solution depends on the index of performance. If the IP changes, so will in all probability the solution. Furthermore, to know one has the "right" solution means one has an algorithm for deriving the optimum solution given the form of the system and the optimizing criterion. Both of these expectations are well-founded perhaps with respect to simple systems described by mathematical relations, but unfortunately neither may be expected to be present in a typical large-scale systems analysis.

Here is another problem created by leaping to the "correct" option, even if you *know* the "correct" answer. In today's adversarial environment, one must be careful to leave an "audit trail" that documents the clear and objective process by which the "optimum" choice was made. A leap directly from the customer's requirements to the solution will often open the analyst and the client to the likelihood of a successful legal protest. This means time and money wasted, the very things you were trying to avoid by leaping to the answer.

The client is quite unlikely to accept the concept of the index of performance, as we have said above, and a step-by-step analytic process of optimization is not likely to exist. Let us examine a situation. In the Woodward Avenue subway study discussed in more detail in a later chapter, a systems team was asked to examine the desirability of a new subway line for Detroit. The Mayor was unable to choose from among the following plausible operational goals which were suggested as the reason for considering this project.

1. Decrease traffic congestion on lower Woodward Avenue?
2. Decrease travel time to and from downtown?
3. Arrest urban decay?
4. Stimulate new construction along Woodward?
5. Other?

Which would you choose? The Mayor said, "All of the above!" Yet, as we will see, the Woodward Avenue subway solution was the optimum for only one special index. A more robust solution exists that is superior for almost any other combination of indices. The analysis team chose to illustrate the alternatives by constructing a computer simulation for Detroit. Seven different criteria could be applied using this computer simulation, which utilized experimental origin and destination transport data and land-use data covering the urban Detroit area. Using the simulation, one could study any artery and apply any index of performance or combination thereof. This permitted the Mayor to look at the effect of any choice he wished to make. Only after he had "experienced" several solutions did he decide on his preferred index. This resulted in the "right" location for a new subway, which was not Woodward. Note that we were using the simulation to construct scenarios that helped the Mayor to reevaluate his understanding of the situation. We will see more of this conceptual tool in the chapter on scenarios.

Even after the index has been established, one needs ingenuity to invent candidate scenarios to be evaluated. Furthermore, as we have just seen, it may be impossible to take these two phases sequentially. Rather, it may be necessary for them to be handled iteratively and together. Very rarely, if ever, is the problem a simple one of optimizing the parameters in a fixed structure. The structure itself is usually at question in a large-scale system study.

We will devote Chapter 5 to suggestions of how to go about developing a field of candidate solutions. One of the most effective of these procedures is the Options Field/Options Profile method, which, as we will see, is a refinement of Zwicky's Morphological Box approach. We should not, therefore, go into methodological details here; it should be pointed out that even among those who accept the concept of developing a field of options, the size of the initial field is often unduly restricted. We don't want just one or two options with which to start the analysis, we may need several hundred. Most of these initial candidates soon fall out of the feasible solution set, but it is not good SA practice to eliminate options before the analysis begins. As an example, the planning for a replacement for the Woodrow Wilson Bridge (over the Potomac River) in the mid-1990s resulted in over 100 possible alternatives in the early iterations, and in subsequent iterations the number was quickly reduced by an order of magnitude. The initial alternatives demonstrated excellent outscoping and represented a very diverse set of possibilities.

2.5 RANKING ALTERNATIVES

This step conjures up the notion of a score for each option and a simple comparison thereof. And indeed on occasion it may be this simple, but rarely so. Consider the relatively simple problem of providing yourself with transportation for the journey to work. You may infer from this question that it is merely a choice from among two or three new car models. But isn't the location of your home with respect to your workplace part of this question? Perhaps you should live nearby and walk to work. Or, perhaps you should live on a public transit line to avoid the cost of a second car.

Perhaps you should buy a bicycle or Moped or a used car. But just suppose you exclude all the above possibilities and move directly to a new car choice. This decision in itself would be rather curious, however, because one would appear to start by excluding a number of plausible choices on an emotional basis and then attempt to evaluate the remainder on a rational basis. Is that rational?

Be that as it may, one would then proceed to weigh comfort, resale value, prestige, immediate operating cost, long-term operating cost, safety, and so on, on a single scale. This can be done, and "decision theory" proposes a reasoned procedure for its accomplishment. Yet one must see that even this "simple" choice is fraught with complexity if approached on any level except the most heuristic and intuitive.

By the way, we seem to have created an argument here against the systems approach. If such a "simple" problem can be rendered so complex by our proposed method, how can we expect a level-headed person to accept such a process? We will consider this issue in more detail in a later chapter.

2.6 ITERATION AND THE "ERROR-EMBRACING" APPROACH

The concept of iteration is a natural one for a person trained as an analyst of closed-loop automatic-control systems (servomechanisms) to suggest. Such devices operate by comparison of the actual state and the desired state. The difference is called "error" and this error signal is used to drive the actual state toward the desired state. Extending this philosophy to large-scale system design, it would seem natural to compare the results of the first iteration to the ideal or normative (i.e., measure the error) and to repeat the analysis in order to reduce the difference. We know from the design of servomechanisms what a powerful concept this is. But application of this technique to large-scale systems flies in the face of popular wisdom.[5] Consider how risky this whole idea seems.

Conventional wisdom says the following: "Look before you leap." "Don't move until you are sure." "Avoid risk." "Don't make a fool of yourself." But the systems approach specifically suggests the opposite. In SA we tend to suggest that one should not take too much time with each step in the first iteration. Rather it seems more effective for the analysis team to crash all the way through, so that it will better understand the problem. One could say this in another way. "Develop an error signal." SA takes what Michael (1972) calls an "error embracing" approach. Yet as he points out, *"Political men and rational men avoid error acknowledgment like sin—which, indeed, it smacks of in our society."*

Doesn't it somehow seem to you wasteful, dangerous, foolhardy even, to proceed rapidly, almost carelessly, into the unknown? Indeed it does in our culture. And why? Because we have learned through painful experience that the potential upside gain from success is less valuable than the downside risk of failure. This tribal memory is a safe guide if we are in a marginal survival state.

There, one or two important failures could be so costly as to endanger the continued existence of the group. Thus, in a survival state, one must sacrifice the possibility of rapid improvement to ensure one's continued existence absolutely. By the way, this seems to say that developing nations should beware of international bankers from developed nations, bearing system study recommendations as gifts.

Here is still another point of view. Let's ask what is the usual class of index of performance within which a control system is designed? The automatic control engineer is often taught to design for minimum response time. He is taught that a "good" system is one in which the error (or some function of error) is brought to zero in a minimum time. He is taught to manage the initial error, but not to fear it. He expects to compute the stresses imposed on the system by this rapid reduction of error and to design the system to withstand them.

How different is the political system or the social system? There "error" denotes waste, mismanagement, or "sin." Why? Perhaps because the energy and force required to bring such error to zero in a minimum time might expose the social system to stresses it could not withstand. Perhaps also the force required for such error reduction is not available to the typical politician or manager.

Perhaps further, society has discovered that it does not wish to allow any controller or leader to be able to gain such power. As usual, the Greeks had a word for it. *Ostracism* was the practice in Periclean Greece of voting to forbid public office for 10 years to especially persuasive or powerful individuals, on the grounds that by their overpowering personal magnetism and political influence they would possibly subvert democracy. Modern examples of national wartime political leaders being sent away when the emergency ends come to mind.

To reduce error in minimum time is often not an acceptable criterion for a social system. Perhaps society has found from bitter experience that the only safe criterion is to operate within a strictly limited correctional force or energy level. If society cannot stand the forces and resulting rapid changes (revolution?) needed to bring the difference between the descriptive (existing state) and the normative (desired state) rapidly to zero, to dwell on this difference or error would be counterproductive. Society might consider it to be the act of a rabble-rouser or revolutionary. It might be thought best simply to move carefully and quietly in such a direction as to improve things eventually.

Here is a social system example of this phenomenon. It was no surprise to the mayor of a small city of the author's acquaintance that many low-income houses in town failed to meet official housing standards. But the city is moving as fast as it can to build new low-income housing. In the meantime, would it be useful for a systems analyst to focus publicity on the "error"—that is, the difference between the descriptive scenario (existing housing) and the normative (future planned housing)? We think not. In fact, the passage of time provides confirmation.[6]

We can see from all this that the value system of the social system designer and that of the automatic control system designer are possibly in direct contradiction. If this is so, we need not wonder at the resistance shown by social systems and other large-scale complex organizations to "error-embracing" methodologies. No wonder that such systems display a marked aversion to the notion of error management, feedback, iteration, and indeed the whole notion of system planning in general.[7]

Thus far in this section, it appears that we have gotten so wound up in telling you about the downside of the error-embracing approach that the explicit advantages of iteration may have been neglected. In a word, iteration is efficient. Here are three specific ways in which iteration promotes efficiency:

1. *Powerful Aid in Getting the Study Started*. Every system team with which we have worked has commented retrospectively that it wasted an unreasonable amount of time and effort in getting started with problem analysis. Starting a system study is like being parachuted in to explore a trackless wilderness. If you waste time in carefully examining every tree and rock in your landing area you may never find your way out. Never mind the details at first; climb a tree or hill, get a quick, long view to get yourself oriented.

2. *Minimizes Fear of Making Initial Errors*. One hates to build on a shaky foundation or to walk on thin ice. However, if a similar cautious initial approach is taken in a system study, the chances of completing it on time and within budget are greatly reduced.

3. *Minimizes Wasted Effort on Unnecessary Subtasks and Extraneous Dead-Ends*. This is perhaps the most important value of the iterative, error-embracing approach. Only those tasks needed to achieve the goal are done.

2.7   THE ACTION PHASE: THE LIFE CYCLE OF A SYSTEM

Systems Analysis as we have described it thus far can be considered as just the first step in the overall life cycle of the system being designed. This system life cycle is portrayed in Table 2.2. We should conclude from this exhibit that the SA phase cannot properly be conducted in isolation, ignoring the fact of the system life cycle. Yet this is precisely how many objects in our modern world are designed. It is perhaps a belated recognition of this fact that has produced public support for the system's point of view. Society seems finally to recognize that to view problems out of context and in isolation often generates more serious and costly side effects than the benefits promised for the original system. Nuclear energy is certainly a prime example of this situation, although not the only example by far.

The life cycle of a system as portrayed in Table 2.2 highlights certain important aspects in system design but obscures others. The life-cycle point of view emphasizes that system analysis and design must consider matters such as system maintainability, periodic system upgrades, decommissioning, dismantling, and replacement. All of these matters are often neglected. On the other hand, this viewpoint seems to imply that the life-cycle process is linear and straight-through, in that iteration is deemphasized.

Production of computer software is an application area in which professionals have come more rapidly to recognize the impact and importance of the life cycle concept than professionals in many other areas of design. Software design routinely and explicitly includes the life cycle concept in the production process. The MITRE Corporation has studied the cost of software production and MITRE's estimate of the relative cost of the various phases of a system life cycle in shown in Table 2.3.

The MITRE life cycle cost tableau in Table 2.3 might be taken to imply that the life-cycle steps are linear, progressive, and independent. This would be an

TABLE 2.2. The Life Cycle of a System

Problem Analysis

Requires all of the six major phases of the system analysis thus far described, even the action phase, although this is implicit.

System Design

Produces a step-by-step procedure, called the "Transition Scenario," for building the system. Steps should be formalized as mileposts to be met during design and construction. Engineering blueprints and specific operating requirements are produced in this step. Problem Analysis says what must be done, while System Design says how to do it.

System Construction and Installation

This step includes production of software source code, debugging, documentation, and Alpha and Beta site testing.

Acceptance Testing and Operation

Covers the sea trials of a naval weapon, for example. The Federal Aviation Administration, FAA, does type certification of new commercial aircraft before commercial use is permitted. In this step, the system is turned over to the regular operating team. In a nuclear reactor installation, the electric utility operating staff begins hands-on operation, first under supervision from the manufacturer's installation team, and then solo. Generally, certification includes checking that operating efficiency and other performance criteria have been met.

Maintenance and Periodic Upgrading

Regular maintenance is a necessary feature to be considered in the original system design. The B-52 currently operating in the USAF has been almost completely redesigned and rebuilt as compared with the aircraft introduced over 55 years ago. This process is explicitly considered in the production of computer software; note the version number attached to software products, MS-DOS 3.1, Word 4.0, Lotus 2.0, WordPerfect 5.0, and so forth. If the original system is designed like a plate of spaghetti, it will be extraordinarily costly and difficult to upgrade. The anticipation of periodic upgrades is an element in good systems design.

Decommissioning, Dismantling, and Replacement

One of the most serious failures of the nuclear engineering profession is its neglect of this absolutely essential step in the original Analysis and Design phases.

TABLE 2.3. Total Life-Cycle Cost of Phases of Digital Computer Software Production[a]

Life-Cycle Phase	Share of Life-Cycle Cost
Establish scope of project	3%
Requirements specification	9%–20%
System design	8%
Coding	10%
Integration testing	15%–30%
Acceptance testing	5%
Operations, maintenance, and version upgrades	50%

[a] Note that about half of the total system cost occurs after the system has been accepted by the client.
Source: MITRE Corp.

erroneous conception, although common in the design of earlier generations of software, and other physical devices. This naïve "straight-through" design concept is common throughout engineering design and continues to be the source of many difficulties. It could be called an "anti-system" viewpoint.

EXERCISES

2.1 In Section 2.1 under "Establish Criteria for Ranking Alternative Candidates," the authors apparently object to permitting the analyst to delay establishing selection criteria until after alternatives have been analyzed. What's wrong with letting the analyst choose "...his own judgment criterion after the fact, so as to place his own creation in its best light?" Isn't this just good salesmanship?

2.2 Explain the difference between a functional alternative and a technological alternative. Give examples of each in a specific application area of your choice.

2.3 Compare and contrast the six phases of system study with the steps given by Hall (1962) and Chestnut (1965). Develop a direct comparison chart.

2.4 John Dewey (1933) suggests "five phases of reflective thought for the solution of a problem." List these steps and compare them with the six phases in a system study given in this text. Discuss.

2.5 Polya (1957) gives four steps in problem-solving. Compare and contrast with the six phases of this text and with Dewey's method.

2.6 The text mentions VoIP as a potential functional alternative for some intra-city business travel. Suggest two other situations in which you can conceive of possible functional alternatives. Describe each situation in about 250 words.

2.7 The text mentions modern leaders who were "ostracized" after the emergency was over. Does this apply to Winston Churchill? Charles DeGaulle?

2.8 Systems Rules-of-Thumb. Here are some sample observed rules-of-thumb from systems practice:
   - NIMBY (Not in My Backyard): People don't want anything built near them that they consider inappropriate.
   - BANANA (Build Absolutely Nothing Anywhere Near Anyone): Keep things just the way they are.
   - Ancient Burial Ground: Any physical system that requires land will always result in an ancient burial ground being discovered. *Note*: There are direct analogies to non-land-based systems.
   - Snail Darter (Ref: Tennessee Valley Projects): A rare (almost extinct) small percoid freshwater fish will be discovered wherever you try to build any system.

Note: There are direct analogies to non-physical-based systems—also called the Quinio Checkerspot rule.

• Build Systems and Non-Users will converge around the new system. Consider the new DIA airport.

Generate two (real) examples of each.

CASE STUDY: METHODOLOGIES OR CHAOS? PART A

Memorandum

Select one of the classical "systems engineering" documents:

• MIL 499B
• NASA Langley Systems Engineering Handbook for In-House Space Flight Projects
• NASA Systems Engineering Handbook
• Defense Systems Management College: Systems Engineering Management Guide
• EIA/IS-632: Systems Engineering
• IEEE Std 1220–1994: Standard for the Application and Management of the Systems Engineering Process

Your goals are:

1. To produce a brief "summary" of the document—a summary that cuts to the essence of the implicit or explicit methodology and captures it in a single page "graphic" (your choice of how to present it—be creative and insightful).
2. To produce (a single page) a list (with some brief explanation) of the critical issues (assumptions, problems, etc.) associated with the methodology (as the group sees them).
3. To develop a "mapping" (again, single page) of the document into the standard six-step methodology in this chapter (again, be creative).
4. To develop a glossary (one page) of critical "key" terms from the document.
5. To prepare a 10-minute briefing of your results.

CASE STUDY: METHODOLOGIES OR CHAOS? PART B

Memorandum

Select one of the following concepts:

Team 1: TQM: Total Quality Management
Team 2: BPR: Business Process Reengineering
Team 3: SI: Systems Integration
Team 4: CE: Concurrent Engineering
Team 5: Chaos Theory
Team 6: Capability Maturity Models (CMM)
Team 7: The Fifth Discipline (Senge)
Team 8: ERP: Enterprise Resource Planning

Your goals are:

1. To produce a brief summary of the concept—a summary that cuts to the essence of the concept or methodology and captures it in a single page "graphic" (your choice of how to present it—be creative and insightful).
2. To produce (single page) a list (with some brief explanation) of the critical issues (assumptions, problems, etc.) associated with the methodology (as the Team sees them).
3. To develop a "mapping" (again, single page) of the concept or its application into the standard six-step methodology in this chapter (again, be creative!).
4. To develop a glossary (one page) of critical "key" terms for the concept.
5. To prepare a 10-minute briefing of your results.

CASE STUDY: WAL-MART CRISIS!

Memorandum

TO: **Consultants**

FROM: **Thorny Ellwood, Managing Partner**

DATE: **10 January 2003**

Wal-Mart has taken an option on a parcel of land on the Shenandoah River on the outskirts of Front Royal (VA) where they wish to build a new superstore. They have requested zoning variances for the rezoning of 121 acres at the southwest corner of the intersection of U.S. 522/340 and Va. 55.

Mr. Karr, a planner for the Front Royal Planning Department, has until Thursday to recommend a preliminary course of action to the Front Royal Town Council at their emergency meeting. It is assumed that the variances and abatements requested are within the power of the Department to recommend to the Town Council for approval.

Our company, *Strategic Consulting*, has been retained by Mr. Karr to develop a preliminary systems analysis briefing and present it at Thursday's Town Council meeting. Fifteen minutes are allocated on the Town Council meeting agenda. Due to the concerns of the Town Council, Mr. Karr wants to initially keep this quiet and not involve any other members of the Front Royal government, the local community, or Wal-Mart. He wants a professional "outside" and independent analysis.

Please have a draft presentation for me tomorrow morning @ 9:00 AM.

NOTES

1. For a discussion of the systems thinking issues in the Big Dig, see Chapter V in Hughes (1998).
2. For more information, see McDonald (2004).
3. See, for example, Plutarch, *Lives*, especially "Pericles" (Plutarch, no date).
4. See an interview with Jobs in Anonymous (2004).
5. For a successful application see H. M. Sapolsky (1972).
6. Note: Most of those substandard shacks have been replaced by vastly superior, low-cost housing.
7. The rise of TQM (Total Quality Management), BPR (Business Process Reengineering), Six Sigma, and The Fifth Discipline (Senge) have introduced some of these concepts into the vocabulary of organizations. For a discussion beyond management implications, see Jervis (1997).

Chapter 3

Goal Development

3.1 SEVEN STEPS IN GOAL DEVELOPMENT

The most difficult, unfamiliar, and tension-producing phase in system analysis, and the one to which ultimate success is most sensitive, is the first—goal development. The excitement level of the system team is generally at a peak in this initial phase, and it may be difficult for the team coordinator to restrain her people until they understand where they are going. Production of computer software is an excellent example of this problem. The pressure to begin source coding early in the system analysis process is almost unbearable.

> "Let's just jot down a few rough ideas in code to get things going."

> "I think we ought to do a little rough coding to see what we've got here."

> "The head shed likes to see action, so let's get a little code in the works. We can always dump it later if we don't like what we get."

> "You know, we don't seem to be making much progress on this project with all this goosing around with goals. So I came in over the weekend and wrote a little code. Here, let me show it to you . . . . "

Writing code first is a "bottom-up" approach that was typical 30 years ago in software design. It has been rejected by modern software houses because it commonly leads to disaster. If the team gives in to the notions above, it is on the way to producing more "spaghetti code" with many loops and "GO TO" statements. The code produced

How to Do Systems Analysis. By John E. Gibson, William T. Scherer, and William F. Gibson
Copyright © 2007 John Wiley & Sons, Inc.

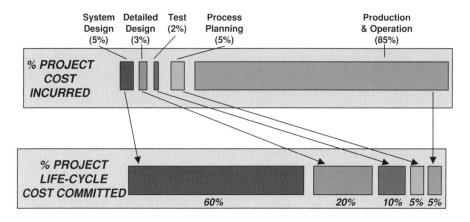

Product Life Cycle Costs are *COMMITTED* Long Before They are *INCURRED*.
When You Spend the First 8% of Your Project Budget,
You Determine 80% of the Cost of Your Product.

FIGURE 3.1 Project costs. (Source: Andersen Consulting, January 1993.)

is likely to be full of bugs and individual idiosyncrasies that will bedevil the program throughout its whole operating life. Furthermore, the initial direction chosen will bias the work on the project. It takes a great deal more effort to undo wrong work and to change stubborn minds once they are made up than it does to do it right in the first place.

The MITRE Corporation manages three federally funded research and development centers (FFRDCs) for systems study work. MITRE has examined the lifetime cost of computer software production and utilization. We have given some of the results of this study in Chapter 2. We note from the MITRE data that what it calls "the analysis phase" represents only about 10% of the total lifetime cost of the typical software system. Furthermore, MITRE also finds that to determine the "scope" of a software project represents only 3% of its estimated lifetime cost. Because MITRE's "scoping" phase is somewhat broader than our Goal Development step, *we estimate that goal development represents less than 1% of the total lifetime cost of the typical software system* (see Figure 3.1). Thus, while goal development, a component of the system design, is a small part of the total cost, it results in a critical commitment of resources. It is possibly even more important to young software professionals who look forward to long careers, and experts are confident that this is the <u>only</u> step in software production that cannot be automated.[1]

Thus we can see that goal development in systems analysis (SA) is an exceedingly sensitive activity. It costs little, but if it is not done correctly, the whole project could be committed to an incorrect solution, possibly irretrievably. Here is an example of just such a debacle. In the early 1960s, there was a flurry of interest in the immediate construction and operation of a commercial SuperSonic Transport (SST) aircraft by the United States. But when one pushed beyond self-serving, bureaucratic ambitions, it was clear that no clear functional goals could be discovered for this proposed program. The FAA wanted to establish a bureaucratic beachhead in the sponsorship of aerospace research while NASA wanted to retain its research mandate. Boeing, Lockheed, and other airframe manufacturers wanted R&D funding, and so on, but no functional purpose was apparent.

Gibson took part in this debate and Horwitch, in *Clipped Wings* (Horwitch, 1982), the definitive account of the process, was kind enough to say that his article in the July 1966 issue of *Harper's* magazine was "extremely influential" in triggering the wave of national public concern over the project.[2] Be that as it may and for whatever reasons, the American SST project was stopped, but the Anglo-French "Concorde" design, equally plagued with goal confusion, was allowed to keep going.

It was apparent to some analysts from the first that Concorde could not make money and Gibson said so, but the Anglo-French team for various reasons did not stop. Now, 40 years later, the cost of the Concorde folly is clear. Even though many of the design costs of Concorde are buried deeply enough never to come to light, we do know that simply to cover direct design and production costs, the break-even point was a production run of 64 airframes. In fact, only 20 were ever built and not all of these were placed in service, and commercial flights ended in 2003. The Concorde project was recently called the most expensive fiasco in the history of international commercial aviation. A systems goals/feasibility analysis pointed this out well in advance.

Goal Development is the most sensitive step in SA, and to organize this vital process we propose the seven detailed steps shown in Table 3.1. We use an iterative approach in the following discussion—first Table 3.1, then a short description immediately following, and then a more elaborate definition of terms and discussion in the remaining sections of this chapter. Still further iteration on the more difficult concepts, such as "generalization," is given in Chapter 10.

Generalize the Question. The general system planner generalizes the question because he knows that the client seldom, if ever, understands his own problem. It must be generalized to phrase it correctly and, even more importantly, to place it properly in context. Lack of contextual integrity often frustrates planners who limit their concerns to technical solutions in socially relevant problems. The designer who

TABLE 3.1. The Term "Goal" Is Used Interchangeably in This Text with the Term "Objective"

The Seven Steps in Goal Development

1. Generalize the question.
2. Develop a descriptive scenario.
3. Develop a normative scenario.
4. Develop the axiological component.
5. Prepare an objectives tree.
6. Validate.
7. Iterate.

applies a conventional engineering approach to urban freeways, or high-powered automobiles, or supersonic aircraft cannot help feeling a sense of bafflement when she completes her technical assignment successfully, only to have it rejected on other than technical grounds. She says, "But I gave you what you asked for." Society is equally frustrated by this because, if it is honest, it realizes that it <u>did</u> ask for the object. Yet all realize, after the fact, that something is very wrong. The client misinterpreted his problem, and the designer failed to appreciate this fact in time. Generalization attempts to avoid this difficulty.

Develop a Descriptive Scenario.   Describe the situation as it is. Tell how it got to be that way. Point out the good features and the unacceptable elements of the *status quo*. This exercise will help broaden and deepen the team's understanding of the generalized problem. This is another attempt to give the work contextual integrity. One way to initiate this process of generalization and description is a group "brainstorming" or "brainwriting" session. A list of descriptive phrases can be generated quite quickly, and then the full prose narrative can be elaborated at leisure.

Develop a Normative Scenario.   Describe the situation as it will be when the project is fully operative.

Develop the Axiological Component.   The normative scenario lists conditions as they should be when the project is complete. Thus it contains within itself a value system. However, it often is very difficult to discover the values of the sponsor, and even after the discovery process the analyst may discover that the sponsor's set of values may be incomplete and/or conflicting.

Prepare an Objectives (Goals) Tree.   The objectives tree, or goals tree, is a chart of objectives, with the most general at the top and becoming more specific as it branches below. The statements in the boxes should be action statements of goals. Questions, difficulties, and the like are out of place in the chart. The objectives chart should be a graphical presentation of the goals and values obtained in the previous steps. However, we usually find that this elaboration reveals new goals or values that were not previously apparent. Generally speaking, the system group will find little difficulty in beginning the objectives tree, but difficulties grow as the work progresses. Thus, the situation is the reverse of that encountered with the axiological component. Among the things to watch for are the following:

- Make the general goal (objective) concrete and related to the problem. Do not let it become merely a vague platitude.
- Allow space for future expansion of the tree by including an "other" box at each level.
- Do not become sidetracked by including personal goals of individual team members or of the study itself. The objectives tree should show the client's goals and be action-oriented.

Validate. The first five steps in goal development should be developed quickly and possibly in a single group session. Then at a more leisurely pace, the validation step is addressed. Initially, validation may merely be evaluation of the material produced in the first team session to detect omissions and internal inconsistencies. This is then followed by data gathering and formulation of the mathematical model to be used (see Section 3.9). In later iterations, the client should be allowed to react to the objectives and consideration should be given to open hearings on the objectives of a public system.

Iterate. The first group session focuses on developing the top-level goals for the system. But the result must not be expected to be useful as is. A group should not feel obligated to the material it has developed in the first iteration. The first run-through should be looked upon as merely a thought-starter. Therefore, the team should not allow itself to be bogged down in the first run-through by worrying about precise definitions and delineations. Several iterations on goal development will surely be needed in the SA.

3.2 ON GENERALIZING THE QUESTION

What do we mean by the word "generalization" and why do we propose doing it? Generalization might mean "expansion," or "extension," or "broadening," and we mean all of these things. Generalization often means going from the specific to a broader class, and we mean this as well. We discuss the whys and wherefores of generalization in Chapter 10. The outcome of proper generalization is a well-defined, quantitative model of the client's "matured" problem, plus consideration of the roles of the five or more classes of actors defined in Section 10.10 of Chapter 10. Furthermore, it includes consideration of the impact of the proposed system on non-users and on the environment, as well as provision for its graceful degradation and ultimate retirement. By "matured" problem, we mean the problem statement accepted by the client after it has been refined and carefully stated by the analyst.

Proper generalization is often a key ingredient to the successful analysis of systems. The British OR pioneers in World War II, for example, generalized the convoy-deck-gun question properly, and their solution of the case was successful. Naturally there are limits to how far one can generalize. To generalize too far will broaden the topic to the point that it will be difficult to solve in the time and with the money available. One also runs the risk of alienating the client by appearing to generalize excessively. The client will often be tightly focused on a very specific crisis. If the system analyst takes a relaxed and broad view of the client's problem, the client may object strongly.

One must admit furthermore that, in the past, some system analysts have used this generalization dictum to expand the problem beyond all recognition. This usually results in a failure to provide a satisfactory solution on time and within budget. As a result, one often hears arguments against funding another study to produce another report. The usual speech goes as follows:

"We don't need another study to produce another report to gather dust on the shelf! I've had enough of these stalling tactics. I say we know what the problem is. Let's stop wasting time and money and get on with the solution."

This is easy to say in theory, but it is difficult to do in practice. Let's consider an example. In this and subsequent chapters, we will discuss a system study of a proposed Woodward Avenue Subway. In that case, the Mayor of Detroit, Jerry Cavanaugh, just before leaving office, recommended that a new subway be constructed along Detroit's major radial artery. The new mayor had to take a position on this very specific proposal only a few weeks after entering office. What should he do?

Suppose the new mayor has called you in as a system analyst to take a look at this question. How would you begin? If you follow the approach of this text, you would attempt to define the goals of the proposed solution. That sounds rather simple in this case, doesn't it? But, you will find that there are pitfalls. The first step in goal development is to generalize the question. Cavanaugh recommended a 4.5-mile subway from Cobo Hall on the Detroit River, up Woodward Avenue to the New Center area, at which the GM Building and the Fisher Building are located. To generalize the question, should we consider an 8-mile subway along Woodward to the State Fairgrounds and the City Line? Or perhaps a 12-mile subway out to Birmingham and Bloomfield Hills? How about a 22-mile subway out to the city of Pontiac? What about other modal choices such as buses or trolley cars (so-called "light rail")? What about the other six or seven major arteries? What about a regional transportation study in the six-county area including Detroit? What about a statewide or nationwide transportation study?

Presumably, one must stop somewhere in this ascending series of ever more complex transportation questions. We choose to generalize the 4.5-mile Woodward subway question up several steps to a study of Detroit's major arterial transport needs. But, as you will see, generalization initially was strongly opposed by the client. Nevertheless, this generalization proved to be a wise move because, given the client's final choice of goals, one would *not* choose to satisfy them by the Woodward subway alternative.

The notion of generalizing the question in order to lend it contextual integrity and to define it properly was considered quite bizarre when it was introduced some years ago (Gibson, 1973, 1977). It is diametrically opposed to the usual engineering approach to problems, which consists of subdividing the overall problem into easily solved elements. Yet it is clear that generalization is rather a standard procedure in non-Western societies. Japanese businessmen, for example, insist on examining the contextual integrity of proposed agreements with American firms, much to the annoyance of American managers anxious to "close the deal."

American business people, coming as they do from a relatively low contextual society, can comfortably think in terms of isolated "deals" or separate transactions. The Japanese businessman, on the other hand, more correctly considers individual transactions in context. Thus he is less likely to make an agreement which, while profitable in the short run or in isolation, could work in his firm's detriment in the long run. Automatically, he generalizes the problem, because this is the correct thing to do given his traditions. We Westerners now seem to be learning to generalize the problem, but only after making mistakes, from failing to do so in the past.

3.3 THE DESCRIPTIVE SCENARIO

The descriptive scenario, "DS," describes the current condition to be corrected or improved by the system we are starting to design. We still aren't sure we have a solid grasp of the client's problem and we are in only the first few days of the study. To help us gain this grasp, the team meets to describe to itself the current situation. Let us focus for a moment on this first working meeting of the team because it illustrates not only the issue at hand but also a deeper issue. In your mind's eye, how do you see this meeting progressing? Does the team leader have an agenda? Does he go around the table for ideas? Is there a free-for-all discussion with people throwing out ideas for criticism and reactions? Are there votes?

We assume that you are approaching this matter *de novo*. Yet we also presume that you can see one or another of the scenes suggested above, and we also predict that you think the particular format of the meeting doesn't really matter.

> "What's the big deal? We have meetings all the time. Just call the meeting and let's get going."

Now go back and read the imaginary quotes on rushing into coding in software projects that we used to open this chapter. We set you up for this. You should have seen it coming, but you probably didn't. If you accepted any of the suggested approaches above, or agreed with the imaginary quote just above, you really didn't understand what we were saying about rushing to code at the beginning of this chapter.[3]

Running a meeting isn't nearly as simple as it appears, and there is good reason for business people and other professionals to hate meetings. We will go into the various types of meetings and how to run them in Chapter 8. For now, let us assume you have carefully prepared for the meeting and have decided to use one of the accepted methods of idea generation such as "brainwriting" or "brainstorming."

Brainstorming is a technique which was developed about 30 years ago (Rawlinson, 1981). We suppose that Rawlinson and others had spent many working hours in badly run meetings and, after some thought, developed a set of rules for unleashing the creativity of people. Perhaps the most important rule in brainstorming is NO CRITICISM. Team members are encouraged to build on each other's ideas and to add their own twists, but no one is allowed to speak negatively. Negative criticism dampens the flow of ideas and it turns one away from the positive act of idea generation into an analytic and judgmental mode of justifying statements. This not only slows things down, but also tends to make everyone more careful and conservative.

An improvement over "brainstorming" is brainwriting (Geschka et al., 1973). A brainwriting session is quite different from a brainstorming session. Instead of loud talking and laughter, a brainwriting session takes place in absolute silence. Five or six people sit around a table with sheets of paper in the center. At the top of each sheet is a "trigger question." Each person takes a sheet and writes a sentence that relates to the trigger and returns the sheet to the center and takes another. One reads the preceding comments and makes a positive contribution, then repeats the process. The developers of Brainwriting were experienced Brainstormers and they had observed that many of the best ideas from the most thoughtful people do not emerge in the brainstorm hurly-burly. They sought to develop a process that retains the strengths of brainstorming and eliminates its weaknesses. We will return to brainstorming and brainwriting in Chapter 5.

"Trigger questions" for an initial brainwriting session in the first phase of the Detroit subway case might be some of the following:

> "Describe Detroit public transportation as it now exists."
>
> "What's wrong with Detroit that a new subway could cure?"
>
> "Why a subway? Why not a new trolley car system? They work in San Francisco and San Diego, don't they?"
>
> "What's the point of spending more tax money on urban transportation? Aren't there more important things in life?"

The output from the brainwriting session will need to be edited, of course. Ideas will have to be classified and a narrative developed to flesh out the bare bones. This editing is more of a cognitive than emotional exercise, and thus it need not be carried on without pause from the brainwriting. After the DS narrative has been edited and digested by the team, we are ready for the next phase.

3.4   THE NORMATIVE SCENARIO

The normative scenario, "NS," may be thought of as paired with the descriptive scenario, "DS." In contrast to the DS, the normative scenario describes the situation as it will be when the project is fully operative. The normative situation will preserve the positive features of the DS and change as many of the negative features as possible. Thus, the normative grows out of the descriptive. It need not be limited, however, simply to correcting existing deficiencies. In fact, the real purpose of dwelling on the preparation of this section is to prompt the group to build innovatively upon the DS and to surpass it. We need encouragement to visualize the potentialities of the situation. This is not to say that we should ignore financial and physical limitations, but rather that imaginative combinations will often reveal entirely new possibilities not contained in mere extrapolations. Here again a group interaction session is recommended as a way of obtaining an initial list of normative phrases.

The first time a group tries to develop an NS, the tendency is to take the bad things in the DS and simply reverse them. A good set of triggering statements for the normative brainwriting session will promote a more imaginative approach. In the Detroit subway study, we want to do more than correct current transportation deficiencies. It won't be sufficient to reduce crime in the streets, arrest urban decay, stop the slide in property values, make commuting easier, and so on, although all of these things are to be desired. Let us examine a concrete example of positive normative thinking here. We will be talking later in this chapter about Fitch's "Goals for an Urbanizing America." One of the strengths of Fitch's thinking is that he moves beyond simply correcting deficiencies in current American cities into making the urban environment attractive, inviting, and dynamic. The Detroit subway SA team found Fitch's concepts of great value in developing its normative scenario.

3.5 THE AXIOLOGICAL COMPONENT

The normative scenario describes conditions as they should be when the project is complete. The words "should" and "ought" are signals that we are talking about personal goals or "values," and the dictionary definition of "axiological" is "... related to or pertaining to human values or beliefs." The normative scenario therefore implies an underlying set of values upon which the NS depends. Unfortunately, these values initially may be implicit and most probably incomplete and conflicting. But, unless the potential conflict in these latent values is uncovered and resolved, the success of a public system is in danger. This is especially so if the problem being addressed is even mildly partisan or controversial. Furthermore, the *team's* values will probably have been intermixed with, and may even have crowded out entirely by, the client's values.

Rokeach (1973) defines a value as a conviction that "a specific mode of conduct or end-state of [human] existence is personally or socially preferable to an opposite or converse mode of conduct or end-state of existence." Robbins (1988), in quoting Rokeach (1973), points out that human values are generally relatively stable and enduring. Apparently, one tends to modify childhood values but rarely changes them totally. "Attitudes," on the other hand, says Robbins, "while based on values, are more specific and less stable" (Robbins, 1988). One holds a relatively small number of basic values, but hundreds or even thousands of attitudes about specific situations or conditions.

Many people find it difficult to discuss personal values. This is especially so of engineers and other analytically minded individuals. To talk about values may seem to such people as attacking them. Other individuals may find a discussion of values boring and irrelevant. Indeed, for some well-specified problems, a value analysis would be unnecessary, but the well-specified problem is the result of general system planning and does not precede it. After an initial difficulty in initiating discussion on values, we would expect to have an intense involvement and possible strong disagreements within the SA team. Because it probably will become apparent that the initial value discussion has deepened the controversy rather than resolved matters, it may be difficult to pass on to the next phase. Progress seems to be accelerated, however, if the team does move on without attempting to resolve all of the tensions set up by the value discussion.

We do <u>not</u> suggest that the analyst conduct a discussion with a client concerning his or her values. Fortunately, values can be elicited indirectly. Just as we will often find that a client cannot or will not provide an explicit IP, *a fortiori*, this is so for values. One of the strengths of an interactive computer simulation of a system and its environment is that it permits the client to play "what-if?" games and thus to exhibit choices. Decision analysts have become skilled in this technique as well. In multiple-objective interactive decision analysis, the client is not asked explicitly for a preference structure or personal values, but rather is asked to express a preference between two choices at a time. From this process, values may be inferred.

It may seem that we have things backward here. If the normative scenario and subsequent system planning depend on the value set of the client, a logical way of proceeding would seem to be to set down a consistent set of operative values and from them deduce a normative scenario. Then one could note the difference between specific items in the normative list and the existing situation (i.e., the descriptive scenario) and thus form specific action tasks to correct the deficiencies (i.e., a transition scenario). Unfortunately, this apparently simple deductive approach is impractical because a consistent set of operative values does not exist.

It is difficult to convey to a literal-minded, analytic, judgmental audience just how tentative the findings are of sociologists on questions of public values. A number of years ago, Gibson was asked to lead a team of Battelle Institute analysts into the area of urban system analysis. Battelle is one of the best of the privately owned engineering research institutes in the world. It was at the time a leader in metallurgy and air traffic control and was an early investor in the Carlson patents and developer of xerography, and so on. It had also moved into analysis of "softer" public issues such as Appalachian regional development, urban development, crime control, and the like, and now also does considerable health care and security work.

The "Battelle New City Team" was internally funded and was designed not only to explore a potential new area of research funding for Battelle, but also to train its SA professionals in this new field. Among the team members were three experienced sociologists. When the team got to the normative scenario development and the axiological component, the rest of the team turned to the sociologists for guidance and leadership.

The team was disappointed. The sociologists continued to take notes, to bring up new issues, and to engage the rest of the team in lively discussion, but there was no closure, no resolution, and no direction. As a prototypical engineer, Gibson pressed the team sociologists for a normative set of values to give the team guidance in our design of the New City. It became a friendly but spirited contest of wills. The sociologists seemed to delight in contemplation of this "messy problem," but the rest of the group wanted to get on with the job. The sociologists became irritated:

"Jack, why is it that you engineers insist on displaying this curiously low tolerance for ambiguity? Can't you people handle conceptual conflicts?"

Gibson had to smile at this. He had never heard of raising to a positive value one's failure to do one's job. He resolved to try that line on his next engineering boss when he started getting pressed for results. Then he did two things. First, he had a calligrapher design a huge banner to hang across the meeting room:

> Sociology Is Not a Normative Science
> It Is a Descriptive Art

This pleased the sociologists. They felt it captured their point. Next, they were asked:

"Why do you sociologists exhibit such a pathological resistance to closure?"

Each team member had demonstrated their characterological stereotypes with this joshing. They had exaggerated each other's personal mind set, or value structure, if you wish. Engineers like to "solve" problems. Sociologists like to "understand" social issues. Mathematicians like to define terms. For an engineer, "understanding" is useless unless it leads to action. The sociologist, on the other hand, understands what a fragile methodological framework he or she is working with and correctly refuses to extend this framework beyond its narrow boundaries.

If we turn to the sociological literature, we find support for the position taken by the Battelle sociologists. For example, Williams in his standard text, *American Society*, discusses "values" in Chapter 11, entitled "Values and Beliefs in American Society" (Williams, 1960). After defining what he means by "values," he is ready to address the subject of the chapter title, but first he says (Williams, 1960, p. 417), "In most of what follows, therefore, we shall not be dealing with values, but rather with the *evaluations* in which values can be discovered."

For many of us, the concept of "values" is sufficiently abstract that we have trouble dealing with it. We turn to sociologists for help and we are told by a leader in the field that even when he is talking about "values," he isn't really talking about "values," but only about underlying "evaluations" by which values may be discovered. That is, he attempts to escape to still another level of abstraction.

An important reason for articulating the values implied in the normative scenario is to sensitize the analysis team to its own members' values. It must be remembered that the client's values are not to be overridden by those of the analysts. Also, the client may feel more threatened by questions of value than by non-axiological matters. If the analyst places too great an emphasis on questions of value early in his relationship with the client, he will risk being thought impractical and possibly incompetent. *The analyst will probably never be able to ask the client directly to articulate his value set.* Rather, the team must infer the values of the client from his behavior.

Because the axiological component appears difficult and nebulous, there is a temptation to ignore it. This temptation is particularly intense for conventionally trained engineers. But to ignore the issue is to court failure. Let us cite two examples, one quite specific and the other rather general.

In Chapter 5, we will discuss the Forrester Urban Model as an example of the use of computer simulation as a means of generating solution options. Forrester is a brilliant and creative innovator. He was a pioneer in digital computer simulation of large-scale systems. Yet he consistently ignored the axiological aspects of his models and opened himself to intense criticism thereby. In fact, the controversies generated by Forrester by his inappropriate responses to questions raised concerning value issues in his models obscured the very real technical advances he had made.

We have pointed out that human values appear to be relatively stable. This is certainly true of the rigid, authoritarian, "Tayloristic" value set of American engineers. The Tayloristic value set continues to be inculcated in American engineering education and is intensified by its implicitness and unacknowledged universality.[4] Tayloristic American engineers appear to qualified external observers as responsible in large part for the failure of the American manufacturing sector to respond adequately to foreign competition. Here is what Mr. Konosuke Matsushita of the Matsushita Electric Industrial Company said to an American engineering audience (Stevens, 1990):

> "We are going to win and the industrial west is going to lose; there's nothing much you can do about it because the reasons for failure are within yourselves. Your firms are built on the Taylor model; even worse so are your heads. With your bosses doing the thinking while the workers wield the screwdrivers, you're convinced deep down that this is the right way to run a business. For you, the essence of management is getting the ideas out of the heads of the bosses and into the hands of labor.
>
> We are beyond the Taylor model; business, we know, is now so complex and difficult, the survival of firms so hazardous in an environment increasingly competitive and fraught with danger, that their continued existence depends on the day-to-day mobilization of every ounce of intelligence."

3.6   DEVELOPING AN OBJECTIVES TREE

The Objectives Tree, "OT," is a graphic display of the goals of the system. It will be found particularly useful in helping analysts and decision makers to clarify and organize a rational set of goals in the early stages of the effort. Then, in later phases of the design, the OT helps in reporting progress and in maintaining a goal-directed effort while discouraging nondirected excursions.

The OT is a special form of a hierarchic logic structure and falls within the area of mathematics called graph theory. It is possible to develop an algorithmic approach to the construction of a hierarchic tree, given elemental goal statements and connective relations (Warfield, 1973a,b). Such a procedure may be desirable in exceedingly complex analyses containing dozens of elemental goal statements. The automated approach, possibly computerized, may serve as a check on the correctness of the formal logic in a graph constructed by hand. We will not pursue algorithmic construction of trees further here, however, for the following reasons:

- Manual construction of the OT serves to stimulate the analysis team to broaden its concept of the problem and to create an attitude of initiation and creativity among the team members. To filter this interaction process through a computer algorithm often serves to dampen the enthusiasm and creativity of the analysis team.

- To construct the OT is also to begin thinking about interactions of activities and the relation of objectives to a value structure. Both these matters will become team concerns in subsequent phases. Thus, this early interaction will be beneficial.

- To aid in communicating the goals of a large-scale planning effort to decision makers, interested observers, and involved citizens, it is desirable to keep the tree simple. Hand construction of the OT serves this purpose by causing the participants to think through and compress their objectives during analysis.

Statement Format. A first step in the construction of an OT is to state tentative elemental objectives for the project, using the following semantic structure:

$$\textbf{To} \text{ (action word)} + \text{(object)} + \text{(qualifying words)}$$

Below are several elemental objectives developed in the initial phase of a study aimed at improving the quality of life in a particular urban area:

1. To (kill) (rats) (in the city)
2. To (improve) (urban lifestyle) (for all Americans in this decade)
3. To (eliminate) (racial prejudice) (in American cities)
4. To (prevent) (police brutality) ( )

Each of these examples of elemental objectives is semantically acceptable as an isolated statement and would be processed by a computer algorithm for objectives tree construction. These objectives are typical, however, of early thinking by inexperienced urban analysts in that they are disordered, vague, improperly qualified, incomplete, and subjective. The deficiencies in these objectives are made more obvious in part because we require a uniform statement format. Naturally, a team leader will be careful in criticizing suggested goals statements such as these in order not to interfere with the flow of ideas and to minimize subjective reaction from the analysts who produced them.

We will see momentarily how the process of tree construction will address the questions of incompleteness and possible conflicts in the goals. But before moving on, let's improve these statements by making each tighter, more objective, and more specific. We need not strain for perfection in this second round because the system analysis process is iterative and we will have ample opportunity to continue the refinement process.

We can see that one wants to kill rats with minimum side effects and low cost, that to aspire to improve the life of all citizens is a lofty but imprecise goal, that it is more practical to seek to "reduce" objective discrimination than "eliminate" a prejudicial mind set, and that "police brutality" is a rather inflammatory phrase. Here are suggested revisions for the original four examples:

1′ To (reduce impact of) (rats) (economically and safely)

2′ To (improve) (urban lifestyle) (for many Americans in this century)

3′ To (reduce) (racial discrimination) (in housing patterns)

4′ To (assure) (fair, equitable law enforcement) (for all minorities)

The reader need not accept these modified statements as improvements; in fact, some of the modified statements may seem to have regressed from the original bold formulations. The modified statements are more measurable and limited, but they are not "attention grabbers." Because they are more pointed, they may contravene one or more of the reader's value elements. For example, 2′ seems to limit the housing improvements to "some" Americans. Precisely which "some?" The analysis process is working as we hoped, if you have begun to become engaged in it.

Next, we want to suggest some aids to improve the individual objectives after they have been written by team members on individual cards. Because the initial development of objectives is done in a "brainstorming," or preferably in a "brainwriting," mode, we do not want to imprison the team with a lot of rules. It is important that the session be free-flowing. When the flow of ideas has begun to slow down, it is the proper time to use the following check points:

- Use of the proper semantic form will assist in developing action-oriented statements.
- Difficulties are not goals nor are non-goal-oriented statements acceptable.
- Do not be concerned with possible conflicts among suggested objectives or with polishing elements once they are in proper form.
- Goals that display biases of specific team members are acceptable initially. They should be combed out in successive iterations, but to forbid them initially may cause good suggestions to be blocked.

Linkage Semantics. Now that a number of individual objectives have been captured on three-by-five cards, we are ready to assemble them into a tree. To link the individual goals together to form a tree, a single, precise phrase must be chosen to define the linkage between them. If one chooses to show arrows pointing upward between boxes, such phrases as "will assist in" or "will contribute to" are satisfactory. If the arrow points down, "includes" or "implies" may be used. For a technical reason discussed below, avoid the phrase "is necessary (to) (for)." Only one definition of the linkage may be used in a simple tree, and this definition must not be changed during construction.

We once observed an urban system planning experience that became intensely frustrating for its participants because the analyst broke these rules. A group of public-spirited citizens had volunteered to meet and discuss urban goals. The young system analyst (none of the authors) who "facilitated" the meeting exhibited an excessive need for control throughout the morning session and he engaged in an overlong explanation of "his" method, but finally he let the citizens begin to formulate their goal statements for the city. After an hour or so, the analyst perceived that he had made a poor choice of the linkage phrase for the OT, and he announced a change. This threw the group into such confusion and resentment that most of the volunteers did not return after a break to continue the session. System planning sessions tend to generate intense involvement, and this emotion must be carefully and constructively contained if the process is to be successful.

Tree Structure. Now that we have the statements in the proper form and have chosen a linkage statement, we are ready to arrange the elemental goal statements in hierarchic order. This is almost sure to be a difficult task initially, but may be eased by asking the team members to print their statements on index cards and to arrange the cards on a table. Some teams prefer to break up into subgroups of two or three members each to work on separate subtrees before combining the trees. One seeks a hierarchic ranking of the goals, with higher and more general goals above and more specific ones below.

One should not be surprised to find it difficult to generate general goals that at the same time do not become vague or fuzzy. Conversely, as the objective elements become more specific, one must guard against becoming too detailed in certain sectors while ignoring other sectors entirely. To satisfy the graph theoretic definition of a tree, our objectives structure must not reenter or close back on itself. Rather, from one general goal, the structure should open outward as one proceeds down through branches showing more specific objectives (see Figure 3.2).

Sometimes one finds a specific objective which seems to fit into several branches, possibly at different levels. In such an instance, we find it advisable to cast the two or more similar statements in somewhat different words to reflect the different higher objectives they serve rather than closing the diagram on one statement. This not only seems to aid in clarity but also permits computer verification of the logic, should this be desired.

To be an effective tool for SA, the most specific, detailed level of the objectives tree must be concrete and measurable. It is not acceptable for the specific goal level to be vague and amorphous.

Simple Example. We want to give you several more suggestions on OT construction, but it occurs to us that it would be useful to examine a simple example of goals tree construction. As is the usual situation, Figure 3.2 opens outward as one moves down any branch. Of course, most real-life trees open outward as one moves upward. One can take this as an indication that graph theoreticians live in an upside-down world or that we are looking at the tree's roots rather than its crown, or both.

The tree in Figure 3.2 represents the goals structure for a project in which Gibson was involved and which was directed at organizing an effort to reduce the rat population in a city. He was asked by his University President to visit with officials of a nearby city to help them develop a federal grant proposal-writing effort.

Figure 3.2 is the outcome of the first planning meeting. It didn't develop in a logical step-by-step manner. Rather, it started by talking about the problem and each time one of the participants mentioned something that sounded like a goal, it was written down. The conversation wandered from level to level; sometimes it would be at a

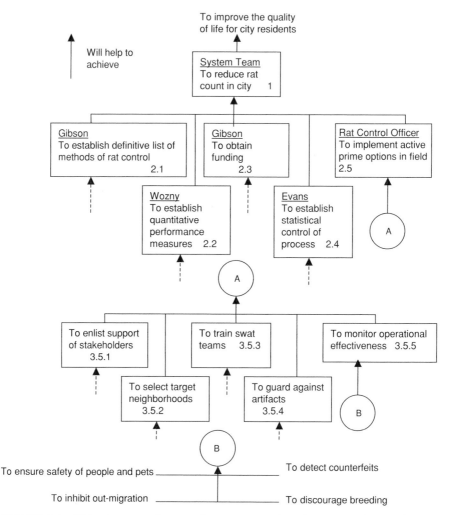

FIGURE 3.2 Objectives tree for an urban rat control project. Note the numbering scheme for the goals. Associate each goal with its next more general goal. Each objective must have an owner. By designating this owner and requiring that the tree consist of goals of a single owner or team, we are able to disentangle into separate trees the goals of different owners such as the client's tree, the team members' tree, the users' tree, and so forth.

high level of abstraction and at the same time another attendee might be talking about brands of rat poisons and someone else would be talking about publicity in the city newspaper.

But, gradually a half-dozen goals were written down on three-by-five cards and they were arranged on the conference table—no lectures were needed. The team just did it. Other participants began to add ideas to the tree and they easily caught on to the meaning of the various levels of the tree. So what you see in Figure 3.2 isn't complete, but it is a start. In a well-developed tree, each of the branches would be developed to approximately the same level of detail.

When the process started, **To Monitor Operational Effectiveness** was at a higher level than is currently shown. Evaluating current methods is an obvious activity if one is thinking in a chronological sequence. Soon, however, the team came to see that "current practice" is really just one support for a more general goal, **To Implement Active Prime Options in the Field**. Another supporting goal is **To Enlist Support of Stakeholders**.

Establishing **Quantitative Performance Measures** seems rather obvious, as is **To Obtain Funding**. However, one might question why **To Establish Statistical Control of Process** is at such a high level. Further analysis through iteration might indicate that this goal should go down into a more operational level. It achieved the high level shown in Figure 3.2 because one of the attendees made the point that statistical control must be established early in the effort because it is impossible to impose statistical legitimacy after the fact. That is, if the necessary data are not collected, one cannot create the needed data afterwards.

To Monitor Operational Effectiveness is elaborated in more detail than several other branches because we had several individuals in the meeting who were interested in the subject, and we wanted to capture their knowledge. **To Ensure the Safety of People and Pets** during the process is an obvious goal, but Gibson was fascinated with the item **To Discourage Breeding** when it was suggested. It turns out that in several rat control projects in other cities a "bounty" was paid for the tails of dead rats. This didn't work because enterprising locals decided to increase their income by setting up rat-breeding programs by placing garbage in the cellars of abandoned houses. **Migration** is more specifically "out-migration." The team didn't wish merely to drive our rats out of the neighborhood and inflict them on nearby locations. **Counterfeits** refers to those rats killed elsewhere and brought in to claim a bounty.

Four Tests of OT Logic. After the first few elemental objective statements have been written on cards and arranged in hierarchic order in accord with the generality of the statement, there are four tests to be applied to the tree. These tests can be applied repeatedly as the arrangement is modified and statements are added. Each test should be made on each statement in the tree:

- Each goal statement should provide a more explicit and detailed goal than the statement above it in the hierarchy. It tells "how" one proposes to reach the immediately higher goal. Thus, reading <u>down</u> any branch, each goal statement must answer <u>how</u> for its immediately superior goal.
- Reading <u>up</u> any branch, each higher statement answers <u>why</u> the goal below it is needed.
- Reading <u>across</u> the goals at a given level under any one general goal, ask are <u>all</u> these more specific goals needed to accomplish the more general goal?

- Reading <u>across</u> the goals at a given level under any one general goal, ask what <u>other</u> specific objectives at this level are needed to accomplish the more general objective?

Who Owns the Goal? In the initial development of goals, special care must be taken to identify the ownership of all goals by labeling them as shown in Figure 3.2. Different trees will be produced depending on the ownership of the goals and confusion could result if ownership is not clearly stated. For example, suppose you are a part of a team analyzing a mass transit proposal for a city. The mayor may be your client and his personal subjective goal structure might include "to be reelected." A subjective goal for a team member might be "to keep my job." Of course, such incongruities should be detected and discarded immediately. It should be obvious that goals must be professional and related to the system objective, yet we have seen OTs constructed by novice system analysts in which exactly these selfish, personal goals appeared.

Some goals inconsistent with the overall thrust of the analysis will not be easy to detect. Certain goals may be introduced that are not directly relevant to the overall objective but which, when decoded, translate into "to be reelected" or "to keep my job." Furthermore, when the goals are written on separate cards, given owners and organized into a tree structure, one may discover that the goals form two or more separate trees.

In the early stages of the Detroit Subway system study, for instance, three separate trees were discovered entangled in the initial set of goal statements. One consisted of team objectives such as delivering the final report on time. Another tree turned out to be citizens' goals such as "to provide faster, more economical transport to the city center," and a third tree consisting of still other goals was identified as those goals of the Federal Department of Transportation but which differed both from local citizens' goals and team goals. This is a good example of the importance of proper role differentiation.

3.7   FITCH'S GOALS FOR AN URBANIZING AMERICA: AN EXAMPLE OF OBJECTIVES TREE CONSTRUCTION

In Fall 1968, *DAEDALUS*, the journal of the American Academy of Arts and Sciences, published a special issue entitled "The Conscience of the City." Nineteen American intellectual leaders contributed papers to this special issue. It was, and is, widely admired as an important statement and still is used as a text in a number of college courses. We will take one of the position papers from this collection to use in an exercise in interpretive structural modeling. L. C. Fitch proposed "Eight Goals for an Urbanizing America" (Fitch, 1968). He analyzed and justified each of his goals and it certainly appears, on first reading the paper, that it would provide a simple exercise to aid in introducing the objectives tree concept to our students. As we will see, it proved considerably more complex than first thought (see Figure 3.3).

It will be important for us to remember in this exercise our position as analysts. Our aim is *not* to substitute our goals for Fitch's. Rather it is to take his prose narrative

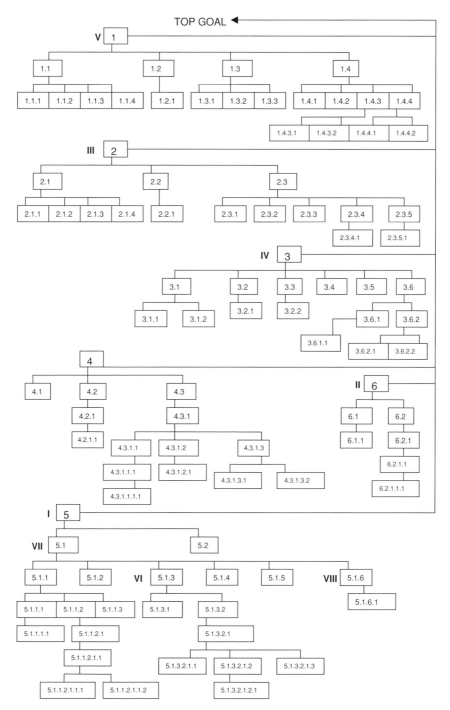

FIGURE 3.3 A tree organization of 105 goals extracted from Fitch's narrative. Fitch's original eight are shown in roman numerals. The top goal and number 4 are implied by Fitch's narrative (Fitch, 1968).

and produce from it an accurate interpretive structural model. This process should produce a clarification of the interactions and an ordering of Fitch's goals by their importance. It may also uncover gaps as well as internal inconsistencies unsuspected by Fitch due to his use exclusively of the narrative form. Our analysis may also make explicit the implicit axiological basis within which Fitch works.

A first reading of Fitch's paper reveals that each of Fitch's eight goals is stated in multisentence form, sometimes in a paragraph over 100 words in length. We also note that some of his eight goals are partitioned by Fitch into several parts. Some of his goals include means, while others do not. Indeed some of his goals would seem to defy measurement. It also appears that his eight goals are not all at the same axiological level. Some are vague and generalized, while others are specifically targeted and restricted in scope. Finally, as one scans the several pages of text that support and explain each of the eight "goals," one discovers dozens of additional goals.

These observations served as indicators that the process of interpretive structural modeling of the Fitch paper might not be as straightforward as was first thought. But it also seems clear that if Fitch's "goals" are to be transformed from vague platitudes into an action program, an analysis such as we will perform is a necessity. In Table 3.2, we list Fitch's eight stated goals in his own words.

Some variation in an analysis of a set of such complex statements is to be expected, because different analysts will break out Fitch's complex goals into different groupings of simpler goals. Nevertheless, the wide divergence initially encountered in an analysis by different system teams was a source of some surprise to the authors. Finally, after a detailed three-stage analysis by cooperating teams was conducted, a major source of the initial difficulties became clear.

Whereas individual analysts produced 30 or even 40 individual goals from Fitch's original eight, and several system teams working separately found 50 or even 60 goals, the final merging of the various separate team goals resulted in *105 separate goals*! No wonder then that Fitch's proclamation of "eight" goals was initially confusing to analysts. These 105 goals of Fitch are listed in Table 3.3, and Figure 3.3 shows the goals organized into a hierarchical tree. Fitch's original eight are followed with their roman numeral in parentheses.

System analysts sometimes meet resistance from administrators trained in the "liberal arts tradition" at the idea of taking apart their ideas and pressing them onto the Procrustean bed of our analysis technique as in the Fitch goals analysis. We appear by our process to be jettisoning years of tradition and their training in developing a fluid and persuasive prose style. When we analysts get through, all of the verve, life and wit seem to be gone. Not to speak of the freedom to express oneself in one's own style. And all of this is true.

But we suppose that it has to do with one's purpose in writing. Is it to attract attention to one's skill at turning literary arabesques? Or is it to persuade and then to achieve a concrete goal? Suppose you were a government official or staff person asked to implement Fitch's program, given his narrative. Isn't the potential for massive confusion and ineffective effort, as well as misuse of resources, apparent? Yet this exercise is not nearly as complicated as some legislation enacted by Congress.

TABLE 3.2. Fitch's Eight Goals for an Urbanizing America

I. "An urban society with values, environment and service systems that respond fully to the needs and wants of families and individuals; a society drawn to the 'human scale.' This society should be open, with freedom of choice, freedom to move up occupational and social ladders, and opportunity to participate fully in economic and political life. It should be a pluralist society in that it honors cultural differences which particular groups wish to maintain. It should offer a variety of ways of life and opportunity to choose among them."

II. "A national commitment to the work of developing the urban frontier, as pervasive and compelling as the national commitment to developing the western frontier in the nineteenth century. Such a commitment must draw on federal, state, and local governments, business, and labor, and educational, religious, and other organizations. It must be based on a heightened sense of common interest among all urban dwellers with increased communication and natural understanding across class lines, and a general concern for the wellbeing of each community."

III. "Eradication of poverty and increase of productivity by:
   a. providing job opportunities for all who wish to work and opportunities for able older people to continue contributing to society;
   b. raising the levels and extending the coverage of social insurance and public assistance programs to promote incentives and stable family life; and to be more responsive to need."

IV. "Extending new meaning to the traditional American ideal of equality of opportunity by making available to all citizens:
   a. lifelong educational opportunities through a system designed to give each person incentives and facilities to fully develop his own capabilities and to contribute to society;
   b. decent and adequate housing;
   c. health and medical services adequate to allow each person to achieve his full potential productivity and sense of physical wellbeing;
   d. a variety of recreational and cultural outlets."

V. "Extending the meaning of individual freedom to include:
   a. freedom from personal aggression, security of person and property in public and private places;
   b. freedom from the physical and psychological damage caused by environmental aggression, including obtrusive noise, polluted air, overcrowding;
   c. freedom from the threat of uncompensated losses by public action for the benefit of others, whether in the name of public welfare or of 'progress';
   d. freedom from discrimination under the law: assurance of opportunity for defense against prosecution, protection against loss of rights owing to property or other personal circumstances, and protection against exploitation of poverty and ignorance."

VI. "Application of modern technology to the improvement of amenity, efficiency, and beauty of the urban environment, and development of new concepts and techniques for guiding metropolitan growth."

VII. "Maintenance of central cities as vital, healthy centers of knowledge and culture, of management and commerce, and of residence for city lovers."

VIII. "Metropolitan development planning for efficiency and aesthetic appeal, and for conservation of urban natural resources and regional ecology."

Source: Fitch (1968).

TABLE 3.3. 105 Goals Extracted from Fitch's Narrative[a]

1. TO EXTEND THE MEANING OF INDIVIDUAL FREEDOM (V)
   1.1 to include "freedom from discrimination" in the meaning of freedom
      1.1.1 to assure opportunity for defense against prosecution
      1.1.2 to assure protection against loss of rights owing to poverty or other circumstances
      1.1.3 to assure protection against exploitation of poverty and ignorance
      1.1.4 to protect the poor from arbitrary treatment of government bureaucracies, including the legal system
   1.2 to include freedom from uncompensated losses in the meaning of freedom
      1.2.1 to reexamine the concepts of "progress" and "personal interest"
   1.3 to include freedom from physical and psychological damage caused by environmental aggression in the meaning of freedom
      1.3.1 to abate polluted air
      1.3.2 to abate overcrowding
      1.3.3 to abate obtrusive noise
   1.4 to provide freedom from personal aggression, security of person and property in public and private places
      1.4.1 to eradicate slums and poverty
      1.4.2 to initiate parole and penal reform
      1.4.3 to change the role of the policeman
         1.4.3.1 to recruit minority policemen who will serve in minority neighborhoods
         1.4.3.2 to better the public opinion of police
      1.4.4 to change police technology
         1.4.4.1 to take into account the mores of the community as to which laws should be enforced
         1.4.4.2 to make connotations of law enforcement terms more pleasing to the public
2. TO ERADICATE POVERTY AND INCREASE PRODUCTIVITY (III)
   2.1 to provide job opportunities for all who wish to work
      2.1.1 to provide opportunities for able older people to continue contributing to society
      2.1.2 to make more employment accessible to ghetto residents
      2.1.3 to provide improved information on the labor market
      2.1.4 to provide specific job training and other measures to equip and rehabilitate workers for jobs
   2.2 to promote incentives and stable family life and to be more responsive to need
      2.2.1 to raise levels and extend coverage of public assistance programs
   2.3 to strengthen the whole income maintenance system
      2.3.1 to reduce the discrepancies among states in levels of public assistance benefits
      2.3.2 to raise social security payments to above-poverty levels
      2.3.3 to provide foundation income for all households
      2.3.4 to eliminate the present disincentives embedded in public assistance programs
         2.3.4.1 to create a system that creates work incentives (not destroy them)
      2.3.5 to provide work which uses the imaginative and creative talents of the laborer
         2.3.5.1 to create a new work ethic

(Continued)

TABLE 3.3. *Continued*

3. TO EXTEND NEW MEANING TO EQUALITY OF OPPORTUNITY (IV)
  3.1 to provide a variety of ways of life and the opportunity to choose among them
    3.1.1 to make available lifelong educational opportunities
      3.1.1.1 to make supplemental programs available to those who need help
      3.1.1.2 to provide better educational opportunities
      3.1.1.3 to persuade the children of ignorance to want education
    3.1.2 to design a system to give each person incentives and facilities to contribute to society
      3.1.2.1 to have the educational efforts reach into the home and the community
        3.1.2.1.1 to include the indoctrination of parents and the cultivation of community attitudes in the educational process
  3.2 to make available decent and adequate housing
    3.2.1 to provide better housing for the lowest economic plane
  3.3 to allow each person to achieve his full potential productivity and sense of wellbeing
    3.3.1 to make available adequate health and medical services
  3.4 to provide freedom to move up occupational and social ladders
  3.5 to foster individual freedom of choice and lifestyle
  3.6 to make available a variety of recreational and cultural outlets
    3.6.1 to provide a society which honors cultural differences
      3.6.1.1 to create increased communication and mutual understanding across class lines
    3.6.2 to increase access to outdoor recreation and open space
      3.6.2.1 to provide recreation for adolescents
      3.6.2.2 to ensure that beaches are open to all people
4. TO HAVE GOVERNMENT PLAY A VIABLE ROLE IN IMPROVING URBAN AMERICA (IMPLIED)
  4.1 to have the federal government assist in obtaining funds for urban development and renewal
  4.2 to induce state governments to respond more adequately to urban areas
    4.2.1 to induce state governments to provide financial support to meet urban development needs
      4.2.1.1 to have civil relations between public servants and the public
  4.3 to create effective local government responsible to citizens' needs and wishes
    4.3.1 to provide the opportunity to participate fully in economic and political life
      4.3.1.1 to promote changes in local government necessary to meet the needs of expanding metropolitan areas
        4.3.1.1.1 to encourage the poor to take part in political control of the government
          4.3.1.1.1.1 to encourage the poor to look to political organization for assistance in meeting pressing needs
      4.3.1.2 to provide leadership from the community
        4.3.1.2.1 to provide a social environment for courtship
      4.3.1.3 to make the city more responsive to individual needs and to foster individual freedom of choice of lifestyle
        4.3.1.3.1 to have the community provide leadership in defining the goals of the urban community and in mobilizing resources to get them done
        4.3.1.3.2 to have citizens accept their problems and not evade them

TABLE 3.3. *Continued*

5. TO CREATE A SOCIETY DRAWN TO HUMAN SCALE (I)
  5.1   to maintain central cities as vital, healthy centers of culture, of management and commerce, and of residence for city-lovers (VII)
     5.1.1 to concentrate physical and social renewal and development programs in specific limited areas
        5.1.1.1 to provide stable and changing historical and contemporary communities
           5.1.1.1.1 to provide communities of low-density and high-density, of single, multiple and mixed dwellings
        5.1.1.2 to offer a greater variety of choices of residence and ways of life to people of all racial and income groups
           5.1.1.2.1 to preserve neighborhood values and traditions
               5.1.1.2.1.1 to maintain cultural differences which reflect pride in race, origin and group accomplishments
                    5.1.1.2.1.1.1 to provide neighborhoods which are homogeneous
                    5.1.1.2.1.1.2 to provide neighborhoods which are mixed as to income, racial, and ethnic characteristics
        5.1.1.3 to reclaim people in order to revitalize central cities
     5.1.2 to place high priority on fiscal reform to relieve cities of public assistance and other special social service costs
     5.1.3 to apply modern technology to the improvement of amenity, efficiency, and beauty of the urban environment (VI)
        5.1.3.1 to provide for coherent relationships or strategies for mutual benefit between cities and their surrounding areas
        5.1.3.2 to provide for efficient spatial relationships between residential, employment, and other activity centers
           5.1.3.2.1 to bring beauty, style, convenience, interest, and other values of environmental design to the city
               5.1.3.2.1.1 to provide outdoor play and recreation facilities on rooftops or open floors
               5.1.3.2.1.2 to provide pedestrian shopping and recreational areas
                    5.1.3.2.1.2.1 to develop arcaded sidewalks
               5.1.3.2.1.3 to separate vehicular and pedestrian traffic
     5.1.4 to institute a public policy for new town building
     5.1.5 to join public and private financial and technical resources to create new towns and cities
     5.1.6 to plan metropolitan development for efficiency and aesthetic appeal and for conservation of urban national resources and regional ecology (VIII)
        5.1.6.1 to define new concepts of urban resources—open space, air and water
  5.2   to have from business, labor, and other private sectors, as well as public leadership, a commitment to the values served by a city of human scale

(Continued)

TABLE 3.3. *Continued*

6. TO MAKE A NATIONAL COMMITMENT TO THE WORK OF DEVELOPING THE URBAN FRONTIER (II)
   6.1   to organize federal, state, and local governments
        6.1.1   to coordinate business, labor, and other groups to work for a common interest
   6.2   to achieve a heightened sense of common interest
        6.2.1   to have all citizens working for a common interest
               6.2.1.1   to achieve a general concern for community wellbeing
                      6.2.1.1.1   to achieve mutual understanding across class lines

[a]Each of these goals is given in Fitch's own words. Only two exceptions were made. The highest goal and Goal No. 4 were inferred by the analysts in order to tie the tree together. This objectives tree exercise on Fitch's goals proved to be extraordinarily difficult. We had no idea in advance that over 100 distinct goals were buried in Fitch's narrative.

This example, through its simultaneous simplicity and complexity, should be a good argument for this analysis device.

3.8 CONTENT ANALYSIS OF FITCH'S GOALS

Structural Analysis of Fitch's Goals. Now that we have a graphical representation of Fitch's goals, we are ready to begin an analysis. First, let us make a structural analysis: We must infer a single top-level goal to Fitch because he does not explicitly articulate one, even in his title. A likely possibility seems "to improve urban America." Five of Fitch's original eight goals lie at the second level, immediately in support of this implicit top level goal. But, *a priori*, one would expect Fitch's eight major goals to make up the totality of his second level goals. But this is not so, which indicates that Fitch has allowed more specific objectives to creep into his original eight. Further examination shows one of his original eight at the third level and two at the fourth level. Thus it appears that Fitch's goals lack balance, in that some of his eight are at a high axiological level and others are rather specific.

Next, we note that the graphical model of Fitch's goals is irregular in depth. We find that the branch containing Fitch goals numbers I, VII, and VI is elaborated down to the eighth level of detail. Other major branches are elaborated respectively to the fourth, the fifth, and the sixth level. Thus certain branches are terminated at a rather high level of abstraction. For example, we are left with "to assure opportunity for defense against prosecution" (1.1.1) under "to extend the meaning of individual freedom" (1) but no details on how to accomplish this.

On the other hand, "to develop arcaded sidewalks" (5.1.3.2.1.2.1) will help "to provide pedestrian shopping and recreational areas" (5.1.3.2.1.2), which will help "to bring style, convenience, interest, and other values of environmental design to the city" (5.1.3.2.1), which will help "to provide for efficient spatial relationships between residential, employment, and other activity centers" (5.1.3.2), which will help "to apply modern technology to the improvement of amenity, efficiency, and beauty of the urban environment" (5.1.3), which in turn will help "to maintain central cities as vital, healthy centers of knowledge and culture, of management and commerce and of residency for city lovers" (5.1), which will help "to create a society drawn to human scale" (5).

A third structural concern with Fitch's analysis lies in the possible incompleteness of his goals. When using a tree to synthesize a set of objectives, we recommend that an objective called "other" be included at each level in each branch. This signals to the analyst and the reader that the tree is incomplete. When a particular branch is deemed complete by the analyst, the term "other" is removed. On the other hand, when one uses this diagrammatic approach to analyze the work of a third party, one must be careful to avoid projecting one's own goals on the author's work. Therefore, in this analysis of Fitch, we have not added our own suggested goals to his work, with the two high-level exceptions noted, which were needed to hold the tree together. Nor do we feel free to read Fitch's mind. He does not indicate that he believes his goals to be samples or examples. We are led to believe that he considers this a complete set of goals. It isn't essential that Fitch lay bare the structural process by which he arrived at his goals. On the other hand, he must permit his work to be subjected to rational criticism and it appears from our structural analysis that his goals do not form a complete set.

Finally, it must be pointed out that Fitch's goals are in some measure redundant. Of course, Fitch may repeat himself if he wishes for emphasis or for other stylistic reasons, but these tactics don't seem appropriate for developing a set of goals. It seems fair to assume that this redundancy is unconscious. Consider the goals under 5.1.1, for example. Here Fitch asks for variety and homogeneity, along with continuity and change, in living patterns. These are understandable options, but it would appear that, had Fitch the benefit of examining the resulting tree, he might wish to organize his thinking in a simpler pattern without these overlaps.

To bring this structural analysis to an end, we argue that the objectives tree shows that Fitch's goals are not balanced, are irregular in depth, are incomplete and, in some measure, are redundant. We have not exhausted the power of graphical analysis, however. We could proceed to correct the structural criticisms just made. Of course, any critical reader adds and subtracts, as well as accepts and rejects, parts of a paper as he reads it. But developing a tree permits a systematic evaluation. There is no reason why the author should not conduct such an evaluation for himself. Then whether he chooses to expose the skeleton or framework of his analysis (i.e., the tree) or to rest with the elaborated surface narrative is a matter for his own choice.

While an author is not responsible for extreme interpretations placed on his work by lazy-minded readers, he certainly has an interest in conveying his real meaning as precisely as he can. It was Gibson's experience while lecturing on Fitch's paper that many people form a more balanced view of his proposals from the objectives tree than they do by skimming his prose and fastening on phrases which strike their attention. It might also be true that an author such as Fitch, if provided with a diagram of an early draft of his narrative, might wish to reorder his priorities or areas of emphasis.

Linguistic Analysis. We have used the tree to discover certain structural concerns about Fitch's goals, and we have mentioned that the graphical analysis aids in making a balanced appreciation of the axiological component of a narrative. The third purpose for which this graphic approach is an important aid is in a linguistic analysis. That is, it helps to highlight parallels or the lack of them. It also pinpoints sloppy thinking and dangling phrases.

Under the rubric of "extending the meaning of freedom" (1), for example, Fitch appears to class not only protection from certain bad things such as discrimination (1.1) and loss of rights due to poverty (1.1.2), but also equal access to certain benefits, which in the past have sometimes been deemed due only to those who earn them. Examples would be relief from overcrowding (1.3.2), and the absence of slums and poverty itself (1.4.1).

Fitch also appears to call for a reinterpretation of our social and economic system, but we will postpone explicitly axiological concerns for a moment. Fitch is open in announcing his intention of "extending the meaning of freedom," and the diagram permits us to see what he means by this. He is less open about his meaning under "eradicate poverty and increase productivity" (2), and this also becomes apparent. Fitch includes "specific job training. . ." (2.1.4) and includes "making jobs more accessible" (2.1.2), but it is not clear what he means by "promoting incentives and stable family life and being more responsive to need" (2.2), because this is as far as he takes these notions, with the exception of proposing to "raise levels and extend coverage of public assistance programs" (2.2.1). It appears that, having once mentioned "productivity," Fitch thereafter ignores it to concentrate on arguments directed toward equity.

Analysis of Axiological Component. It does not require a graph to examine Fitch's value structure. But an objectives tree does clarify and simplify the analysis. For example, consider Fitch's goal III, "to eradicate poverty and increase productivity." Reading Fitch's narrative, certain phases seem heavily value-laden. The lead sentence of his first paragraph on page 1148 in Fitch (1968) may serve as an example. "Poverty is a relative not an absolute condition—people measure their well-being by comparison with the population at large, not by how far they are from starvation." On the contrary, Banfield says on page 1235 of the same issue of *DAEDALUS* (Banfield, 1968) that one should "define poverty in terms of objective 'hardship' as opposed to 'inconvenience' or 'relative deprivation'. . ."

The reader may feel that these two authors provide typical examples of doctrinaire liberal versus the doctrinaire conservative positions, but remember that as system analysts our job is to capture accurately the *author's* position and not contaminate it with our own. As system analysts, however, we must be concerned with the difficulty of measuring relativistic goals.

An examination of the tree in Figure 3.2 under Goal III seems to indicate that while Fitch is concerned with "providing a foundation income" and "raising social security payments to above poverty levels," he is also concerned with "providing job opportunities for all who wish to work" and "making employment accessible and providing job training and job information." Thus Fitch is concerned with the balance of the poverty eradication program and how it will be paid for. Then when the reader returns to Banfield, the apparently hard-line sentence quoted above finishes with "... and bring all incomes up to this nearly fixed level." Then Banfield goes on to advocate the negative income tax. Thus, while there is a difference between Fitch and Banfield, neither one is simplistically one-sided or doctrinaire.

One can see that Fitch maintains strongly the position of the government as a support resource. In this philosophy it is the state's place to plan and to support and to nourish and to encourage and to train and to reward. Negative reinforcement (i.e., punishment) is withheld. Thus Fitch visualizes a world in which everyone is self-actualized. We see phrases such as "... work for those who want it," "... work which uses the imagination and creative talents of the laborer," and "... people accept their problems and not evade them (4.3.1.3.2)." We are to "... persuade the children of ignorance to want education" (3.1.1.3) and to "... give each person incentives to fully develop," and so on.

Banfield, in contrast, begins with the individual and argues only for that minimum governmental structure necessary to provide essential services. One author sees the bureaucratic system as potentially capable of providing almost total support for the individual; the other sees this proposed total support structure as a prison and an inefficient one at that. In practice, the pragmatic positions of these protagonists may not be far apart, as we have seen, but their basic philosophy is in global opposition. Some readers may be a little surprised that this graphic process can be used for an objective analysis at a prose narrative. It surprises many arts scholars, we know. Perhaps it has occurred to you that many problems between contending individuals arise because of the imprecision of the prose narrative form. Much of contract law is based on this flaw. Couldn't many disagreements among nations be traced to this cause as well?

3.9 VALIDATE

Following each pass through of the steps in goal development, the system team should validate and consolidate its findings. While the preceding steps are creative and emotional, validation is analytic and judgmental.

In the process of validation, we begin to outline the elements of the data base that will be needed in the analysis and we begin to formulate the analytic model to be used. In other words, the analytic OR component begins to be emphasized here.

Depending on the psychological type of each member of the system team, either creative or analytic activities are more appealing. It is important that one learn something about oneself and attempt to counterbalance one's natural tendency in this regard. We have deliberately ruled out, previous to validation, activities such as criticism, editing, corrections, selection, comparison, weighting, evaluation, and so on. Now is the time to emphasize those judgmental activities.

We sometimes find system team members who have a heavy judgmental component in their personal value structure. They can hardly control themselves during the first few "outscoping" steps in the goal development process we have been outlining. These individuals should be assigned leadership in the validation process. They like to do it and may do it well. They will also see that they "asked for" the assignment by being so eager to criticize when it really wasn't appropriate. Thus, they may also learn to temper their critical enthusiasm in future rounds of analysis.

3.10 ITERATE

Remember that we suggest iterating in this first phase of the study and then we also include iteration as one of the final major phases as well. We have discussed the central position of the process of iteration in SA in Section 2.6. Because we know we will iterate, we can proceed rapidly through the steps, gaining new perspective as we go. At this point in the analysis, we suggest that you iterate only once or twice on goal development, because at this early point in the SA, you are clarifying your own position, and this isn't nearly as important as clarifying the client's position. Further iteration on the steps in goal development will prove even more useful after completing several of the other major phases in SA.

CASE STUDY: DISTANCE LEARNING IN THE FUTURE?

Memorandum

TO: Systems Analysis Consultants (SAC) The Department Chair[5] of the Systems and Information Engineering Department at the University of Virginia is concerned with the future of engineering education, specifically with the delivery of an SE education at UVa.

He has heard of, directly and indirectly, innovative new ideas in the extended or distance delivery of education. One such program is, of course, the UVa SE Accelerated Master's Degree Program, and there is also the televised graduate engineering program (CGEP). Our TV program is designed to offer outreach and continued education to numerous sites throughout the East.

He would like to brief the Dean in the next couple of weeks on this issue. He has asked my SAC teams to perform a systems study on where extended engineering education at UVa, focusing but not limited to SE, should be in the year 2008 and beyond.

Concerns of his include decreasing engineering student enrollments, retraining the U.S. work force, the future and direction of the SE discipline, technology directions and potential, and funding of programs. It is his belief that we must start positioning ourselves now for the future, but he's not sure if there is a problem. Unfortunately, he feels that he and his faculty are biased and would like a fresh, professional look at the situation.

He has requested that we brief him tomorrow on our recommendations. I remind you that he is a steadfast believer in the systems methodology and expects a thoroughly professional briefing.

HISTORICAL CASE STUDY: GOALS OF 4C INC.[6]

The College CAD/CAM Consortium (4C) was founded by 12 U.S. Schools of Engineering and funded by a two-phase grant from the National Science Foundation in 1980 for a total of $705,000. Additional funds were to be sought from nongovernmental sources such as foundations and industry. The founding purpose of 4C was to promote the development and widespread use of interactive graphic software in all branches of engineering education in the United States. Within several years, the membership of 4C grew to 22 Schools of Engineering. 4C was incorporated as a nonprofit organization in early 1985.

In the spring of 1985, the new President of 4C Inc., Dean Wayne Chen, of the University of Florida, directed Pat Egan, a consultant, to draft a renewal proposal to NSF. The new director of NSF, Eric Bloch, formerly a corporate executive at IBM, is known to be supportive of CAD/CAM, and the purpose of 4C seems directly in line with the widespread desire to improve industrial productivity in the United States. President Chen argued that even if the grant proposal is not funded, that the preparation process will help focus the goals of 4C and help to organize and focus its membership.

At a meeting of the Executive Committee of the Board of Directors of 4C Inc. in Baltimore in October 1985, final plans were laid for the first annual national 4C conference, which was to be held at North Carolina State University in March 1986, and the first draft of Egan's renewal proposal was reviewed. It was generally agreed that the computer world had advanced very rapidly since 1979 when the first 4C proposal was drafted. The IBM PC did not exist at that time, for example. Thus it seemed apparent that the goals and methods of 4C should be reviewed and possibly modified for the future effort.

A jumbled list of old goals and new possibilities were jotted down by Pat during the meeting, but he wasn't very clear on how to proceed further. He could poll the 4C membership, but that could take months. In the airplane on the way home, Egan decided that he should turn to a few trusted, broad-gauge system thinkers for their ideas.

The "jumbled goals list" is given below as thought starters. Please organize these objectives and edit the material for inclusion in the 4C proposal for renewed funding.

Some Possible 4C Goals

- To expand 4C membership more rapidly
- To encourage industrial participation
- To include all colleges (not limited to technical)
- To prepare engineers to solve current problems in a modern environment
- To increase national productivity
- To promote innovation
- To document properly all of the 12 original modules [i.e., graphic software designed by founding member institutions]

- To encourage the daily use of the 12 modules [i.e., institutions' software packages]
- To increase interaction among universities, industry and government to promote the currency and effectiveness of CAD/CAM instruction
- To improve the quality of engineering education
- To create a cooperative approach in professional engineering education involving common goals, shared knowledge, and a shared commitment
- To develop a framework for sharing instructional materials among institutions with varying curricula
- To foster the smooth introduction of CAD into the engineering education process
- To design protocols that will guide the development of machine-independent, transportable software and a mechanism for documenting and validating such software
- To develop an effective, nonprofit distribution system for approved software
- To develop recommendations for a compatible base of hardware and software that will allow the graceful expansion of computing facilities throughout the next decade
- To reinforce the native graphic sense of engineering students and to emphasize the holistic elements of engineering design and synthesis
- To reinforce the emphasis on discrete mathematics and computerized design as opposed to the continuous math and applied physics base of the past
- To subsidize more software module development
- To act as a "Good Housekeeping Seal of Approval" and a distribution agent for independently produced software and to abandon subsidized software production
- To encourage an annual national conference at which software modules can be displayed and new developments discussed
- To become financially independent of NSF support as soon as possible
- To encourage use of electronic mail for communication among 4C schools
- To set up hardware standards for industry
- To award prizes (perhaps funded by outside sources) for software development
- To double the number of 4C members in 1986
- To submit an excellent proposal to NSF by January 1986
- To send out small teams of 4C officers to seek industrial support
- To permit some commercial displays at the annual meeting
- To encourage academic credit for faculty software development
- To write articles in the national technical press and give general interest papers at ASEE conferences to publicize the work of 4C
- To seek out and merge with other organizations
- To seek to cooperate with other organizations
- Other

NOTES

1. Informal testimony to the National Academy of Science committee on USAF software production productivity, 1986–1987.

2. Apparently, Horwitch gained access to internal NASA correspondence on Dr. Gibson's article using the Freedom of Information Act. To Gibson's surprise, he found for the first time from the Horwitch book (Horwitch, 1982) that over two dozen reports, memos, and other internal documents had been generated by NASA in attempting to rebut the some 50 concerns that he had raised. While none of his findings were contravened by NASA, the position he took in the *Harper's* article did threaten his consulting opportunities with the space agency and other federal agencies for the next several years.

3. Many things about SA seem like simple common sense if you haven't seen the alternatives to SA in action. In other words, simply reading about SA makes everything seem so simple and obvious that you may be lulled into a false sense of confidence.

4. American engineering educators would almost certainly brand as reprehensible any suggestion that they would "brainwash students" or "inculcate values." Examples of such activity would be labeled as merely training in "professional attitudes" and as absolutely essential for our continued success as a profession.

5. This is a fictional character and is based on no person living or deceased.

6. This case does not illustrate either good or bad management practice, nor does it necessarily represent the position of the College CAD/CAM Consortium. It is meant solely to provide a basis for classroom discussion. For more information, see Beckert (1986).

Chapter **4**

The Index of Performance

4.1 INTRODUCTION

In this chapter we discuss the process of setting up success criteria for the project. Another name frequently given to this step is the "Project Requirements and Specifications" phase. The essence of this concept is, *"If we can't measure it, it's not worth doing,"* but more on that later. Unfortunately, as discussed in Chapter 2, the Index of Performance is often a neglected or misused concept. As Dilbert illustrates in Figure 4.1, it's easy and common to select metrics that direct us to the wrong solution. This point was driven home to us on a consulting venture for a call center where the metric used for evaluation was so wrong as to drive the business into the red.[1]

Before we begin, however, we will address several possible concerns. First, it may appear that we are delaying matters with overly formalistic procedures. We have already made a first cut at determining the goals of the system, so why can't we go ahead now and solve the problem? That is, why not start now to design the system solution? If this were an information or software system, one might ask,

"Can we start coding now, please?"

The answer is,

"No, because we don't know how the client wants to measure success."

How to Do Systems Analysis. By John E. Gibson, William T. Scherer, and William F. Gibson
Copyright © 2007 John Wiley & Sons, Inc.

FIGURE 4.1 Dogbert's tech support.

The analyst may think he or she does but, if so, it is because we are substituting our own opinion for the client's success measure. Take for instance the design of a simple software compiler for batch processing jobs in a single language. No fancy stuff here. How will you decide which of the four candidate programs to buy? The choices are given in Table 4.1.

We hope you have decided that you can't make a choice yet, because you have insufficient information. You don't understand the environment in which this utility is to work. If you did make a choice, you did so by substituting your personal Index of Performance for that of the client. That was anti-systems behavior and thus a mistake. On the other hand, it would be a mistake to go to the other extreme of simply asking the client to make the choice. Rather, what you need is a performance-requirements analysis.

It is your job as a system analyst to work with the client to translate the client's needs into system specifications. At this point one might ask, "Doesn't this put the analyst in a subsidiary role? Why couldn't the client just go ahead and make his own choice of compiler?" Exactly. You are helping the client to solve his problem. But, in this trivial example, it was easy and a system analysis possibly wasn't needed. In more complex situations, we will have plenty to do, without trying to usurp the role of the client as well.

This example illustrates one reason for not moving directly to system design at this point. There is another point to be considered; not only would it be premature to try to pick the optimum system at this point, it is even premature to compile a list of

TABLE 4.1. Four Simple compilers[a]

Program	Description
A	Fewest lines of source code.
B	Fastest to produce an executable program.
C	Slower, but has most complete error diagnostics.
D	Least costly to purchase.

[a]All come from reliable vendors and are in use at other DP centers.

candidates. System analysts have learned from experience that if a list of candidates is developed at this point, prior to IP design, individual analysts and perhaps the client may "fall in love" with one or another of the possibilities. That is, one makes an emotional, subjective response for or against one or another of the candidates, without sufficient evidence (as you may have already done!). From then on, these individuals may become advocates for their favorite solution rather than remaining objective analysts. It may sound silly to say that one "falls in love" with an inanimate object, but it seems to be an accurate description of an emotional attachment that actively resists quantification or justification.

The Detroit subway case discussed in Chapter 2 and throughout the text is a good example. The Mayor's office "knew" in advance that the subway was the correct transport mode, that Woodward was the correct artery, and that the strip between the Detroit River and the New Center area was the correct location. Yet when the client was asked by what optimizing criterion he had reached this conclusion, the client was unable to give reasons for his choice.

System analysts who say, "I don't know why I like candidate C, I just do," seem to place themselves in the same category as individuals who say, "I don't know much about art, but I know what I like." On the other hand, we cannot expect the client to produce, unaided, her Index of Performance. That is a technical job of the system analyst.

A client recently provided another insight on the matter of determining criteria *before* doing the options analysis. We were doing an urban solid waste recycling study and the systems team was complimented by the client for its calm and objective analysis and for setting up the objectives and sticking to them during the options analysis (Warfield, 1976, 1989). The client remarked that this is a very emotional issue for citizens and that he often received phone calls at home on weekends from emotional voters. He had grown accustomed to advocates who pushed pet ideas with no facts and no evidence of objective analysis. It seems evident from these comments that some public officials view favorably a calm, objective, fact-based study when one is offered. However, if a hidden or nonpublic agenda exists, the decision maker may not want a clear Index of Performance.[2] For an excellent and still, sadly, very relevant discussion of this and related issues, see Churchman's 1979 book *The Systems Approach and Its Enemies* (Churchman, 1979).

4.2 DESIRABLE CHARACTERISTICS FOR AN INDEX OF PERFORMANCE

The ideal Index of Performance has the following five characteristics:

- Measurable
- Objective
- Nonrelativistic
- Meaningful
- Understandable

Measurable. This might seem to be an obvious characteristic, yet it is often ignored in practice. We have discussed Fitch's Goals for an Urbanizing America, and we think we can agree that Fitch had thought long and deeply about the problems of urban America. Yet look at the number of Fitch's goals for which no measurement technique was or is currently available. It is essential that quantitative measures be established for each of the various concepts employed in system planning.

Here is another example of the same problem. President Eisenhower commissioned an important National Goals development program during his term of office. When Biderman studied the results, he concluded that the final report contained many unmeasurable goals. He reports (Biderman, 1967) that "... [over 40 percent of the] 82 quite explicit statements of specific goals in each of 11 domestic areas, established by the President's Commission on National Goals ... have no pertinent indicator data available." Thus, even (and perhaps, especially) at the highest level of policy-making, serious misunderstandings on the necessity for indicators exist.

President Reagan's Persian Gulf policy of "reflagging" and escorting foreign oil-tankers was questioned in July 1987 by James H. Wells, then Secretary of the Navy, in an internal memorandum to then Secretary of Defense, Caspar Weinberger. *"What are our objectives?"* Wells asked, *"When do we know we have achieved our objectives?"* (Anonymous, 1987). Exactly.

President Bush outlined the goals for the 2003 war in Iraq by stating *"Our coalition has a clear goal, understood by all—to see the Iraqi people in charge of Iraq for the first time in generations."*[3] This notion may be understood by all, but is not measurable (see the final property of a metric).

It is difficult to see how one can achieve an objective for which there is no generally accepted success measure. At the very least, it means that the objective is vague and ill-defined. It probably also means that honest and possibly intense differences of opinion can arise as to whether the objective has been achieved. Success in Iraq, in the first or second war, is clearly disputed. Weinberger's response to Wells, according to *The Washington Post*, was a "process" response. That is, Weinberger suggested that success was achieved with each successful ship passage through the Gulf. Obviously, from a SA perspective, this is not so.[4] A process goal is relativistic, see below, and is almost always unsatisfactory. Do not let yourself get caught with process goals, if you can help it.

Fitch's urban goals analysis is certainly open to this criticism. When Fitch calls for "air pollution abatement" (1.3.1) or "elimination of obtrusive noise" (1.3.3), one can imagine establishing measurable standards. Indeed, significant progress has been made since 1968 in both these areas. But how are we to measure "the connotations of law enforcement terms more pleasing to the public" (1.4.4.2), or the "achievement of personal full potential" (3.3)? This is not to say that Fitch should not employ these value-laden concepts. Rather, it is to say that prior agreement on what constitutes achievement of such goals should be obtained before instituting expensive ameliorative or remedial programs. The analyst not alert for this trap may get eaten alive.

Objective. "Objective" is similar to, but not the same as, "measurable." Objective means that all observers will agree on the observed quantity. Suppose we have a room full of people. We can take it that the number in the room is a measurable quantity, but is the number of overweight people in the room measurable? Of course, but only if we can agree on an objective measure of "overweight," such as a BMI (Body Mass Index) greater than 25. We may have a goal to have "well-trained reservists" for the military; however, without a measurable goal of the reserve function and the definition of well-trained, we don't have an objective measure. Many of Fitch's goals are not only nonmeasurable in principle, but are not objective, because two observers can disagree on the meaning of the same observation. Note that this problem is present in the Persian Gulf policy discussed above.

Nonrelativistic. A simple example of this characteristic is a goal such as "increase minority enrollment by 10%," a goal that is relativistic and lacks any clear reference point. This is especially important because we know that many social reformers, Fitch included, are relativists. Thus their "real" goal may be a moving target. Furthermore, relativists may not only resist giving an absolute target, they may object in principle to the concept, possibly because they are following a hidden agenda. There is a great deal of Argyris Model-1 behavior in public systems (Argyris, 1982). The literal-minded analyst who ignores hidden agenda items in public policy issues can be ground up in the process. We're tempted to go on here at some length with anecdotal evidence about the dangers of hidden agendas, but we feel sure that you already see the point.

Meaningful. One would think this goes without saying, but not so. In fact, failure to attain this attribute often produces what the medical community euphemistically calls an "iatrogenic illness," that is, a disorder brought on by the treatment process itself. The "systems approach" has been imposed on many public and governmental operations without the full cooperation of the individuals concerned. These individuals sometimes feel forced to conjure up something "countable" even if it isn't meaningful. A common example is in the academic tenure and promotion processes, which often use countable metrics, such as the number of papers published and research dollars, without respect to quality, impact, or contribution. Thus, they may compound the problem rather than solve it. Building on the "increase minority enrollment by 10%" goal, we could improve the goal by anchoring it by revising it to "increase minority enrollment by 10% in the next two years, as defined by the number of minorities enrolled on the first day of the fall semester . . . " Once again, though, this may fail the meaningful test if the true goal is to recruit *and retain* minority students and might be subject to gaming in order to check-off a measurable goal.

We're reminded of a time, almost a hundred years and a dozen or so wars ago, when one of the authors (Gibson) was in Army basic training. He was issued two pairs of boots and was required to alternate their wear. To make it easy to check on recruits, one pair of boots was required to be laced in the usual crisscross manner, and the other pair was required to have the laces going straight across from one eyelet to its pair. Thus, one pair of boots had laces looking cross-hatched and the other square. But suppose one pair of boots was at the repair shop? On alternate days, then, one would appear to have on the wrong boots. What to do? Simple enough for Army bean counters. Each night, the recruit with only one pair of boots was required to re-lace them! Thus producing uniformity on morning parade and nonsense in the process.

Another example we enjoy is when Milwaukee police changed their definition of a "solved" homicide. In order to reduce the number of unsolved cases, a slight redefinition of "solved" was required. They searched old cases, and if the leading suspect was deceased, then the case was considered solved. Hence they were able to meet their goal of 80% solved cases (Spivak and Bice, 2000).

Understandable. An index can be so complex that, even if it meets all of the other requirements, its effectiveness is impaired by difficulty in interpretation. Decision Analysis can be marred with this problem. It may be possible to get a feeling for the difference between a probability of 0.5 and a probability of 0.1. It is unlikely, however, that a respondent can sense the difference between a rare event probability of 0.0001 and 0.000001. Yet tiny probabilities of exceedingly unlikely events can have an impact if the cost of incurring the event is catastrophic, as in a nuclear power plant explosion or terrorist attack, for example. This problem of noncomprehensibility has often flawed the use of decision analysis in nuclear power plant location studies.[5] John Allen Paulos has written extensively in his *Innumeracy* books about the rampant lack of numeracy in the U.S. public [see, for example, Paulos (1988)]. This innumeracy problem was brought to the forefront in 1990 in a debate that raged in the popular press in the "Ask Marilyn" column that ran in many newspapers and *Parade* magazine (September 9, 1990). The columnist had given the correct answer to the classic *Monty Hall* probability problem, and she was savaged by numerous letters from Ph.D.s and University faculty members claiming, in the harshest terms, that she was wrong. These letters, given their source, are a reason to believe Paulos and to be afraid of the state of contemporary mathematical literacy. They also give us even more reason to make sure that our goals are understandable!

Then there is also the Bowl Championship Series (BCS) poll, a confusing mix of weighted polls that even diehard college football fans find confusing and difficult to understand.[6] Combining ordinal and cardinal numbers (from various polls), a ranking is produced that is used to decide which teams participate in which postseason games (see Chapter 6 for more on this). Serious money is at stake, because the game payouts to the schools/teams range from the hundreds of thousands to millions of dollars. Confusion and concern over the results in the past produced a new system of rankings and playoffs for the 2006 season.

The requirement for "understandability" was given new meaning for us when a client pointed out that, outside of financial circles, even the simplest economic criteria are well beyond normal comprehension. This means that we must take extra care to explain *why* we suggest a particular criterion and that the analyst must give simple definitions of such criteria without forcing the client to ask for such definitions. We will discover in this chapter that, even within the business management community, there is little, if any, understanding of such concepts as present net worth, and so on. The vast majority of business decisions are often made, even today, without applying objective criteria or by the use of erroneous criteria.

4.3   ECONOMIC CRITERIA

It is possible to argue that the Index of Performance idea is not all that revolutionary, but rather is merely an extension to a wider sphere of the concept of a quantitative measure of efficiency, which is standard in business and economics. If we exclude questions of equity for a moment, economic efficiency is the ultimate measure of all commercial enterprises and increasingly government activities.[7] Outcomes must be directly measurable in dollars or convertible to this measure. Fortunately, many system studies can be evaluated by economic criteria as well. Indeed, if this were not so, SA would not have been adopted so enthusiastically by business managers.[8] Commercial enterprise represents a large job pool for SA graduates, and many systems Ph.D.s accept faculty positions in M.B.A. programs, as well.

Even though measures of economic efficiency are the most often used of all criteria, the specifics are not simple. Many common criteria do not correctly measure economic efficiency at all. Perhaps the most illustrative study of the actual practice of practical business people is the survey performed by Schwartz and Vertinsky (1977). Although this study was done in the 1970s, it illustrates the complexities of criteria selection. They found that over 50 decision criteria for judging the acceptability of new development projects are in use, but the following six were the most common:

- Probability of success
- Payback period
- Internal rate of return (IRR)
- Cost relative to total budget
- Impact on market share
- Availability of government funding

Obviously, the *"probability of success"* is not a direct measure of economic efficiency, nor is *"cost relative to total budget."* Rather, they are measures of risk and are not necessarily either the complete or correct risk measures. *"Impact on market share"* is not a direct measure of economic efficiency either, but because share is related to long-term profitability, it can make good sense as an indirect measure.[9] Possibly some of the business people using a "probability of success" criterion are sophisticated enough to compute an expected monetary value (EMV) for the venture using the probability, but in most instances we think not.

Consider a simple decision facing a T-shirt seller. Mr. Jensen has an opportunity to sell T-shirts at an upcoming football game, and there are three possible sales outcomes: low (2000 sold), medium (6000 sold), and high (10,000 sold). Each outcome is equally likely (i.e., 1/3). Profit from sales is based on a complex formula, resulting in a profit of $0 for low sales, $15,000 for medium sales, and $100,000 for high sales. Assuming the goal is to maximize profit, what is the expected profit for Mr. Jensen's venture? The answer is easy: We expect to sell 6000 shirts (1/3*2000 + 1/3*6000 + 1/3*10,000 = 6000), so we expect to make $15,000. But Mr. Jensen knows better. But more on this later.

"Availability of government funding" will reduce the investment of internal funds required and thus will improve the efficiency of the investment, but this is merely one of many cost factors. All costs should be considered, although this one is different in that it can be externalized—that is, ignored as an internal cost. Thus, it directly reduces corporate costs. *"Internal rate of return"* is a common measure of economic efficiency, but it is a faulty one. The quantitative justification for this statement is examined in greater detail below (see Section 4.8). *"Payback period"* is commonly thought of as a measure of economic efficiency but it is not, nor is it adequate for this purpose. It is, however, useful for measuring risk, in a very restricted set of circumstances.

A study similar to Schwartz and Vertinsky in the 1990s compared the change in use of five common economic measures from 1978 to 1991 (Remer et al., 1993). The criteria they examined, all economic this time, were:

- Net present value (NPV)
- Internal rate of return (IRR)
- Return on original investment (ROI)
- Return on average investment (RAI)
- Return on investment (RI)

They note a shift in the dominant technique from IRR to NPV; however, all techniques were used across the companies surveyed and IRR still saw significant use. Typical contemporary books will list economic measures (NPW, IRR, ROI) along with other measures, such as benefit–cost analysis, payback periods, discounted cash flow, life-cycle analysis, MAPI (Machinery and Allied Products Institute—the "Challenger and Defender" idea), and proprietary techniques [see Bowman (2003)].

If you think about the implications of the preceding paragraphs, they should be rather disturbing. We think we have just said that none of the six most common measures of economic efficiency explored in the Schwartz and Vertinsky study for business ventures were adequate, and only recently has there been a nonexclusive shift to NPV. *Benefit–cost ratio* and *net present value* (NPV) are two more common measures of economic efficiency but they did not appear on the Schwartz and Vertinsky list in the 1970s, and IRR still is frequently presented in texts and other sources without comment on the issues that surround it. We will discuss all of these explicit measures of economic efficiency, but first we want to remind you of the definition of the basic concepts of compound interest. We present this discussion to motivate the thinking behind these criteria and discuss some of the history to illustrate the context and complexity of economic performance indices.

4.4 COMPOUND INTEREST

The defining relation for compound interest is as follows:

$$F = P[(1 + i)^n] \tag{4.1}$$

or in symbolic form,

$$F = P[F/P, i, n] \qquad \text{(symbolic form only)}$$

where F represents future value, P represents present value, i represents interest rate per period (decimal), and n represents number of periods (not necessarily years). Equation (4.1) is the basic definition of compound interest and all of the other more complex relationships found in texts on engineering economics and elsewhere can be derived from it. The second form is a standard shorthand notation often seen in texts. It is only a shorthand notation and cannot be used for computation.

The more complex relationships for calculating such things as constant annualized payments, and so on, were of considerable utility when the most convenient way of handling compound interest problems was by means of table look-up, but they are of less importance today, given the availability of hand-held devices and ubiquitous computer spreadsheets. Note that the quantity in Eq. (4.1) enclosed in square brackets depends only on the interest rate and the number of periods. Because this is so, a table could be constructed for this bracketed quantity as a function of i and n. A similar table can be constructed for other relationships, thus converting compound interest calculations to (a) simple multiplication of a specific compound interest factor found by table look-up and (b) a total amount of money.

A common way of portraying the economic factors in business decisions is by means of a cash flow diagram as shown in Figures 4.2 through 4.5. Investments or costs [i.e., negative (outward) cash flows] are shown as arrows pointing downward, and returns [i.e., positive (inward) cash flows] are shown as arrows pointing up. Equation (4.1) could be applied to each of the future values in any of the cash items in the figures to find their equivalent present worth, given the assumed interest rate of course. In the cases of projects X and Z below, uniform annualized payments are involved, for which a special relation can be derived and tabulated to make such calculations convenient. These constant annual values are conventionally designated by the letter A.

$$A = P[i(1 + i)^n / ((1 + i)^n - 1)] \qquad (4.2)$$

or

$$A = P[A/P, i, n]$$

where A represents the value of constant annual payments.

The question of the discount rate, or interest rate, is an important one. Usually the Chief Financial Officer (CFO) of an enterprise will set a *minimum attractive rate of return* (MARR) or the *opportunity cost of capital* (OCC). MARR is the return, below which the organization will not consider investing in a venture. In a strict, technical sense, MARR and OCC need not be identical.

4.5   FOUR COMMON CRITERIA OF ECONOMIC EFFICIENCY

Internal Rate of Return.   Abbreviated variously as IRR, ROR, and IROR, internal rate of return has a distinguished history, apparently having been championed originally by John Maynard Keynes. R. de Neufville and J. H. Stafford mention that it is used by "sophisticated design agencies in a number of countries such as Mexico and France" (de Neufville and Stafford, 1971). We further know that its use is widespread in engineering construction in the United States (Wohl, 1979). AT&T's *Engineering Economy*, which the telecommunications industry considered its Bible for engineering economics, seemed to support its use (AT&T, 1971). In fact, Au and Au quote surveys that show upwards of three-quarters of the world's business enterprises considered IRR their principal measure of economic performance (1975) (Au and Au, 1983). IRR, as mentioned earlier, is still used extensively and often without understanding of the assumptions and implications (see example in Section 4.6).

Internal Rate of Return is defined as that (fictitious) interest rate that will cause a particular series of cash flows to have zero present net worth (PNW). PNW is a very important concept. It is defined as the net sum of the positive and negative cash increments, after each of these increments, whenever each occurs in time, has been translated to the present time using Eq. (4.1) or its equivalent. When used to compare two or more ventures, the venture with the largest IRR is presumed to be the optimum one. IRR is very popular in business circles for three reasons: First, because it is believed to be correct; second, because it appears simple to calculate; and, third, because it apparently does not require an assumption about the discount rate. Unfortunately, this popularity is now known to be unjustified, because all three of the reasons just cited are false.

Why is the IRR still potentially troublesome? If we enter the cash flow in Table 4.2 into Excel™ (function IRR), we get the answer as 13%, the interest rate that makes the NPV of the cash flow equal to 0. Excellent and correct. What Excel has done is solve for the roots of a fifth-order equation. Unfortunately, it has not identified or warned us of the fact that there are two real roots for this cash flow, the other being 69%. If you use the "guess" option in the Excel IRR function and guess 80% (.80), then you will get the 69% IRR. We don't know about you, but we prefer a return of 69% to 13%, so that's our choice .... In this case any interest rate between 13% and 69% results in a positive NPV.

Benefit–Cost Ratio.   The *B–C* ratio has several definitions. The first, and most elementary, is the ratio of the present value, PV, of the benefits of a venture, divided by the PV of the costs. When used to compare several ventures, it is presumed that the venture with the highest *B–C* ratio is the optimum, although this assumption is, in

TABLE 4.2.   Cash Flows for IRR Calculation

Year 1	Year 2	Year 3	Year 4	Year 5
−200M	400M	−100M	200M	−350M

fact, not true. Other definitions of *B–C* ratio that account separately for capital costs and operating costs are sometimes used. *B–C* ratio is popular in civil construction projects, especially dams and waterways funded by the Federal government and supervised by the U.S. Army Corps of Engineers. The use of *B–C* ratio for such work was mandated by the U.S. Congress in 1936 and it continues to be used, despite its impaired theoretical basis.

To calculate the *B–C* ratio, one must assume a discount rate (interest rate) for the funds involved. Often an artificially low discount rate is set by law in federal construction projects, rather than the use of the current prime rate or other measure of the actual cost of money. The rationale given for this procedure is that public works last for generations and return benefits to the nation for decades. It is argued that to judge such projects using the current (higher) prime lending rate would discount (devalue) such future benefits, thus obscuring the real value of such projects. However, de Neufville and Stafford quote a study indicating that as high as 80% of federal construction projects would be rated as noneconomic if more realistic discount rates were assumed (de Neufville and Stafford, 1971, p. 173). One will note that this discussion of the "proper" discount rate for public projects involves value-based positions.

Present Net Worth. PNW (or net present worth, NPW; equivalently, annual worth or future worth) of a venture is defined as the sum of the individual discounted costs and benefits involved. As in the calculation of the *B–C* ratio, one must assume a specific discount rate, usually the MARR, in order to find the PV of each cash increment.

Payback Period. This term is perhaps the most popular of all criteria for measuring the economic efficiency of a proposed venture. We know, for example, that it outranks even IRR in the Schwartz and Vertinsky survey. The main appeal of Payback Period seems to be its simplicity. No discounted cash flows are involved. One simply sums the raw cash items, one by one, as they occur in the project over time. The number of time periods from the present to the point at which the project moves "out of the red" (from a negative cash position) and "into the black" (to a positive cash position) is defined as the payback period. Not only is payback period impossible to justify as a measure of economic efficiency on any theoretical grounds, it is obviously meaningless if additional costs are mandated at periods after the ostensible payback period. While payback period is not an accurate measure of economic efficiency, it can be shown to be a crude measure of risk exposure.

We have now defined the four common indices for measuring economic efficiency, but two problems (at least) exist in applying any of them. The first problem is with the specific definitions of the criteria. We have mentioned that several definitions of *B–C* ratio exist and that more than a dozen definitions of ROI [return on investment] (still another common measure) are in use (Peters, 1979). Obviously, consistent results are impossible if the definitions themselves are inconsistent. The analyst must be wary, therefore, when using these measures, to make explicit definitions of terms.

The second problem is potentially even more serious. Given that these four criteria and others exist—ROI for example—can there be a conflict in which one criterion points to one investment opportunity as economically optimum and another criterion selects a different project as economically optimum? And, if such a conflict should arise, how is it to be resolved?

We will see immediately below that there indeed is a problem, but before we get to this demonstration, we want to make one or two "editorial remarks."[10] The first of these remarks is that the active and continuing controversy over the correctness and range of applicability of these economic efficiency criteria may be taken as an example in microcosm of the difficulties faced by system analysts in combating strongly entrenched error. Note that we are discussing here a particularly straightforward issue in that it can be, and has been, resolved purely by the application of rigorous analysis.

Thus, this is not a difficult problem such as one confronts in addressing a question of prudential balance between social equity and economic efficiency in a broad or even a narrow arena. Neither is it a question of which set of human values should prevail, nor is it an issue of individual suffering for the common good. Nor is this a complex issue in which some, possibly vital, data are missing or in doubt. We have here only an issue in mathematical deduction. How then can the results be denied?

We system analysts are dealing with practical people in the world of work. Active managers and engineers have little patience with long-winded theory. They demand simple "If-Then" rules. They don't want to bother with the restrictions on rules of thumb and thus they can get into trouble by ignoring these limits. Furthermore, for the most part, they are creatures of habit and reject change. So it is, for more than 50 years, theorists have known the B–C ratio and IRR criteria are faulty (Lorie and Savage, 1955). Yet the majority of federal decisions that use any objective criterion at all (a small minority) are made using the B–C ratio. And many business decisions that depend on economic factors are still made using internal rate of return, an equally faulty rule.

We do not have room here to do more than give a few indicators on the issue. Thus we suggest that the reader involved in economic decisions consult Au and Au (1983) for theoretical and computational details, Bussey (1978) for a seminal discussion of economics and industrial projects, and Wohl [1981; also see Wohl (1979)] for an interesting discussion on IRR use and the reactions to it in civil engineering circles. Kerzner (2001) gives a practical discussion on economic selection criteria in his extensive project management tome, and Blanchard and Fabrycky (2006) give a thoughtful discussion on economic considerations in systems engineering. With all of the advances in systems analysis techniques and tools of modeling and simulation, the key challenge and difficulty is still determining the appropriate measures, especially economic.

4.6   IS THERE A PROBLEM WITH MULTIPLE CRITERIA?

Let's take a moment to demonstrate that the multiple economic criteria currently in use present a problem. We are seeking the evaluation criterion that will select the one venture from among many that maximizes the value of the owners' equity or investors' wealth. Suppose we could construct a set of relatively simple cash flows to which we apply various selection criteria. Then suppose that not all of the criteria indicate the same choice for the optimum choice. We think we could then agree that we have a problem to which the solution may not be evident. We have constructed such a critical example and give it now.

We will apply the four popular criteria to each of four series of cash flows. We will find that each criterion indicates that a different project is the best choice for the economically efficient optimum. Obviously, this cannot be true. Thus we demonstrate beyond all doubt that it is essential to select the proper optimization criterion. The following are four investment opportunities from which we are to select the one that provides the maximum economic benefit.

Project W. A special project requires that a Windows-compatible computer software package be made available for a stand-alone microprocessor installation for occasional backup use over the coming year. The package can be leased for $100 for the year and will yield an estimated $115 in annual benefits. At the end of the year, we plan to convert our design office to a distributed processing system with a standard software set. No future use is anticipated for the leased software package.

Project X. Our engineering design office has requested that it be allowed to purchase a used car for in-town courier service. The auto will cost $3000 and is expected to return $1500 net benefits each year for 3 years. The machine will be junked at that time and will have no salvage value.

Project Y. Our bank has proposed a rather unusual long-term investment opportunity. For a $500 zero-coupon bond purchased now, it will pay $12,295 at the end of 20 years. You have been asked to evaluate this unit investment for our firm.

Project Z. A new network testing device will cost $5000 initially and will return $1200 net revenue annually for 10 years. It will then be junked with no salvage value expected.

Our company controller has decreed that all investments will be evaluated over their lifetime at a 15% discount rate, our corporate MARR. Evaluate these four projects for maximum economic efficiency by application of (a) IRR, (b) *B–C* ratio, (c) PNW, and (d) Payback Period.

Project W: Microprocessor Software Lease. See Figure 4.2. The rate of return is defined as that discount rate for which the present value of benefits equals the present value of costs. Thus, for this project we seek i such that

$$\$100 = \$115(P/F, i\%, 1)$$

Generally, a trial-and-error approach to this calculation is required or the use of a software package such as Excel^{TM} (or more sophisticated financial analysis packages) is needed, although this happens to be a particularly simple case. We can see that an

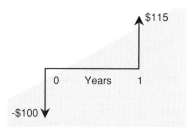

FIGURE 4.2 Cash flow for Project W.

interest rate of $i = 15\%$ satisfies the equation

$$\text{IRR} = i = 15\%$$

The benefit–cost ratio at $i = 15\%$ is found as follows:

$$B/C = \$115(P/F, 15\%, 1)/\$100 = \$100/\$100 = 1.0$$

The NPW is given by

$$\text{NPW} = \text{NPB} - \text{NPC} = \$100 - \$100 = 0$$

If one wishes to draw a smooth curve to represent instantaneous cash flow, then the payback period is slightly less than 0.5 years (exactly 0.465 years). Such an interpolation process really doesn't make sense, however, because we are operating under an accounting convention that permits cash transfers to be made only at the end of each interest period. For these projects, the interest period is at year end, or end of year, EOY. Thus, the payback period is one year.

Project X: Courier Service Used Auto Purchase. See Figure 4.3. The IRR for project X occurs at an i for which the following relation holds:

$$\$3000 = \$1500(P/A, i\%, 3)$$

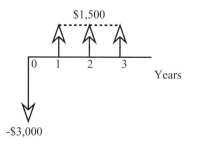

FIGURE 4.3 The Cash flow for Project X.

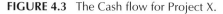

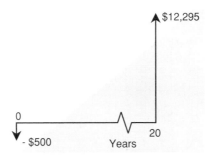

FIGURE 4.4 Cash flow for Project Y.

Trial and error will produce a solution for this equation at

$$\text{IRR} = i = 23.3\%$$

NPW at $i = 15\%$ may be found as follows:

$$\text{NPW} = -\$3000 + \$1500(P/A, 15\%, 3) = -\$3000 + \$1500(2.283)$$

$$\text{NPW} = \$424.50$$

$$B/C = \$1500(2.283)/\$3000 = 1.14.$$
$$\text{Payback Period for Project X} = 2 \text{ years}$$

Project Y: Zero-Coupon Bond. See Figure 4.4. In exactly the same fashion, we can calculate the following:

$$\text{IRR} = i = 17.3\%$$
$$\text{NPW} = -\$500 + \$12{,}295(P/F, 15\%, 20)$$
$$= -\$500 + \$12{,}295(0.0611) = -\$500 + \$751 = \$251$$
$$B/C = \$751/\$500 = 1.5$$

Payback Period = 20 yr (not 0.8 yr)

Project Z: Network Testing Unit.

$$\text{IRR} = 20.2\%, \qquad B/C = 1.2$$
$$\text{NPW} = \$1022, \qquad \text{Payback} = 5 \text{ yr}$$

See Figure 4.5. In Table 4.3, the results are given with the best choice for each criterion indicated by **boldface**. In this example, we have four projects, each of which is optimally efficient according to one criterion and nonoptimal in any other sense. This

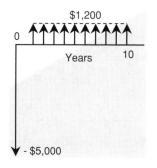

FIGURE 4.5   Cash flow for Project Z.

admittedly artificial example illustrates confusion among the various criteria. Which is the "correct" criterion and what does "correct" mean? This example does not tell us which is the "correct" result. However, it is universally agreed by economists that NPW is the fundamentally correct criterion, and therefore Project Z is the optimum for economic efficiency.

Note that the form of the cash flow in each of these projects is particularly simple, consisting of a single investment at time zero followed by a flow of benefits. This illustrates that the results are not due to "non-normal" cash flows as is sometimes erroneously claimed. Nevertheless, there are other concerns with this example. One might note that the project lifetimes are unequal. This is a valid objection. However, an annual net worth, ANW, that is equivalent to NPW can always be computed and ANW places the comparison on a fair annual basis. This does not change the result here. In general, one needs to establish a common length of time over which to make the comparison. We eliminate any concern with unequal lifetimes in the example given in Table 4.4. There, we have two cash flows over the same lifetimes that require the same initial investment and for which NPW and IRR criteria differ as to the proper choice.

Another point upon which we must be clear in constructing a truly definitive and rigorous example is the mutual independence of the projects, as opposed to

TABLE 4.3. Four Projects Evaluated for Economic Efficiency by Four Common Criteria[a]

Project	Payback	IRR	B/C Ratio	NPW $	Net Annual Worth ($)
W	**1 Year**	15%	1.0	0	0
X	2	**23.3**	1.14	424.50	185.70
Y	20	17.3	**1.5**	251.00	40.10
Z	5	20.2	1.2	**1022.00**	**203.90**

[a]Each criterion indicates a different optimum project, shown in boldface and underlined. Net annual worth is to be preferred to NPW in comparing projects with different lifetimes, but this does not change the result in this example.

TABLE 4.4. Two Cash Flows Over the Same Period of Time and Requiring the Same Initial investment[a]

Project	Initial Investment	EOY 1	EOY 2	EOY 3	EOY 4	EOY 5	NPW	IRR
A	−$10,000	$3000	$3000	$3000	$3000	$6000	**$1548**	20.7%
B	−$10,000	$7000	$7000	$500	$500	−$2000	$1000	**23.9%**

[a]The NPW criterion and IRR differ as to which project maximizes economic efficiency. The Optimum project is shown in boldface.

their possible mutual exclusiveness. Still another limitation in this example is the assumption of a fixed MARR over the lifetimes of the projects. Moreover, we need to know if the amount of available capital can limit the number of projects to be selected. To develop more rigorously these and other points of possible concern would require several chapters. Thus, we refer the interested reader to Au and Au (1983) and to Bussey (1978) as mentioned above.

4.7 WHAT IS WRONG WITH THE *B–C* RATIO?

Logically speaking, all we need do after having demonstrated that other criteria differ from NPV (a.k.a., PNV, NPW, PNW) is to show, or cite a reference that shows, that NPV correctly optimizes wealth. But, as we mentioned in Section 4.5, we are not dealing with logic. Your client in the federal government, accustomed to using the *B–C* ratio is almost sure to ask, "But what's wrong with the *B–C* ratio?" The same is true in private practice for IRR (see Section 4.8).

Some clients will dismiss discussion of efficiency and focus on social equity. But does *B–C* ratio properly address this matter? No, not necessarily. As Quade (1975) points out, use of the *B–C* ratio combined with an unrealistically low discount rate has resulted in billions of dollars devoted to water "reclamation" projects in the Far West of the United States, with a much lower benefit per person than spending the same amount on the same type of project in the southeast. He argues that encouraging cotton farming in Texas and California through the allocation of Federal funds has raised the price of cotton and also has forced newly impoverished laborers (mostly black) from Southeast farms to migrate to Northeast urban ghettos.

Furthermore, the *B–C* ratio does nothing for distributive justice. A dollar allocated from Federal (i.e., taxpayers) funds to large and wealthy corporate farms counts the same as a dollar allocated to tiny, marginal subsistence family farms in the same area (de Neufville and Stafford, 1971). Thus the use of the *B–C* ratio cannot be argued on the basis of equity or distributive justice.

Strictly from the point of view of economic efficiency, the *B–C* ratio is flawed on several counts. First, we note that often individual cash items can be interpreted as either an additional benefit or a reduced cost, and the converse is also true. This "interpretation" influences the calculated *B–C* ratio and thus possibly the ranking of the project. Here is an example.

TABLE 4.5. Cash Flow in Soft Coal Strip Mining Venture

EOY	Amount	Comment
0	−$5,100,000	Initial cost of site preparation
1–10	$1,200,000	New annual operating benefits
10	−$2,000,000	Cost of recontouring the site

In strip mining soft coal, an initial investment for site preparation, such as removal of overburden, is incurred. Then a series of net annual operating benefits should result, followed by the federally mandated cost of returning the site to the "original contour." Table 4.5 gives the EOY cash items to be considered:

Assume a MARR of 15% has been mandated and calculate the *B–C* ratio.

$$\text{NPB} = 1.2(P/A, 15\%, 10\text{yr}) = 1.2(5.02) = \$6.02 \text{ million}$$

and

$$\text{NPC} = 5.1 + 2(P/F, 15\%, 10) = 5.1 + 2(0.247) = \$5.59 \text{ million}$$

thus,

$$B/C = 6.02/5.59 = 1.0769$$

However, calling the reclamation cost a negative benefit results in the following:

$$\text{NPB} = 1.2(5.02) - 2(0.247) = 5.53$$

$$\text{NPC} = 5.1$$

$$B/C = 1.0843$$

While the difference in this example is not large, it could be in another case. Furthermore, it is well known that one cannot rank the profitability of ventures by comparing their *B–C* ratios. That is, there is no assurance that a venture with a higher *B–C* ratio will be more profitable than a venture with a smaller ratio. In part, this is due to the ambiguity just pointed out, but a more serious and fundamental reason is that, as we saw in Section 4.6, the project with the highest *B–C* ratio need not have the highest NPV.

It is possible to rank projects by calculating incremental *B–C* between pairs, and Au and Au (1983, Chapter 7) discuss the rules to be followed in this cumbersome process. But even then, the *B–C* ratio rule may fail in the face of capital limits (capital limitation is the usual case). Bussey (1978, Section 8.5) gives an example of precisely such a failure.

Lorie and Savage (1955) first pointed out that this problem occurs because of the differing implicit assumptions made in the *B–C*, IRR, and NPV criteria as to the reinvestment of cash benefits developed during the life of the ventures. NPV implicitly assumes immediate reinvestment of all intermediate benefits at the MARR [see Bussey, 1978, Section 8.7]. On the other hand, the IRR criterion implicitly assumes reinvestment at another, presumably unobtainable rate [see Bussey, 1978, Section 8.9].

Finally, we note that the *B–C* ratio incorrectly optimizes the per unit investment, while the NPV maximizes total wealth. The implication is simply demonstrated. For simplicity and without losing generality, assume a zero discount rate. Suppose you have a choice between the following two simple investments: In case A you invest one dollar and receive a benefit of $2 at the end of the period; in case B you invest $10 and receive $12 at the end of the same period. We see by inspection that in case A the *B–C* ratio is 2 and the NPV is $1. In case B, the *B–C* ratio is only 1.2, but the NPV is $2. Which would you rather have, a profit of one dollar or two?

4.8 CAN IRR BE FIXED?

The short answer is, *"Yes, but not as easily as many people think."* In the first place, only since 1955 have we had clear evidence that IRR will not necessarily produce the correct choice when used as the criterion for selecting from among independent options under capital rationing. Even as recently as the 1980s and the early 1990s, the subject was controversial among experts (see Wohl, 1979, 1981); thus perhaps it is not surprising that some older practitioners and current textbooks even today do not understand or portray the current understanding of the correct state of affairs.

Given that the Net Present Worth of an investment (NPW) is the fundamental criterion, one must agree that only if IRR can be brought into agreement with NPW can it be trusted. Some authors are under the (erroneous) opinion that this agreement can be achieved through the use of the marginal IRR or Incremental IRR, abbreviated "IIRR." The Green Book of the old AT&T (AT&T, 1971) is an advocate of IIRR and is guilty of this error.

The Green Book makes it clear that comparison of the IRR values calculated for a set of projects cannot be used directly to determine the economically most efficient. However, the Green Book states that calculating the marginal or incremental IRR, pair-by-pair, though admittedly tedious computationally, can be so used. Unfortunately, it is not difficult to construct examples that contradict this *ad hoc* modification. Furthermore, the IIRR *ad hoc* patch requires that one know the "cost of money to the firm"—that is, the operative discount rate, and the "minimum attractive rate of return" (MARR). In other words, the hope of using IRR to eliminate the need to assume a discount rate has also vanished.

As to the matter of the complexity of calculation when using IIRR, the Green Book points out that pairwise comparison of many proposed projects rapidly grows tedious. The number of pairwise comparisons needed is "$n(n-1)/2$," where n is the number of projects to be compared. If 10 projects are to be considered, and this is not at all out of the ordinary, the number of incremental IRR calculations is 45. Each of these calculations must be done by trial and error just as the basic IRR calculation is done.

The IIRR procedure is an *ad hoc* heuristic rule that is meant to permit the use of the IRR procedure to select the best (largest) NPW project. Unfortunately, this *ad hoc* procedure doesn't always work. In other words, it is possible to construct an example in which applying the basic IIRR rule of thumb (which we do not intend to give here because the rule is insufficient) selects a project that has a negative NPW. The Green Book doesn't know this. Wohl does and gives several such examples in Wohl (1981).

On the other hand, Wohl (1979) has gone on to construct an even more complicated set of rules based on the IIRR. Probably the most accessible exposition of this modified IIRR technique is given by Au and Au (1983). Of course, by this point, as Wohl (1979), Au and Au (1979), and any rational person would admit, we have far exceeded all reasonable bounds. No one would actually apply the Wohl rules in practice, least of all Wohl himself. Wohl is simply demonstrating just how impossibly complex it is to use IRR or IIRR or even the correct (Wohl-modified) IIRR. A glance at the first and last paragraphs of Chapter 8 in Au and Au (1979) will remove any lingering doubts on this score.

In his Section 8.8, Bussey (1978) points out the specific technical, and hidden, assumption that causes IRR sometimes to fail. It turns on the matter of how interim cash benefits are reinvested. Use of IRR to select from among competing projects implicitly assumes reinvestment of these interim benefits at a rate equal to, or higher than, an already artificially high (and unattainable in practice) rate called "Fisher's rate of return over cost" (Fisher, 1930).

One sometimes is met with the argument that while it may be true that IRR can be shown not always to work correctly (and one wouldn't know this without an elaborate calculation), it is usually correct for the "normal" cash flows encountered in practice. This is a nonsensical argument, of course, because it leads to the circular reasoning that if IRR doesn't work in a particular instance, the cash flows can't be "normal." If one accepts that sort of argument, there is an even simpler method that sometimes leads to the correct result. Just flip a coin. It is sometimes thought that trouble occurs only in those cases in which the cash flow is "strange" and IRR is multivalued. Not so. IRRs can be multivalued even if the cash flows of individual ventures are simple and the IRRs for individual projects are single-valued.

At the end of the day, the analyst will always look at the economic criteria through many lenses. We may look at NPW, measures of the variance of the cash flow, the maximum and minimums of the cash flow, extreme event statistics, and so on. Further discussion of this multiple criteria aspect will be presented later in this chapter and in Chapter 6.

One final point. The analyst who comes to this discussion without practical experience may feel that this section is much ado about nothing. If the *B–C* ratio or the IRR is wrong, it's wrong. Why not just say so and move on, or perhaps don't even mention the criterion at all? We have had our say on this point at the end of Section 4.5. But, if you remain unconvinced, you owe it to yourself to read the discussion following Wohl's paper (Wohl, 1981). That should help persuade you that error is stubborn, intransigent, and tricky. Several of Wohl's opponents have published books in which the IRR error is made, but you wouldn't know that from the discussion. Their ox has been gored and they don't intend to give in. One lesson for the system analyst may be that a simple declaration of the truth as you see it will not cause those who disagree with you to faint. Your proclamation of "unassailable truth" may not be the end of the argument, but rather just the beginning.

4.9   EXPECTED MONETARY VALUE

The expected monetary value (EMV) of a particular event is defined as "the monetary value of the event, if it occurs, times the probability of occurrence." We can use the EMV concept to temper the raw estimate of the net present worth of a particular venture if it is successful, by the risk involved. In fact, we may wish to break up the overall probability of success into statistically independent components. EMV is a concept that is used further in Chapter 6. Consider the following examples:

Project A: Hotel Reservation System. Suppose you manage a computer software production house and you have before you two proposals for new ventures. The first is a hotel billing and reservation system. The analyst estimates that you can sell 100 copies of this system if it meets all of the performance specifications, the product announcement is on time, and you meet the announced shipping date. Sales will fall significantly, it is estimated, if the product is late or cannot actually perform all of the tricks that have been promised. Unit sales price is to be set at $1,250,000. Your production VP has estimated that her people have an 85% chance of meeting all of the technical requirements in the time available. Your marketing VP estimates a 75% probability of meeting the sales quota within the time horizon given.

$$\text{EMV} = 100 \text{ systems} \times \$1,250,000/\text{system} \times 0.85 \times 0.75 = \$79,687,500$$

Project B: University Student Record System. Venture B is a University student record system that will keep student grades, do class scheduling, and do tuition billing. A systems study indicates likely sales of 250 units at a unit selling price of $700,000. The production VP places a 70% probability of successful on-time product roll-out and Marketing estimates a 60% chance of meeting the sales target.

$$\text{EMV} = 250 \text{ systems} \times \$700,000/\text{system} \times 0.7 \times 0.6 = \$73,500,000$$

We see from the calculation of the Expected Monetary Value for the two proposals that although the Gross Sales for Project B are greater than that for Project A (i.e., $175 million vs. $125 million) when risk estimates are included, Project A is the recommended choice under the EMV criteria; other criteria will be discussed later.

Let's look at another example—the *54 Thousand Dollar Question*—back to selling T-shirts. Consider the distribution in Table 4.6 for sales of T-shirts at events. To keep things simple, we are not considering time value of money.

As analysts, we are quickly able to calculate the expected number sold as 18,500 (sum of the probabilities and projected sales). Our accountants have determined the

TABLE 4.6. The $54,000 Question

Projected Sales	Probability
0	.10
5,000	.10
10,000	.20
20,000	.30
30,000	.20
40,000	.10

profit (Π) associated with this venture as

$$\Pi(\$) = -100,000 + (\# \text{ sold} > 20,000)^* 38.50$$

For example, if 10,000 shirts are sold, our profit is $-\$100,000$, and with 30,000 sold, it's $285,000. Once again, if our goal is to maximize the expected profit (Π), should we take this venture? Our expected number sold is 18,500, and plugging in we get

$$\Pi(\$) = -100,000 + (0)^* 38.50 = -100,000$$

It's a clear loser. Once again, we've fallen victim to a common probability fallacy. Consider Table 4.7. Thus, the expected monetary value (EMV) is actually $54,000, and the venture looks potentially promising.[11] Once again, this is a result of Jensen's Inequality.[12] Obviously, in an actual decision we would need to look at the broader perspective, such as risk. Are we willing to have a maximum loss of $30,000? Are we willing to have a 70% chance of losing money? Classic measures would look at the mean and variance of such a venture. It would be negligent if we, as the analyst, only considered/presented the decision-maker with an EMV and not the other considerations. Moving beyond EMV (and standard deviation), for example, we might look at the maximum loss of the T-shirt venture ($-100,000$) or at the probability of losing money (.70, or a 70% chance of losing $100,000!). So, even though the EMV is significant, it's not clear what the decision should be, and the client's goals are essential if an informed decision is to be made. As we've stressed, it's the analyst's job to make these "trade-offs" clear to the client. More on this is presented at the end of this chapter and in Chapters 5 and 6.

TABLE 4.7. The $54,000 Question Revisited

Projected Sales	Probability	Net Profit	Expected Profit
0	.10	−100,000	−10,000
5,000	.10	−100,000	−10,000
10,000	.20	−100,000	−20,000
20,000	.30	−100,000	−30,000
30,000	.20	285,000	57,000
40,000	.10	670,000	67,000

4.10   NONMONETARY PERFORMANCE INDICES

Civil engineers have become, from necessity, quite sophisticated in dealing with the public and with private clients. Mechanical engineers, electrical engineers, aerospace engineers, and others often work for large industrial organizations and may rarely, if ever, meet the client in person, or be required to deal with other stakeholders, but civil engineers usually deal directly with clients and the public. Yet even experienced civil engineers are often forced into confrontations with segments of the stakeholder population. Why?

Environmentalists, advocates of the poor, anti-nuclear activists, and others argue that "the system" as represented by design engineers does not represent them. Often, these activists are able to enlist concerned bystanders in their cause. This sort of confrontation occurs so commonly that we really ought to give it some thought. Could such confrontations be caused by the design process itself, rather than any specific error made by individual engineers? We would argue the answer is, "yes."

The normal bottom-up design procedure assumes that the nominal, "official" client has clearly-defined goals, and that these goals are articulated in the design specifications. Conventional bottom-up engineering design begins and ends with these design specifications. But, it appears that using this pure bottom-up design methodology almost ensures conflict in all but the most simple design cases. Conflicts can arise with nonclient stakeholders because they are excluded from consideration, as in the activists' example above. And a bottom-up approach will also, in all probability, generate conflicts in the long run with the clients themselves.

Classic examples of these phenomena are NIMBY (Not In My Backyard) and the newer BANANA (Build Absolutely Nothing Anywhere Near Anyone).[13] Look at any construction project (search the Internet to find examples easily, and verify), and you'll see that almost every construction project is slowed down by the discovery of "something" on the property (maybe a snail darter or a burial ground) or by the people or business near the site. Our favorite example is the relatively new Denver International Airport (DIA), where, after its construction in a very rural area in the 1990s, many people moved near the airport for obvious reasons: access, jobs, and so on. Subsequently, in the 1990s, the new neighborhoods around the airport complained and took legal action about the airport noise.[14] If you move into "Airport Acres" (fictitious name) then should you be surprised by aircraft noise? Should the systems analyst be surprised by the resulting complaints? Absolutely not—completely predictable!

The bottom-up approach can lead to a climate of conflict because, insofar as performance criteria are concerned, it appears that the designer is permitted only the following three options, all of which are flawed:

1. Work with implicit goals as embodied by the client in concrete design specifications.
2. Ignore potential conflicts until and unless they occur, and then handle on an *ad hoc* basis.
3. Work with monetary criteria—that is, to minimize cost and/or maximize revenue.

On the other hand, with the top-down design approach, we can develop nonmonetary goals by working with the client, using various techniques such as "generalizing the problem" and emphasizing the axiological component.

If the option set above is complete, one can see why designers and clients are forced or at least encouraged toward monetary criteria as a palliative. There is no way for the designer to include nonmonetary criteria in a design if the client's value system is unknown. As a substitute, when financial criteria are obviously inadequate, implicit values are sometimes converted to design constraints or to specific design specifications. There is nothing wrong with converting nonmonetary criteria to design specifications—provided that the client will be steadfast, having made this reduction. Unfortunately, when the client makes this conversion, it is often imperfect and the designer will be faulted for this error. An example of this implicit process may serve to make this point more concretely.

Suppose you are an architect designing a house for a client. You can talk with the client and attempt to make explicit her value structure, so that you may take it into consideration in your design, or you can let the client dictate to you specific design constraints. Here are some explicit design constraints *in lieu* of values:

"I want a house all on one floor."

"I want a formal dining room and a large entry-way and living room."

"I want lots of counter space in my kitchen."

These are specific embodiments of implicit values. If your client really knows what she wants when she gives you these explicit design directives, there may be no problem with the completed house. If, however, her embodiment of her implicit goals doesn't seem to work once the house is completed, <u>you</u> will get blamed. And one would argue that you deserve the blame.

Suppose the implicit value behind specifying a house "all on one floor" is that one of the residents has arthritis or a hip condition that makes stair-climbing difficult. But if you don't check this, you might consider "all on one floor" an aesthetic preference and supply a single-floor design with many steps up to the front door and steps up to the house from the garage. You have a house on one floor, but it may still be unsatisfactory.

Perhaps your client wants a large living room because she does a lot of entertaining, but you don't ask why and you fail to include a large coat closet for guests in the front hall.

The client may have asked for lots of counter space in the kitchen because he is a gourmet cook, but you don't know this and you fail to build in sufficient cupboard space for the exotic pots and pans and other special cooking utensils owned by the client.

This house design example is trivial and we hope you haven't been wasting your time thinking out how you would solve these specific design issues. That would be missing the point. The point we are trying to illustrate is that the analyst may totally miss the client's real values if she lets the client translate implicit values into specific design requirements.

Yet this is precisely what engineers who follow the conventional bottom-up procedure require of their clients. Is it any wonder that controversy is often the result? We find it more surprising that conflicts don't occur more often. The reason, we suspect, is that engineers and systems analysts temper their rigid bottom-up design process with experience and wisdom. All hail to them for this. But it would seem to be preferable to build into our design procedures our best thinking, instead of being forced to use our best thinking to avoid the errors produced by inadequate procedures.

A simple approach to dealing with multiple, non-monetary criteria will now be discussed.[15] More elaborate approaches will be covered in Chapter 6. Suppose that early dialogues with the client have elicited several nonmonetary criteria. Not all of these criteria will be equally important, thus ask the client to pick the most important criterion and give it a "weight" of 10. Then give lesser weights to the others as the client directs. The client may hesitate to give these weights, but he can be reassured that he can change the weights later on, if he doesn't like the results. The next step is to develop the options, perhaps using one of the methods suggested in Chapter 5.

Then each option can be rated on a scale of 1 to 10 for each of the criteria. This rating need not be done by the client initially, but the client should become involved once the options are narrowed to the top few. Now each of the ratings can be multiplied by its weight and a sum taken over all of the weighted values for each option. The result is the score for each option. Here is the step-by-step process.

1. List the client's nonmonetary criteria.
2. Give the criterion rated most important by the client a 10.
3. Weight the remaining criteria with weights less than 10.
4. Give each option a rating for each criterion.
5. For each option, multiply the criteria scores by weights.
6. Find the sum of the weighted values for each option.

In Table 4.8, we give an example of this exercise for a set of four performance criteria, ALPHA, BETA, GAMMA, and DELTA, applied to Options 1 through 3. The client has rated ALPHA as the most important criterion and thus it has been given a rating of 10. BETA is rated 7, and so on. The value of ALPHA earned by Option 1 is 7, and thus its weighted value is 70, and so on. Apparently Option 1 is to be preferred, because its score is higher than the other two options.

We don't want to lose sight of the object of this exercise. The point isn't to take the evaluation process away from the client and to give it to a decision tool. Rather, we are trying to help the client express his implicit values through the weighting and rating process by informing him of associated trade-offs and their implications. Thus, suppose that the client looks at the scores for the three options in Table 4.8 and shakes his head.

"I don't like this. I think I really prefer Option 3."

TABLE 4.8. A Simple, Single-Pass Weighting Process for Nonmonetary Criteria[a]

Criterion	Weight	Option No. 1		Option No. 2		Option No. 3	
		Score	Weighted Value	Score	Weighted Value	Score	Weighted Value
Alpha	10	7	70	8	80	5	50
Beta	7	8	56	6	42	7	49
Gamma	4	4	16	8	32	10	40
Delta	4	7	28	2	8	3	12
Totals			170		162		151

[a]More elaborate rating procedures are discussed in Chapter 6.

The system analyst doesn't say something such as

"Well, that's what the decision software shows."

or

"What do you mean you don't like it? Those are your weights we used."

Rather we say something like *"Fine, that's no problem. You weren't sure of the meaning of the weights you assigned tentatively anyway. Let's go back now and see what the weights should be to make Option 3 come out on top."*

Then, once the weights are adjusted and Option 3 is the top scorer, the analyst goes on to say, *"O.K., that's fine. Option 3 is now ahead of the others and you said you liked that. But, now let's check the weights of these criteria. Are you comfortable with these new weights? Originally they were different you remember."*

This process may cycle several times. The client varies the weights and notes the effect on the options. One hopes the process converges to a satisfactory set of weights and an options choice with which the client is comfortable. The whole process is designed to help the client express his value structure through the rating process, perhaps with the term "value" never having come up.

But, before we go further, let's talk more about generating options.

EXERCISES

4.1   Who is C. Argyris and what is his Model 1 mode of managerial behavior?

4.2   The text says that the system analyst can be "ground up" by hidden agenda items. What does this mean? Give examples.

4.3   A certain program is to be evaluated for economic efficiency. The investments (costs) and returns are given in Table 4.9 below. Evaluate *B–C* ratio, NPW, Payback Period, and IRR for discount rates of 5%, 10%, and 20%. Comment on the attractiveness of this program.

TABLE 4.9. Investments and Returns

EOY	Amount
0	($10,000) Initial investment
1–10	$5,000 Annual returns
10	($45,000) Salvage cost

4.4 *Newsweek* for January 12, 1981 (Sheib, 1981) pointed to a U.S. House of Representatives statement that "estimates that decommissioning a single nuclear reactor plant could cost as much as $100 million." The estimated operating life of a nuclear electric generating station is 30–40 years. Some utilities have established sinking funds—money taken from earnings and set aside for future use—to cover decommissioning costs. How much money should a utility deposit annually in its nuclear plant decommissioning fund if it assumes a 40-year life, a $100 million decommissioning cost, and a discount rate of 10%? Is the discount rate a particularly sensitive parameter?

4.5 Some years ago, the U.S. Equal Employment Opportunity Commission (EEOC) and Ford Motor Company agreed to settle a seven-year complaint, with Ford spending millions to make up for past discrimination against women and minorities (French, 1981). Ford agreed to spend $383,000 each month over a five-year period beginning January 1, 1982. Assuming EOM payments, calculate the NPW as of January 1, 1982, of this settlement. Assume constant dollars and a discount rate of 10%. Litigation delayed this settlement for seven years. Does this delay have an economic value to Ford? To the beneficiaries?

4.6 In Section 4.10, we suggest that the analyst work with the client to change the weights in the process of evaluating options until the client is satisfied with the outcome. How is this any different from the charlatan consultant who merely asks the client what he or she wants and then produces a report to confirm that prejudice? How can the analyst prevent the biased client from fooling himself and/or the analyst? Is this situation any different from that faced by professionals such as doctors, lawyers, or psychiatrists?

4.7 Read the Sky High Airlines Case (following). Reflect on the issues in the case in light of the automated baggage handling system that was installed in the Denver International Airport (DIA) and the final decision regarding the automated system. Also, reflect on the impacts of 9/11 on the case. (*Note:* The case is dated prior to 9/11, as well as prior to the Eastern Airlines bankruptcy.)

4.8 FEMA (Federal Emergency Management Agency) has the following goals (http://www.fema.gov/):

- Goal 1: Protect lives and prevent the loss of property from all hazards.
- Goal 2: Reduce human suffering and enhance the recovery of communities after disaster strikes.

• Goal 3: Ensure that the public is served in a timely and efficient manner.

Examine these goals, given the 2004 hurricane season, and their associated measures to see if the desirable characteristics in Section 4.2 are achieved.

4.9   Find several examples of NIMBY and BANANA. How could a proper systems analysis process have eliminated or reduced the issues that resulted?

CASE STUDY: SKY HIGH AIRLINES[16]

Sky High Airlines is a large scheduled carrier with routes covering most of the continental United States. Sky High management has felt that its baggage handling problems are not unlike those of many other major trunk airlines. Several years ago, however, this issue came into high visibility.

Early in October of that year, Ms. Joyce Roberts, Administrative Assistant to Mr. Peter Brice, Corporate Vice President for Terminal Operations, at Sky High, asked George Smith to meet with her. Smith was a newly hired systems analyst at corporate headquarters, and Roberts wanted to brief Smith about a possible baggage handling problem at the airline.

The Initial Meeting

"Thanks for dropping by on short notice, George. Coffee?"

"No thanks, I'm fine. What can I do to help?"

"Well, E.W. is boiling about baggage handling at Sky High. My boss, Peter Brice, attended E.W.'s staff meeting as usual yesterday and Webber seemed quite upset, from what Peter reported to me later. I don't know if we have a real problem here or just the perception of one and neither does Peter. We want you to take a look at it and come back in a day or two and give Peter and me a briefing. We want to know what you have found out, and what you think we ought to do about it."

With that, she handed Smith Exhibit 1. Smith left and immediately phoned the corporate library and asked them to round up what was available on the airline baggage problem and to get something to him within 24 hours. Next, Smith called the director of Sky High's terminal operations at Hartsfield airport in Atlanta and flew over the next morning to discuss the matter with him. On his return the following day, Smith wrote a memo to the file (see Exhibit 2). He also received a list of reprints from the library and was disappointed to see that they were rather old (see Exhibit 3). What should Smith do next?

Exhibit 1

Sky High Airlines Corporate Headquarters

Memorandum

From: Peter Brice, Vice President for Terminal Operations

To: File

Re: Staff Meeting 9/2/19–. Baggage Handling

Date: 9/3/19–

I. Attending:

> E. Webber, President
> W. Pruitt, V.P., Public Relations
> K. Priest, V.P., Flight Operations
> Self

II. Opening Remarks by President:

E.W. and his wife just back from separate vacations in Alaska for salmon fishing and New York City for shopping, respectively. Unfortunately:

1. Sky High lost his best fly rods, thus ruining his fishing trip. The rods haven't yet been found.
2. Wife's new fall wardrobe, purchased expressly for this trip, was routed to Moline, Illinois.

Lengthy remarks followed, including an old story on how Pan Am screwed up back in 1973 by routing all of the luggage to a Mr. Mazatlan in Singapore from a flight to Mazatlan, Mexico. Mazatlan is in the Mexican state of Sinola, and the baggage clerk mislabeled the baggage tickets "Mazatlan/Sin." Unfortunately, "Sin" is the abbreviation of Singapore. While this wasn't a Sky High flight, we interconnected a number of passengers and took a lot of grief afterwards.

III. President's Remarks on the Costs of Such Foul-ups:

Mr. Webber noted three kinds of costs:

(My comments in parentheses, P. B.)

A. The direct cost involved in paying lost luggage claims and damaged bag claims amounts to more than $5 million annually for Sky High. (We are estimating $5.3 million, in fact.)

B. There are associated costs of mishandling bags—for example, time/expense for our employees tracing bags and cost of delivering recovered bags to passengers, plus the cost of emergency travel kits, toothbrushes, and so on.

C. The public relations cost, lost revenue, irate customers, and so on.

IV. Pruitt (P.R.) and Priest (Flight Ops.) view the issue:

A. The trouble is that the low rate of pay for baggage handlers plus the alternating boredom and rushing cause a high rate of mishandled bags. None of the other lines know what to do either. (We mishandle about 1 out of 80 bags, or about 1.25%. Can we improve this? How? What cost?)

B. Passengers are ripping us off. They are making outrageous claims about the value of items in lost luggage. We must be subsidizing half the camera makers in Japan. Then we're stuck with bags full of dirty underwear.

C. Not sure that our employees aren't stealing from luggage either. What about supervision?

V. Pruitt and Priest view solutions:

A. Lengthen time required of passengers to be at check-in counter. Say we require 30 minutes to check-in bags before flight time, rather than current 20 minutes. That would give us more time to do the job right. (Ouch! I don't like that. Full fare business people would howl. Of course, many of them don't trust us now. They represent most of the carry-on luggage. Thank the stars for small favors.)

B. Let's get on Eastern's computer system for tracing lost luggage. (That might work; look into it).

C. Get on BAGTRAC. (That's not up and running yet, and so far mostly international carriers have signed up, but we'll follow it.)

VI. Problem Assignment:

A. Problem is in my lap. Solution is my responsibility.

B. Mr. Webber wants some idea of size of problem and what we really want to do about this issue (and how to tell if we have solved the problem), by the next staff meeting.

C. He also wants a detailed study on specific alternatives ASAP but knows that is several weeks away.

Exhibit 2

Sky High Airlines Corporate Headquarters

Memorandum

From: George Smith, System Analyst

To: File

Re: Interview with Director Terminal Ops. Hartsfield, 9/4/19–

Date: 9/5/19–

Mr. R. Mathieu, Director of Terminal Ops at Hartsfield/Atlanta, was interviewed yesterday to get his view of the issue. The following information was gathered at this interview and from review of corporate data:

I. Sky High Airlines

Sky High Airlines is a major American trunk carrier. It flies into most of the major cities in the country, JFK and LaGuardia in NYC, O'Hare in Chicago, Hartsfield in Atlanta, Miami International, and so on, as well as many second-tier cities, such as Byrd Field in Richmond, and so on. Hartsfield is our busiest terminal, and that is one reason I wanted to see it in operation. There is a vast new terminal planned for this field, but it won't be ready for several years.

Total revenue passenger miles for Sky High approached $20 billion last year with about 25 million tickets sold. Total passenger revenues were about $4 billion last year with net operating revenue of $250 million and total net income of $25 million. Total number of employees is about 34,000, approximately 30% of whom are aircraft and traffic servicing (ground) personnel.

Sky High has about 240 aircraft available for service. Approximately 25% of revenue passenger miles are accounted for by wide-bodied Boeing 747s, and the remainder is split fairly evenly between regular-bodied B-737s and B-727s.

II. Baggage Handling

Sky High uses three types of baggage tags: (1) thru-flight, (2) intra-line, and (3) interline. Thru-flight tags are attached to bags of passengers who will not change planes in the course of their trip; intra-line tags identify bags of passengers who will change planes but remain on Sky High; interline tags are for use on bags of passengers whose flights connect with other airlines. These cardboard tags are color-coded and have labels printed for the larger airport destinations but must be made out by hand for smaller destinations. The tag is affixed to the bag by elastic strings looped around the bag handle. On the tag is the flight number and the final airport destination (three letter code) of the passenger (and also any connecting flight numbers and intermediate destinations). Sky High also has special tags for luggage that has been previously damaged when checked, and it makes available stick-on tags for the passenger's name and address. Tagging with name and address has recently become mandatory in the United States.

III. Claim Procedures

Sky High has an in-house computer tracing system for lost bags, which, although similar to the Eastern tracing system, is not linked to the Eastern system (the Eastern system is used by several other U.S. carriers) or to any other airline's system. In both the Sky High and the Eastern systems, if a bag is declared missing, the owner's name, flight number, and a brief description of the bag and its major contents are fed into the computer system. As unclaimed luggage is located, information on these bags is fed into the system and the computer periodically searches for matches. In tracing a lost bag, the passenger's itinerary is also considered so as to get the bag to the passenger if possible and, if not, to return it to the passenger's address.

IV. Problem Areas

Sky High Airlines encounters three particular types of problem rather frequently in the area of baggage handling. First, false or inflated claims are often lodged, sometimes by deliberate planning and other times by "honest" persons attempting to take advantage of an opportunity. Second, the quality of work performed by the baggage handlers is sometimes poor. This is more often true at larger airports, especially during rush hours. Finally, passengers are often ignorant of the time constraints imposed upon baggage handling by airport/aircraft operating procedures. Often, passengers will rush up to a gate at the last moment and attempt to check their bags. Weight distribution on the plane, loading diagrams, or ground equipment scheduling requirements, if violated, can set off a chain reaction causing confusion and delays.

Exhibit 3

Sky High Airlines Corporate Headquarters

Memorandum

From: Dedi Pancake, Corporate Librarian

To: George Smith

Re: Your request of 9/3/19–, on Baggage Handling Information

Date: 9/5/19–

1. Airports. <u>Architectural Record</u>, Nov. 1974, pp. 133ff.
2. Airports. <u>Architectural Record</u>, Nov. 1973, pp. 135ff.
3. Bublan, E. J., Layout dictated Texas airport systems. Oct. 22, 1973, pp. 111–115.
4. Computer controls carts over complex route. <u>Modern Materials Handling</u>, March 1974, pp. 50–53.
5. Davis, C., Unified baggage handling systems at Seattle–Tacoma. Meeting Preprint 1452, Joint ASCE–ASME Transportation Engineering Meeting, July 26–30, 1971, Seattle.
6. Doty, L., Automating the airline system. <u>Aviation Week & Space Technology</u>, Oct. 22, 1973, pp. 40–43.
7. Eastern, Braniff buy baggage X-ray unit. <u>Aviation Week & Space Technology</u>, Feb. 26, 1973, pp. 27–30.
8. Elson, B. H., Experience sifts system costs, benefits. <u>Aviation Week & Space Technology</u>, Oct. 22, 1973, pp. 116–117.
9. Elson, B. H., West Coast Airport Ready for 1980s. <u>Aviation Week & Space Technology</u>, May 14, 1973, pp. 27–30.
10. Greer, G. (Ed.). Lost luggage: How smart travelers cope with the problem. <u>Better Homes and Gardens</u>, May 1972, p. 34ff.
11. Hake, B. H., Baggage handling: Passenger and baggage processing at air terminal. <u>Journal of the Aerospace Transport Division, ASCE</u>, Oct. 1963, pp. 29–44.
12. <u>Handbook of Airline Statistics, 1975 edition</u>, Civil Aeronautics Board, Washington, D.C., Nov. 1975.
13. Horonjeff, R., Analyses of passenger and baggage flows in airport terminal buildings. <u>Journal of Aircraft</u>, Oct. 1969, pp. 446–451.
14. Kukar, J., Advanced baggage handling and processing concepts. AIAA Paper 70–917, July 1970.
15. Prokosch, W., Implications of mechanical systems on airport terminal design. SAE Paper No. 700259, April 1970.
16. Schneider,   G.   E.,   Eastern   spurs   prompt   service,   cost   cuts. <u>Aviation Week & Space Technology</u>, May 27, 1974, pp. 31–35.

17. Stein, R. J., Eastern installs baggage code system. Aviation Week & Space Technology, Feb. 26, 1973, pp. 27–28.

18. Hawkins, W. J., How they're routing your baggage by laser. Popular Science, May 1971, p. 34.

19. No alignment problems in this sorting system! Modern Materials Handling, Jan. 1974, p. 57.

20. Stein, R. J., Ground technology competes for funds. Aviation Week & Space Technology, Oct. 22, 1973, pp. 129–131.

21. Watkins, H. D., Computer filling crucial passenger role for airlines. Aviation Week & Space Technology, Oct. 22, 1973, pp. 44–45.

22. Where the hell is my bag? Newsweek, Sept. 3, 1973, pp. 73–74.

23. Worcester, R. E., Baggage handling: Airline baggage handling systems. Journal of Aero-Space Division ASCE, Oct. 1963, pp. 21–27.

24. Yager, S., Analysis of passenger delays at airport terminals. Transportation Engr. Jour., ASCE, Nov. 1973, pp. 909–921.

CASE STUDY: BRIDGES—WHERE TO SPEND THE SECURITY DOLLARS?

Thursday, 26 January 2006

The Virginia Commonwealth Transportation Commissioner has decided to allocate $100 million to bridges for the protection against terrorism, and he wants recommendations in 10 days. Your manager's boss, the Chief of Policy, Planning, and the Environment, has asked your manager to prioritize the bridges in the state and produce a list of the top 30 bridges for consideration. Since all work flows downhill, your manager has asked you, for Monday's meeting, to develop a preliminary ranking of the state's bridges (the top 30) and to explain, via a PowerPoint™presentation, the criteria you've selected and the method used to rank the bridges. Given the short timeframe, the only data to be used are the National Bridge Inventory (NBI; http://www.nationalbridgeinventory.com/).

Note: The following site has an NBI data dictionary: http://massroads.com/nbiDesc. htm

CASE STUDY: MEASURING THE PROCESS AND OUTCOMES OF REGIONAL TRANSPORTATION COLLABORATION

The FHWA Office of Operations recently drafted a white paper entitled "The Tangible Benefits of Regional Transportation Operations Collaboration and Coordination" (available in libraries and on the Internet). The white paper attempted to characterize and illustrate the tangible benefits that can be derived for each of the agencies and jurisdictions that participate in the regional transportation operations collaboration activity. Five case studies were highlighted in the paper and show a range of collaboration activity from an effort between four county road maintenance agencies to a multistate wireless network that integrates transportation and criminal justice information for a multitude of agencies. Based upon interviews with some key champions of each collaboration case, the white paper was able to identify some important common benefits such as cost savings, savings in procurement, expanded service area coverage, new funding opportunities, and formalized regional operations structures. Because of the limitations of time, resources, and research capabilities, the white paper was limited in the number of sites that were studied and was unable to investigate and quantify further any of the benefits identified.

FHWA has released a task order contract to continue this effort. The purpose of this task order is to support the FHWA Office of Operations. Also, it is to investigate and develop the work done in the existing white paper; it will conduct the necessary research to analyze, quantify, and document the benefits of regional transportation operations collaboration that were identified. The research will be packaged into a reference manual, with case studies, to meet the needs of the transportation community. The results will be prepared for both electronic posting on the web and publication in hard copy. For 508 compliance, please use the standards 1194.22 and 1194.31.

Our company has been hired, as a subcontractor, to develop an initial set of system metrics for measuring the process and outcomes of regional transportation collaboration. At our first meeting next week, they would like to see our initial set, with justifications.

CASE STUDY: BASEBALL FREE AGENT DRAFT

Part A: Ranking Free Agents

Team 28 General Manager, Marc Bock, has asked you, our new intern team, to help select which free agents our team should pursue in this year's free agent draft. His concern is not about searching for a position player, but the best athletes to help our team win more games next season. He would like you to determine, from the 40 available free agents, the top 10 (in order) we should pursue. He would also like a presentation on why/how this order was created. The only data we have to work with are the player and team data in Figures 4.6 and 4.7.

Part B: Draft Day (optional team exercise)

Bock has also asked his intern teams to make draft selections on draft day. On draft day, each of the student teams will decide which player they will select for each of the eight draft rounds. The draft order will be determined randomly once, and then reversed after each round (i.e., the team that gets the first round first choice will have the last choice in the second round, etc.; this is typically referred to as a "snake draft" process). Your draft goal is, with a $40M budget, to improve the team performance as much as possible. Once you've expended your budget, you will not be able to draft any more players (i.e., if you spend $40M on your first four draft choices, your draft is over). A maximum of eight players can be drafted, per team; once a player is drafted, they are unavailable for all teams. Each team will have a maximum of 90 seconds to make their draft selection for each round—if no selection is made within 90 seconds, the selection is lost. Computers are allowed in the draft room. Our GM would also like your draft strategy included in your presentation.

Our team performance models have been determined by the front office statisticians and will not be divulged; however, their goal is to win more games and they have developed performance models to help them predict improved performance. Based on your drafted players, we will determine which student team has improved our team the most. Winning teams will be determined immediately after the draft and awarded appropriately.

Terms:

AB	At bats
R	Runs scored
H	Hits (all)
2B	Doubles
3B	Triples
HR	Home runs
RBI	Runs batted in
SB	Stolen bases
CS	Caught stealing
BB	Base on balls, or walks
SO	Strikeouts, whiffs, or Ks
BA	Batting average (H/AB)
OBP	On-base percentage (H + BB + HBP)/(AB + BB + SF + HBP) (SF and HBP are assumed zero if unavailable)
SLG	Slugging percentage TB/AB (see TB below)
TB	Total bases (Singles +2*2B + 3*3B + 4*HR)
OPS (Pitch)	On-base plus slugging: on-base average pitcher has allowed plus slugging percentage allowed (pitching stat)
K/BB	Strikeouts/base on balls ratio (pitching stat)
K/9	Strikeouts per 9 innings (pitching stat)

Team #	R	AB	H	2B	3B	HR	BB	SO	BA	OBP	SLG	SB	CS	K/BB	K/9	OPS	Win
1	855	5555	1544	319	24	214	548	1085	0.278	0.344	0.46	111	47	2.370	6.45	0.715	105
2	850	5546	1500	314	33	183	705	874	0.270	0.357	0.438	43	23	1.860	6.3	0.755	91
3	840	5643	1505	303	23	215	645	1133	0.267	0.345	0.443	100	27	2.130	6.58	0.778	86
4	833	5577	1531	331	34	202	568	1181	0.275	0.345	0.455	44	33	1.360	5.94	0.843	68
5	803	5570	1503	304	37	178	587	1158	0.270	0.343	0.434	86	32	1.960	6.36	0.729	96
6	803	5468	1458	294	36	187	590	999	0.267	0.342	0.436	89	30	2.440	8	0.745	92
7	789	5628	1508	308	29	235	489	1080	0.268	0.328	0.458	66	28	2.470	8.27	0.715	89
8	768	5573	1521	304	32	139	566	910	0.273	0.342	0.414	52	25	2.560	6.74	0.749	87
9	761	5542	1450	226	30	203	536	1092	0.262	0.332	0.423	102	41	2.050	6.6	0.732	93
10	750	5518	1380	287	28	194	599	1335	0.250	0.331	0.418	77	25	1.730	6.18	0.830	76
11	718	5486	1447	275	32	148	499	968	0.264	0.329	0.406	96	43	2.180	6.98	0.735	83
12	684	5532	1376	289	20	185	512	1159	0.249	0.317	0.409	107	23	1.650	6.07	0.740	71
13	680	5483	1428	267	39	142	415	1066	0.260	0.321	0.401	63	40	1.870	6.8	0.758	72
14	634	5483	1358	295	32	135	540	1312	0.248	0.321	0.387	138	40	2.310	6.85	0.737	67
15	635	5474	1361	276	27	151	496	925	0.249	0.313	0.392	109	38	1.770	6.42	0.772	67
16	615	5544	1401	295	38	135	441	1022	0.253	0.310	0.393	53	32	1.730	7.23	0.790	51
17	949	5720	1613	373	25	222	659	1189	0.282	0.360	0.472	68	30	2.530	7.02	0.727	98
18	897	5527	1483	281	20	242	670	982	0.268	0.353	0.458	84	33	2.380	6.6	0.759	101
19	865	5534	1481	284	19	242	499	1030	0.268	0.333	0.457	78	51	1.920	6.37	0.791	83
20	860	5615	1492	323	34	227	500	1099	0.266	0.329	0.457	69	36	1.790	6.12	0.776	89
21	858	5676	1565	345	29	184	606	1009	0.276	0.351	0.444	94	55	1.930	6.84	0.787	80
22	842	5736	1614	319	18	169	528	949	0.281	0.345	0.432	101	41	1.590	6.74	0.752	78
23	836	5675	1603	272	37	162	450	942	0.282	0.341	0.429	143	46	2.320	7.2	0.740	92
24	827	5623	1531	284	54	201	518	1144	0.272	0.337	0.449	86	50	1.880	6.22	0.781	72
25	793	5728	1545	336	15	189	608	1061	0.270	0.343	0.433	47	22	1.900	6.32	0.741	91
26	780	5623	1494	310	24	191	513	982	0.266	0.332	0.431	116	46	2.610	6.85	0.729	92
27	719	5531	1438	290	34	145	513	1083	0.260	0.328	0.403	58	31	1.570	6.05	0.782	67
28	**720**	**5538**	**1432**	**261**	**29**	**150**	**461**	**1057**	**0.259**	**0.322**	**0.397**	**67**	**48**	**1.710**	**5.620**	**0.828**	**58**
29	714	5483	1416	278	46	145	469	944	0.258	0.320	0.405	132	42	1.590	5.86	0.780	70
30	698	5722	1544	276	20	136	492	1058	0.270	0.331	0.396	110	42	1.800	6.39	0.779	63

FIGURE 4.6 Team data.

Player #	Salary	AB	R	H	2B	3B	HR	RBI	SB	CS	BB	BA	OBP	SLG
1	$ 18,000,000	373	129	135	27	3	45	101	6	1	232	0.362	0.609	0.812
2	$ 9,333,000	498	102	150	38	3	42	111	8	3	101	0.301	0.418	0.643
3	$ 14,000,000	592	133	196	51	2	46	123	5	5	84	0.331	0.415	0.657
4	$ 11,600,000	547	115	190	49	2	32	96	3	0	127	0.347	0.469	0.62
5	$ 20,000,000	568	108	175	44	0	43	130	2	4	82	0.308	0.397	0.613
6	$ 5,000,000	598	104	200	32	0	48	121	7	2	53	0.334	0.388	0.629
7	$ 4,200,000	518	118	158	28	8	31	93	12	3	118	0.305	0.436	0.569
8	$ 7,780,000	500	109	157	32	4	34	124	4	3	72	0.314	0.409	0.598
9	$ 4,580,000	582	94	175	47	3	41	139	0	0	75	0.301	0.38	0.603
10	$ 6,500,000	544	104	172	40	3	30	106	9	7	127	0.316	0.45	0.566
11	$ 3,160,000	482	96	150	41	3	28	109	3	2	68	0.311	0.41	0.583
12	$ 11,000,000	612	124	206	39	2	39	126	15	3	52	0.337	0.391	0.598
13	$ 10,600,000	574	118	173	47	1	30	105	40	5	127	0.301	0.428	0.544
14	$ 6,000,000	547	99	174	32	1	36	103	0	2	49	0.318	0.373	0.578
15	$ 2,333,000	550	111	187	41	0	27	104	11	6	66	0.34	0.419	0.562
16	$ 7,000,000	584	109	174	34	2	31	108	3	0	88	0.298	0.39	0.522
17	$ 2,200,000	522	97	166	37	10	20	97	12	5	52	0.318	0.379	0.542
18	$ 3,400,000	487	94	151	38	2	24	69	17	5	30	0.31	0.361	0.544
19	$ 2,100,000	511	80	164	35	1	22	88	3	0	56	0.321	0.396	0.523
20	$ 6,800,000	571	101	185	44	2	24	99	2	2	46	0.324	0.381	0.534
21	$ 4,780,000	653	107	203	40	2	34	150	4	1	48	0.311	0.36	0.534
22	$ 2,000,000	591	103	180	37	0	31	99	11	5	54	0.305	0.366	0.525
23	$ 6,521,000	527	72	176	32	2	19	86	7	4	41	0.334	0.383	0.51
24	$ 326,000	579	83	174	53	1	16	87	2	1	81	0.301	0.385	0.478
25	$ 365,000	579	83	183	33	3	23	86	0	0	47	0.316	0.37	0.503
26	$ 2,500,000	620	108	208	47	2	16	76	5	3	58	0.335	0.391	0.495
27	$ 8,000,000	621	123	189	35	6	20	94	19	8	76	0.304	0.38	0.477
28	$ 4,500,000	690	114	216	33	9	22	99	12	3	44	0.313	0.353	0.483
29	$ 3,920,000	481	67	146	31	1	16	62	1	2	36	0.304	0.353	0.472
30	$ 445,000	568	105	151	34	0	46	102	6	1	108	0.266	0.388	0.569
31	$ 6,500,000	606	78	190	37	3	15	63	8	5	55	0.314	0.37	0.459
32	$ 312,500	462	56	145	36	5	9	76	8	0	39	0.314	0.378	0.45
33	$ 6,530,000	704	101	262	24	5	8	60	36	11	49	0.372	0.414	0.455
34	$ 2,600,000	562	68	174	36	3	15	80	2	0	24	0.31	0.348	0.464
35	$ 1,850,000	652	82	201	41	12	11	59	8	4	26	0.308	0.335	0.459
36	$ 3,950,000	503	74	150	21	0	17	55	7	4	27	0.298	0.345	0.441
37	$ 8,571,000	574	86	183	32	0	3	51	11	8	60	0.319	0.399	0.39
38	$ 2,400,000	678	100	221	22	12	3	49	45	24	45	0.326	0.374	0.407
39	$ 1,000,000	553	91	170	22	3	5	38	26	5	36	0.307	0.349	0.385
40	$ 340,000	523	76	156	23	3	5	47	5	4	31	0.298	0.348	0.365

FIGURE 4.7 Player data (from mlb.com and other sources).

NOTES

1. See *Performance Management for a Call Center*, Darden Case Study, by Fuller, Scherer, and Pfeifer.

2. See CBO Testimony, Statement of Robert A. Sunshine, Assistant Director for Budget Analysis Assessment of the Air Force's Planto Acquire 100 Boeing Tanker Aircraft, before the Committee on Armed Services United States Senate, September 4, 2003.

3. www.whitehouse.gov, news releases, May 2004.

4. Some observers might assert that it was this sort of sloppy thinking that led to the butchery of our Marines in Lebanon; see, for example, Bartlett (1987).

5. Extreme event statistics can help ameliorate this problem; see Haimes (1998).

6. See http://www.bcsfootball.org/index2.cfm?page=rankings.

7. For example, the rise of CAIV (cost as an independent variable) in the 1990s in government decisions and the requirement on military projects to "make the business case,"—that is, justify, on economic grounds, a new or replacement system.

8. An excellent example of this is the Information-Based Strategy (IBS) used to grow Capital One into a financial giant.

9. However, Apple Computer is a good example of low market share, less than 5%, with good profitability.

10. As if this whole text weren't some sort of an editorial comment!

11. We note that when presented with this example in a graduate engineering class, only 1 in 30 calculated the correct EMV, with the 29 others falling into the trap that was set.

12. Jensen's Inequality: $E[\Pi(x)] \geq \Pi E(x)$ for a convex function Π. If Π is affine, then $E[\Pi(x)] = \Pi E(x)$. See, DeGroot (1970).

13. See, for example, Maize and McCaughey (1992) and Heyes and Liston-Heyes (2005).

14. See Whitmore (2005) and Martinez (1998).

15. A basic form of "rate-and-weight," which will be elaborated on in Chapter 6.

16. This case does not necessarily illustrate either good or bad management practice. It is meant solely to provide a basis for classroom discussion.

Chapter 5

Develop Alternative Candidate Solutions

5.1 INTRODUCTION

By this point in the system analysis we have established, at least tentatively, the goals of the client and the index of performance by which the client will judge the success of the installed system. Now we are ready to grapple with the problem of developing viable alternative solutions. We are still in an out-scoping mode. We are not trying yet to focus on a particular solution. Rather, we intend to range over the obvious possibilities and also seek to enlarge our option field beyond the obvious. This phase, as with the problem definition phase, is critical and is a reason for the failure of many systems efforts.

5.2 THE CLASSICAL APPROACH TO CREATIVITY

Polya (1957) points out that we must continually change our viewpoint of the problem as we proceed with the solution. He distinguishes four main problem-solving phases. First, says Polya, we must *understand* the problem. That is, we must have a clear appreciation of what is required in the solution. Often, if one attempts to restate the problem in one's own words, it becomes clear that one's initial understanding is really incomplete or erroneous. Every teacher is aware of this phenomenon. It isn't until you have taught someone a concept that you understand it yourself.

Second, we must understand how the parts of the problem are interconnected. For example, what are the connections among the "givens," the "constraints," and the "objectives?" Polya calls this *making a plan*.

How to Do Systems Analysis. By John E. Gibson, William T. Scherer, and William F. Gibson
Copyright © 2007 John Wiley & Sons, Inc.

TABLE 5.1. Dewey's "Five" Phases of Reflective Thought

0. A state of doubt, hesitation, perplexity, mental difficulty
   (Dewey, 1943, p. 12, "pre-reflective")
1. Suggestions immediate but conflicting
2. Blocked suggestions, intellectualization
3. Guiding idea or hypothesis formed
4. Reasoning, evaluation of hypothesis
5. Testing hypothesis in action, verification

Third, we *carry out the plan*, and finally we *look back* on or *review* the completed solution. Polya devotes his whole book to specific suggestions in each category. It is interesting to note how often one of Polya's simple suggestions such as "draw a picture," "restate the goal in your own words," "focus on the goals," or "have you used all of the data?" will suggest a solution.

Often in our impatience, we leap to premature conclusions or panic and fail to attack the problem in a calm, methodical way. We grasp at straws and seek magic formulae instead of using our intellect. It is a well-known psychological phenomenon that a person under pressure tends to regress to a more primitive level of thinking. If you recognize this in yourself while it is happening, you can sometimes break the spiral and move back to a higher intellectual plane.

John Dewey, the famous American educator–philosopher, also devoted a whole book to the question of how we think creatively, and in it he suggests the "five" phases of reflective thought given in Table 5.1 (Dewey, 1933).[1]

Dewey is more rambling and discursive than Polya, and his concepts seem not so clearly formed. Dewey's "third" phase, for example, is clearly the central point, but Dewey merely says, "... the idea just comes or it does not come; that is all that can be said." (Dewey, 1933, p. 109) This isn't of much help and it really isn't even true.

Wallas (1962) captures the essence of what might be called the classical approach to creativity in his four steps, given in Table 5.2.

Each of us is tempted to think of ourselves as unique and possessed of inimitable life insights. Thus, it sometimes comes as a surprise when we find that what we thought of as a personal and possibly unique experience is really a human universal. Most of us have had the experience of working very hard on an intractable problem. Something seems to be missing, but we know not what. Intense, unremitting pressure does not cause the problem to yield and finally we give up in disgust and turn to something else, perhaps an evening of relaxation. At first, we find it hard to unwind

TABLE 5.2. Wallas' Four Classical Steps in Creativity

1. Preparation. Learning about a problem and defining it.
2. Incubation. The waiting period for the ideas needed to solve the problem.
3. Illumination. The occurrence of usable ideas.
4. Verification. The testing and application of ideas from the previous step.

but finally we lose ourselves in the other activity. Then, unbidden, perhaps after a good night's sleep or a day at the beach, the solution comes to us, complete, simple, and obvious.

The concept of incubation is present in the description of the working methods of many creative artists and scientists. It does not follow, however, that we can count on illumination. One is sometimes tempted to quit before exhaustion and to count on incubation and illumination. This almost always fails to work. One cannot take shortcuts or pull one's mental punches. You must put in an intense effort to solve the problem straight through if incubation is to follow, but even then there is no assurance that it will.

5.3 CONCEPTS IN CREATIVITY

There are three modes of thought involved in the modern approach to developing alternatives, and there is a class of tools that matches each mode (see Table 5.3). The first might be called the *unstructured search mode*. In this mode, we range freely and attempt to bring in new and unconventional approaches as well as more conventional ideas. Tools in this first mode include, among others, "brainstorming," "brainwriting," and so-called "dynamic confrontation."

These group stimulation tools are attempts to institutionalize a common folk phenomenon. You probably have had the experience of finding yourself stuck with a problem and began to explain the issue to a sympathetic listener. Part way through the explanation and before your listener has made any comments, you suddenly realize what is missing and how to correct it. Another common occurrence is that, after your explanation, your listener suggests something that is perfectly obvious but that you have overlooked. A third variation is the useful suggestion from a listener that is so wild and uncharacteristic of your own approach that you know you would have never thought of it.

TABLE 5.3. How to Develop Alternative Scenarios[a]

Tools For Creativity	
Phase	Tools
Unstructured search mode ("out-scoping")	• Brainstorming • Brainwriting • Dynamic confrontation
Examine various combinations of elements	• Zwicky morphological box • Options field
Assemble elements into complete candidate solutions	• Options profile • Computer simulation • Delphi?

[a]Other possibilities also exist. Geschka (1983) mentions "creative orientation," for example, and "careful examination and development of specifications."

The second mode of thought in the creativity phase of SA is *examination of various combinations* and subsystem elements, with the idea of possibly creating new and untried combinations. We seek to include unconventional combinations along with the more conventional solution approaches. Tools for this second mode of thought include Zwicky's "morphological box" and a modification of Zwicky's tool called the "options field" approach. In the third mode of thought, we want to *assemble the elements into complete candidate solutions*. In this final mode, the tools to be used include dynamic interactive computer simulation, and "options profiles."

Why do we find it desirable to work through idea generation by means of brainwriting and then through combinations of solution elements with morphological boxes? Why not go directly to creating complete solutions? Because we find that creating "complete solutions" initially often results in premature in-scoping. "Complete solutions" offered at this point tend to be old and tired ideas. They seldom, if ever, are imaginative or take full advantage of the situation.

There are a plethora of books on creativity, which range from engineering and management-oriented to the development of personal creativity skills. Lumsdaine and Lumsdaine (1995) and Cougar (1995) give thorough treatments of all aspects of the subject of creativity, while authors such as de Bono (1970) (e.g., lateral thinking), Adams (1986), Gardner (1978), and Bransford and Stein (1984) all directly address the individual's problem-solving and creativity skills in an informal fashion. One well-known method is the Pugh Method, which is a team-based method for generating creative solutions and is popular in the engineering design community (Pugh, 1991). Other authors, such as Evans (1991), directly address the issues of creativity in building analytical models. There is also a significant literature on the concept of "critical thinking," which, although important in systems analysis, is different. Critical thinking involves applying the principles of scientific thinking (hypotheses, evidence, completeness, etc.) to evaluate ideas and potential alternatives in order to ensure their reasonableness. Our focus is different in that we leave the details to others named above and instead discuss the relevance to systems analysis and present several examples.

5.4 BRAINSTORMING

"Brainstorming" has been around for 35 or 40 years. It is a group process designed to create new solutions to problems [Geschka et al. (1973); for a "how to" see Harrington-Mackin (1994)]. One might say that it is designed to bridge the gap between "left-brain" and "right-brain" people. There are only a few rules and generally the participants enjoy the sessions (see Table 5.4). It seems to be desirable to hold a brainstorming meeting away from the normal place of work. This reduces interruptions and seems to free people up a little from the normal social inhibitions of the workplace. A good idea would be to ask the participants to arrive at the session, held perhaps in a hotel meeting room or conference center, in casual leisure clothes. It is important that participants be told that they cannot receive messages (instant or delivered) or cell phone calls during the process. Some insecure people deliberately

TABLE 5.4. The Main Rules of Brainstorming[a]

- Proven group process for producing new ideas
- Trained leader, called a "facilitator," absolutely necessary
- Sessions informal, no bosses, use first names
- Hold away from usual workplace, in casual clothes
- No interruptions; can't leave the meeting
- No criticisms, no categorizing, no organizing of ideas
- Building on "main idea" with "helpers" encouraged
- Facilitator not a traffic cop, everybody talks as they please, but positively about ideas
- Take a break after an hour or so, but wait until new idea creation is slowing down
- After one or two sessions can move to an evaluation and categorization mode

[a]Brainstorming looks easy, but it is important to use a trained facilitator, preferably from outside your organization. The facilitator is a process person and need have no content knowledge. Some participants grow to detest the process and should not be forced to remain. Others don't mind being present, but they can't stop being critical. That inhibits the process and must be prevented.

seem to arrange to have their secretary call them out of meetings for "important phone calls," and so on, to demonstrate to themselves and others, perhaps, how needed and important they are. That isn't allowed in a brainstorming session.

It is not necessary that the participants know each other prior to the meeting, and it is desirable that no "bosses" are present. The facilitator should ask that participants introduce themselves by first name or nickname and perhaps put this on a name card. It is expected that participants will build on and add to ideas of others. Typically, no record is kept of whose ideas are used. It is a good idea to pin up large sheets of flip chart paper on the walls around the room to record the ideas as things get moving rapidly. If the group is fairly large, say more than six or eight people, as one idea starts building, a participant can record the main idea and "helper notions" on a flip chart while other members of the group are moving along on another main idea.

It is important that the facilitator *not* act as a traffic cop on the ideas. We don't need categorization and focusing. Rather, we need to encourage the free flow of concepts in the early iterations, even if it is hard at first to see how a particular "helper notion" connects to the main idea. The facilitator should expect to have to get the ball rolling at first. She should throw out an idea that is a little unusual to start things off if no one else volunteers a starter suggestion. Then the facilitator seeks to get others to add helper notions.

Generally, one or two participants catch on quickly and then others join in. However, a few individuals dislike the whole concept and refuse to participate. Others seem to find it impossible to resist criticism and running evaluations of ideas as they are suggested. Eventually, persistent nonparticipants and critics may have to be eliminated from the group if they cannot be converted. But this is a last resort (for one thing, to do so converts the facilitator into a policeman, which contradicts her role as enabler). It must be made clear from the beginning that no criticisms or judgmental statements are allowed, and experienced facilitators try to invite people to participate with this in mind. "Idea killers" need to be discouraged, and possibly identified or

TABLE 5.5. Drawbacks of Brainstorming

- A trained and skilled facilitator is an absolute necessity for successful brainstorming. Brainstorming is an emotional and stressful process, and the possibilities for bent egos and hurt feelings are numerous.
- Many individuals are uncomfortable with a verbal free-for-all. Such personalities are likely to resent being pressed into participating in a brainstorming session.
- Some of the most vocal and voluble participants enjoy themselves but don't necessarily make the best contributions, yet the facilitator may be hard-pressed to cut them off without creating a dampening effect on the others.
- Slow-talking persons are sometimes the most thoughtful, but they risk being overridden by more voluble personalities.
- No matter how skilled and effective the facilitator, only one person can talk at a time in a brainstorming session. All the others are in low gear or in neutral while they wait their turn.

noted during the process. Process observers can play a critical role in improving the process for future sessions [see Harrington-Macklin (1994, p. 12)].

After an hour or so, it is a good idea to take a break and walk around outside to stretch one's legs. On reconvening, the facilitator should expect to have to prime the pump again and thus should have held some ideas in reserve for this purpose. We can see that the role of the facilitator in brainstorming is crucial to the success of the process. The facilitator must have the right personality and have careful training in advance. *Lack of trained facilitators is a major cause of failure in the brainstorming process.*

Usually, two one-hour sessions are about all that participants can take. After a lunch break, the participants should be asked to move to an evaluative role and take the various ideas developed earlier and put them in categories, perhaps working from the flip chart records. It is often found that this process rekindles the flow of ideas and also results in modifications and improvements of the original concepts. Table 5.4 provides a summary of the main points in brainstorming.

There is no doubt that brainstorming is an effective technique and that, under the right set of conditions, does work. However, it has several serious drawbacks (see Table 5.5). We recall one instance with NASA and issues regarding the use of the Deep Space Network (DSN). In a brainstorming idea generation session, there was one individual who was internationally renowned and recognized by anyone in the science community. Regardless of the quality of the facilitator and the process, there was, a priori, virtually no possibility of the open generation of ideas given the presence of this individual in the meeting. This was not due to the malevolence of an individual, but the inherent problems with brainstorming.

The lack of parallel processing in brainstorming is a serious functional difficulty with the method. The other personality difficulties can be overcome with proper selection of players and training for facilitators, but series processing of ideas is fundamental to the method. All in all, there seems to be a real need for an idea creation process that retains the positive features of brainstorming and reduces or eliminates the drawbacks. Brainwriting is a prime candidate for this post.

5.5 BRAINWRITING

In all of these idea generation techniques, someone must edit the product. A trained facilitator will be very helpful in this step as well as in running the session itself. Following a quick editing, a hard copy of the rough edited output should be circulated to individual team members for their further comments.

We have already introduced brainwriting in Section 3.3, thus little more need be said here about the basic technique. It is not to be assumed, however, that brainstorming and brainwriting are totally interchangeable techniques. In the first place, these two techniques appeal to different personality types. Brainstorming appeals to ebullient, outgoing extroverts, persons who are stimulated by group interactions and who are a bit impatient with detail. Brainwriting, on the other hand, appeals more to the quieter, more intellectual individual, especially those who shrink from verbal combat.

Brainstorming is an excellent technique for a group seeking new products or a totally new way of doing a job (Geschka et al., 1973). It is a technique appropriate for those individuals who tend naturally to the top-down mode. Brainwriting is more appropriate when it is desired to capture from a group knowledge that the group possesses, but which may not have been fully articulated. It is also more effective in a situation in which there may be hidden conflicts within the group or an imbalance of power as illustrated in the NASA DSN example.

One of the reasons that brainstorming seems so effective when persons are first introduced to it is that one is often taught brainstorming in an artificial situation such as a seminar or the like in which the participants have no history of conflict or any hidden agenda items. But this is not usually the case in realistic environments. Here is an example from our consulting experience: A government agency, head decided to invest in strategic planning for the agency, and the first phase was quite successful. Under the guidance of an outside consultant—not us—the planning staff was led through the development of what we call the descriptive scenario and the normative scenario.

This consultant calls the normative scenario the "preferred future" and the process, "preferred futuring." We like this term. In fact, it seems more graphic than our own. Developing this "preferred future" scenario, or "architecture" as the agency had become accustomed to calling it, took over a year because opinions and inputs were solicited from agency professionals throughout the nation and not merely the Washington-based central staff. An excellent final report was produced and, overall, it was a very credible professional systems effort.

The central planning staff of the agency then produced alternative transition scenarios for reaching this preferred future using the brainstorming technique, but this process failed. The Strategic Planning Initiative Team, or the so-called SPIT team, was made up of three individuals from the strategic planning office of the agency and the remaining 8–10 members were representatives of the various operating divisions of the agency. All of these individuals were senior administrators, some with line responsibilities; others were senior staff individuals from the operating groups. Interestingly, the average service to the organization was over 30 years! The leader of the SPIT team, a member of the strategic planning office, was a dedicated senior professional committed to building consensus. But the planning process bogged down. The team retained an outside consulting firm to facilitate the next phase, and we were asked to become a member of this group.

The first meeting of the new consultants with the SPIT team was pleasant from a social point of view because the team members knew each other and each was obviously a committed and knowledgeable professional. On the other hand, it seemed that progress might be difficult because the team members brought massive exogenous needs into the meeting room. These team members could not be expected to put aside their loyalty to the operating divisions each represented. Yet these operating divisions exist because of the demands of the status quo. Obviously, the way the agency will go about its business in 2020 A.D., the target year of the preferred future scenario, will differ dramatically from the status quo, but this change could threaten the future existence of one or more of the operating divisions.

Furthermore, this Federal agency had recently undergone a substantial reduction in force.[2] Reminding team members that each individual would be retired for more than a decade before the target date of the preferred future did no good. Thus it is understandable if the SPIT team members found it difficult or impossible to divorce themselves from present exigencies for the purposes of this planning activity.

We suggest that this conflict is implicit in any real organization and must be resolved if planning is to proceed. It is not sufficient for strategic planning to be relegated to a corporate staff group. Eventually the results of the planning effort must be internalized and acted upon by line managers. We will see later in this chapter how P. Wack and the corporate planning group at Royal Dutch Shell found it difficult to involve line managers in the results of planning scenarios in this situation.

The SPIT team leader was determined to seek consensus as the process unfolded. Team members were unwilling to "play the game under protest." That is, when a consultant suggested that the team go ahead with the planning process in order to see what would come out, this suggestion was rejected. The chairman supported the rejection because he felt that each team member had to be willing to proceed before the next step could be taken.

Team members often attempted to test interim results by asking how the result would impact their operating division in the current environment. When a consultant suggested that a concept designed for 2020 A.D. using as yet undeveloped technology might not be relevant to today's tactical environment, this suggestion was rejected. It seems reasonable to characterize these operating managers as dedicated bottom-uppers, and as consumed with detail. But isn't this precisely the behavior an operating manager should have?

We broke this log jam by using brainwriting. Controversy over issues raised in brainstorming was thus avoided. No one team member could monopolize a meeting by monologues on tactical issues. Consensus could be delayed until all the data were in. All in all, the brainwriting session was judged as a major success and as responsible for moving the planning effort off dead center. Now the rest of the story—as warning and caveat. During our first brainwriting session, one of the sheets that members were using to list ideas disappeared during the brainwriting session. We discovered that the sheet addressed one of the functional areas of one of the team members, and she didn't like the ideas/words being written on the sheet. She had stuffed the sheet into her purse.[3] This could be one benefit of computer-based brainwriting or at least a recommendation for active monitoring of the process.

5.6 DYNAMIC CONFRONTATION

Geschka et al., (1973) mention this technique, calling it "creative confrontation," and Zwicky in his book *Discovery, Invention, Research* (Zwicky, 1969), calls it the method of "Negation and Construction." The Geschka article provides an excellent introductory survey of the field, but it is flawed by the complete absence of references. One really needs to read Zwicky to gain a sense of the flavor of his prose. He makes no small claims. Another advocate of dynamic confrontation is Andrew Grove, President and a founder of Intel, a highly successful Silicon Valley semiconductor chip manufacturer (Grove, 1984).

The process of dynamic confrontation differs somewhat from user to user, but the essence seems to be to deny or contradict or attempt to prove false each main claim or assumption as it is made in a presentation. Presumably, this questioning of standard assumptions puts everyone on his or her mettle, forcing the reevaluation of conventional wisdom and requiring each participant to think through every claim. In this respect, dynamic confrontation is the polar opposite of brainstorming. In the latter case, we were forbidden to criticize; in the former, we are required to do so. Dynamic confrontation is an adversarial process and would appeal, no doubt, to the legal-type mind.

One of the major issues about dynamic confrontation is that it is constrained by cultural norms and, for that reason, may not be appropriate for all environments. In some Dutch or Japanese organizations, where achieving consensus is more important than individual goals, the use of dynamic confrontation would be extremely counterproductive and in violation of cultural norms. Even in a U.S.-based organization, Grove makes clear that he is aware that some individuals don't like to see themselves contradicted, but he assures us that so long as the contradiction is focused on the idea and not the person, tempers do not fly out of control.

Perhaps so, but Grove is widely known as a very bright and also a hyper-aggressive individual. Possibly he and Zwicky, who also immensely enjoyed playing the intellectual gadfly, are simply attempting with sophistry to justify their self-indulgent behavior. One may be amused to note that, in one issue, *FORTUNE* magazine published an article in which Grove outlined his ideas on dynamic confrontation (Grove, 1984), and in its very next issue, *FORTUNE* published a poll in which Grove was named as one of the 10 toughest bosses in America (Flax, 1984).

5.7 ZWICKY'S MORPHOLOGICAL BOX

Zwicky (1967) argues that we make ourselves prisoners of convention, thus impeding our creative processes. He suggests what he calls the "morphological approach" to

TABLE 5.6. A Morphological Phrase Maker[a]

A	B	C
Integrated	Management	Options
Total	Organizational	Flexibility
Systematized	Monitored	Capability
Parallel	Reciprocal	Mobility
Functional	Digital	Programming
Responsive	Logistical	Concept
Optional	Transitional	Time-phase
Synchronized	Incremental	Projection
Compatible	Fourth-generation	Hardware
Balanced	Policy	Contingency

[a]Judicious use will improve most reports. Select at random one word from each column and insert where indicated. (Source unknown; see http://www.dack.com/web/bullshit.html for a more humerous version).

force ourselves out of these self-imposed shackles. The method of the morphological box is representative of the second step in developing alternatives. In this technique, we first attempt to define all of the functional classes that make up the basic subsystems. These classes should be functional rather than technological. Next, exhaustive lists of technological alternatives in each class are developed. Next, combinations are made by picking one example from each subsystem. Zwicky feels that it is essential to exhaust the combinations. Finally, each combination is carefully examined with emphasis given to making even the unusual combinations work. One recognizes in advance that most combinations will prove impractical, but the idea is to stimulate original thought.

This idea of combining elements at random is the basis of a well-known children's toy consisting of a book with separate flaps. On the uppermost set of flaps, a variety of cartoon heads are drawn. One finds a number of grotesque bodies on the middle set, but finds a variety of legs and feet on the bottom set. Children are entertained by the unexpected results obtained from selecting various combinations.

Another humorous example of this morphological process is a set of words from which one may construct high-sounding phrases. Table 5.6 gives one example. These jokes and toys touch on an important point, however. The humor of these toys is in the unexpectedness, and that is precisely the direction in which creativity lies.

Suppose we now turn to a more serious example of the morphological approach. Let us attempt to stimulate our thinking about new modes of personal transportation. The major subsectors of a personal transportation device appear to be four, namely, the propulsion sector, the suspension sector, the guidance system, and the passenger compartment. We are using the word "personal" here not in the sense of a private vehicle, but only to focus on human passengers rather than a device for bulk material transport. Zwicky's approach suggests that we list all conceivable ways of accomplishing each sector without regard for practical limits or consideration of the other

TABLE 5.7. Morphological Approach to Passenger Transportation Device[a]

Suspension Sector		
1. Air ducts	2. Air cushion	3. Magnetic field
4. Steel wheels	5. Rubber tires	6. Legs
7. Capacitive	8. Anti-gravity	9. From a cable
10. Float on water	11. Hot air balloon	12. Crawler treads
13. Like a snake	14. Slide on grease	15. Other

[a]This list is one of four. It is for the "Suspension" sector. The other three sectors for which lists must be produced are "Propulsion," "Guidance," and "Passenger Compartment."

sectors. Table 5.7 shows how such a set of lists might be started. How does one create such lists? Probably by brainwriting or brainstorming. The first few ideas may come from conventional existing systems. Then perhaps one begins to think of the ways in which birds and insects propel themselves. And of course some ideas will be inserted as "jokes."

But remember, no criticism while the list is being created. List construction is an out-scoping or divergent mental experience. Then examining the combinations one-by-one is an in-scoping or convergent mental exercise. One's critical faculty is appropriate in the latter situation but not, as we know, in the former.

Perhaps the "freeing" effect is achieved by tricking one's mind. One is accustomed to conventional means of transportation, and if one permits oneself to think of complete transportation units, apparently incongruous combinations may be suppressed, simply because one doesn't want to appear silly before one's colleagues and oneself. But, when one considers only one sector at a time, who is to say what is silly? One is released from artificial bounds.

We have a suggestion you may wish to keep in mind when examining the various combinations. Don't ask, "Will it work?" Don't ask, "What do you think of the following combination?" Those are "killer phrases" designed to bring out the critical faculty. It is better to say, "Do a preliminary design of a device with the following attributes . . . ." The latter approach relieves assignees of responsibility for practicality and may help to free up their thinking.

5.8 THE OPTIONS FIELD/OPTIONS PROFILE APPROACH

One of the values of a powerful idea is its ability to stimulate further thinking. By this measure, Zwicky's morphological box is very powerful. One of the useful modifications of Zwicky's concept is the so-called Options Field/Options Profile approach (Warfield, 1980). In essence, this modification simply suggests that as one selects elements from the morphological categories, one should impose some ordering principle on the selection. One might tend to do this automatically, but a reminder may be of some value. Zwicky's morphological approach is not identical to the Options Field approach, but it is very close. The Zwicky approach focuses on discovering new combinations, while the Options Field approach seeks to display existing but latent

TABLE 5.8. Some Possible New Telecommunication-Related Business Ventures[a]

Possible New Telecommunication-Related Ventures		
Cellular telephone	Cable TV	Electronic mail
Burglar alarm service	Fire alarm service	Voice mail
Call waiting feature	Call forwarding	Auto redial
Satellite home TV	Bypass LD service	Wide area computer net
Telemarketing	Teleconferencing	Video-conferencing
Video-text service	Video classrooms	Video newspaper
Video yellow pages	Electronic office	Electronic schools
Emergency medical alarm	Paging service	Other

[a]This is by no means a complete list.

combinations. Note that it is vital to define correctly the morphological sectors. In the case of the design of a physical object, the functional subsectors may be obvious, although not always. In many large-scale system problems, this morphological division is not at all apparent. How do we handle this issue?

Suppose you are a manager in a telecommunications enterprise, charged with analyzing new business ventures for your company. You have developed a list of potential new ventures (see Table 5.8). Perhaps this list is the outcome of a brainwriting session, or possibly you have been collecting ideas from the literature and by attending conferences, or whatever. In any case, you have a list. Now, what are you going to do with it?

Of course, we could test each item in Table 5.8 for its potential match with our corporate objectives. Indeed, this is the most common procedure. However, there might be a better way. Suppose we were to take the following steps:

- Develop a Morphological Field, or so-called options field, on which the following profiles can be traced.
- Corporate Profile. Select the attribute(s) in each sector that best describe(s) our organization.
- Venture Profile: Aggressive Posture. For a specific venture such as those listed in Table 5.8, select the attribute(s) in each morphological sector that would be required for rapid entry into a market segment.
- Venture Profile: Conservative Posture. Attribute(s) desirable for a more cautious market entry.

Our first problem is to define the critical features that define our organization. That is, how do we generate the morphological sectors that make up a functional description of our business? We don't want specific descriptors yet, rather we seek the names of general categories. How do we know what categories should be used? We suggest that you define as many features as you feel appropriate. In case of doubt, include the sector. Then, as you proceed with the process, you may find that one or more of those morphological sectors initially defined seem to have no part in subsequent steps. That is, certain categories appear never to play a definitive role in the decision process. These nonactive sectors might be omitted from future analyses.

In Figure 5.1, we show an options field designed to describe the functional attributes of typical telecommunications ventures. We have chosen to display 10 attributes in the options field. The sectors were chosen to focus on what we believe will be the key elements in a strategic marketing plan for a specific venture and a specific company. There are two options profiles shown in Figure 5.1. One profile represents our evaluation of the present condition of our *organization*. The second profile represents our evaluation of the attributes needed for an *aggressive entry into the market* for this venture. A third profile could be added that illustrates the requirements for a slower, more conservative entry into the marketplace.

All of the profiles mentioned above should be shown on the same field. This approach will highlight good and bad matches. Presumably, the aggressive approach will entail higher risk and a more rapid expenditure of funds in the early phase, including perhaps the use of external funds. At the same time, it should reduce the time necessary to recoup our investment and serve to secure our marketplace against the assault of possible competitors. The more conservative options profile will take longer for the venture to break even, but will require fewer outside financial resources and is apparently less risky.

Which profile should we recommend? The considerations involved may be segmented into two categories: (1) the external marketplace and (2) the internal posture, that is, the corporate culture of our organization. Suppose we know that our organization in the past was dedicated to slow, careful growth and that it prefers to finance this growth from internally generated funds. Then, on the basis of this examination of the internal "corporate culture," perhaps we should not recommend an aggressive strategic market orientation that will require external funding, either equity or debt, as well as possibly the need to recruit a number of new key personnel from outside the organization.

But now let us further suppose that the conditions of the external marketplace seem to dictate that an aggressive strategy be pursued. Presume that one or more competitors is currently in the market or is contemplating entry. This intensified competition will increase the cost for us to capture our anticipated market share and may even exclude for us the possibility of success unless we act quickly. Three possibilities present themselves, as shown in Table 5.9.

The specific example we are considering illustrates the issue of a mismatch between the current corporate value system and the requirements for a successful market entry with this venture. A detailed venture analysis (not presented here) reveals that a substantial unmet market demand apparently exists for this venture in the target metropolitan area. However, one competitor already exists and another is contemplating entry. Thus a slow, conservative introduction financed with internally generated funds is unlikely to be successful. Therefore, our organization must move aggressively or not at all.

We are familiar with two major financial services firms, namely the two investment management arms of insurance companies, which needed to make significant, aggressive investments in their infrastructures. The major difference between the two

VENTURE PROFILE

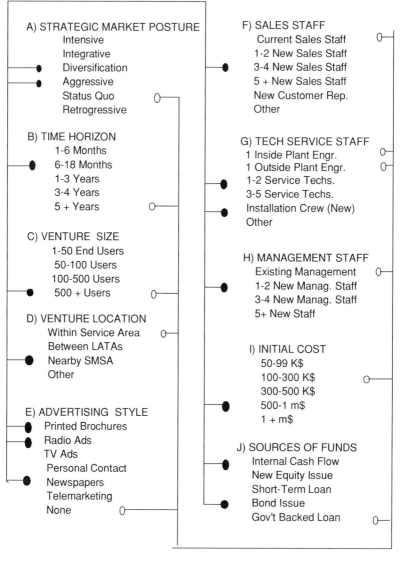

A) STRATEGIC MARKET POSTURE
   Intensive
   Integrative
   Diversification
   Aggressive
   Status Quo
   Retrogressive

B) TIME HORIZON
   1-6 Months
   6-18 Months
   1-3 Years
   3-4 Years
   5 + Years

C) VENTURE SIZE
   1-50 End Users
   50-100 Users
   100-500 Users
   500 + Users

D) VENTURE LOCATION
   Within Service Area
   Between LATAs
   Nearby SMSA
   Other

E) ADVERTISING STYLE
   Printed Brochures
   Radio Ads
   TV Ads
   Personal Contact
   Newspapers
   Telemarketing
   None

F) SALES STAFF
   Current Sales Staff
   1-2 New Sales Staff
   3-4 New Sales Staff
   5 + New Sales Staff
   New Customer Rep.
   Other

G) TECH SERVICE STAFF
   1 Inside Plant Engr.
   1 Outside Plant Engr.
   1-2 Service Techs.
   3-5 Service Techs.
   Installation Crew (New)
   Other

H) MANAGEMENT STAFF
   Existing Management
   1-2 New Manag. Staff
   3-4 New Manag. Staff
   5+ New Staff

I) INITIAL COST
   50-99 K$
   100-300 K$
   300-500 K$
   500-1 m$
   1 + m$

J) SOURCES OF FUNDS
   Internal Cash Flow
   New Equity Issue
   Short-Term Loan
   Bond Issue
   Gov't Backed Loan

COMPANY PROFILE

FIGURE 5.1 An options field and two options profiles for the analysis of a new venture in the telecommunications business. One profile is of the company, a small independent telephone concern. The other profile is for aggressive entry into a specific market with a specific new venture.

TABLE 5.9. Three Options for Market Entry with a Specific Venture and an Enterprise with a Conservative Corporate Culture

Option	Analysis
I. Reject this venture	This option accepts the inconsistency between the requirements dictated by the external market place for aggressive entry and the existing corporate value structure. It is the most likely alternative.
II. Aggressive market entry	Entry using an aggressive posture satisfies the needs of the market but is not consistent with existing corporate culture. It should be recommended only if all of the following three conditions are met. (A) Corporate management is aware of and accepts the added risk. (B) The investment required will not be an impossible burden should failure occur. (C) Management is committed to a change in the existing corporate culture or understands that the venture under consideration must be operated as a nonintegrated subsidiary.
III. Low-key market entry	Entry using a nonaggressive posture seems doomed to failure because competition exists in the market. Thus this option must be eliminated.

[a]Aggressive market entry is dictated by the existence of competition already in the market.

is that one is a mutual insurance company (i.e., it was owned by its policy holders), while the other is a stockholder-owned firm. The latter was able to make the decision to accept the incremental risk and make the investments; the former was not able to overcome the institutional inertia and accept the risk, nor was it committed to an evolution in its corporate culture.

In the short-term horizon, the mutual-owned firm generated better financial results. However, by the third year, the stock-owned firm generated consistently better results, with a more diversified product line. The prevailing corporate culture of the former firm was dominant, but suboptimal, in this situation. However, woe betide the analyst who thinks that the "right" solution might be the "appropriate" one, given the culture.

Examination of Figure 5.1 clearly illustrates a rather complete lack of overlap between our current corporate posture and the actions needed for aggressive entry.

5.9 COMPUTER CREATIVITY

Given the important role that creativity plays in the formulation of alternatives, we then face the question of computer-based automation of some or all of the creativity and generation functions. Group Decision Support System (GDSS) is the term that comprises the end-user technology, analytic decision techniques (alternative ranking), human facilitation, customized facility layout, specialized equipment, and underlying process that a group of decision-makers employs for the purpose of generating ideas, analyzing courses of action, and making decisions (Desanctis and Gallupe, 1987) [see also Group Support Systems (GSS)]. The critical issue in GDSS implementation and effective usage is the human–computer interaction it necessitates. Problems can arise in two areas from the interaction between users and the computers in a GDSS. First, communication and participant interaction among users can be negatively affected by a poorly designed system (Bui and Jarke, 1986). Second, the preference elicitation and idea expression of users can be hindered if the system has a poor interface (Matsatsinis and Samaras, 2001). GDSS computer tools can play a vital role in the systems analysis process; however, we believe, especially in the early stages of problem definition and alternative generation, that the old-fashioned flip-chart and tape method is preferred. As powerful as some of the software tools are, our experience leads us to recommend a manual process.

In a recent session with an aerospace company, we filled the four walls of the conference room with sheets of paper and handwritten ideas. The team of five was highly engaged and making connections across the sheets around the room, using the human ability to process visually and manage disparate visual information. It's not obvious or believable that a software product (of the kind listed below) could have enabled the process that resulted. There are potentially powerful creativity tools, some web-based, but the critical key to success is clearly facilitation. We would be remiss in not mentioning that numerous software packages can be purchased, including Group Systems II, Logical Decisions for Groups, Solution Genie, MeetingWorks, and so on, but we reiterate that they are tools only. Many of these tools also have decision analysis features appropriate for the *rank alternatives* phase, which is covered in the following chapter and is in our opinion the most valued aspect of such tools.

A well-designed GDSS can improve brainstorming, enhance collaboration, increase self-reflection, create a trusting environment, and promote group learning (Froehle et al., 1999). Much of this value comes from the use of brainwriting as opposed to brainstorming, which is clear in the features that were identified in the use of GDSS tools: participant anonymity, multiple simultaneous input and processing, instant and permanent documentation, skillful group facilitation, and the ability to include members in different places (Froehle et al., 1999). Obviously, the GDSS systems can play a role in situations where the group is distributed geographically. Face-to-face GDSS groups, however, are more truthful than distributed GDSS groups and members are less likely to start "flaming" in the meeting (Barkhi et al., 2004).

In complex detailed systems design (e.g., satellite transponders or aircraft control systems), GDSS tools can play a critical and successful role. In large-scale, complex systems analysis, however, such tools tend to be minor players, especially in the early, critical phases of the analysis.

5.10 COMPUTER SIMULATION: A TOOL IN OPTION DEVELOPMENT

One of the most powerful techniques for developing alternative solutions is the process of dynamic modeling of the problem and its environment using a computer. Such computer simulations are sometimes called "scenarios," although the term "scenario" would perhaps be better applied to the narrative description of a particular solution produced by the simulation process. In practice, unfortunately, usage of the term "scenario" is mixed.

Computer modeling has become such a powerful tool since its introduction in the late 1950s that it could even serve as a paradigm of the whole of systems analysis. One of the early practitioners of digital computer modeling and the person most responsible for its widespread popularity is Jay W. Forrester (i.e., *systems dynamics*). Indeed, computer models of the economic dynamics of industries (Forrester, 1961), cities (Forrester, 1969a), and even the entire world (Forrester, 1971a), are often called "Forrester-type models." On the other hand, one should not think that dynamic simulation began with the "Forrester-type model." In the late 1940s and early 1950s, the analog computer became a practical simulation device and was used for this purpose in hundreds of engineering laboratories in the United States. The systems dynamics efforts continue to be strong today, especially in the business literature [with the highly popular works of Senge (1990) and his concept of the *Fifth Discipline* (systems thinking)] and in numerous business modeling books [see, for example, Sterman (2000)].

The crude calculators that existed prior to World War II were rare and experimental in nature but, based on major military research expenditures, the electronic analog computer became practical soon after the war. It was 10 more years before the digital machine became reliable. Although the analog computer is in many ways more ideally suited to the modeling and solution of the differential equations used to model physical situations, it has been completely replaced by the digital machine during the past 30 years. This has come about because of the versatility, accuracy, and economy of the digital machine and especially because of the ease of programming.

Only in one minor respect is the replacement of the earlier analog device by the more modern digital machine regrettable. The very ease of programming digital machines has promoted a drift away from careful identification of intermediate physical variables in modeled systems and the intimate knowledge of the situation required for this process.

The analog modeler was forced to live with the problem and to build the model, physical variable by physical variable. This skill and intimate knowledge of the problem saved many modelers from making the horrible mistakes that became common in digital modeling in the 1960s when computer "experts" were let loose with large budgets to model the world. Whereas analog modeling requires detailed knowledge of the problem, its variables, and parameters, the ability to program a digital computer seems only to require the ability to operate a keyboard. This was particularly true in building the large-scale military simulations that require the integration of very disparate systems of simulation systems—thus, GIGO.

5.11 WHY A DYNAMIC SIMULATION FOR CREATING OPTIONS?

The labor and cost of constructing a large-scale computer simulation of a complex, interrelated set of variables is not to be underestimated. The IIASA world energy model, for example, took 225 person-years of labor and a total research budget exceeding

$6.5 million (Keepin and Wynne, 1984). Even to collect the data required to establish the initial conditions and to set the parameters of a realistic computer simulation model can be very expensive and time-consuming. Thus, while simulation is an exciting technological frontier, unless dynamic modeling provides a more effective way of solving complex problems than alternative approaches, the required investment in time and money can hardly be justified. Here are several arguments for the development of computer simulation models.

Examination of Complex Interactions Becomes Practical. The basis of Systems Analysis is the careful examination of complex interactions. Other solution regimes usually require the division of complex problems into smaller subunits and the analysis of these subunits in isolation. This is true in the classical "Engineering Method," for example. But failing to consider problems in their context and with all interrelations leads to suboptimization at best, and total failure at worst.

The economist Kenneth Boulding said, "I have discovered the real name of the Devil. It isn't Lucifer. It is suboptimization." (Boulding, 1985) By suboptimization, Boulding meant the optimization of one small, accessible element of a complex problem to the neglect of the overall context. Boulding lived in Colorado and he could well have been thinking of the construction of dams and waterways in the West without considering the overall impact on the nation.[4] It may be trite, but it is certainly true, that technology has given modern society more powerful tools than it knows how to use wisely. Possibly to have a tool that is capable of simulating the interrelationships and cross-impacts in complex problems may be of assistance in counteracting some of the negative impacts of suboptimization.

Validation by Generalization Made Practical. We have argued that in order to lend contextual integrity to a specific solution, one should embed the specific problem in the next more general situation. Yet this is often difficult to do because of the added cost of the more complete analysis. For example, to validate the analysis of a specific urban transport element, one probably should embed it into an analysis of the overall urban transport system. Yet to handle the additional data and variables would be difficult and expensive and probably impossible without a computer simulation.

Significant Increase in Ease of Exploring Options. Examining alternatives is an essential feature in SA. Often hundreds of combinations should be explored, but this may be practical only with a computer simulation. We have talked several times about the proposed 4.5-mile Woodward Avenue subway system in Detroit, from the New Center area downtown to the Detroit River at Cobo Hall. Suppose the result of your analysis of this issue is a negative recommendation. Your client will ask for proof and after he is convinced, his next question should be, "Okay, then what should we do to improve the transportation system in the city? How about an 8-mile subway? 16 miles? How about a different route? How about buses? How about . . . ?" A properly constructed computer simulation will help the client to think about these other possibilities.

Provides Opportunity to Explore Prime Options in Depth. Complex systems often cannot be constructed and tested before installation. Thus complete examination of all of the possible impacts is difficult, even with simulation, but simulation does improve matters. Furthermore, there is even a more important reason for examining prime options via dynamic simulation.

Helps the Client to Develop a Feel for the Impact of His/Her Decisions. This is hard to do without a dynamic simulation. If the client can be allowed to manipulate the critical variables in a simulation and to observe personally the impact on various outputs of these parameter variations, he gains a perception of the solution space available in almost no other way. We saw this in the Detroit subway simulation. The client, possibly for the first time, really understood the effect of different solutions on the key variables when he could adjust the parameters and rerun the simulation for himself.

We gained this same effect also in an early simulation of the automobile industry. Auto engineers and managers began by examining the simulation with deep skepticism, because they did not fully accept the process by which the model was constructed. Only after they began to see results that they knew were representative of reality in familiar cases did they begin to trust the model's extrapolations into new territory.

Enforces a Disciplined Approach to Problem Definition. If a computer simulation can be made to run correctly once, much of the total potential value has been gained, even if it is never run again. This is so because the discipline required to understand the object being simulated completely and the knowledge gained through this process is of major importance. Also, such a simulation mandates the use of an index of performance (metric), bringing that critical issue to the forefront.

5.12 CONTEXT-FREE SIMULATION MODELS?

An intriguing proposal that has been suggested time and time again is the concept of a context-free database of simulation models. A typical suggestion is to assemble all available data on a subject and to cram it somehow into a computer. Then, when asked a question, the "giant brain" will somehow be able to return all relevant information with the speed of light, it is claimed. It isn't only those who are ignorant of how computers work that make such absurd claims. Many who should know better have done so. For example, the National Science Foundation became involved in this fallacy when it advocated construction of a physical and social inventory of the Chesapeake Bay region.[5]

"The inventory—an ambitious attempt to look at the bay region as a single system—will catalogue many thousands of 'entities,' from algae and airports to schools, power plants, and wetlands, as well as their characteristics and the processes by which they interact. The enormous amount of data to be generated by this cataloguing procedure will be stored in a computerized data bank as part of an information system that, the authors of the report hope, could be useful both to researchers and to officials of regulatory and management agencies concerned with the bay."[6]

Proposals such as the Bay data bank are common, and represent a trap for novice system analysts. Not only is conversion of randomly collected data to a common base a massively complex job, but also the design of a search scheme to recover the data once they are computerized is no small problem. Perhaps more important than such technical concerns, however, is the following more general problem. Any computer model or database can be isomorphic with physical reality at only a few isolated points at best. Thus, it seems merely primitive common sense to choose beforehand, and with great care, the class of questions to which the database is to be responsive. It seems clear on the face of it that there can be no such thing as a general-purpose computer model or database independent of the class of questions to which it is designed to be responsive, that is, context-free (Gibson, 1972). Gray et al. (1972), Hoos (1984), and Babcock (1972) have produced a strong critique of Forrester's urban modeling that includes reinforcing this same point.

A multi-million dollar study, the Detroit Transportation and Land Use Study (TALUS) (1969) for was fatally flawed with this same error and ran out of money before useful results were obtained.[7] Hamilton et al. (1969), report on a Battelle Susquehanna Basin System simulation study that recognized and avoided the context-free trap. Note the date of the report of the Battelle study (1969) and recognize that the Susquehanna River represents the main fresh water inflow to the Chesapeake Bay. Now check the date of the proposed RANN Chesapeake simulation (1971). Would it be fair to say that the authors of the RANN proposal were unfamiliar with the relevant literature? It seems to us that this is the sort of professional irresponsibility that gave system analysis a bad name in the early 1970s.

If permitted, data collection and simulation will expand to use all of the time and money available in a system study, and, if more time and money is allocated, will absorb that as well.[8]

5.13   BOTTOM-UP SIMULATION OR TOP-DOWN?

Broadly speaking, as with system analysis, there are two general approaches to simulation in common use. These may broadly be characterized as the "bottom-up approach," and the "top-down." The bottom-up approach is the technique normally favored by engineers. In this approach, the object to be simulated is first divided into subsystems and then each of these subsystems is characterized in complete operational detail, including all of the intermediate physical variables and parameters. Then the subsystems are interconnected and any bugs are ironed out. This is the correct, and indeed the uniquely correct, approach if the simulated system is a free-standing unit. For example, we would feel quite uncomfortable flying in an airplane for which the designers took any other approach in their simulation studies.

On the other hand, there are many systems simply too large ever to be constructed at one time. And often these large-scale systems are too complex ever to be simulated in a fully detailed overall computer model. The Chesapeake Bay is one example, cities

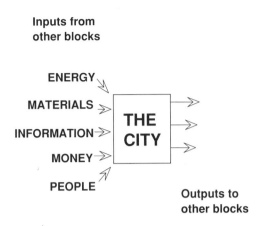

FIGURE 5.2 The city modeled as a single node. This representation of a city might be adequate in a regional model that does not require representation of variables internal to the city.

are another, whole urban transportation systems possibly another, and so on. When such complex large-scale systems are modeled using a bottom-up approach, failure is often the result. We have mentioned one failure mode; the modeling team runs out of time and money before completion. But other sorts of failures are also possible. The computer may be found to be inadequate to handle all of the variables required, certain data may be unavailable, the cross-couplings may be unknown, and so on. For example, no presently available computer is large enough or fast enough to permit weather prediction with reasonable accuracy for more than a few hours in advance.

Sometimes full microscopic detail of a very complex system is necessary if the results are to be of value. If so, the problem is beyond current technological capabilities. This is true in weather modeling, for example. In many instances, however, a top-down approach to the simulation may be taken.

In the top-down approach, the overall system is characterized by a few critical variables or subunits and then successively more complex models are made of critical subsystems. Take the modeling of an urban environment as an example. In Figure 5.2, we have represented the city as a node with a few critical input and output variables. This representation might be sufficient in a regional model that includes many cities and other regional ecological artifacts, such as rivers, watersheds, or point pollution sources, such as major factories, and so on. It would be possible to relate the various input variables to the output variables in Figure 5.2 by developing the required transfer functions and cross-couplings by methods well-known to those versed in the state of the art. The level of detail in Figure 5.2 would not be adequate, however, if variables internal to the city must be traced.

If we are interested in the internal workings of the city, the next level of detail is needed. This next level of complexity might be represented as shown in Figure 5.3. Now the general variables of Figure 5.2 are used appropriately to drive a number of sectors that represent the city in more detail. The boxes in Figure 5.3 have as outputs

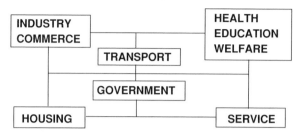

FIGURE 5.3 A simple six-sector model of a city. This model has six sectors and would represent a more complete simulation. We would assume that few, if any, variables internal to the six sectors will be needed.

a number of additional variables that represent the internal workings of the city, but suppose we need still more detail, on the internal operation of the transportation sector, for example. In that case, the transportation sector model could be expanded as shown in Figure 5.4. And this process can be continued as needed.

We must be prepared to sacrifice apparently valuable detail in those sectors not under intensive study in order to gain a general understanding of the system as a whole. To describe a spaceship as "a point mass moving in three-dimensional space" may be sufficient for many purposes, but it cannot reveal if the craft is tumbling, nor could such a model be used to help design its attitude control system. Similarly, we cannot expect to observe even gross behavior of the urban transportation system in a city model consisting of a single black box.

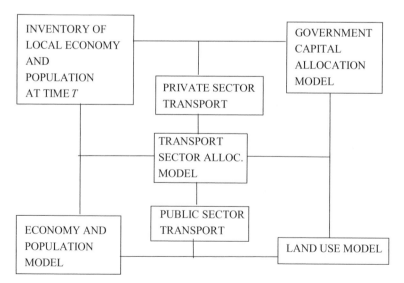

FIGURE 5.4 A more complete representation of the transportation sector. We assume that transportation is our main interest, thus that sector has been elaborated upon.

Note that in the top-down approach we do *not* begin with elemental blocks that describe small components of the system in great detail. Rather we begin with the gross behavior in order to obtain a functioning simulation quickly. Also, note that an additional benefit of this approach is that the model is susceptible to testing and modification as it is being developed. Nevertheless, the top-down approach is difficult to accept, even by some of those who lay claim to being "system thinkers." The multi-million dollar Doxiadis analysis of Detroit regional development (not to be confused with the TALUS study mentioned previously) contains an example of this issue.

One of the Doxiadis working papers describes a hierarchic construction of a general system model of the Detroit Urban Region using a rather elaborate bottom-up analytic formulation (Sheather, 1969). However, the attempt had to be abandoned when it was discovered that many of the required coefficients were not and could not be measured. The report concludes that, "perhaps then it is best to abandon this mathematical model for one that emphasizes the process by which the system functions irrespective of the measure or presence of the individual components."

5.14 LESSONS FROM THE SUSQUEHANNA RIVER BASIN MODEL

In 1967, a systems group at Battelle Institute completed a dynamic computer simulation model of the Susquehanna River Basin using the same computer language, DYNAMO, as employed by Forrester in his urban and world dynamics modeling. The Battelle Susquehanna Model (BSM) has three main sectors—demographics, economics, and water flow—and it permits considerable variation in constraints, assumptions, and parameter settings (Hamilton et al., 1969). It is of the same generic class as the Forrester models. We discuss BSM here for its intrinsic value, but more importantly for the lessons we can learn about the process of developing a dynamic computer simulation model.

It is difficult to determine exactly how Forrester went about the initial formulation of the Forrester Urban Model (FUM), discussed in the next section. Forrester does tell us in his Preface that he owes initial inspiration to the lucky accident of John F. Collins, past mayor of Boston, having an office nearby when he was appointed visiting professor at the Sloan School of Management. One sees a parallel here to the field of "expert systems," in which it is recognized that the individuals developing the "expert system" on the computer must have access to a recognized human expert in the field in order to discover the heuristics used by the human expert.

In the case of BSM, we see the more typical case of a continuing interaction between a systems team and the clients, a group of electric utilities serving the Susquehanna basin. The Battelle team grasped that river flow was an important variable, and that long-term management of the Susquehanna and its basin is important to the life of the region. This realization is a result of the Battelle team generalizing the goals of the clients. The clients did not bring this realization with them initially. The sequence of steps in the client dialogue appears to have been approximately as given in Table 5.10.

It might appear that the definition of three major sectors in the BSM model was obvious. This is not so, however. We can see from Appendix A of Hamilton et al.

TABLE 5.10. Steps in the Initial Problem Definition Phase of the Battelle Susquehanna River Basin Simulation Model Project

1. Sponsor agrees on a dynamic simulation of the Susquehanna Basin to determine the role of water supply on the development of the region's economy.
2. Decision to include regional economic variables and water resources as sectors within the same model.
3. Recognition that population levels and demographic factors will influence economic and water sectors.
4. Elaboration of employment demand and supply. Skill spectrum of region working population recognized as important.

(1969) that this seemingly straightforward order was imposed only *ex post facto*. In the original BSM model there were only two sectors, economic and water. Only subsequently was demographics recognized as a critical factor. Further study showed that a complete water audit and other aspects of the water sector had been overemphasized initially. Still another early emphasis in the project, later deemphasized, was data collection.

Figure 5.5 shows the three major sectors of BSM. The water sector builds a water budget for a number of critical points along the main branches of the Susquehanna. Water withdrawn by various industries is tied to the employment sector by coefficients that relate water use per employee, industry by industry. Water returned by industry and rainfall is added to the budget as appropriate. Pollution injected at a point can be followed downstream by means of flow and diffusion calculations. Other sectors have equivalent budgets and the cross-coupling among sectors shows the overall

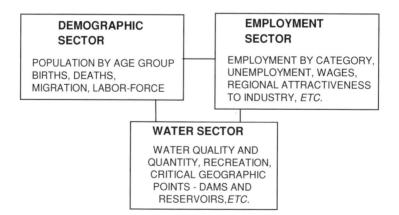

FIGURE 5.5 The three major sectors of the Battelle Susquehanna River Basin simulation Model. The text describes the iterative process used by the Battelle systems team to arrive at the specific three sectors described here. The text by Hamilton et al. (1969), contains a wealth of information on modeling philosophy.

TABLE 5.11. Concepts Utilized or Discovered in the Battelle Susquehanna Study

- "There is no such thing as a general [purpose] regional model." One builds a model to supply answers to a class of questions defined *a priori*.
- An iterative approach should be used. One learns to understand the problem by working it. One must be willing to modify the model as understanding deepens.
- It is important to build the first-cut model rapidly. Time used in perfecting interim steps toward a first-cut model is wasted. One cannot understand the problem until the first-cut model is running, if then.
- A model should be constructed to be used. <u>A model should seldom, if ever, be considered as the output of a study</u> (Hamilton et al., 1969, p. 4).
- A model is not a device for producing optimal or single-valued projections. Rather, it is a means of facilitating understanding of complicated interactions relative to policy-making (Hamilton et al., 1969, p. 55).
- "... One should be careful not to just build a model of a region without an end in mind. A model is a means to an end; not an end in itself... the goal is understanding of the specified phenomena, and not the model itself" (Hamilton et al., 1969, p. 101). **This point is so important and so at variance with common thinking it is hard to overemphasize it**.
- "Use of the model simply to make projections is fraught with danger. Some projections will be good for one purpose and not for others. Many potential users will not understand how the projections were derived and will expect unreasonable accuracy.... Major plans may be made as though the numbers were God-given" (Hamilton et al., 1969, p. 111).

Source: Hamilton et al. (1969).

impact of various incidents, heavy rainfall, unemployment in a given industry, and so on.

Our purpose here is not to discuss technical details of BSM, but rather to focus on the process of model-building itself. We have already mentioned a number of principles discovered or employed by the Battelle team. Table 5.11 gives several additional points.

5.15 THE FORRESTER URBAN MODEL (FUM) AND SOCIETAL VALUES

In his seminal text on urban dynamics, Forrester takes a block diagram approach to modeling what he called the fundamental processes of the city over a 250-year time period (Forrester, 1969a). These fundamental processes are business activity, housing, and the working population. Forrester (1969a, p. 17) argues that these are the fundamental processes that determine the development of the city. "These three subsystems are more fundamental than city government, social culture, or fiscal policy." Forrester sees a temporal progression in each of these categories. New industry is created, becomes mature, declines, and is demolished. Luxury homes for managers are built, decline to worker housing and finally to slum housing and are finally demolished. Some worker homes and slum housing are created directly. Labor arrives and departs the city. Labor may also upgrade to managerial status or downgrade to unemployed. Some managers arrive and depart without being upgraded from labor and some unemployed arrive and depart directly. All of these basic elements are interrelated according to Forrester.

Engineers and scientists have little or no difficulty in understanding the technical aspects of the Forrester model. On the other hand, by our training and nature, we are likely to overlook an entirely different problem in the dynamic simulation of a social organization. We tend to be unconscious of implicit value structures and the biases they can introduce. Forrester's Urban Model (FUM) provides an example of such a problem.

Forrester argues that his model simulates the fundamental control processes of a city, and so it does—but only from one point of view. Forrester assumes that we will accept this point of view without question; that is, he doesn't bother to justify it. In fact, he does not admit that he has taken a position. He works as if his is the only correct view. He seems to be under the impression that his implicit value structure and consequent policies are the values and the policies of all right-thinking people. Thus, he never feels the need to articulate these values and policies or to subject them to analysis. Fewer than a dozen pages of *Urban Dynamics* are devoted to discussing the structure of the model and its philosophy, but from p. 14 et seq. of Forrester (1969a), we seem to be able to gather the following:

- "The World" is an infinite source and sink for all variables. People move into and out of the "the city," depending on whether world conditions are more or less favorable than those in the city. Only these two entities exist.
- Changes in housing stock, population levels, and industry levels are the central processes involved in the growth and stagnation of the city. Changes in city government, social culture, and fiscal policy are less fundamental.
- Aging housing and declining industry cause population migration from the city.
- If a low-cost housing program exists, it creates housing for the underemployed directly.

Many other direct cause/effect assumptions are implicit in Forrester's model. How should we approach the discussion of this model? We cannot refer to Forrester because it is plain from the text and his subsequent writings that he has not developed a philosophic objectivity about this model. He becomes defensive and answers objective criticism on an inappropriate level (Forrester, 1969b, 1970b, 1971). For example, in a generally complimentary review of Forrester's book, Kain raises several specific technical concerns as well as some general policy concerns. Forrester ignores the policy issues and moves directly to a technical defense. It appears that the questions of value structure and implicit, sometimes quite well-hidden, assumptions cannot be ignored in large-scale modeling.

Remarks on FUM will be divided into the following three levels: The most general is The Axiological Level, or the implicit value framework; next is The Policy Level, implicit or explicit goals developed from the axiological level; and, finally there is The Structural Level, consisting of specific technical elements of FUM and their interconnections.

The Axiological Level in FUM. The implicit value system in FUM is hidden. Forrester in fact was perhaps unconscious of the fact that he was working from a value structure. Here are some of the values that appear to be operative.

- Dedication to the World of Work. Forrester subscribes to the concept that individuals are attracted to the city and leave it, based on immediate economic wellbeing. Forrester's urban world is subsumed in the world of work.
- The Concept of Progress. FUM people subscribe to the concept of moving upscale economically, or leaving the city. This implies acceptance of the principle of deferred gratification.
- The Frontier Concept. FUM ignores the idea of an urban community living in harmony with its environment. Rather, it trades with the world to seek advantages. There is no attempt at urban renewal, for example. Industry and housing are started, mature, and inexorably decline.
- Defensive Economic Imperialism. The city does not expand or contract. Land area remains constant.
- Permanence of Value Structure. FUM models the city over a 250-year period. Forrester writes of 20-year transients during which "good" policies may show temporary "bad" effects—that is, for most of the transient. But the value structure is fixed.

The issue here is not whether we "like" these values or whether Forrester likes or dislikes them. We ask only whether we have correctly extracted the values from the model and whether they correctly represent reality over the period 1900 A.D. through 2150 A.D. Forrester could argue that this is a "base-line model," which represents in a limited way the value structure in 1900 A.D., and that a drift in values from these base assumptions explains why cities appear to be in trouble today. Forrester could then suggest that variations in the base-line model be explored to determine their effects. This is a standard scientific process and has been taking place since Forrester's original publication. Perhaps this is what Forrester intended all along, and his show of intransigence and defensiveness was merely to get the systems community stirred up. If so, he succeeded.

The Policy Level in FUM. Many policy decisions are buried in FUM. Sometimes the policies are in accord with the value structure discussed above and sometimes not. These contradictions are not intentional and could have been avoided had Forrester proceeded properly in the axiological component, rather than ignoring it. Here are some of the policies buried in FUM.

- Increase City Attractiveness for Laborers and Managers. This policy is consistent with the value of economic imperialism. The policy is implemented in five steps: provide jobs, arrange upward economic mobility, provide good worker housing, destroy slum housing, and lower taxes.

- Drive Away Underemployed. This is accomplished in two steps. Destroy slum housing and decrease taxes, thus reducing support and benefits for underemployed.
- Balance City Budget. "(1) Low-income households cost the city more in taxes than they pay, whereas the city makes a profit on high-income households. (2) Growing businesses are an unqualified good because they pay taxes and, by assumption, cost the city nothing in services. (3) Increases in local taxes and increases in local government expenditures produce 'adverse' changes in the city's population and employment structure" (Kain, 1969).

Is it possible to argue that some of these "values" are merely artifacts due to the model limitations? For example, because only the city and the world exist and the world is an infinite resource, if the city becomes attractive to underemployed individuals, the world can supply an infinite number of them. Forrester (1969a, p. 123) appears to foreclose this argument:

> People are the fundamental generator of municipal expenditure. People require welfare. People require police and fire departments. People require transportation. People use schools. People demand city services. Unless people are economically able to support these services and be politically responsible for authorizing them, the urban system is almost sure to be self-defeating . . . and then only if the revenue is highly correlated with the people who require the expenditure will the city have a self-regulating system which generates a population able to sustain a healthy city and to pay for the urban services they desire.

Apparently, however, Forrester is somewhat uncomfortable with the consequences of this policy statement, because he goes out of his way to say, (Forrester, 1969a, p. 8) "Although the policies of slum demolition and new-enterprise construction in Figure 1.3 have reduced the underemployed population, this has not been done by driving underemployed from the city . . . . At all times after the inauguration of the new policies, the underemployed arrival rate into the city is higher and the departure rate is lower than before the policy changes."

Yet, when we examine his Chapter 5 as directed to corroborate this claim, we find it clearly not to be true. In his Figures 5.1, 5.4, 5.8, 5.10, and 5.12, we find that the departure rate increased and the arrival rate decreased, sometimes permanently, and at least for 20 years. Why is Forrester uncomfortable with this tactic of using underemployeds as trading stock—sending them away and recalling them to serve a higher need? Possibly it clashes with a value he feels he should hold or which is proclaimed by others. Perhaps with a more clearly articulated value structure, Forrester could have remained more objective about these (distressing?) results, or he might rearrange his value set, or work to eliminate the cause. Forrester might be comforted if he knew that Saint Thomas More, in *Utopia*, utilized the same process in order to regulate the economic well-being of his ideal city. So perhaps this result isn't as "counterintuitive" as Forrester seems to think.

The Structural Level in FUM. Suppose we focus on only one small part of FUM to illustrate a portion of a structural analysis. Forrester develops an "attractiveness-for-migration multiplier" (AMM) by multiplying five other factors, each of which is the product of other factors and which are operated upon by nonlinear gains and time constants. AMM is one of the simplest of seven main factors in the model. While each individual concept in FUM is relatively simple, it is difficult to retain one's faith in the model as assumption after assumption, loop after loop, and nonlinearity after nonlinearity is added. A reality check is to examine limiting cases. How does the simplified model behave? Forrester does not indicate that he applied these tests.

Forrester makes much of the "counterintuitiveness" of the results of FUM. Possibly they are only counterintuitive in the sense that they are not true. We have forced the model to deal with land as a fixed and therefore valuable resource. Thus, why should we be surprised when this forces difficult (and unrealistic) choices? One may be forced by this constraint, and the imposed requirement to maximize wealth, to optimize by removing underproductive population sectors. Why should we be surprised that, with fixed land area, we are forced to replace slum housing, a negative wealth-producing factor, with tax-revenue-producing factories in order to maximize wealth?

5.16 EXTENSIONS AND VARIATIONS

We have taken considerable space to discuss a model that was superseded several decades ago and which was widely regarded as unrepresentative and unrealistic almost immediately upon publication. Why? First, because this type of modeling is intrinsically attractive. It takes a top-down approach that offers rewards commensurate with the effort. That is, we appear to get rough results for a rough model and better results as we refine the model. It is the recommended approach in large-scale-system analysis and is widely used. Thus we would like to focus on the concept if not the specific results.

The second reason for flogging this apparently dead horse is that the hard lessons the many critics of the Forrester Urban Model have tried to teach seem not yet to have been learned.[9] Forrester's errors of the 1960s were repeated in the IIASA energy model of the 1970s (Forrester, 1970; Keepin, 1984) and in the Nuclear Winter model of the 1980s (see below). In each instance, millions of dollars were wasted and perhaps, more importantly, world opinion was tricked into advocating public policy choices based on bad science.

Had systems simulation progressed beyond its early and obvious errors into a state of hard, rigorous, objective science in the past 30 years, we would need only to salute Forrester for the brilliant innovator he is. Unfortunately, his modern followers seem to be amplifying his early errors and to be even more careless with truth, until now, one believes a large-scale system simulation at one's peril. We will close this chapter with one more simulation horror story and finally add one positive example.

The "Nuclear Winter" Model. In the fall of 1983, a media event of major proportions was set rolling by Carl Sagan, the well-known TV science personality, who was a Professor of Astronomy at Cornell. Based on a totally inadequate, simplistic, one-dimensional computer simulation, it was predicted that a single tactical nuclear exchange in Europe could raise such a dust cloud as to affect global weather seriously for a year or more. Subzero temperatures and elimination of one or more growing seasons, it was claimed, would trigger "... an extinction event equal to or more severe than that at the close of the Cretaceous Period when dinosaurs and many other species died out ...."

Although substantial criticism of the simulation's shallowness was lodged informally almost immediately by a number of respected scientists, Sagan and company proceeded to hire a Madison Avenue PR outfit and to produce alarmist predictions in print and for TV (Seitz, 1986). Now, the model has been thoroughly discredited, but the damage done to the integrity of simulation modeling could be serious and long-lasting. Are we seeing similar issues with the global warming models that are prevalent today?

Royal Dutch Shell Petroleum Demand and Supply Model. Prior to 1965, Royal Dutch Shell planners began to be disturbed with what they felt to be a lack of corporate preparation for troubled and uncharted waters ahead in the world supply and demand for petroleum products. They decided to abandon their traditional forecasting approach to long-range planning and to adopt a scenario generation approach (Wack, 1985a,b).

The two articles by Pierre Wack cited above provide an excellent case study of the difficulties of introducing the scenario concept to managers. The Shell planners placed a high probability on an upheaval in petroleum supplies due to world conditions. This predated by several years the formation of OPEC. But the reaction of high-level line managers within Shell, with whom this highly confidential prognosis was shared, surprised and perplexed Wack and his planning associates. Rather than dismay or disbelief, for which the planners were prepared, the line managers seemed aloof and disinterested.

How could these bright and dedicated managers seem unconcerned when the planners predicted catastrophe ahead? Wack postulates that the planning scenarios were excessively general when first presented. The managers found it hard to relate to their own shorter-range concerns. Wack did not abandon the scenario approach. Rather, he and the team disaggregated their general scenario into separate and specific pieces, each of which addressed short-term operating issues faced by each manager.

Thus, rather than a generalized question such as, "What should Royal Dutch Shell do about the impending problem?", each manager was asked what he planned to do about several specific issues within his personal span of control. This did the trick. Interest became intense. Probing questions were asked about the scenarios, and planning initiatives were accelerated. Partly as a result of this forethought, Shell survived the turbulent initial OPEC price-advance period with less harm than most of the other international oil majors.

5.17 WHERE TO GO FROM HERE?

Creative alternative generation is critical to successful systems analysis efforts. Through practice stories, historical cases, and representative techniques, we have, hopefully, illustrated the inherent complexities in this critical step of an analysis and warned of the potential pitfalls. Given a robust set of alternatives, we can now proceed to the phase of a systems analysis: ranking the alternatives. We must, however, keep in mind the iterative nature of this process and realize that we are likely to revisit the development of alternative candidate solutions.

EXERCISES

5.1 Section 5.6 ends with some skeptical comments on dynamic confrontation as a management tool. Yet, on the other hand, is there evidence that being agreeable and seeking corporate harmony above all will get the job done? Psychologists tell us that a fundamental life-process is that of challenge and response.
Clearly, one can cite examples and anecdotes "pro" and "con" for each approach. But, rather than an anecdotal analysis in this exercise, we wish to take an SA approach to the issue. Under what specific work-environment conditions would the confrontation management style likely to be successful and where would it likely be less successful? Repeat for a high interpersonal interaction, "feel-good" style.

5.2 Consider the elements of a conservative entry into the new business venture shown in Figure 5.1 and plot the option profile. Does that profile give a closer match to the corporate culture profile? Suppose your client decides on the aggressive market entry shown in the option field shown in Table 5.9. What specific steps would you as the analyst suggest, in order to improve the probability of success?

5.3 Consider that we are going to start an internet site from scratch. Use brainstorming and/or brainwriting in teams to generate ideas for the new business. Then use the Options Field method to determine several Options Profiles.

5.4 During the past decade, there has been considerable discussion about the issue of illegal immigration from Mexico into the United States. Recently (2006), a major effort has been launched to build a significant fence the length of the border. Use the Options Field method and generate several options profiles for a barrier to entry from Mexico into the United States. How does this relate to Chapter 3 and the concept of iteration?

CASE STUDY: WINNEBAGO

A U.S. couple in their early fifties is considering purchasing a Winnebago (http://www.rvlife.com) type vehicle for their vacations. However, they are not sure if this is a wise choice.

Prepare an analysis for them.

CASE STUDY: DISTANCE LEARNING IN THE FUTURE?

Revisiting this case from Chapter 3, generate candidate alternatives.

HISTORICAL CASE STUDY: REAL-TIME TELEVISION LINK WITH MARS ORBITER[10]

The chief responsibility of the National Space Agency (NSA) Subgroup Coordination Division is to coordinate the design of space component subsystems of space flight vehicles. Currently, Subgroup Coordination is concerned with the feasibility of a real-time television link (RTTV) for a manned Mars mission. The story begins when Subgroup Coordination becomes aware that NSA center management is concerned about the success of the proposed RTTV. Subgroup Coordination has 10 days to extract itself from its dilemma.

People Involved

Gordon G. Lattimer—Division Chief at Subgroup Coordination. A long-time propulsion engineer at NSA, quite competent and close to retirement. His space experience began with the Mercury Project over 30 years ago and he was recently moved to his current assignment.

Marian A. Hammil—Director of Space Mission Operations and an excellent coordinator. One major job is to keep upper division NSA management aware of ongoing scientific development projects scheduled for future flights.

Henry R. Wilson—Division Chief of the Scientific Data Collection group. His main task is to determine what data should be taken and how information should be converted to a format which allows evaluation.

David B. Downs—Director of the NSA Public Relations Office. His job is to make sure NSA's space achievements reach the public eye in a favorable light. His job can be critical when funding is a problem in Congress.

Dr. Hla Shwe—Division Chief of the Hardware Development Division. His main responsibility is to oversee the development of space hardware for future flights.

Supervisors 1, 2, and 3—All supervisors in Subgroup Coordination are under Mr. Lattimer.

Exhibit 1

National Space Agency

Space Vehicle Design Center

TO: Gordon G. Lattimer, Division Chief
          Subgroup Coordination, NSA

FROM: Marian A. Hammil, Director
          Space Mission Operations, NSA

RE: T.V. Link on Proposed Manned Mars Mission

DATE: January 10, 20–

It appears from the latest briefing that the manned Mars mission slated for later in this century is proceeding on schedule. Because of the tremendous success of our lunar TV. link in the Apollo series, NSA feels that RTTV would provide valuable scientific information, permit greater ground/spacecraft interaction, and greatly enhance the public relations value of the flight, an important element for the maintenance of an ongoing space program.

Preliminary analysis indicates that existing RTTV systems, left over from Apollo, will not be adequate for the manned Mars Mission and that a totally new system must be designed. For this reason, NSA management would like Subgroup Coordination to do a preliminary analysis of the feasibility of an RTTV link for the Mars Mission. It is believed that this report would go a long way in determining the extensiveness of the effort necessary to design the RTTV link. Current plans call for NSA to supervise the entire mission and will continue in that role throughout post-flight analysis.

Sincerely yours,

Marian A. Hammil

Exhibit 2

National Space Agency

Space Vehicle Design Center

TO: Marian A. Hammil, Director
           Space Mission Operations, NSA

FROM: Gordon G. Lattimer, Division Chief
           Space Mission Operations, NSA

RE: Yours of January 10 on the RTTV for the MMM

DATE: July 10, 20–

We have been aware for some time of the critical nature of the RTTV in the public's perception of the success of NSA's MMM. Therefore the enclosed preliminary report on the feasibility of this "pacing technology" has been prepared by my Division, and is enclosed for your information.

Sincerely yours,

Gordon G. Lattimer

Exhibit 2— Continued

National Space Agency

Space Vehicle Design Center

PRELIMINARY REPORT ON THE FEASIBILITY OF RTTV LINK ON
MANNED MARS MISSION

SUBGROUP COORDINATION DIVISION, July 5, 20–

The first space photographs of Mars were taken by the unmanned Mariner IV in July, 1965, on a flyby mission. In 22 minutes, the television camera secured 19 useful photographs covering a strip 320 km wide and 4800 km long (approximately 1% of the surface). Manned missions to Mars are planned in the next 25 years.

The above history brings us to the present status of the Mars exploration program. Today, the Viking program is in full swing. The purpose of this program is to determine planet composition and whether or not conditions are favorable for the existence of life. Viking data are still being processed at this time, but it is expected that this one program will produce a vast measure in our knowledge concerning Mars. It is also assumed that data from this program will be used for the determination of a landing site for manned exploration.

Because of the success of the television communication system that accompanied Apollo astronauts, it is felt that this capability should be included in the Mars mission. It is hoped that this study will serve to outline the major areas of design that will need to be considered in a more detailed manner when mission objectives are more definite. The final result should be a communication system concept that will achieve the required performance (real-time video transmission from Mars to Earth) with minimum weight and minimum volume, with components and subsystems that can be developed within the available time span. Before realizing the end result, it was decided to commission this study to determine the primary feasibility of a real-time TV link between Mars and the Earth.

The first accomplishment of the study was to define the major subtasks. They are as follows:

1. Systems integration
2. R. F. modulation
3. Optical modulation
4. Video
5. Aiming

6. Power system
7. Configuration

Each of these areas has been investigated in this report in a very limited manner. The intent is to provide a preparatory survey for a more detailed analysis follow-on study to be initiated immediately.

System Integration. The purpose of the system integration subtask is to steer the subsystem design effort toward the system objectives and select from the resulting candidates subsystems that best meet overall system objectives. This task will need a well-defined method of approach established in order to assure progress will be made in an orderly fashion to the desired result. It is believed that this process will allow for the division of the total effort into small categories so that specific assignments can be made to project groups. With the task split, it is necessary to identify the interactions and establish the necessary communication. Proper procedures will allow for the orderly selection of optimum alternatives along with the smooth interfacing of the subsystem.

Radio-Frequency Modulation. The purpose of this portion of the study is to define the constraints on a wide-band communication link between Mars and Earth using a radio-frequency signal. Attention will be focused on the Mars/Earth link, because this is the most difficult aspect of the communication system due to the large space loss. The space loss will be the most significant constraint on the system because the distance between Mars and Earth varies from 54×10^6 to 400×10^6 km with the minimum distance occurring every two years. The picture information will have to be transmitted over a period of 1–20 days. An attempt to shorten the transmission distance by adjusting the launch date would disrupt the overall mission profile by drastically increasing the length of the mission and/or energy requirements. Current mission profile plans indicate a transmission distance of 140×10^6 km.

Another problem will be that of telemetry bandwidth. Commercial television requires a bandwidth of 4.5 MHz and the design objective of 5 MHz was selected in order to provide for other information which will accompany the real-time pictures.

The command bandwidth could also cause problems. The command link will not be transmitting pictures to the spacecraft. Rather, the uplink information would probably consist of a good-quality audio signal. A high-quality audio signal would require a bandwidth of 6000–8000 Hz using FM modulation. Quality bandwidth would be limited by the human ear capability. A quality audio-command signal would probably be a requirement because of the desired accuracy of information transmitted and the positive psychological effect on the crew. Thus, the telemetry link remains as the critical factor in this communication system.

Other problems come into play when selecting the carrier frequency. The selection of this parameter has a direct effect on the cost of the communication system. Space loss increases as the frequency is squared, and the attenuation due to the Earth's atmosphere must be added.

Antenna gain is another variable that is frequency-dependent. For a given-size antenna, antenna gain may be increased as the frequency is squared. The antenna beamwidth would decrease, but this beamwidth reduction benefits the system performance as long as it is large enough not to impinge upon the pointing system capabilities. It has been determined that for the frequency range being considered and feasible antenna size for the spacecraft, the bandwidth imposes no restrictions on the antenna gain and frequency trade-off.

There are also political constraints on the radio-frequency spectrum, as well as physical. The spectrum has been divided by international agreements. The International Telecommunication Union in Geneva, Switzerland, is the principal agency for establishing international agreements. Allocations for radio astronomy, space research, scientific research, industrial uses, satellite communications, meteorological satellites, space telemetry, space commands, and aeronautical navigation were made, and deep-space telemetry command and tracking were allocated the range from 2.11 to 2.30 GHz.

Optical Communication. Interest in laser developments is greatly enhanced by its potentially advantageous use in communication. The high-intensity, low-dispersion beam of light radiation that emanates from the laser is capable of providing a high information rate transmission with applications ranging from near to deep space communication. The requirements for light energy transmission and its accurate modulation appear to be satisfied by current laser systems. Perhaps more emphasis is now being placed on the design of peripheral equipment to bring laser communication to fruition for specific applications. The requirements of the ultimate communication system will then make more specific demands on fundamental improvements and peripheral techniques.

Laser communication techniques will compete directly with the microwave techniques for the transmission of wide bandwidth high information rate data. Although the state-of-the-art microwave technique is superior, there are indications that the inherent advantages of high-intensity and low-power requirements of the laser can be exploited by continued research and development. Although the communication systems will differ in type and quality, they all have certain elements in common: the power source, modulator, transmitter, and receiver. The most important aspect of the design, given the laser source (includes power supply), will be the modulation techniques used in the development of a communication system. Methods for optical modulation will be one area of intense research before the system will become space-qualified. Transmission and reception are usually considered separate entities, but their function can be carried out by one piece of equipment—the telescope. Telescope design will be another area of detailed research later in the project.

Video Systems. The characteristics of the video system determine the operating bandwidth, and consequently, the degree of sophistication, of the overall communication network. Some of the criteria needed in order to determine the optimum video system properly within limited size and weight constraints will be presented here.

It should be kept in mind that, no matter what the mission profile, the basic goal of any communications network is to transmit to the receiving station the most scientifically useful information possible within the established limits. The quality of the information received is dependent on the acquisition system—in this particular case, the cameras.

The question of what type of information would be most valuable for man's purposes should take into account the following:

1. The real advantage of a wideband communications system is to return information back to earth at a real time rate.
2. Because the mission will be manned, it can be assumed that at least part of the payload will be returned to Earth. Therefore, ultra-high-resolution reconnaissance pictures that are not immediately needed can be stored on film and returned with the astronauts.
3. Despite real-time or high rate transmission, the tremendous distance over which the signal is broadcast will cause at least a 10-minute lag in the receipt of the image.

Because of these considerations, it is believed that further video system design will be broken down into four subsystems: (1) short distance (from Mars surface) camera systems, (2) long-range (orbiter) camera systems, (3) signal preparation systems, and (4) storage systems. Each of the above systems will require detailed design work in the future.

Antenna Aiming Subsystem. Prompt and accurate transmission of the television pictures back to Earth is a prime mission requirement, as the manned space capsule travels in its orbit about Mars. Precise pointing of the transmitter antenna toward Earth will be required. The question that must be posed is: what positioning accuracy is required and what system can best be selected to obtain this position accuracy? It is generally accepted that positioning accuracy will be dictated by the type of system selected to control the position of the antenna. The problem is one of controlling the antenna aiming error. As an example of the seriousness of the error, a 24-arc-second aiming error would cause a beam of light directed at the center of Earth to miss Earth completely.

It is believed that the final system will be one of the following:

A. *Astro-inertial Control System.* This system is a self-contained control system; that is, it requires no aid or cooperation from equipment external to the capsule.
B. *Laser Beam Control System.* This system has the spacecraft continually tracking a laser beacon located on Earth.

C. *Earth-Capsule Radio Command Control System.* This system uses a radio signal to control the error. The principal problem with this system is the large time lags between Earth and the capsule caused by the transmission of information at the finite speed of light. This problem has been solved to a large extent. As the capsule travels through space, it will transmit its instantaneous antenna position back to Earth. These data will be fed into an Earth-based computer. The computer will process the data and, after the prediction is performed, the future spacecraft antenna position will be transmitted to the capsule. Stepper motors will then be activated to position the antenna precisely.

The astro-inertial and radio command systems are on the shelf, but the laser beam control system will need substantial design work.

Electrical Power Systems. By definition, the electrical power system consists of "all equipment which generates, converts, controls, and distributes electrical power within the spacecraft, whether it be generated from batteries, fuel cells, photovoltaic devices, and so on." Included in this definition is (a) the radiation shielding required when nuclear heat sources are employed, (b) consumable fuels with their tanks when chemical fuel cells (or engines) are used, and (c) systems using solar concentrators, or cells, as a heat source which require energy storage devices (generally batteries) for dark periods of operation.

All systems provide for peak power demand by utilizing reserve primary power or by relying upon batteries. If batteries are used, they are recharged during a low-power-demand period. Reserve primary power units, either running at low output or in a standby mode, are generally provided as part of the basic power system in order to improve system reliability by redundancy. The degree of redundancy varies for different missions, as well as for the different types of power systems, depending upon the development status of the system and past experience with it.

A great variety of potential power systems involving different energy sources, storage, and conversion techniques is available. Power system weight will be an important criterion used in system selection; however, it is not impossible that heavier systems may be selected for other reasons, such as freedom from nuclear radiation, or experience with a specific system higher reliability, or the availability of existing hardware or technology.

Various space missions require several specific types of spacecraft modules, each of which can be categorized by its function in the mission profile. All of the modules provide electrical power for environmental control, life support, communications, and spacecraft operations; whereas electrical power for experiments and data processing is usually provided only in the mission module and excursion module. The mission duration and flight environment, as well as the operating characteristics of the power system, generally dictate the type of power systems considered for each of the modules. In addition, the propulsion system used for the mission influences the power system choice; for example, missions using nuclear propulsion generally use nuclear power systems because of the possibility of utilizing the same radiation shield, thereby reducing the power system weight.

There will be three types of spacecraft modules needed for the mission. Each one is presented with a short discussion of its particular needs.

Mission Module: The function of the mission module generally consists of housing for the entire crew for the duration of an orbital flight and/or providing round trip transportation of the crew between Earth, lunar, or Mars orbit. The mission module is usually not recovered from these types of flights. Because a great deal of time is spent in the mission module, its power supply will run almost the full duration of the mission. This allows the consideration of almost all types of power sources.

Excursion Module: The excursion module provides the round trip transportation between an orbiting mission module and the Martian surface. The characteristics that affect the power system selection are that it must:

1. undergo the deceleration and acceleration loads associated with a manned landing,
2. provide for the support of only part of the crew, and
3. operate in what is still an unknown environment.

Earth Re-entry Module: Earth re-entry modules represent the vehicles by which the crew is returned to Earth. These modules generally use atmospheric braking, thus requiring the power system to operate under high deceleration loads. The power system considered for these modules generally operates only for a few hours at a relatively low power output. Silver–zinc batteries are the most probable battery power source of re-entry power.

The selection of a spacecraft power system for a specific mission is a function of:

1. environmental conditions—that is, acceleration, radiation, and so on,
2. power requirements of the mission, and
3. mission duration.

The above questions must be answered for each particular module before the matching of power supplies with spacecrafts can occur.

There are several types of power systems available to the design engineers. Various systems will be presented with brief comments about each.

Solar Power Systems. Solar radiation, the only free source of power in space, covers a range of frequencies including visible light. Basically, there are two types of systems. They are as follows:

Solar Cells. Solar cells are not light in weight and must be directed at the sun at all times. Without constant sunlight, no power is available. Solar cells are very costly and subject to damage in space because of their sheet-like nature.

Solar Concentrators. Solar concentrators can be extremely light. The major problem is that they must be pointed accurately at the sun. There are some design problems at present, which means cost estimates vary widely.

Nuclear Power Systems. Nuclear systems convert the thermal energy available from nuclear reactors or isotope decay into electricity by utilizing the same conversion cycles employed with solar power systems. The primary advantage of the nuclear systems is that high power can be generated for a long duration without being dependent on the position relative to the sun; radiation being the main disadvantage. The shielding requirements for manned spacecraft are much less if a radioisotope heat source is used, rather than a reactor; however, in either case, the shield design is strongly influenced by factors such as external spacecraft operations and properties of the outside environment.

Chemical Power Systems. Chemical power systems include engines connected to turbo-alternator units, fuel cells which combine reactants producing electricity directly and batteries which store electrical energy. All of the chemical power systems are limited to short duration power demands because of their high specific weights. There are two types of chemical systems that will be considered.

Fuel Cells. Fuel cells can be designed to operate on a variety of reactants; however, the hydrogen–oxygen fuel cell has received major emphasis in the manned spacecraft program because of its high efficiency and because potable water is obtained in addition to electricity.

Batteries. Primary batteries (non-rechargeable) are generally considered for spacecraft power systems when the power level cell is receiving the greatest consideration; advanced designs using other compounds are also being considered.

Configuration. The configuration of a spacecraft and the propulsion modules are completely determined by the mission requirements and objectives. Although there are generally several competing methods of achieving a particular task, one will prove to be the obvious choice when all of the facts can be considered against the overall mission constraints and objectives. It would seem then that choosing the correct configuration is a trivial task. The difficulty lies in obtaining all the facts concerning the decision and identifying the mission objectives. In many cases, the mission objectives themselves may not be completely specified. If, for example, it is learned during the course of design and development that some additional, previously unconsidered but desirable, objective could be had at a bargain price and the money were available, it could be included. On the other hand, a prime objective might be deleted if, during the course of the program, some unforeseen technical problem could not be solved in the time frame allotted. The "facts" or pertinent information concerning a task or design may require extensive analysis, tests, or experimentation or combinations of these to learn. In some cases, the information comes easy and in others it is never obtained, due to the difficulty or expense involved.

Some of the steps required to arrive at a configuration to achieve a specific goal are presented. In general, the only information required to configure an object is its size. The size and shape of all the objects that constitute a spacecraft depend on their functions. It is therefore necessary to determine what functions must be performed to accomplish the mission objectives. When the functions have been identified, a device can then be configured to perform that function. Because one of the mission objectives is to travel to Mars, the velocity increment requirements dictate that weight is of prime importance. This says that not only the function and size of the object must be determined, but also its weight.

Summary. It is hoped that this preliminary study will provide Subgroup Coordination with added insight into design projects of the future concerning a real-time TV link with Mars. At this point, it is felt that a better understanding of mission objectives is needed before detailed design work can be carried out.

Exhibit 3

National Space Agency

Space Vehicle Design Center

TO: Gordon G. Lattimer, Division Chief
          Subgroup Coordination, NSA

FROM: Henry R. Wilson, Division Chief
          Scientific Data Coordination

RE: Manned Mars RTTV Link Report

DATE: July 20, 20–

The report reviewed by my office seems to be quite indefinite on the matter of image quality. It should be pointed out that there are several methods of storing high-quality image information for transmission at a later time. That is, for scientific purposes, high-quality real-time TV images are unnecessary. In fact, the goal of designing for a real-time communication link seems to be quite wasteful, because this goal can be easily met through the use of data storage and delayed transmission. As Subgroup Coordination is aware, this alternative would decrease bandwidth requirements that would permit a much reduced radiated-power level. For this reason, our group believes that low-quality real-time images would be sufficient, and then high-quality images could be transmitted with a time delay. Indeed, perhaps the entire RTTV concept is faulty.

Sincerely yours,

Henry R. Wilson

Exhibit 4

National Space Agency

Space Vehicle Design Center

TO: Gordon G. Lattimer, Division Chief
        Subgroup Coordination, NSA

FROM: David B. Downs, Director
        Public Relations, NSA

RE: Feasibility Report of RTTV Link for Manned Mars Mission

DATE: July 21, 20–

Our office supports wholeheartedly your efforts to design a real-time TV link for the Mars Mission scheduled for the end of this century. In order for the American public to fully participate in these missions, it is necessary for them to achieve a feeling of presence. This feeling can be achieved quite effectively through the use of a real-time TV link. In order for this link to be successful, image quality should be as close as possible to that experienced by commercial television. For this reason, high-quality image transmission must be a top-priority goal of any real-time TV link designed for the Mars Mission. It is important that NSA realize that the American public pays the bills for these missions and that a good relationship with the public is essential to continued NSA support. For this reason, anything short of a high-quality real-time TV image could cause a lack of public participation in the project. NSA must constantly show that their efforts are done with the intention that the taxpayer is the audience and the ultimate judge of its effort.

Sincerely yours,

David B. Downs

Exhibit 5

National Space Agency

Space Vehicle Design Center

TO: Gordon G. Lattimer, Division Chief
         Subgroup Coordination, NSA

FROM: Dr. Hla Shwe, Division Chief
         Hardware Development Division, NSA

RE: Feasibility Report on RTTV Link for Manned Mars Mission

DATE: July 28, 20–

Our office was slightly confused by the report issued from your group. It seems that the study just completed has little or no appreciation for the technical problems involved in such a system design. Some of the problems mentioned just briefly should be examined in heavy detail before proceeding on with the system design. For example, the problem of antenna pointing is substantial and should be solved before the feasibility analysis proceeds. What if the antenna pointing problem cannot be solved? This would make the concept on a RTTV link meaningless, because it would be technically impossible. For example, my rough calculations indicate that a pointing accuracy of 0.01 seconds of arc would be necessary if the beam from the space capsule is to hit the Earth at all! This is close to, if not beyond, the current state-of-the-art of pointing systems. For this reason, it is our belief that a highly intensified study be initiated to do the same basic report over in much greater detail. However, this time, specialists should be called in when needed to solve technical problems as they arise. This would give the finished report more integrity and stability that would allow it to stand alone. After all, NSA staff consists of many highly experienced specialists who could lend their expertise to such a study rather than relying on people with only a passing familiarity with some of these areas to do this type of work.

Sincerely yours,

Hla Shwe

Exhibit 6

National Space Agency

Space Vehicle Design Center

TO: Gordon G. Lattimer, Division Chief
          Subgroup Coordination, NSA

FROM: Marian A. Hammil, Director
          Space Mission Operations, NSA

RE: TV Link on Proposed Manned Mars Mission

DATE: August 20, 20–

It has come to my attention that there are problems concerning the determination of the preliminary feasibility of a TV link on the manned Mars mission. It appears that certain fundamental questions are being asked which should be answered before any more effort should be expended. Some of the problems which need to be solved for the RTTV link to become reality are quite critical and may be the pacing developments of the entire mission. It is for this reason that clarification must get underway as soon as possible.

Because of the need for immediate results, I have been informed that a tiger team may be formed by NSA Headquarters to attack this matter. This of course disturbs me because a tiger team operating in my directorate is a nuisance and is potentially embarrassing. I have convinced my superiors to give you 10 days to attempt a solution to the dilemma. I hope that this matter will receive your immediate attention and support.

Sincerely yours,

Marian A. Hammil

Exhibit 7

National Space Agency

Space Vehicle Design Center

TO: Supervisors, Subgroup Coordination, NSA

FROM: Gordon G. Lattimer, Division Chief
            Subgroup Coordination, NSA

RE: RTTV Link for Mars Mission

DATE: August 22, 20–

Enclosed in this memo you will find copies of all feedback received on the preliminary report concerning the feasibility of a real-time TV link for the upcoming manned Mars mission. The criticism indicates mixed feelings as to the success of the report. The major problem at hand is to determine the status of the feasibility of a real-time TV link with Mars so development can proceed on schedule. Because of the seriousness of the dilemma, a meeting has been scheduled in order to discuss this problem. The meeting is scheduled for 1300 hr today (August 22, 20–).

It is imperative that at this meeting we make the right decision on this critical issue. The threat of a tiger team being formed in 9 days does not give us much time.

Sincerely yours,

Gordon G. Lattimer

[Dialogue from the August 22 meeting at Subgroup Coordination. Mr. Lattimer chaired the meeting.]

(Meeting began with a brief account of the history of the problem—omitted here.)

Lattimer: "As you can see, our dilemma is quite acute. We are in a bind as far as time goes, and as far as progress toward our original goal: the feasibility of a TV link with Mars. Quite frankly, gentlemen, I'm at a loss, and that is why I called this meeting. The project as stated in the January 10 memo from Ms. Hammil seemed so specific, but evidently it was not specific enough. Now we are faced with a problem that no NSA supervisor would enjoy, the formation of a tiger team. I was a tiger team member two years ago that examined a critical issue at another NSA site. I assure you that it is not a pleasant experience for the people being investigated. At best, a tiger team is a nagging headache and it could make us all look like a bunch of fools. We have only 8 days to come up with an answer. So what did we do wrong and what are we going to do about it so that our heads don't roll?"

Supervisor 1: "Perhaps there are forces or values operating in this project that we did not see. Our problem may be one of breadth and not depth."

Supervisor 2: "No, that can't possibly be the answer. We should have come up with a specific system in our report. Our main problem stems from our inability to reconcile choices of alternatives so that specific designs could be offered. If we had offered a specific detailed design, we would have received almost no criticism, because the design would have been definite and criticism would have been useless."

Supervisor 3: "The next question is, could we design an optimal system without articulating the values of all potential groups?"

Lattimer: "I am hesitant to bring in all concerned groups, because we might not be able to handle the conflicts. Perhaps there is someone who has had problems similar to those we are facing."

Supervisor 1: "Perhaps the System Engineering group over in Building 4 could help us on this problem. They made a significant contribution to the Apollo mission on problems that needed quick solutions."

Lattimer: "I'm inclined to agree with you on this. Let's get in touch with these people and give them what we've got and let them wrestle with it awhile. I can't help but feel we have missed something fundamental somewhere, and they may pick it up. The study we did on the feasibility of a TV link with Mars was definitely inadequate, and they may come up with something better. We need to make sure they understand the urgency of the situation so that we can meet the 8-day deadline with substantive results."

Supervisor 1: "My only objection is what if they don't give us what we want? If we give them only 4 days, then we have a 4-day cushion."

Supervisor 3: "I agree, let's not put all our eggs in one basket."

Lattimer: "I have an even better idea: Why don't we give them 4 days and do our own study in the meantime. This way in 5 days we can meet and compare the reports. This way, we will have 3 days to review our position."

Supervisor 1: "Sounds good to me."

Supervisor 3: "I'll buy that."

Supervisor 2: "I'm still against it. They will produce a vague study with no direction and no substance. It will be littered with jargon and far-reaching goals and beautiful graphics, you know how those systems types operate. Their report will be totally useless from the operations standpoint. We should do a detailed design of an antenna system, for example, before we even waste any more money on the project."

Supervisor 3: "I agree with Gordon. Let's give these guys our dilemma and information, and let them fly with it awhile."

Lattimer: "I guess it's settled then. I'll get in touch with them today and give them what we've got."

Supervisor 1: "I just hope that we get what we need in 8 days. If we don't, it's going to be very tough on us."

Exhibit 8

The Tiger Team Concept

In order to rescue bogged-down projects at NSA, several strategies are used. One of them is to call in the outside contractor and present him with the circumstances and ask for recommendations. The contractor investigates the situation, and writes a report for NSA. The report should outline the problem and what to do to get the project back on schedule.

Another approach is to have NSA appoint its own special in-house, interdisciplinary team to do the same investigation. This approach has been called the "Tiger Team" method. The team members can be selected from all over NSA. It is the Tiger Team's job to critically examine the situation and determine what action is needed to resume the regular project schedule. A Tiger Team has little time and no patience. It is looked upon as an emergency remedial operation and is an invasion of ordinary management procedures. An NSA manager seldom survives more than one Tiger Team attack.

Exhibit 9

Glossary of Terms[11]

1. *Antenna Gain*: Sometimes called the gain factor, this is the ratio of the power transmitted along the beam axis to that of an isotropic radiator transmitting the same total power.
2. *Bandwidth*: In an antenna, the range of frequencies within which its performance, in respect to some characteristic, conforms to a specified standard. In a wave, the least frequency interval outside of which the power spectrum of a time-varying quantity is everywhere less than some specified fraction of its value at a reference frequency.
3. *Configuration*: A particular type of a specific aircraft, rocket, and so on, which differs from others of the same model by virtue of the addition or omission of auxiliary equipment.
4. *Dispersion*: The process in which radiation is separated into its component wavelengths.
5. *Frequency*: Of a function periodic in time, the reciprocal of the primitive period. The unit is the cycle per unit time and must be specified.
6. *Frequency Band*: A continuous range of frequencies extending between two limiting frequencies.
7. *Gain*: A general term used to denote an increase in signal power in transmission from one point to another.
8. *Isotropic Radiator*: An energy source that radiates uniformly in all directions.
9. *Modulation*: The variation in the value of some parameter characterizing a periodic oscillation. Specifically, variation of some characteristic of a radio wave, called the carrier corner wave in accordance with instantaneous values of another wave, called the modulating wave. Variation of the carrier frequency is frequency modulation.
10. *Spectrum*: Any series of energies arranged according to wavelength.
11. *Telemetry*: The science of measuring a quantity or quantities, transmitting the results to a distant station, and there interpreting, indicating, and/or recording the quantities measured.

HISTORICAL CASE STUDY: A HIGHWAY VEHICLE SIMULATOR RFP FROM DOT[12]

Dave Whitlock had plenty to think about as he walked back from lunch at the Executive dining room at National Electronics Corporate Headquarters. Whitlock had been made Vice President of Technical Marketing a few months previously, after a rapid rise in managing a high-tech R&D group doing business for N.E. with the Department of Defense. He knew that Ed Hargrove, Senior VP at N.E. for many years, had been helpful in his promotion. But he also knew that Ed had his eyes on John Gilbert's job as President.

Corporate Background

National Electronics is a diversified manufacturer of high-technology electrical and related products with important interests in man-made and natural resource materials and varied service businesses. Products and services are divided into nine segments: Consumer, Major Appliances, Industrial Systems, Power Systems, Aircraft Engines, Materials, Natural Resources, Technical Products & Services, and Financial Services.

National Electronics employs over a quarter of a million people around the world. Total sales for the nine segments in 1984 was $28.9 billion, with net earnings of $2.3 billion. Of the 18 key businesses in these segments, 15 were number one or two in market share. The three companies that were not in the top 1 or 2 were Transportation, Industrial Electronics, and Construction Services.

The Simulator RFP

As Dave entered his office, he closed the door and began thinking about his lunch-time conversation with Hargrove.

"Dave, I think you know I was in Washington last week and had lunch with Frank O'Dell. He is in the Highway Design Division of DOT. Of course, we don't do anything with that end of DOT. Almost all of our work is with the DOT research center in Cambridge. We have done little or no hardware design work for DOT. Most of our work has been in the modeling and impact study area. One reason for this is the research climate at DOT has been heading that way for the last 5 years. But we are mainly a hardware development company. Our accomplishments in hardware design are numerous, because we started in the appliance business and moved out.

"Well, Frank mentioned to me that they, the Highway Division at DOT, are going to issue an RFP next month on the task of designing and constructing a highway vehicle simulator (HVS). About 15 years ago, we had a guy working here at National Electronics who thought we should be in HVS design. Sort of a Link trainer for automobiles, I guess you could say. We wrote all kinds of proposals on HVSs with no success at all. Several were built by other people across the country, but the profit incentive for us looked marginal so we got out of it. In fact, we dropped it completely and ate 100% of the research cost as a bad venture.

"Stay with me, Dave, the story gets more interesting. As you know, our company has built several flight simulators over the last 15 years and our interest in this field is growing. It has been my contention that prowess in this field would make us competent to design an HVS of high quality and wide set of uses. About a year-and-half ago, I mentioned this to Dick White. Dick, as you know, is in charge of reading unsolicited proposals at DOT, and because most of our work is pioneering, we deal with him fairly often. I mentioned the HVS idea to him and I argued that new advances in technology might make the design of a realistic HVS a reality. I tried to point out to him our track record in pioneering research on flight simulators, both aircraft and spacecraft.

"White told me that they had done everything there was to do and knew everything there was to know about HVSs at DOT. He said flight simulators are successful because pilots key on instruments and not visual cues most of the time and this is not true in the auto environment. In autos, you have a rich visual field. I tried to tell him of the new advances in optics and how visual cues could be produced with realism. Dick completely turned me off the idea and said no such proposal would have a snowball's chance in hell of getting out the door at DOT. Well, I dropped the idea at once. No use wasting points. It looks as if the two groups at DOT don't talk to each other and we could get burned if we respond."

"Well, Ed, just a rough look at the situation tells us we have a small dilemma. We, more than any other company in business, are qualified to answer that proposal. What's more, we could even market scaled-down versions of an HVS, if it works, to driver training labs in every high school in the country! The profit potential here is certainly promising. A whole new market like that would certainly be an asset to our company."

"Yeah, but there is a risk involved in the thing, Dave. O'Dell thinks it will work and White disagrees violently. O'Dell is young and doesn't have much power at DOT, but White is in pretty solid because of the pioneering research he has sponsored in the past. Dick White has influence and he knows how to use it. Regardless of the profit of HVSs, we cannot afford to make an enemy out of Dick White. I don't want National Electronics to be involved in any internal war in DOT. Yet I feel the HVS idea is worth going after if we can get it with no ill feelings. If O'Dell makes it work at DOT he will become powerful and it would be in our best interests to have him on our side. There is no better way to do that than have National Electronics be the prime contractor for DOT's HVSs."

"Yeah, Ed, I see your point."

"The next question is what do we do about it? If we don't answer the RFP and the HVS idea becomes profitable for someone else, we will hear about it."

"Especially with all our previous experience at it. Not to capitalize on it could be embarrassing if it becomes someone else's profit."

"One other possibility is to answer the RFP and fail to get the contract and make Dick White mad in doing it. Even if we get the HVS contract, it is only one contract and we may lose future contracts with Dick White if we are not careful. So our best situation is to win the contract for HVS and still maintain strong ties with Dick White. Then we have both White and O'Dell in our pocket."

"Well, Ed, you've been at National Electronics for 30 years, and I've been here only 6 years, what are you going to do about it?"

"Oh, I have an idea."

"Let's hear it then."

"Dave, the man that gets the HVS contract and doesn't do any damage to the rest of our relationship at DOT will be an outstanding prospect for a great career at National Electronics. So far, the Marketing Division you head has done pretty much routine stuff. When I started that group and brought you in, I had hoped it would become an important part of our company's decision process in venture analysis. It seems to me this will never happen until the group identifies a highly profitable market passed over by regular channels. That's why I think your group should spend a week or so scoping out this concept before the RFP is published and see what you come up with. Essentially, do a market feasibility study of HVS first. This should tell us about the state-of-the-art and current marketability. From that, we should be able to project future marketability along with how many people will buy the product at a given price. By doing this, we should be able to determine potential profits in HVS production. If this study proves out, we can push for writing the proposal. During the next 3–4 weeks we can also watch the situation at DOT with White and O'Dell."

"I agree with you, Ed, that the only way the Marketing Division can get out front is by identifying a product that eventually becomes a substantial success. Our budget has been very small and we are understaffed for this type of work, but we can give it a hard try. I'm anxious to keep my career moving and I can see a chance to come to the front with this idea."

"Yeah. Well, you know John is going to retire in the next year and I would like to replace him as president. An outstanding success in this venture won't guarantee me the top spot, but it won't hurt me either. The new president will be hired from within, because that is National Electronics' past tradition. Our people must understand that if the RFP comes out they won't have much time to produce something very convincing so that upper-division management will agree to spend more money to write a proposal to DOT."

"Well, Ed, I'll report to you every now and then and give you the final report with an oral presentation in about 10 days."

"I'll be expecting it, Dave."

References on HVS

Bartucci, J. F., and Horton, J. A. (1969). Goodyear Aerospace Corporation, Development of lightweight infinity optics display for field evaluation, Technical Report AFHRL-TR-6913; August. Air Force Human Resources Laboratory, Air Force Systems Command, Wright-Patterson Air Force Base, Ohio.

Bidwell, J. B. (1967). Driving modeling and driving simulation. Proceedings; *Mathematical Models and Simulation of Automobile Driving*, M.I.T., Sept.

Collacott, R. (1973). *Simulators: International Guide*, Addison-Wesley, Reading, MA.

Cripe, R. A. (1973). Making a road simulator simulate. Paper #720095, Society of Automotive Engineers, Automotive Engineering Congress, Detroit, Michigan, Jan. 10–14.

Gold, T., and Workman, J. D. (1964). Research in the application of windshield projection displays to the all-weather landing task. AIAA Paper No. 64-347.

Hulbert, S., and Wojcik, C. (1975). Research activities at the UCLA driving simulation lab. *Highway Research News*, No. 17, Feb. pp. 111–14.

Lox, B. H. (1967). Some indications for and against simulation research. Proceedings; *Mathematical Models and Simulation of Automobile Driving*, M.I.T., Sept.

The NDC Dispatch (1974). Newsletter of National Driving Center, W. L. Roberts, Director, Vol. 1, No. 2, Oct. NDC developing advanced driving simulator.

Notice of Request for Proposals, Highway Simulator Specifications: Design Study. *Commerce Business Daily*, Oct. 16, 1975.

Obermayer, R. W., and Vreuls, D. (1972). *Measurement for Flight Training Research.* Manned Systems Science, Inc., Northridge, California.

Operation and Maintenance of Transportation Facilities: Statements of Research Problems. Special Report 158, Transportation Research Board, National Research Council, Washington, D.C., 1975.

Parrish, R. V., Dieudonne, J. E., Bowles, R. L., and Martin, D. J., Jr. (1973). *Coordinated Adaptive Washout for Motion Simulators.* NASA Langley Research Center, Hampton, Virginia.

Szalai, K. J. (1971). Motion cue and simulation fidelity aspects of the validation of a general purpose airborne simulator. NASA Technical Notes, NASA TN D- 6432, Washington, D.C., Oct.

NOTES

1. One may perhaps be forgiven for wondering as one examines Dewey's numbering scheme in the table, remembering his towering impact on American public education, if perhaps Dewey is not one cause of the trouble modern primary teachers and students seem to exhibit with numbers and counting.
2. This may seem unlikely given the typical growth of the Federal bureaucracy, but it is nevertheless true.
3. A personal note (from WTS)—I had never seen Jack get so angry! He had to take 30 minutes and walk around the building to cool-off.
4. Boulding was also President of *The Society for General Systems Research* [now the International Society for the Systems Sciences (ISSS); see http://www.ifsr.org/members/isss/] and one of the founding fathers of systems thinking along with Bertalanffy and others. Much of this original work emerged from biologists and other natural, physical systems. This community is, in many ways, divergent from the "systems engineering" community in the United States, which is centered on INCOSE and their perspective on the discipline.
5. Another interesting example is a recent attempt to build a single model of the entire human physiology—The Archimedes Project—by Kaiser Permanente. Reflect on this in light of our observations in this section.
6. Anonymous (1971) is an article describing a proposed initial study by N.S.F./RANN.
7. For contemporaneous reports on the cancellation, see *The Detroit News*, 18 Jan., 4 Feb., 12 Feb., 19 Mar., 28 Mar. 1969.
8. Consider the efforts (and resulting struggles) in the 1990s (and continuing today) of the U.S. military to build ubiquitous warfare simulation models.
9. Consider the history of the models on global warming as another example.
10. This is a retrospective case circa 1990—consider the material as classified documents recently released. No connection with actual government agencies nor real individuals is intended. The case does not illustrate either good or bad judgment and is meant solely to provide a basis for classroom discussion.
11. Adapted from *Dictionary of Technical Terms for Aerospace Use*, NASA, Scientific Technical Information Division, Washington, D.C., 1965.
12. No connection with actual government agencies nor real individuals is intended. The case does not illustrate either good or bad judgment and is meant solely to provide a basis for classroom discussion.

Chapter **6**

Rank Alternative Candidates

6.1 INTRODUCTION

If the criterion for ranking the alternative options is a simple quantitative relationship such as NPV, then the ranking is easy. But this is a simple case. The problem becomes more interesting, however, when there are additional factors to be considered. Such additional factors would include incommensurate side effects, parameter sensitivity effects, and external critical incidents, as well as probabilistic risk and uncertainty.

Incommensurate Side Effects. Side effects would include such factors as constraints or limits on resources or dependency relations, for example. As an example, a dependency relation might require that certain operations be completed before others start, and so on. A more important side effect is the impact of each option on non-users of the system.

Sensitivity to Parameter Variations. A particular option might score very highly on the index of performance when all system parameters are set at their design center. However, this same system might be highly sensitive to moderate variations in key parameters. Such a system could be called "pseudo optimal."

Subject to Likely Critical Incidents. Sensitivity of the IP to variations of parameters internal to the system is one matter. But this is a somewhat different beast. Here we refer to sensitivity to variations in external parameters, that is, the operating environment of the system.

Probabilistic Risk and Uncertainty. The theory of Decision Analysis has been developed to deal with the probabilistic nature of reality.

How to Do Systems Analysis. By John E. Gibson, William T. Scherer, and William F. Gibson
Copyright © 2007 John Wiley & Sons, Inc.

6.2 RATING AND RANKING METHODS

Procedures for selecting "the best choice" or "acceptable options" from among a field of candidates are commonplace in many fields of endeavor. Voters in a democracy select their leaders, entrepreneurs select business opportunities for investment, universities select from among applicants for admission, and so forth. It will not surprise one to learn that there exists a vast literature on the matter of making optimum choices. But some of the conclusions drawn in the literature may be surprising.

There are two polarities in the area of decision-making. One extreme is the totally holistic, intuitive approach.[1] This is the approach traditionally used almost exclusively in industry. "Actually in all the companies we have examined the decisive factor in the final analysis is almost solely managerial judgment" (Gee, 1976). In contrast are the analytic techniques often advocated by academic decision theorists. Unfortunately, these analytic techniques usually require data that are difficult and expensive to obtain, and have other drawbacks that will be discussed subsequently [see Wallenius et al. (2000)]. Thus, the middle ground between the purely intuitive and the rigorously analytic approaches has become more popular.

The academic literature on decision-making methods numbers in the thousands with the flood continuing to rise.[2] Surveys of the literature, which cite hundreds of articles each, number in the dozens and date back to post-World War II. Very little, however, appeared before World War II, and much of this subsequent march forward was led and characterized by Herb Simon (Simon, 1978). As an example of the early literature and possibly the peak, Clarke cites 171 references (Clarke, 1974). To cope with this flood of verbiage, several authors have introduced classifications for the various methods. There isn't complete agreement concerning these classification schemes of course, but the idea makes sense. As one might expect, earlier methods of decision-making are relatively pure examples of one or another group, while later methods attempt to combine the advantages of several groups and thus are more difficult to classify. In the classification scheme below, we combine what seem to us the best features of Clarke's method (Clarke, 1978), and the Moore–Baker scheme (Moore and Baker, 1969). This is a five-category classification with the categories becoming progressively more quantitative and analytic.

Ranking Methods. A ranking procedure can be as simple and intuitive as the application of managerial judgment to the available options, which is the method Gee and Tyler tell us is the most widely used technique. It is also possible to develop more elaborate ranking schemes such as the "Q-sort," "Dollar-metric," "Standard Gamble," and the like (Pessemier and Baker, 1971). The central principle of all ranking methods is pairwise comparison. This is the simplest conceivable process and lends a sense of confidence because it is the intuitive judgment process used by lay persons.

It is interesting that one particular attribute of pairwise comparison appears as a drawback to decision theorists and at the same time as an advantage to managers. That is, one need not reveal the basis on which the choice between each pair is made. Experienced managers usually feel that they know more about their sphere of managerial responsibility than they can articulate. Decision theorists sometimes argue that ranking processes do not exclude irrelevant and emotional matters and do not force the consideration of all rational factors. Managers, including those in the public sector, value ranking processes for precisely these same reasons. The analyst argues that the results of a pairwise comparison process cannot be replicated if the decision-maker refuses or is unable to reveal the basis for judgment. This is the most telling argument against the pairwise ranking processes.

Scoring or Rating Methods. An obvious outgrowth of simple ranking is the use of explicit scoring criteria. Each criterion can also be given a weighting commensurate with its importance. Analysts consider scoring methods a definite step forward because they force the criteria and their weightings out into the open. Practical decision-makers are concerned, however, with this very point. We have heard lower-level managers say that if they are given advanced notice regarding the scoring procedure to be used by upper management, they can always find a way of beating the system.

By "beating the system" one means to produce a high score for a particular option even if under normal circumstances it might score lower. One does this because one has an interest in a particular option, or for other reasons irrelevant to the process. Analysts can respond by producing more elaborate rating schemes, but this defeats the purpose of simplicity and reduces intuitive appeal.

Economic Rating Methods. One may consider economic criteria as only an important subclass of scoring methods or as a separate category. Economic rating methods employ calculations such as NPW, IRR, and the like, and were discussed in Chapter 4. An important attribute of these economic rating methods is their market orientation. It is possible to incorporate pure economic criteria such as NPW into somewhat more elaborate indices. For example, one might use the probability of technical success of a proposed new venture and the probability of commercial success (assuming these two are independent) along with the estimated return of investment as follows.

Index

$$= \frac{[\text{Probability of technical success}] \times [\text{Probability of commercial success}] \times [\text{ROI}]}{[\text{Estimated total cost of project}]}$$

To be meaningful, the estimates of technical success and commercial success must be carefully defined in advance and the tendency to overestimate these probabilities avoided. Gee and Tyler (1976, pp. 114, 117) recommend taking 60% of estimated earnings and requiring approximately 50% annual return before taxes.

Formal Optimization Methods. Many methods of mathematical optimization, usually requiring computers, exist. Linear programming, non-linear and integer programming, dynamic programming, pseudo-random search (genetic algorithms, simulated annealing, Tabu search), neural networks, real options, and so on, have been adapted to the process of rating alternatives. *There exists, however, little evidence known to us of practical decision-makers utilizing these advanced techniques in the real world.* Typically, if they are used, it is for lower-level operational decisions and not strategic decisions (e.g., for scheduling airline crews/flights and not for relocating one's corporate headquarters) [see, for example, Farrell (2001)]. Provided that one can formulate one's problem analytically, and all of the needed data exist, and the decision-maker will cooperate in the process, these techniques are excellent. Nevertheless, even if all of these pre-conditions cannot be satisfied, and this is almost always the case, a mathematical formulation of the problem often clarifies the situation and can lead to further progress.

Decision Analysis. Decision analysis (DA) is an attempt to place the whole of the decision-making process on a rigorous and formal basis. It has been under active investigation in academia for over 30 years, and a few of the elements are now beginning to appear more extensively in practice (Keefer et al., 2004). It is an exciting challenge and it is important that we not overestimate its current practicality, which is slight, thus prematurely causing excessive depreciation. DA will be considered in detail below.

6.3   CONDORCET AND ARROW VOTING PARADOXES

There is a large and analytically precise body of knowledge on the complexities of the voting process and the genuine paradoxes that can exist. But this knowledge is usually ignored in practical decision-making. Practitioners of the deductive budget planning process, such as the users of PPBS (Planning, Programming, Budgeting System) and ZBB (Zero-base budgeting) and the standard texts on these processes ignore the matter. Yet these two methodologies in particular and others as well can present situations in which these paradoxes can occur.

Two of the best-known paradoxes are the Condorcet paradox, and the Arrow paradox, both named for their discoverers. The Marquis de Condorcet (1743–1794), encyclopedist and supporter of the French Revolution, was a fine mathematician and led an interesting life (Durant and Durant, 1967). During his service in the Revolutionary Assembly, he became concerned with the paradoxes that can occur in the democratic processes and voting, including the following paradox that bears his name.

All decision processes require the simple and logical condition of *transitivity*. A *transitive relation* between three states can be expressed as follows. Let the symbol "$\succ$" be interpreted as "is preferred to," or "is greater than," and so on. Then,

$$\text{If } X \succ Y \text{ and } Y \succ Z, \text{ then } X \succ Z$$

The axiom of transitivity says that if X is preferred to Y and Y to Z, then X is preferred to Z. Transitivity is a simple, logical, and necessary condition for analysis. It is to be regretted, therefore, that real life is so often intransitive. Let us now suppose, as did Condorcet, the following symmetrical voting pattern.

Voter 1: $X \succ Y \succ Z$
Voter 2: $Y \succ Z \succ X$
Voter 3: $Z \succ X \succ Y$

We observe that the majority of two voters prefer $X \succ Y$. We also observe that two voters, a clear majority, prefer $Y \succ Z$. Therefore assuming transitivity, it is clear that the majority should prefer $X \succ Z$. However, this is not so!

Certainly the Condorcet paradox is disturbing to a logical individual, but unfortunately there is more. Group preference structures, such as those we have been using, have been analyzed by many workers, among the better known of whom is Kenneth Arrow (Arrow, 1963). Arrow has contributed another result that has an important impact on the majority decision process. Arrow starts with two axioms, the first of which is that a voter is able to express a preference between two choices or is indifferent between them. Second, Arrow assumes transitivity. He goes on to set five more conditions that have to do with relating individual preferences to the majority preferences. These conditions are likewise simple and reasonable (Sage, 1977). Yet Arrow then finds that there exists no social welfare function; *that is, there exists no majority decision process that can always satisfy the basic axioms, if the group must choose from among three or more options.* This is the Arrow paradox, and it is more disturbing in its implications for democratic procedures than is the Condorcet paradox.

Other workers have found restrictions that, if placed on the allowable range of individual voters' choices, result in limited majority social welfare functions, but the basic result, as surprising and unpalatable as it may seem, appears unassailable.

What does all this mean to the system analyst, or to the manager for that matter, faced with taking a simple logical approach to decision-making? Often the manager is faced with more options than can be exercised, given the available resources. Thus, it will become necessary to retain only the top candidates based on some sort of rank ordering. This sort of selection process is a usual, everyday sort of thing, but it presents some unexpected difficulties. The following example is based on the work of Fishburn (1974).

Suppose the seven members of your system team have used a ranking procedure to sift through the options available and have presented to you four candidates ranked as follows:

Best: Option c
Second: Option b
Third: Option a
Fourth: Option x

You have been required by the client to forward not more than three options for review, and thus you drop Option x and forward the following:

Best: Option c
Second: Option b
Third: Option a

The client immediately drops Option a, as seems reasonable if resources are limited, and proceeds with a detailed evaluation of the remaining two projects. You are satisfied

TABLE 6.1. The Actual Preferences of the Seven Team Members in the First or "A" Round of Voting

Team Member	Preference
1	*abcx*
2	*bcxa*
3	*cxab*
4	*abcx*
5	*bcxa*
6	*cxab*
7	*abcx*

with this process and so are your team members. (Finally, you seem to have found a rational client!) But, now let's go back and see what really happened. Your team ranked the four leading projects as shown in Table 6.1.

You decide to use a standard textbook rank-position weighting procedure due originally to Jean-Charles Chevalier de Borda, a contemporary of Condorcet, in which the bottom position gets a weight of 0, the next higher gets a 1, and so on. The Borda sums for the first round, called the "A" round, therefore, are as follows:

$$s(c, A) = 13, \qquad s(b, A) = 12, \qquad s(a, A) = 11, \qquad s(x, A) = 6$$

It seems clear that Option x is the weakest and should be dropped. Thus, without changing the original preferences of the team members, go back to the rankings in Table 6.1, and eliminate Option x. The resulting preferences for what we will call the "B" round are as shown in Table 6.2. The Borda sums for the B round are as follows:

$$s(a, B) = 8, \qquad s(b, B) = 7, \qquad s(c, B) = 6$$

We can see that the rank order of the A round has reversed itself in the B round. So when Option a was dropped, the client actually eliminated the best remaining alternative, not the worst. Please don't be misled by the brevity of this example. The problem does not lie in the particular cyclic vote ordering, nor with the number of votes, nor with the Borda weighting procedure, nor in a computational detail.

TABLE 6.2. The Actual Preferences of the Seven Team Members in the "B" Round of Voting

Team Member	Preference
1	*abc*
2	*bca*
3	*cab*
4	*abc*
5	*bca*
6	*cab*
7	*abc*

TABLE 6.3. Sports Writers' Votes

Team	SW1	SW2	SW3	SW4	SW5	SW6	SW7
A	1	4	3	1	4	3	1
B	2	1	4	2	1	4	2
C	3	2	1	3	2	1	3
D	4	3	2	4	3	2	4

Let's drive this point home with another example from our newspaper's sports pages (modified from French, p. 1988, 23). Consider a group of seven sports writers ranking four teams. Each sportswriter (SW) ranks the four teams from first (#1) to last (#4), as in Table 6.3 (does this look familiar?)

If we tally the votes (a Borda-type sum), then we have the following, since lower is better:

Team A :   17   Team B :   16   Team C :   15   Team D :   22

Thus, the teams are ranked as follows: Team C ≻ Team B ≻ Team A ≻ Team D (where ≻ means ranked higher). If we remove Team D, the lowest ranked team, and the sports writers keep their individual rankings (e.g., SW2 ranking is now Team B ≻ Team C ≻ Team A), then the new overall rankings are Team A ≻ Team B ≻ Team C, and the order has reversed. Borda again.

One critical aspect of this example is also the confusion of measurement notions in that ordinal measures (the SW rankings) are being treated as cardinal measures when the rankings are summed via a Borda scheme. Thus, when the rankings are added, there is an implicit assumption of strength of preference, which is clearly not true nor is it likely intended by the sportswriter. SW3, for example, may feel that Teams C and D are almost identical, while Teams A and B are significantly inferior. The ordinal ranking scale, however, does not allow for this information.

In Table 6.4 is another disturbing example constructed by Fishburn. Suppose now that there are seven options under careful consideration by your team consisting of 13 persons. Using the conventional Borda scheme, the options in Table 6.4 rank as shown in Table 6.5.

TABLE 6.4. Thirteen Voters Distributed Their Votes Among Seven Candidates as Shown in the Table

Number Voting	Order
2	*FEDCBAG*
2	*EDCBAGF*
2	*DCBAGFE*
2	*CBAGFED*
2	*BAGFEDC*
2	*AGFEDCB*
1	*FEDCBAG*

**TABLE 6.5. The Voting Distribution in
Table 6.3 Yields the Ranking Shown Here**

Rank	Option
1	A
2	B
3	C
4	D
5	E
6	F
7	G

This client wishes to see only six candidates and thus you drop Option G. The client then drops three more candidates, D, E, and F, before proceeding with the final evaluation. But none of these three candidates should have been chopped. All of those three dropped by the client were preferred over those retained. To show this, return to the original 13 rankings and eliminate Option G. Then take new Borda sums. The aggregate ordering of the six remaining options is F, E, D, C, B, A, exactly reversing the order of the original seven.

What Fishburn has shown with these carefully constructed counter-examples is that one may not assume that a rank ordering is independent of subsequent trimming of the ordered list. In fact, one can go further. Arrow has shown that unless the selection process is artificially restricted, there cannot exist any rational social welfare function by which rational (transitive) individuals can be assured of arriving at a group priority ranking for a list of options or projects, or people for that matter.

According to Arrow (1950),

> The Possibility Theorem shows that, if no prior assumptions are made about the nature of individual orderings, there is no method of voting which will remove the paradox of voting ... neither plurality voting nor any scheme of proportional representation, no matter how complicated. Similarly, the market mechanism does not create a rational social choice.

6.4   A MULTISTAGE RATING PROCESS

In Section 4.10 we introduced a simple, single-pass weighting and rating system for projects. Under some conditions, there appear to be advantages to adding an additional step or two to the process. For example, suppose that the "client" is not a single individual, but rather is a political constituency. Perhaps the sponsor has requested that an attempt be made to "smooth out" or minimize subjective biases. For example, suppose that the analyst is working with a focus group of concerned citizens on locating a bypass to a congested highway through town. Naturally, those individuals whose homes are threatened by a particular routing will be tempted to vote against that route.

The same problem occurs in locating radioactive waste dumps, new construction, land fills, nuclear reactors, and so forth. It also arises in the evaluation of research projects for future funding in private enterprise and with panels established by Federal research agencies for the same purpose. In Federal funding selection processes, there may be hundreds (even thousands) of candidates and many rating panels made up of different individuals acting in parallel. A process that involves some regularity and objectivity seems essential in such a situation. In general, the object is to elicit objective evaluations from panels, while minimizing bias. No system can be totally foolproof, but one can improve matters if one partitions the process so that an evaluator cannot directly give a final weighted evaluation to a specific candidate. Often evaluators don't want to subject themselves to a logical process but wish, without thinking, to reach through the process as it were, to put a favorite candidate on top, or to eliminate an unwanted candidate, for personal, hidden reasons they choose not to disclose. On the other hand, remember Arrow's quote above on the impossibility of totally rational social choice.

The multistep process described below is aimed at forcing an objective process on the evaluation panel member and making it more difficult to rate an option high or low for undisclosed "subjective" reasons. We would not argue that this approach is perfect or that it is impossible to thwart. Rather, we merely claim that the process makes it easier or more practical to obtain an "objective" and fairly transparent result while at the same time providing a clear audit trail. Here are the steps in the process (Gibson, 1977):

1. A number of "technical criteria" are defined and each candidate is rated with respect to each of them.
2. A number of "use functions" or "social functions" are defined and each technical criterion is rated with respect to each use function.
3. Each technical criterion, and thus also each use function, can be weighted for importance.

The same rating panel need not be used for all of the scorings. The technical criteria can often be evaluated by technicians, because those values are determined by reference to evidence rather than opinion. The weightings, on the other hand, are more subjective, as are the use functions. For these latter activities, therefore, users should do the ratings. All this may be rather vague so far, but an example should clarify matters.

Let us suppose that we are to select the site of a new, large city to be constructed somewhere within the state of Louisiana, possibly to replace or complement New Orleans after its devastation from Hurricane Katrina in 2005. The first step is to define a set of technical criteria that will be of use in the site selection process. Table 6.6 gives examples of criteria that could be applied.

It could be argued that the technical criteria in Table 6.6 are excessively coarse. If this is felt to be so, it is easy to provide more specific indices for a more fine-grained choice. Take "buildability," for example. Table 6.7 gives a more specific breakout for this criterion.

Next, the analyst develops a set of "use functions." In this example, we ask what do people want in their city. Table 6.8 gives a set of generalized social functions for a city.

TABLE 6.6. Examples of Possible "Technical Criteria" to Be Used in Selecting the Site for a New City

1. Exploitable natural resources	6. Available transportation
2. Available land	7. Land acquisition cost
3. Flood/hurricane vulnerability	8. Political climate
4. Buildable sites	9. Available labor
5. Economic climate	10. Other

TABLE 6.7. A More Specific Breakdown for the "Buildability" criterion given in Table 6.6[a]

"Buildability" Break-Out	
A.	Suitable for bearing heavy structures (marshy)?
B.	Good drainage (clay)?
C.	Suitable for excavation (rocky)?
D.	Suitable for construction (very hilly)?
E.	Other (ravines, valuable crop land, etc.)

[a]Even more detailed criteria could be developed. Similarly, detailed break-outs for the other technical criteria could be developed

Now we are ready to rate each of the site candidates with respect to each of the technical criteria. Suppose we take a short list of sites for computational convenience. In Table 6.9 four general sites are listed along with raw ratings for four technical criteria.

Not all technical criteria are always of the same importance. Thus, it is necessary to be able to weight the criteria according to an agreed-upon scale. In Table 6.10 we show a diagonal $[D]$ matrix to be used for this purpose. All of the elements in the diagonal weighting matrix $[D]$ are zero with the exception of those elements on the main diagonal. Each diagonal element weights a single technical criterion, using a three-point scale.

Next we will develop an $[F]$ matrix that relates the social functions of a city to the technical factors given in the $[C]$ matrix. In Table 6.11, we take five example social functions. The matrix allows us to relate each social function to each technical criterion. This $[F]$ matrix also serves to test the entire process in the following sense. Suppose we find that the so-called "technical criteria" don't really influence the human

TABLE 6.8. Some General "Use Functions" or "Social Functions" for a City

1. Work	6. Shopping
2. Outdoor recreation	7. Cultural activities
3. Health care	8. Waste disposal
4. Social welfare	9. Other
5. Education	

TABLE 6.9. The [C] Matrix[a]

Site	Land and Environment	Regional Transport	Political Climate	Water
Site #1	3	1	3	3
Site #2	2	1	2	1
Site #3	3	3	1	3
Site #4	2	2	2	3

Rating Scale: 1, low (bad); 2, medium; 3, high (good)

[a]The [C] matrix rates each site with respect to four sample technical criteria. We have chosen arbitrarily to use a three-point scale in this early round of general site evaluation. More finely grained criteria, smaller individual site candidates and a more detailed (cardinal) rating scale, using five or more values, would then be appropriate

TABLE 6.10. The Diagonal [D] Matrix[a]

Land & Environment	3	0	0	0
Transport	0	1	0	0
Political Climate	0	0	2	0
Water	0	0	0	3

[a]This diagonal [D] matrix will be used to post-multiply the [C] matrix in order to weight the technical criteria in accord with their relative importance to the rating panel. All elements must be zero with the exception of those elements along the main diagonal.

activities for which the city is to be constructed to serve. This would be the situation if most of the elements in the [F] matrix were given low values by the raters. This would indicate that the technical criteria had been improperly selected in the first place.

Now we must be able to weight the relative importance of each of the social functions. This is done by means of post-multiplication of the [F] matrix by the {W} column vector shown in Table 6.12.

Finally, we perform the matrix multiplications shown in Eq. (6.1) in order to find the relative site ratings.

$$\{R\} = [C] \times [D] \times [F] \times \{W\} \tag{6.1}$$

TABLE 6.11. The [F] Matrix[a]

	Work	Recreational	Access	Educational	Social
Land & Environment	2	3	1	1	1
Transport	3	2	3	2	3
Political Climate	2	1	1	1	1
Water	3	3	1	1	1

[a]This [F] matrix relates each social function to each technical criterion. One should be a little concerned at the large number of "1"s in this rating. Have we selected an effective set of technical criteria?

TABLE 6.12. The $\{W\}$ Column Vector[a]

Work	3
Recreation	2
Accessibility	1
Education	2
Socializing	1

[a]This $\{W\}$ column vector weights the relative importance of each of the social functions.

The resulting scores are

$$\{R\} = \begin{cases} 410 & \text{Site \#1} \\ 224 & \text{Site \#2} \\ 408 & \text{Site \#3} \\ 361 & \text{Site \#4} \end{cases}$$

This rating is relative; that is, the numbers shown have no absolute meaning. The important result is the ranking, that is, Site #1 > Site #3 > Site #4 > Site #2. What would follow next is a sensitivity analysis, especially in light of how close Site #1 and Site #3 score.

This is a rather long and involved process and would be recommended only for a case in which many options were to be processed and also where there is reason to believe that a simpler one-pass process might lead to bias on the part of the raters. In the reference from which this simplified example is drawn, involving locating a new city on Appalachia, approximately 397 counties were rated. Furthermore, it is apparent that citizens could be emotionally involved in the site selection for a variety of reasons. Thus, this elaborate procedure seemed appropriate.

One caveat to consider when using these types of models is worth mentioning. Consider another example (again, modified from French, 1988, pp. 80, 81). Suppose that we were evaluating companies regarding their ability to produce software, and we had a five-level rating system (Level 5 the best) similar to the Software Productivity Consortium (SPC) Capability Maturity Model (CMM). Table 6.13 shows the proportion of each company's units at the different levels (columns 4 and 5).

TABLE 6.13. Software Productivity Comparison

			Proportion with Each Level	
Software Level	Scoring System 1	Scoring System 1	Company 1	Company 2
Level 1	5	90	5	30
Level 2	4	75	65	5
Level 3	3	65	5	25
Level 4	2	50	5	35
Level 5	1	30	20	5

The question is to determine which company has a better average software productivity score. If we use Scoring System 1, then we have

$$\text{Company } 1 = 3.3 \quad \text{and} \quad \text{Company } 2 = 3.2$$

Hence Company 1 has a higher average productivity. Alternatively, if we use a different scale such as Scoring System 2, then we have

$$\text{Company } 1 = 65 \quad \text{and} \quad \text{Company } 2 = 66$$

and Company 2 has a higher average. So, the "average" depends on which scale we use; therefore, be careful in selecting and changing scales in any kind of exercise as the above and in future sections of this chapter.[3]

6.5   DECISION ANALYSIS

Decision analysis (DA) is an attempt to bring analytic methods to bear on the difficult problem of decision-making under risk. There is some value in differentiating between "risk" and "uncertainty," perhaps. Specialists would like to reserve the word "risk" for situations in which the probabilities of the possible outcomes are known and the word "uncertainty" for situations in which the probabilities are not known. This is probably an academic distinction without any real difference, however, because the probability of an outcome is never known precisely in a realistic decision problem.

DA is based on extensions of certain propositions from probability theory and utility concepts that economists have used in the past to deal with the way individuals arrive at monetary decisions. Yet DA is not coldly objective and nonpersonal. It attempts to include an axiological component by permitting personal expressions of value to be attached to various outcomes. Moreover, it attempts to deal with the very subtle but important matter of estimating the probabilities to be attached to various outcomes from a decision.

DA makes use of so-called subjective probability theory in order to extend the range of its applicability. Objective probability is the more conventional theory and the more rigorous of the two. Under objective probability theory, there are two ways in which the probabilities of various outcomes may be derived. These are, you may recall, the logical approach in which all possible outcomes are enumerated and thus the likelihood of each assessed and the frequency ratio approach, in which probabilities are defined in the limit. In the real world, however, the probabilities of various outcomes are usually rather vague, initially at least.

Subjective probability theory argues that if an objective probability cannot be calculated because insufficient data exist, then the analyst should first take the best possible informed guess as to the initial probabilities and then correct these initial guesses using Bayesian estimation theory and information gained as the process unfolds. This broadened concept appears to permit us to handle decisions about processes that will only be repeated a few times and even those that are unique. Finally, it permits us to handle the problem of obtaining more information about the process when the cost of obtaining this information is not insignificant.

DA also includes the possibility of using game theory to extend itself to include contests with reasoning, although not necessarily reasonable, opponents. Attempts have also been made to rationalize the decision process with respect to multiple objectives.

All in all, this bill of fare seems rather appetizing to the decision-maker. DA appears to have removed one by one the restrictions that prevent objective statistics and economics from being useful to the real-world decision-maker, by substituting a more general, broadly applicable theory. What remains would appear to be a strong, supple mechanism for reducing ambiguity and the tension that invariably accompanies it.

Yet, perhaps the reader has noted a tentative flavor in the phrasing of this introduction. There are very real practical and theoretical problems with DA, both pure and applied. From a tutorial point of view, however, it appears desirable to establish the case for DA before presenting the case for the opposition. Thus, we will delay listing the possible concerns with the DA process.

To summarize then, there are four major advances that DA appears to offer the decision-maker as compared with the use of objective statistics and conventional probability theory, or a decision based on pure intuition:

- DA encourages the use of all information—"fuzzy data," observations as the process progresses, and so on— for the estimation of probabilities and parameter values. It does so through the use of Bayes' rule and other more advanced estimators.
- DA is designed for once in a lifetime (unique) or almost unique decision situations, as opposed to objective probability theory, which requires a very long run of stationary statistics for the rules to apply in principle.
- Through the use of subjective utility functions, DA permits the decision-maker to incorporate his personal evaluation of the benefits and costs of a particular policy rather than forcing him to utilize the expected monetary value (EMV) of the possible outcomes from the policy.
- DA permits the decision-maker by the use of game theory to evaluate his options when he deals with a rational opponent rather than limiting him to a game against nature.

Much of the current work in DA is based on a set of utility theory axioms proposed by Von Neumann and Morgenstern in their classic text on game theory and economic behavior (Von Neumann and Morgenstern, 1964). Those authors set very precise limitations on the applicability of their work that have not always been observed by those who have followed. It is on these proposed extensions of the work of Von Neumann and Morgenstern that most controversy over DA centers. It is also interesting that the Von Neumann and Morgenstern utility theory axioms are developed in the early introductory section of their book and merely as a preliminary to the development of their theory of competitive games.

It should be unnecessary to add that in an introductory treatment of a complex subject such as this, one cannot expect rigor. We will take a brutally direct application orientation here, even at the possible sacrifice of complete precision. As one would expect in an active field, there has been an immense amount published over the last 50 years since Von Neumann and Morgenstern's original work. An excellent, recent brief introduction to the fundamental thinking is given by Bell and Farquhar, serious contributors to the theory in their own right (Bell and Farquhar, 1986). We will follow them in the next section.

6.6 BASIC AXIOMS OF DECISION THEORY

Before we give the necessary three axioms, we will define the concept of a "lottery." A simple lottery can be represented by the decision flow diagram or decision tree shown in Figure 6.1. The first element of Figure 6.1 is the decision fork represented by a square box. In this illustration, the choice is between playing and not playing. Associated with playing may be a specific cost. If all of the possible outcomes represent a gain to the player, then a cost is often associated with the right to play. A basic

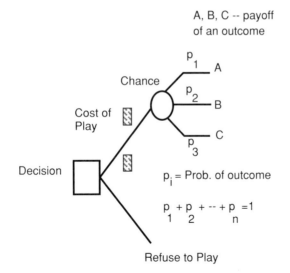

FIGURE 6.1 A decision tree for a simple lottery. A "simple lottery" has a decision point, shown as a square box, at which it is decided to "play" or to "refuse." If one chooses to play, there may be a cost to play, shown as a gate. Then chance acts, shown as a circular node. Any number of outcomes are possible. The payoff for each outcome is labeled as *A, B, C,* and so on. There is also associated with each outcome a probability, labeled as p_1, p_2, p_n, etc. The sum of the probabilities must be unity.

problem in DA is to determine the cost that one is willing to bear in order to participate in the lottery. The next essential feature of the lottery is the chance fork, represented by a circle. Chance will determine which of the possible outcomes will actually occur. With each outcome will be associated a probability p_i of its occurrence. Not all outcomes need be equally probable, but the probabilities must be exhaustive, that is, they must sum to unity. In addition, there will be associated with each outcome a payoff A, B, C, and so on.

As Bell and Farquhar point out, decision-makers do not normally behave consistently with the Von Neumann–Morgenstern axioms. In part, this is due to the vagaries of human behavior, but it is also due in part to the rigidity of the theorems themselves. Fishburn and others have made contributions that simplify and refine the original axioms, reducing the necessary axioms to the following three (Fishburn, 1970).

The first axiom establishes orderability and transitivity. It must be possible to establish a preference ranking among the possible outcomes of the lottery. Let the symbol $\succ$ mean "is preferred to" and let the symbol $\sim$ mean "is indifferent between." Given two outcomes A and B, the player must be able to state that either $A \succ B$, or $A \sim B$, or $A \prec B$. Note that this simple requirement implies the existence of a scale for ordering the consequences. Thus, certain analysts to the contrary notwithstanding, it is <u>not</u> possible to use DA theory to establish a preference among noncommensurate outcomes.

It is further required that the preference ranking be transitive. That is, if $A \succ B$ and $B \succ C$, then $A \succ C$. This appears to be an obvious and simple requirement. One can demonstrate that if the preference scale does not obey this rule, either silly consequences result or one is led to an impasse. As an example, suppose a player has the following preferences:

$$A \succ B \quad \text{or} \quad A \sim B + \$1 \tag{6.2}$$

and

$$B \succ C \quad \text{or} \quad B \sim C + \$1 \tag{6.3}$$

and finally let the player be intransitive, because he feels

$$C \succ A \quad \text{or} \quad C \sim A + \$1 \tag{6.4}$$

Substitute Eq. (6.3). for B in Eq. (6.2). Then

$$A \sim (C + 1) + 1 \tag{6.5}$$

and by Eq. (6.4)

$$A \sim (A + 1) + 1 + 1 \tag{6.6}$$

Now, how can one be indifferent between A and $A + 3$? This argument can be elaborated to show the intransitive person exchanging goods and money until he ends up

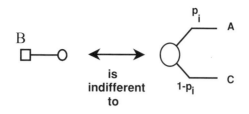

FIGURE 6.2 Continuity.

with the same object with which he started but poorer by the additional monetary considerations. This process is sometimes termed a "money pump."

We will now make several observations based on this axiom. Given that the preference $A \succ B \succ C$ exists, an indifference lottery may be constructed. That is, there exists a simple lottery with outcomes A and C, which for some probability p_i, to which the player is indifferent, with respect to the sure outcome B.

Suppose in Figure 6.2, $A = \$100$, $B = \$25$, and $C = \$0$. Then for some probability, p_i, a player would be indifferent to receiving B or to entering the lottery and letting chance decide between A or C. Given the existence of the indifference lottery, the certain (monetary) equivalent (CME) may be substituted for it.

A *compound lottery* is one in which one or more outcomes of the first lottery is itself a lottery (see Figure 6.3). Given the values of the various outcomes and the probabilities, the compound lottery can be decomposed into an equivalent simple lottery.

The second axiom, on independence, appears to be the source of considerable controversy according to Bell and Farquhar because many behavioral researchers have documented systemic violations of its conditions. Nevertheless, take the simple lottery shown in Figure 6.2. Its EMV is

$$pA + (1 - p)C \qquad (6.7)$$

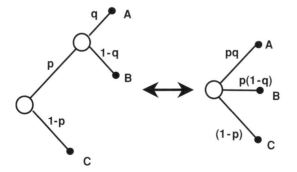

FIGURE 6.3 Decomposability. A simple lottery can be constructed that is equivalent to the compound lottery.

Now suppose prize D is substituted for prize A. The new lottery has a value of

$$pD + (1 - p)C \qquad (6.8)$$

The independence axiom requires that if $A \succ D$, then

$$[pA + (1 - p)C] \succ [pD + (1 - p)C] \qquad (6.9)$$

The first two axioms plus this one on continuity of preference, taken together, means that there exists a <u>utility function</u> that has the following properties. First, the utility function preserves the order of the preferences among the risky prospects. That is, if $A \succ B$, then $u(A) \succ u(B)$. Second, the utility function is "linear in probabilities," that is,

$$u[pA + (1 - p)B] = pu(A) + (1 - p)u(B) \qquad (6.10)$$

This permits the evaluation of compound lotteries by reducing them to an evaluation of their components. "Folding back" (see below) also relies on this property (see Figure 6.4).

Fishburn has developed a revised utility theory called "skew-symmetric bilinear utility theory" that relaxes the independence axiom and does not require transitivity,

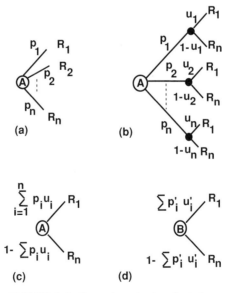

FIGURE 6.4 Several equivalent lotteries.

but we won't go into it here [see Bell and Farquhar (1986) or Fishburn (1982, 1983)].

6.7 PROPERTIES OF UTILITY FUNCTIONS

The "utility" of a concept or an object is its worth or value to an individual. More precisely, we use "utility" in the sense of cardinal utility under risk. Utility is sometimes considered synonymous to "satisfaction." The theory of utility requires that this "satisfaction" be expressible in terms of common referent, usually money, certain authors to the contrary notwithstanding [Von Neumann and Morgenstern (1964); Howard (1976) maintained the contrary].

Utility is a personal, subjective matter. My "need" for $100 is for me alone to say. It is probably different from your need. The "satisfaction" that $100 could bring me today may be different from the satisfaction it could have afforded me 10 years ago. It is precisely this subjectivity that we seek to include in a utility function. This subjectivity is at once the strength and weakness of the concept.

In addition to the subjectivity of a utility function, we wish to emphasize its relative nature. We are not interested in absolute satisfaction (if there is any meaning in such a concept) but rather the relative satisfaction one obtains from one outcome compared with other possible outcomes. One must be able to rank the satisfaction to be obtained from each of several outcomes (i.e., assess the "utility" of each) and to perform the other operations indicated by the axioms given in the previous section. We will delay criticism of this and other elements of the concept of utility until after we have completed the initial development.

Utilizing the utility axioms given above, we can develop certain operational properties of the utility function. Using the orderability axiom, we can assign a utility to each possible outcome of a lottery and establish an order of reference for the outcomes or rewards as follows:

$$R_1 \succ R_2 \succ R_3 \cdots \succ R_n$$

With the continuity axiom, we can then compose a lottery with only R_1 and R_n as prizes and find a probability u_i of winning R_1 such that the player is indifferent between the lottery and a certain equivalent R_i. Using the decomposability axiom, we can find an equivalent simple lottery to a given compound lottery. All this should be obvious from the axiom statements.

Now we will point out a consequence of the axioms that may not be obvious initially. Suppose we have a compound lottery. We know by decomposability that it can be represented as lottery A as in Figure 6.4a. Now let us treat each outcome R_i as a certain (monetary) equivalent and substitute for it an indifference lottery as shown in Figure 6.4b. Note there are only two prizes in this new compound lottery.

By the decomposability axiom, the probability of winning R_1 in the lottery shown in Figure 6.4b is

$$\sum_{i=1}^{n} p_i u_i \qquad (6.11)$$

and thus we have the final form shown in Figure 6.4c. We could have followed the same procedure for a different lottery B, also shown in Figure 6.4d. Both lottery A and B have the same two prizes.

Here is the point of these manipulations. Because the prizes are the same, the player will prefer lottery A only if

$$\sum_{i=1}^{n} p_i u_i \quad \succ \quad \sum_{i=1}^{n} p_i' u_i' \qquad (6.12)$$

We can interpret u_i as the utility of the ith prize, and we have thus shown that one lottery is preferred only if it has a higher utility, where the utility of the lottery is interpreted as the expected utility of its prizes. Thus we have the important relationship

$$u(R_i) \sim p u(R_1) + (1 - p) u(R_n) \qquad (6.13)$$

which is illustrated in Figure 6.5. This will prove fundamental in the manipulation of utilities and will permit us to construct a utility curve for an individual, or a client evaluating project alternatives.

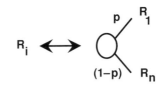

AND

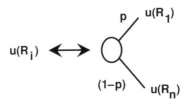

FIGURE 6.5 A relationship fundamental to the manipulation of utilities.

6.8   CONSTRUCTING A UTILITY CURVE

One perfectly acceptable way of constructing a utility curve for an individual is to explain its implications to that individual and let him plot it for himself. Another approach is to observe the player in action and to calculate the utility he unconsciously assigns to individual transactions. But we will develop a third procedure based on standard practices [see Buede (2000), Clemen and Kelly (2001); for the classic work in the field, see Keeney and Raiffa (1976)]. The first variation of this procedure utilizes a series of hypothetical questions based on a simple lottery with equal probabilities for its two possible outcomes. In the second variation, the CME is fixed and the probability which creates a state of indifference is sought. Using both these techniques, we can interpolate between the end-points initially set in the exercise. Extrapolation is equally simple operationally but its meaning is in doubt (see below).

Let us assume we find that the usual monetary range with which a decision-maker must deal lies between $0 and $1000. This is a purely arbitrary number pair. We could pick any two positive or negative dollar amounts with which to deal. The respondent will no doubt agree that the utility of $0 is zero, although really any lower dollar limit, negative or positive, could be assigned a utility of zero. Because $1000 is the arbitrarily chosen upper limit of the decision-maker's normal range, it will be assigned a utility of unity. Thus,

$$u(\$0) = 0 \quad \text{and} \quad u(\$1000) = 1.0$$

Now we will use Eq. (6.13) and the equiprobable lottery as a means of interpolation. The first question is charted in Figure 6.6. For what certain monetary equivalent (CME) would you trade your chance to enter into the lottery shown in the figure? First let us calculate the equivalent monetary value (EMV) of the lottery.

$$\text{EMV} = 0.5(\$1000) + 0.5(0) = \$500$$

It is not obvious, however, that one would be indifferent to a CME of $500 for this lottery. This would be a "fair" gamble and one would expect to come out even choosing either the CME or this lottery after a long (possibly a <u>very</u> long) series of trials. But you will be offered this opportunity once, or at most a very small number of times. We cannot speak for you, but we are risk-averse and would trade the lottery for a

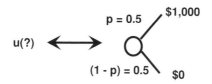

FIGURE 6.6   Interpolation to establish points on a utility curve using the equiprobable lottery technique.

CME equivalent of much less than $500. We have thought about it and feel we are indifferent at a CME of $250. Thus for us, from Eq. (6.13) we have

$$u(\$250) = pu(\$1000) + (1 - p)(\$0) = 0.5(1) + (0.5)(0) = 0.5$$

Your utility for $250 may be different, but this is ours. Now we will repeat the process interpolating between $0 and $250 as well as between $250 and $1000. We are indifferent to an equiprobable lottery with $0 and $250 as possible outcomes and a CME of $100. A lottery with $250 and $1000 as the prizes is indifferent for us to a CME of $500. Thus for *us* from Eq. (6.13) we obtain

$$u(\$100) = 0.5u(\$250) = 0.25$$

and

$$u(\$500) = 0.5u(\$1000) + 0.5u(\$250) = 0.5 + 0.25 = 0.75$$

Similarly for *us* we have

$$u(\$700) = 0.5u(\$1000) + 0.5u(\$500) = 0.5 + 0.375 = 0.875$$

Figure 6.7 shows this set of utilities. The points appear to form a smooth curve. But suppose that one point fell off the smooth curve. Then the respondent could be given some time to think about it and to change his mind if he wishes, but it is not essential that the curve be monotonic. If the whole curve (or a portion of it) fell below the EMV straight line, we would see the player as "risk seeking" in that range. In effect, such a person would be willing to pay more than the EMV for a certain lottery. This might be because he received a psychic return from the suspense (i.e., a gambler) or because his present bankroll is "too small to do him any good," thus he feels himself forced to take a plunge. But the player does not need to "justify" his answers. The analyst's questions are merely to ensure that the player's response is firmly felt.

The mechanics of extrapolating a utility curve are precisely the same as those we have used for interpolation, but the meaning of such an exercise is murky. To demonstrate this, we need merely recall the personal and subjective nature of utilities. Suppose the individual for whom you constructed the utility curve in Figure 6.7 with a range of $0 to $1000 is a business executive. Figure 6.7 might be his current utility curve for personal dollars, but as a venture capitalist he needs a utility curve with a range from, say, 50×10^6 to 500×10^6. It would be exceedingly unlikely that the portion of such a new curve between $0 and $1000 would have the same shape as Figure 6.7. It would also be unlikely that either new curve would have the same shape as the whole of Figure 6.7 with the end-points renumbered. The owner of the utility curve has expressed his preferences under a specific set of circumstances. It would be unwise to assume that these preferences remain fixed as the circumstances change.

The reader should appreciate that we have adopted a personal, stream-of-consciousness style in the narrative above, to convey as strongly as possible the

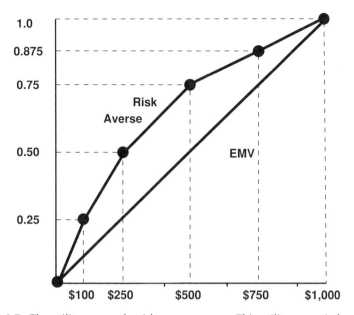

FIGURE 6.7 The utility curve of a risk-averse person. This utility curve is for a single, specific individual, at a single unique point in time and for a specific range of dollars. Theory does not permit exceeding those bounds.

subjective nature of this exercise. The personal opinion of the owner of the utility curve is the whole point. Constructing a utility curve is not an objective, scientific enterprise.

The second variant of utility curve construction based on Eq. (6.13) is mechanically the same except that the CME and both prizes are set, while the participant adjusts the probabilities to suit himself to obtain indifference. One generally has more trouble "believing" in the answers he gives in this latter mode because adjusting the odds is a less familiar activity for most people.

Furthermore, as A. P. Sage has pointed out to us in a personal communication, there are a number of psychological traps one can get worked into in adjusting the odds [see Sage (1992) for a complete discussion]. This is especially so in the case of an inherently very low probability for a disastrous outcome. How can one rely on a utility value assigned to an outcome totally beyond the experience of the assignee? This is the situation, for example, in siting of nuclear plants.

6.9 SOME DECISION ANALYSIS CLASSIC EXAMPLES

One is placed in a certain quandary in discussing practical examples of Decision Analysis (DA). There just do not seem to be many practical examples available. The oil-well drilling problem mentioned by Raiffa and others is a possible exception, but in all probability that is a contrived exercise (Raiffa, 1968). Medicine has produced several example applications (Ginsberg and Offensend, 1968; Pauker, 1976). Nevertheless, most examples in the literature seem rather contrived and simplistic. Of course, simplified examples can be a perfectly valid pedagogical tool for introducing a complex subject. But usually there is a mass of more advanced material looming behind a simple example to which an unsatisfied student can be referred. Such realistic examples seem rare in DA.

For example, of the 16 papers in a special issue of the *IEEE Transactions on Decision Analysis* (Vol. SSC-4, No. 3, 1968), only the one paper, Ginsberg and Offensend (1968), discussed an application of the method by real decision-makers to a real problem. And in that example the procedure was not successful. Recently, there has been an increasing rate of DA applications (as measured by published journal papers on decision analysis applications), especially in newer areas of research such as "value focused thinking" (Keefer et al., 2004). There has, however, to our knowledge, been limited use of formal decision theory (assessment of utility functions, especially nonadditive) and most of the focus is on practical decision analysis such as using the Analytic Hierarchy Process (AHP) (Saaty, 1980; Saaty and Vargas, 2000). Academic research continues to advance the theory on many fronts, but we'll stick to the practical orientation of this text.

The Highway Vehicle Simulator Case: A DA Formulation

By this time, you may have already struggled with whether Dave Whitlock should recommend to Ed Hargrove that National Electronics respond to the Department of Transportation RFP on the proposed HVS National Facility (see "Historical Case Study: A Highway Vehicle Simulator RFP from DOT" in Chapter 5). We won't analyze the HVS case in detail here, but we can use it to illustrate how one might approach the issue from a DA point of view.

We will construct one possible DA tree that could represent the major issues. However, there doesn't exist a single correct DA representation. Various orderings of the possibilities can be made and greater or lesser detail may be used. Naturally, one hopes that whatever representation one develops, the result of the analysis will be unchanged. Figure 6.8 shows an example DA tree. Suppose we assume for the moment that all of the numerical details shown in the figure are removed—that is, that we are starting with a blank sheet of paper. The box at the left is the "Decision to Bid" point. The two possibilities are "Yes" and "No." It will be our objective to establish which of these two choices has the greater weighted utility.

If the choice on bidding is "No," the outcome will be certain. No chance is involved, and thus the outcome probability is 1.0. If, on the other hand, we choose to bid, a number of possibilities come into play. We represent the first of these chances as a circle labeled "Obtain Award." For the moment, don't worry about the numerical probabilities associated with the two possible outcomes. Go on to the next possibility circle, labeled "Marketability of a Follow-on Product." You may recall that the design and construction of a single DOT simulator would not be very interesting financially

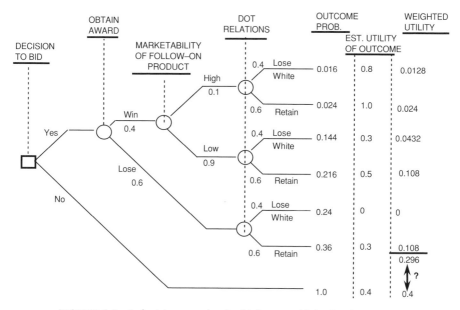

FIGURE 6.8 A decision tree for the highway vehicle simulator case.

for NE. NE would need to have some kind of a follow-on business opportunity to make it worthwhile. One possibility would be a stripped-down simulator to market to high schools for driver training. It is this situation that we represent with this circle.

Obviously, if NE bids and loses the DOT award, this possibility does not exist, so in the "Lose Award" branch, the marketability of a follow-on product does not appear. Next, we consider the question of future DOT relations. Dick White at DOT has been the contract monitor on many NE projects in the past and we value his goodwill. Yet he has expressed concern at the possibility of NE diverting its attention away from work with his Division. We represent this issue by a chance circle labeled "DOT Relations" with two possible outcomes: "Lose White's Goodwill," and "Retain." Notice that this issue appears in all of the paths involved in the "Yes" decision to bid. Apparently, we could have moved the DOT Relations issue back to an earlier point in the DA process. If we had considered it immediately following the decision to bid, it would need to appear on the tree only once. This sort of hindsight is useful in simplifying and editing a tree.

We haven't entered any of the numerical probabilities at any of the chance nodes yet and we will continue to hold off on this matter. Before we enter any numbers, we want to think about the utilities of each of the outcomes. We have shown several procedures for constructing utility curves, but these procedures are only aids. We aren't forced to use them and in this example we choose to take a simple, direct approach. There are seven outcomes shown in Figure 6.8. One is associated with the choice not to bid and the remaining six are associated with various possibilities involved in the bidding process.

Recall that this is a simplified tree in a number of respects. For example, we have decided to omit the possibility of winning the bid but of being unable to produce the simulator on time, within budget, and within specifications. If any of these unpleasant things occurred, NE's profits would be negatively impacted. But, within the limits described, these seven outcomes represent the analysis universe.

Of these seven, which in your opinion is the worst of all possible outcomes? Most folks would say that to bid, and also to lose the competition, and at the same time to lose Dick White's goodwill, would be the worst that could happen. If you agree, give this outcome a utility of 0. Now pick the best of all outcomes and give it a rating of 1.0. We presume you would agree that to bid, and to win the bid, then to find that a follow-on product of high marketability is feasible, and to also retain Dick White's goodwill is the best of all possible worlds. Now by a process of comparing pairs of outcomes, give each of the remaining possible outcomes a utility rating.

We think that losing White's goodwill isn't very important provided that we have a highly marketable follow-on product, and so we'll give that outcome a utility of 0.8, and so forth. Note from Figure 6.8 that we think the utility of not bidding ends up at 0.4. You may not agree with the utilities we have assigned to the various possible outcomes. If so, feel free to put down your own numbers. Remember that the whole concept of utility is subjective.

Now that we have assigned utilities to all of the possible outcomes, we are ready to go back and assess the probabilities associated with each of the chance circles. We assume that the probabilities are independent. That is, the probability at any stage does not affect the probability at any other. Having estimated each of the probabilities at each chance circle, we multiply the probabilities along each path and put this product in the output column as shown in the figure.

Next, weight the raw utilities previously assigned by the probability of each outcome in order to find the weighted outcome utilities, as shown on the rightmost column of Figure 6.8. Finally, sum all of the weighted utilities associated with the "Yes" decision to bid and compare it with the weighted utility of deciding "No." As you can see, we find that a decision not to bid has the higher utility.

Coronary Artery Surgery: A Decision Analysis Application

Pauker (1976) has applied decision analysis to the choice between coronary artery bypass surgery and conservative medical treatment of certain types of heart disease. Chronic ischemic heart disease presents the patient with problems of severe pain and high mortality risk. Coronary artery surgery provides a relatively high probability of short-term pain relief, but at the same time, Pauker says, "operative risks are high and long-term benefits on life expectancy and pain relief remain unproved." "Three main variables determine the value of bypass surgery: (1) the prognosis with medical therapy, which is largely dependent upon the severity of the patient's coronary disease and upon his ventricular function; (2) the potential short- and long-term surgical results, including the operative risks; and (3) the patient's preferences (how he views the relative importance of pain relief and life expectancy). The first two factors affect the likelihoods of the various outcomes, while the last influences the relative desirability of the outcomes."

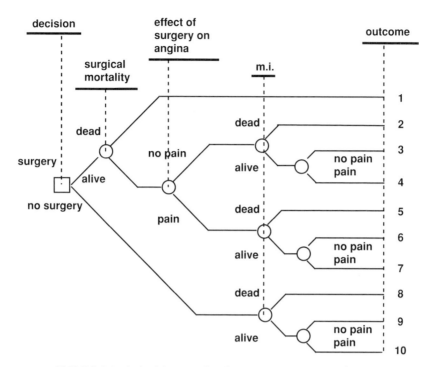

FIGURE 6.9   A decision tree for chronic coronary artery disease.

Pauker assembled the likelihoods (probabilities) from published data and from interviews with experienced heart specialists. The desirability (utilities) was obtained from patient interviews. A decision tree was developed for each patient for each of five years, which represents the time horizon under review. A typical tree is shown in Figure 6.9.

Pauker gives probabilities for these 10 outcomes for a number of different situations. The probabilities depend on the coronary anatomy of the patient, the patient's ventricular function and the results achieved in the past by the specific surgical team (Pauker, 1976, Table 1). We will illustrate the case of a patient suffering from disabling angina, with good coronary anatomy, good ventricular function and a surgical team with good past results. Pauker's probabilities for this situation are given in Table 6.14.

Next, one wishes to obtain the utility placed by a patient on various outcomes. Pauker, in a process similar to the one we have shown in detail above, asks a patient to consider the lottery shown in Figure 6.10 and to assign probabilities such that he is indifferent to the lottery. A number of different types of utility curves result. Pauker characterizes risk-averse patients as "life"-type patients, and those more intent on avoiding pain and thus slightly less risk-averse with respect to surgery are referred to as "pain" patients. Other patients combine these basic characteristics. Figure 6.11 shows typical curves.

Then by multiplying the utility that an individual places on a particular outcome by its probability, one can determine the expected value for the two possible therapies

TABLE 6.14. Probabilities of Various Outcomes for Patients with Disabling Angina, Good Coronary Anatomy, Good Ventricular Function and Good Previous Results by Particular Surgical Team

	Surgery		
	Years Alive	Years Free of Pain	Expectation
1. Perioperative death	0	0	0.03
2. Pain relief but fatal MI	2.5	2.5	0.17
3. Long-term pain relief	5	5	0.41
4. Short-term pain relief	5	2.5	0.24
5. Persistent pain and fatal MI	2.5	0	0.05
6. Spontaneous relief of pain	5	2.5	0.01
7. Persistent pain	5	0	0.09
TOTAL			1.00
	Medical Therapy		
8. Persistent pain and fatal MI	2.5	0	0.23
9. Spontaneous relief of pain	5	2.5	0.10
10. Persistent pain	5	0	0.67
TOTAL			1.00

Source: Pauker (1976, Table 4).

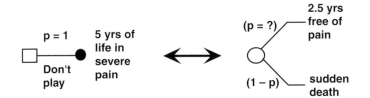

FIGURE 6.10   Assessing the present utility of coronary bypass surgery.

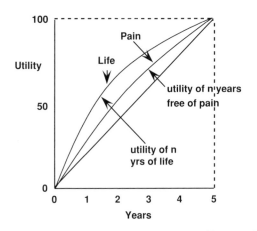

FIGURE 6.11   Utility for two patients of various outcomes. [from Pauker (1976), Fig. 2.]

TABLE 6.15. Value to Two Specific Patients of Possible Outcomes of Two Possible Therapies Under Specific Conditions

Outcome	Patient with "Life" Utility Curve: Utility Experimental Value	Patient with "Pain" Utility Curve: Utility Experimental Value
Surgical		
1	$0 \times .03 = 0$	$0 \times .03 = 0$
2	$80 \times .17 = 13.6$	$62 \times .17 = 10.5$
3	$100 \times .41 = 41$	$100 \times .41 = 41$
4	$100 \times .24 = 24$	$62 \times .24 = 14.9$
5	$80 \times .05 = 4$	$0 \times .05 = 0$
6	$100 \times .01 = 1$	$62 \times .01 = 0.6$
7	$100 \times .09 = 9$	$0 \times .09 = 0$
	Total value 92.6	Total value 67.0
Medical Therapy		
8	$80 \times .23 = 18.4$	$0 \times .23 = 0$
9	$100 \times .10 = 10$	$62 \times .10 = 6.2$
10	$100 \times .67 = 67$	$0 \times .67 = 0$

Source: Pauker (1976).

to the individual. Table 6.15 shows the calculation for the two patients whose utility curves are shown in Figure 6.10, given the conditions of Table 6.14. For the "life" patient under these conditions, medical therapy is indicated, but for the person who places a greater value on the avoidance of pain, surgery is clearly indicated. Pauker goes into this example in much greater detail in his excellent paper, and the interested reader is urged to consult the reference.

6.10 ESTIMATION THEORY IN DECISION ANALYSIS

6.10.1 The Worth of Additional Information

Estimation theory or prediction theory has been an area of major theoretical and practical concern for the past several decades and there is a great deal of material available. We will discuss only two simple discrete cases. First, we take up the unrealistic but relatively simple situation of a perfect prediction and attempt to find out what a perfect prediction is worth. Then, we discuss the case of the imperfect prediction. In the latter example, we mention the process of sequential sampling and when to stop sampling, assuming that each additional sample costs more money.

Suppose that Ajax Metal Products Incorporated is a light metal fabricator that manufactures desks and other office equipment (Gibson, 1989). In the Ajax–San Antonio factory is a sheet metal shear used to cut sheet steel from rolls for construction of four-drawer files and so forth. Mr. Delgado, the General Manager of the plant, is considering the purchase of a new, more powerful shearing machine. He expects the new power shear to be faster and more economical to operate, but he has been informed

TABLE 6.16. Profits for Two Power Shears at Ajax-San Antonio

Sheet Steel	Power Shears	
	Old	New
Good	$800 profit/hr	$960
Bad	$640	$320

that the new shear may be less forgiving if the incoming sheet steel is imperfect. Mr. Delgado knows that in the past the sheet steel supplier has shipped steel in which about 20% of the rolls have imperfections sufficient to halt production on the new machine. He could inspect the incoming sheet steel by unrolling it before mounting on the shear, but this would add production costs. Mr. Delgado has asked for guidance from Ajax Corporate located in Ivy, Virginia, and a young systems analyst skilled in Decision Analysis has flown down to assist him. You walk into Mr. Delgado's office and say:

"Good morning Mr. Delgado. I'm from headquarters and I'm here to help you."

Mr. Delgado hands you a spreadsheet shown in Table 6.16 on which he has estimated his profitability as given. You draw the decision tree shown in Figure 6.12 from the data supplied and recommend the purchase of the new power shears. Next, Mr. Delgado asks whether you would recommend retaining the old shears for emergencies or inspecting the incoming rolls of sheet steel to prevent bad steel from disrupting the production process? What would this information be worth? You diagram the decision process in Figure 6.13.

The upper branch following the first decision box, "do not inspect material," is the same as Figure 6.12. On the other hand, if Ajax decides to "inspect steel," either of two possible outcomes will take place. If the material is "good," the new machine will yield the best outcome of $960 profit/hr. If the material is "bad," the old machine yields the best outcome of $640/hr. To obtain the best overall EMV for the "test material" branch, use the known prior probability of material quality.

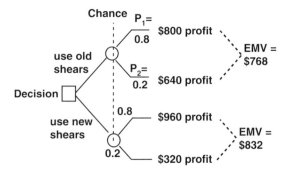

FIGURE 6.12 The Ajax-S.A. power shears purchase decision tree.

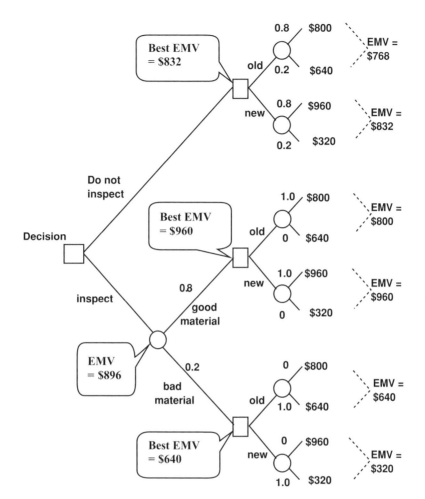

FIGURE 6.13 Possible outcomes given a perfect inspection.

The best EMV for "test material" branch is as follows:

$$\text{Best EMV (with testing)} = 0.8(\$960) + 0.2(\$640) = \$896$$

Thus if inspecting the steel costs less than $\$896 - \$832 = \$64$/hr, it should be done.[4] Although the assumption of perfect inspection is a very strong one and would appear somewhat unrealistic, we now have an upper bound on the value of a prediction. No inspection process could be worth more than $64/hr to Ajax-S.A. But Mr. Delgado isn't finished with you. He knows that no inspection process is perfect. Thus he asks you to include the effect of mistakes made in the incoming steel quality inspection.

6.10.2 The Folded Tree

In order to proceed with this analysis, it will be convenient to discuss a rearrangement of the "normal" decision tree. To show this, let's return to Figure 6.12 and emphasize a specific point. Note that the chance outcomes of the "test material" branch were assigned as 0.8 for "good material" and 0.2 for "bad material." This is a perfectly reasonable assumption based on our prior knowledge of the quality of the material and given a perfect inspection. Nevertheless, it is precisely here that we must pause if the outcome is to some extent uncertain. We will be able to reinspect the steel in the laboratory or have the inspector grade steel of known quality. Thus we could determine the conditional probability of the inspection process given steel of known quality. Of course, this is not the situation in the actual production process. In the plant, we will need the probability of a specific quality of the material conditional on the outcome of the test. Bayes' theorem will permit this calculation.

This situation is represented in Figures 6.14 and 6.15. In Figure 6.14, the "normal" decision tree represents the laboratory determination of the effectiveness of the inspection process given material of known quality. And in Figure 6.15, we show the "folded" tree, with plant test results of the material quality state as an output of the test. The posterior probability is calculated by Bayes' rule. In the theoretical case of the perfect predictor, the result is intuitively obvious perhaps, and all this effort may seem unnecessary. Its value should become clear in a moment, however, as we apply it to the imperfect predictor.

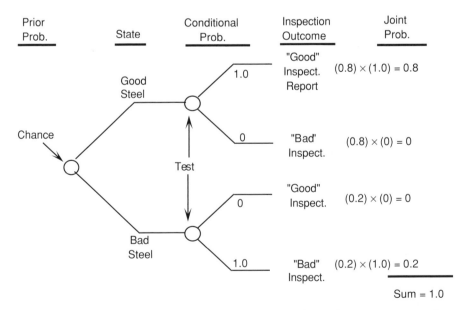

FIGURE 6.14 Normal decision tree for the Ajax power shears decision given a perfect predictor.

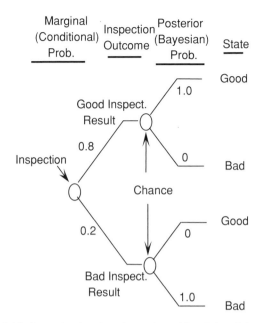

FIGURE 6.15 A folded tree for the shearing unit at Ajax-S.A., giving the desired information in a more convenient form (perfect information).

6.10.3 The Imperfect Estimator

Suppose the steel inspection gives a "good-quality steel" reading 60% of the time when the material is known to be good. This implies, of course, that the conditional probability of a "bad" reading given good material is 0.4. Next, suppose laboratory experiments reveal the conditional probability of a "bad" reading given bad material is 0.90. Thus, the conditional probability of a "good" reading given bad material is 0.10. Figure 6.16 represents this laboratory situation in the form of a "normal" tree and is to be compared with Figure 6.14.

We will use the results of this tree to reconstruct it in the more useful (folded or reversed) form as shown in Figure 6.16, with the state of the quality of wrapping materials (the desired information) as the outcome. The "marginal" probability of a "good" reading may be seen from Figure 6.15 to be $0.48 + 0.02 = 0.50$. We will calculate the posterior (conditional) probabilities.

$P(A_1) = $ prior probability of good material $= 0.8$

$P(B/A_1) = $ conditional probability of "good" test reading, given good material $= 0.6$

$P(\hat{B}/A_1) = $ conditional probability of "bad" test reading, given good material $= 0.4$

$P(A_2) = $ prior probability of bad material $= 0.2$

$P(\hat{B}/A_2) = $ conditional probability of "bad" test reading, given bad material $= 0.90$

$P(B/A_2) = $ conditional probability of "good" test reading, given bad material $= 0.10$

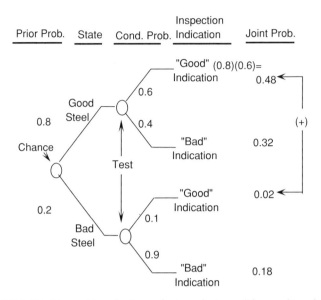

FIGURE 6.16 Normal tree for imperfect prediction of the quality of steel.

Thus, the posterior probability of good quality wrapping material given a good test reading is given by Bayes' rule:

$$P(A_1/B) = [P(B/A_1)P(A_1)]/[P(B/A_1)P(A_1) + P(B/A_2)P(A_2)]$$

Thus

$$P(A_1/B) = \{(0.6)(0.8)/[(0.6)(0.8) + (0.1)(0.2)]\} = [(0.48)/(0.48 + 0.02)] = 0.96$$

As with many numerical examples involving Bayes' theorem, we feel this is a counterintuitive result. An inspection process that is only "right" in 60% of the cases gives a correct result 96% of the time. This isn't the whole story of course, because we can show by the same calculation that even with a "poor" reading the material will be "good" 64% of the time. Nevertheless, we hope you will permit us to be surprised. In exactly the same fashion, the other posterior probabilities as shown in Figure 6.17 may be calculated.

We are now prepared to calculate the worth in dollars of this imperfect inspection process. Figure 6.18 gives the results. Clearly, the expected value of utilizing the additional information provided by the imperfect testing device is $6.40/hr.

6.10.4 Sequential Sampling

Let us review what we have accomplished by inspecting the incoming rolls of sheet steel at Ajax-S.A. The prior probability of good steel was 0.8. From Figure 6.17 we can see that if we get a "good" reading from the testing device, we are 96% sure

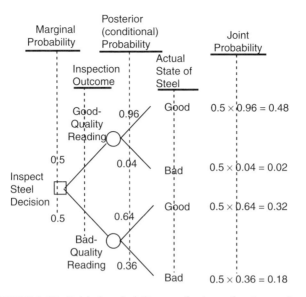

FIGURE 6.17 Folded probability tree for imperfect inspection.

that it is good material. Perhaps this is sufficient precision. However, if the reading is "bad," the probability that the steel is really bad is only 0.36. This is better than no inspection at all of course, because there was only a 0.2 prior probability of bad steel in random roll. Suppose then, if a "bad" reading is obtained, we were to reinspect the roll? It seems apparent that we will obtain a clearer picture of the actual condition of the material, provided the second inspection is independent of the first. Because only a portion of the steel (what portion?) will be subjected to this reinspection, our inspection costs would be held in check. What is the best we could do under this sequential sampling? We already know the answer to this from the perfect inspection calculation.

Sequential sampling has been a field of great theoretical and practical interest in the past several decades. Wald's text is a major theoretical contribution (Wald, 1947), and Shewhart was responsible for introducing the concept of sequential sampling in industrial quality control (Shewhart, 1931). Some students of modern America, Daniel Boorstin for example, give major credit for current productivity standards in American industry, and our current standard of living, to the development of sequential sampling techniques based on probabilistic concepts (Boorstin, 1974). We will leave for the reader the precise calculation of the benefits to be obtained by Mr. Delgado in sequential testing.

6.10.5 Applying Delgado's Utility Curve

We know that most of us are non-EMVers and this certainly applies to Mr. Delgado. He is risk-averse, as are most business people. Thus, he may not be satisfied with the results we have obtained thus far, which were based on maximizing his EMV.

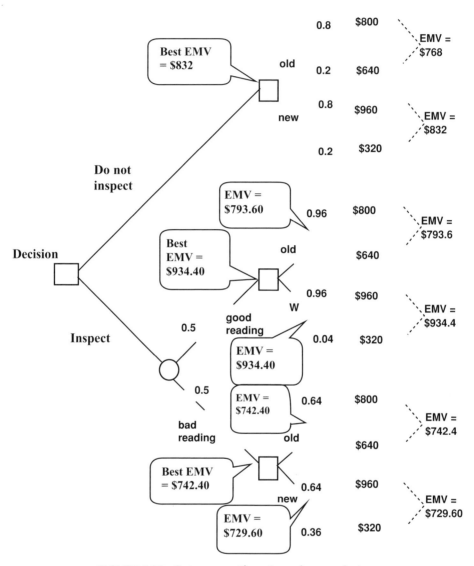

FIGURE 6.18 Outcomes with an imperfect test device.

Suppose Mr. Delgado has established for us the points on his utility scale shown in Table 6.17. In Figure 6.19 we have passed an approximate curve through these points. We have redrawn Figure 6.12 as Figure 6.20 and added Mr. Delgado's utilities. Thus Delgado's expected utility of "using old machine" is given by

$$0.8(0.97) + 0.2(0.92) = 0.96$$

TABLE 6.17. Points in Mr. Delgado's Utility Curve

Delgado's Utility	Hourly Profit ($)
.99	960
.97	800
.92	640
.75	320

And in the same fashion, one may find Delgado's utility for using the new machine to be 0.94. Thus Mr. Delgado should not buy the new sheet steel shearing machine apparently. Perhaps not though. Perhaps the inspection process will improve prospects to the point that the new machine was justified after all from the point of view of maximizing Delgado's utility. We will leave this to the reader to discover.

6.11 SOME PRACTICAL PROBLEMS WITH DECISION ANALYSIS

We have postponed to this point raising objections to the concepts implicit in Decision Theory. Yet, a number of practical and theoretical arguments can be raised against the use of decision analysis (DA) as a practical management tool. Among them are the following.

6.11.1 How to Obtain the Probabilities

This is a standard problem in the use of objective statistics, but it is raised to a new intensity in DA because, by definition, DA is purported to be of use in unique situations

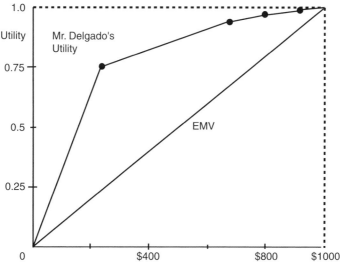

FIGURE 6.19 Mr. Delgado's utility curve.

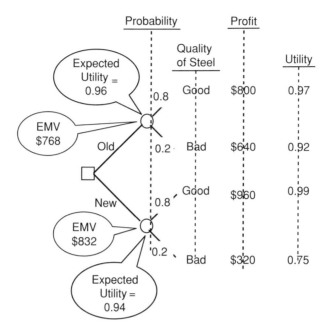

FIGURE 6.20   Redrawn version of Figure 6.12, with Mr. Delgado's utilities added. This leads us to a possibly unexpected result.

or in those with only a few repetitions. The counter argument asks what better tool is available. This is hardly a scientific response.[5]

6.11.2   Institutionalization of Prejudice

Raiffa (1968) introduces a number of dialogues designed to show that different people can have quite different views of risk and arrive at different "decisions." How can we deal scientifically with a process in which two persons can arrive at different results given the same objective "facts?" Obviously, this is outside the paradigm of science, and it appears disingenuous to attempt to disguise this.

6.11.3   Lends False Rationality to Structurally Unstable Situations

The Ajax shearing machine example is completely artificial, of course. By repeatedly refining our technique, we arrive at first one, then the other, conclusion. In reality, we could not know the raw data as precisely as we pretend in this example. At the other extreme, say in nuclear reactor safety for example, we are dealing with incredibly small probabilities of extremely horrible outcomes. Can we "feel" the difference between 10^{-16} and 10^{-20} chances of serious incident? Yet such shifts in these tiny numbers may result in large changes in the results.

More precisely, we argue here that the analyst must ask the decision-maker to produce, or must produce himself, probability values for outcomes for which no quantification procedure can exist. Moreover, the decision-maker must produce value judgments (i.e., utilities) that are psychologically meaningless. Furthermore, Von Winterfeldt and Edwards (1975) show that small errors in utility assessments can lead to gross errors in the final result. Also, there can be considerable lack of belief in the results, given the probabilistic nature of the outcomes (Smith and Winkler, 2006).

6.11.4 Encourages Dealing in Closed Sets

The DA process requires that the real-world problem of the client be reduced to a formal structure (decision tree) and that the analyst name each outcome and evaluate its probability. Yet often the world is indeterminate. A poignant example of this problem was provided unwittingly by Ginsberg and Offensend (1968). The authors gave physicians at the Stanford Children's Hospital methodological assistance in formalizing their decision process as more tests and exploratory operations gained more data on a baffling illness in a child. The reader is led skillfully through this process in the reference; yet ultimately the youngster was found to have <u>none</u> of the illnesses listed on the decision tree.

This is not a rare situation. As a rule in new situations, we cannot enumerate the possible outcomes. In effect here, we argue that the DA process encourages the analyst to adopt a formal structure that does not represent reality in a vital sense.

6.11.5 DA Requires Transitivity

One is told that to be intransitive is to become a "money pump," but this is only true in repeated transactions, which is not the situation DA was designed to handle. In the simple case of repeated transactions, we don't need DA, because we know the "right" answer by prior experience. Unfortunately, the real world is often intransitive; if it wasn't, the Saturday football pool would be easy to beat.

6.11.6 DA Requires Decision-Maker to Reveal Hidden Agenda

An essential part of decision-making in the real world is the decision-maker's (DM) hidden agenda. The DM does not want his opponents to know his future plans or the values which he attaches to certain outcomes. Moreover, the DM often does not want his colleagues and subordinates to have full access to his plans. Full disclosure of all options may involve the organization in continuous debate over relative desirabilities to the exclusion of real work.

Note also that in this problem and especialy in the next one, as well as throughout DA, we are asked to break the first commandment of systems analysis, that is, "the client does not understand his problem." In DA, on the contrary, we declare not only that the client understands his problem, but also that he is the <u>only</u> person who can decide on his own utilities—that is, understand his own problem.

6.11.7   The Utility Curve Concept Is Invalid

Its proponents agree that the utility curve concept is subjective. They further agree that even one's personal utility curve will change from time to time. One can prove to himself by construction that one's curve varies depending on the end-points chosen for the construction process and whether one is dealing with one's own money or one's organization's funds and whether one is buying or selling. Raiffa has shown that one cannot combine the several independent utility curves of individuals to form a valid expression of the group's utility. Obviously, it is nonsense in principle to extrapolate beyond the initially established end-points of the utility curve. Thus one is left with the question, What good is a utility curve?

6.11.8   A Practical Compound Lottery Can't Be Transformed into an Equivalent Lottery

If it could, it wouldn't have been presented as a compound lottery in the first place. This has nothing to do with the so-called "no fun in gambling" axiom. Complex decisions in the real world usually take the form of a compound lottery. But, in almost every case, the prizes and probabilities of the several lotteries downstream from the first decision point are unknown. That is, most real decisions must be based on inadequate and incomplete information. In the real world, one must pay something to enter the lottery <u>before</u> the prizes and probabilities of the next stage are revealed.

6.11.9   Conclusion

A number of difficulties that would seem to block the use of DA in many realistic situations have been cited. Von Winterfeldt and Edwards (1975), put it the following way. Given agreement with all of the axioms and procedures, and in particular the correct assessment of subjective utilities, a DA cannot be wrong. And this they label *"The Decision Analyst's Cop Out."* Because, as they argue, it is in this formalistic reduction of a real-world problem to an unrepresentative model that all the problems lie.

   We find it impossible to argue with the above conclusion from a <u>scientific</u> point of view. Nevertheless, one can make a response from a <u>practical</u> point of view. It all boils down to saying that an imperfect instrument is better than none at all. From a scientific viewpoint, if it hasn't been proven correct, it shouldn't be used. But we have nothing better. Thus, as imperfect as DA is known to be, perhaps it can be used with caution until it is proven or disproved.

6.12   PRACTICAL TRADE STUDIES

OK, so we've partially rejected utility theory but are still left with the problem of making decisions. In Chapter 3, we illustrated a simple method for ranking, and earlier in this chapter we outlined an illustrative process for ranking alternatives. Now, let's go one more round with more discussion on the bottom line of most ranking methods: *rate & weight*. We like to give a definition of decision analysis to our students:

> *To give a mathematical basis for decision-making, allowing hard numbers to be the basis of decisions and not unclear, unspecified, unstated assumptions and beliefs.*

It's interesting to see how many students started writing this definition down; then, after putting the definition on the screen, we start telling them an aside about how students will copy anything put before them on the board (idea borrowed from a classic Doonesbury cartoon). Most, at this point, stop writing, with some laughing. Others will keep writing. But this has been one of the fundamental problems with the use and acceptance of decision analytic tools. In the 1980s we were involved in the development of expert systems to aid physicians in medical diagnosis and treatment selection. There was significant resistance since many involved were operating under the premise of the above definition. So, maybe a better definition is:

> *To give guidance, information, insight, and structuring in the decision-making process in order that better, more "rational," decisions can be made and allow decision-makers to be better informed.*

This is much closer to the value we've seen in the methods and is acceptable to decision-makers. So let's go through a process of a simple trade study and address some of the critical issues of a rate & weight approach. Many books and papers go into considerable detail; however, we want to continue with our application orientation to illustrate critical, practical issues.

Assume that we are going to purchase a car, and want to do alternative ranking via rate & weight. First, we need a set of requirements for the car choice. The requirements will contain all kinds of constraints, performance requirements, derived requirements, and so on. From these requirements we can derive a set of system attributes by which we can evaluate the cars under consideration. Let's assume that we have identified the following attributes:

1. Cargo capacity (cu. ft.)
2. Miles per gallon (MPG)
3. Passenger capacity (# people)
4. 0–60 miles per hour (seconds)
5. Cost (assumes a measure of total cost of ownership [TCO], except gas and oil) ($)

After an exercise of creativity, we have generated the following alternatives. All alternatives are acceptable in that they meet the minimum (or maximum) system requirements (e.g., "must be able to seat at least four adult passengers").

TABLE 6.18. Raw Attribute Scores

Vehicle	Cubic Feet	MPG	Number of People	0–60 sec	$
Minivan	38.4	23	8	7.3	36,900
Performance sport sedan	16.0	22	5	5.9	52,700
Station wagon	35.8	26	5	8.0	30,200
Sport utility vehicle (SUV)	18.6	15	9	10.2	38,400
Family sedan	15.4	28	5	9.1	20,160

1. Minivan
2. Performance sport sedan
3. Station wagon
4. Sport utility vehicle (SUV)
5. Family sedan

What is needed next is to generate performance data for each alternative on each attribute. Such data might come from simulation or analytic models, lab testing, or field testing, and so on. In this simple example, the data in Table 6.18 come directly from the manufacturer.[6]

Next, we have to translate these raw scores into some measure of value. This requires us to decide if more is better (possibly MPG), less is better (possibly cost), or average is better (possibly 0–60). If more is better is selected, for example, we then need to create a "value" function that maps the raw data into value measure. These value functions appear similar in nature to the utility functions discussed earlier, except there is no notion of uncertainty.[7] Consider Figure 6.21, where we have three value functions for MPG. Function A exhibits decreasing returns in that going from 15 to 20 MPG is of more delta value than going from 20 to 25 MPG (i.e., $(V[20] - V[15]) > (V[25] - V[20])$). Likewise, C exhibits increasing returns. Function B is linear with constant returns. Note that the 0–100 scale is arbitrary, and many use a 0–1 scale. Also, there are numerous other possible functional forms, including an "S" shape that exhibits early increasing returns and then decreasing returns.

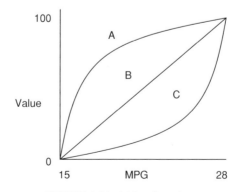

FIGURE 6.21 Value function.

TABLE 6.19. Alternative Values

Vehicle	Cubic Feet	MPG	Number of People	0–60 sec	$
Minivan	100.0	61.5	75.0	67.4	48.6
Performance sport sedan	2.6	53.8	0.0	100.0	0.0
Station wagon	88.7	84.6	0.0	51.2	69.1
Sport utility vehicle (SUV)	13.9	0.0	100.0	0.0	43.9
Family sedan	0.0	100.0	0.0	25.6	100.0

Which function is best? It depends on your preferences. Typically, in practice, analysts will scale linearly (*B*) and then determine the importance of that choice via the sensitivity of the rankings. Also importantly, how does one determine a nonlinear type of value function? There are numerous assessment techniques, such as the midpoint technique, that are fairly simple and effective in use.[8] In our practice, we often limit the choice to a set of maybe five functions (such as in Figure 6.21, with an *A′* and a *C′* added to the diagram), and determine the sensitivity to such a choice, and follow with a more detailed assessment if necessary.

If less is better, the procedure would be similar. If average performance was preferred for an attribute like 0–60, we could use for the *Y* axis something like standard deviations from the mean or the absolute value of the deviation from the mean. Once these functions have been selected, we then can create a value matrix as in Table 6.19. For this example, the starting point has been linear value functions for each attribute.

First we can determine if any of the alternatives outright dominates another; that is, does any alternative do equal or better on all attributes, with at least one better? For this example, the answer is no. Typically, a number of alternatives can be eliminated at this stage as a result of basic dominance. One easy check is that any alternative that scores 100 on an alternative is likely to not be dominated; however, not scoring 100 (e.g., the station wagon) does not imply that it's dominated. It is interesting how one leading consumer reporting magazine often recommends dominated alternatives.

Next, we come to the critical stage—how to determine the trade-offs between attributes. Table 6.20 revisits Table 6.18, showing the maximum and minimum of the attribute raw scores along with the difference of these (termed "delta"). The

TABLE 6.20. Weight Assessment Information

Vehicle	Cubic Feet	MPG	Number of People	0–60 sec	$
Minivan	38.4	23	8	7.3	36,900
Performance sport sedan	16.0	22	5	5.9	52,700
Station wagon	35.8	26	5	8.0	30,200
Sport utility vehicle (SUV)	18.6	15	9	10.2	38,400
Family sedan	15.4	28	5	9.1	20,160
Maximum	38.4	28.0	9.0	10.2	52,700
Minimum	15.4	15.0	5.0	5.9	20,160
Delta	23	13	4	4.3	32,540

TABLE 6.21. Trade-Off Weights and Total Scores

Vehicle	Cubic Feet	MPG	Number of People	0–60 sec	$	Weighted Score
Relative weight:	3	1	3	1	2	
Normalized weight:	0.3	0.1	0.3	0.1	0.2	
Minivan	100.0	61.5	75.0	67.4	48.6	75.1
Performance sport sedan	2.6	53.8	0.0	100.0	0.0	16.2
Station wagon	88.7	84.6	0.0	51.2	69.1	54.0
Sport utility vehicle (SUV)	13.9	0.0	100.0	0.0	43.9	43.0
Family sedan	0.0	100.0	0.0	25.6	100.0	32.6

importance of each of the attributes should depend on these delta values. The smaller the delta, the less important (or less weight) we would assume for an attribute.

Given Table 6.20 and the delta values, we next assess importance weights for each of the attributes. Once again, there are numerous techniques for doing this; however, we prefer initially to start simply [see Buede (2000) for several techniques for assessing these "swing weights"]. Continuing with our example in Table 6.21, we have assigned the least important attribute a weight of 1 (see "Relative Weights" row); then we assessed relative weights from there, with the higher the number, the more important. Once these relative weights have been assessed, we normalize them (see "Normalized Weights" row) and create a "Weighted Score" for each alternative. Given the values scores and normalized weights, we create the total "Weighted Score" for each alternative, along with the product of the weight row and value row for each alternative, which is given in the rightmost column. Use of value scores between 0 and 100 and weights between 0 and 1 allows for easy interpretation.

OK, so now we're done, and the "minivan" is the best choice. No. Now we are ready to get started with the important part of the trade study, which asks the question "Why is the mini van the best?", which leads to a sensitivity analysis. We can ask questions such as:

- Under what set of weights, if any, would the performance sedan be best?
- How much can the value function for cubic feet change (i.e., from a function like *B* to *A*) before the decision changes?
- What are my top two choices and how robust is that selection?
- How much can I change the weight on cost before the rankings change?
- Etc.!

These questions provide the purpose of a trade study—to provide insight into the decision and recommendation. Such questions as those above could be answered by a brute force search over values, or one could use a tool such as Solver in Excel^{TM} to find desired values. For example, a linear program can be set up to determine the answer to question 1, but in this simple case the basic idea is easy to see: Put a significant weight into the 0–60 attribute and the performance sedan will be best. Alternatively, we could add "noise" to the values or weights by using a tool such as Crystal Ball^{TM} or @Risk^{TM} to perform a Monte Carlo simulation. Such an approach would allow for the decision-maker to incorporate uncertainty about raw scores, value scores, or trade-off weights.

A formal, but simple, trade study such as described above can add considerable insight and clarity into the decision process. If a decision-maker insists that a particular alternative is best, they would have to demonstrate which value functions they disagree with and/or with which weights they disagree. If they agree with the values and the weights and not the choice, then are they wrong with their decision logic and must they accept the mathematics? Again, no. If they continue to insist on a different choice, there could be several reasons.

First, there could be a missing attribute that is driving their thinking, and hopefully the discussions would bring this issue to the table. Such a missing or hidden attribute could be very sensitive and high on the political agenda of the stakeholders, so be careful. At that point, the decision could be made to add the new attribute to the trade study or to agree to remove it from consideration.

Second, there could be something deeper going on that is more difficult to address. Inherently in the trade study, we have buried some significant decision-theoretic assumptions about the attributes, mainly notions of independence [See French (1988)]. If, for example, attributes are substitutes or complements (often called "synergies"), then they are not additive and the simple rate & weight additive model we've assumed is not valid. One possible way around this issue is to redefine the attributes in such a way that they are "more" independent or to add a new attribute that may capture some of the synergies. Ideally, from a decision theorist's point of view, we would replace the additive model with a more advanced functional form, such as a multiplicative value model (which has interaction terms between the attributes) [see Keeney and Raiffa (1976) for details on various functional forms].

In practice, however, this complication is very difficult to address and the assessment issues become overwhelming. All of the popular software on the market today for decision-aiding assumes an additive value function given the difficulties in moving beyond such a model, thus all are in effect rate & weight models. The wildly popular and dominant decision tool termed "AHP" (Analytic Hierarchy Process, developed by Thomas Saaty), for example, uses an additive form [see Saaty (1980); for a more recent works see Saaty and Vargas (2000)]. The difference between various tools is the manner in which they assess the trade-off weights and the value functions. Tools based on AHP, for example, use pairwise comparisons to create "positive reciprocal matrices" for which they then calculate eigenvalues, which are normalized to create values and weights (Saaty, 2003). Too complex for us—we recommend a simple spreadsheet, where everything is transparent. One advantage of formal tools, such as Expert Choice^{TM} (based on AHP, see: http://www.expertchoice.com/), is the powerful sensitivity analysis that is built in to the software. The downside, from our perspective, is the lack of transparency in much of the behind-the-scenes machinations.

One can easily also see decision scenarios, which are represented by differing sets of trade-off weights. If we imagine a young family with three children, their

TABLE 6.22. Alternative Weights

Vehicle	Cubic Feet	MPG	Number of People	0–60 sec	$	Weighted Score
Relative weight:	1	3	1	1	3	
Normalized weight:	0.1	0.3	0.1	0.1	0.3	
Minivan	100.0	61.5	75.0	67.4	48.6	63.6
Performance sport sedan	2.6	53.8	0.0	100.0	0.0	29.3
Station wagon	88.7	84.6	0.0	51.2	69.1	66.8
Sport utility vehicle (SUV)	13.9	0.0	100.0	0.0	43.9	27.3
Family sedan	0.0	100.0	0.0	25.6	100.0	69.5

weights might look very much like what we saw in Table 6.21. Alternatively, an older couple that is traveling considerably and concerned more about cost issues might have weights that look more like those in Table 6.22, where the family sedan looks like the preferred choice, followed closely by the station wagon. One could easily imagine other numerous scenarios, such as the performance-minded person mentioned earlier. Without even assessing a set of weights, the analyst could generate several reasoned scenarios and their respective decisions, such as:

- If you are primarily concerned with storage and carrying people, then the first choice is a minivan followed (not closely) by a station wagon.
- If you are primarily concerned with cost issues, then the first choice is a family sedan followed (closely) by a station wagon and minivan.

Alternatively, if carrying nine people was an imperative, then the clear choice is the SUV. However, this begs the question as to whether carrying nine people should have been a requirement, which would have led to a different set of alternatives. Once again, if this is revealed, then the goal of the decision analysis has been achieved. As with all steps in a systems analysis: Iterate! Iterate! Iterate!

Again, the goal of the analysis is to understand why one would choose Alternative A over Alternative B. The above example is simple and obvious; however, in complex trade studies the results might not be so obvious or intuitive. Consider the BRAC (see http://www.defenselink.mil/brac), a major trade study effort that was performed with considerable depth and skill in the decision analytics. In that case, there were 40 attributes and 97 installations (alternatives)—the results which were not necessarily obvious at all.

Another consideration involves the issue of cost. The decision-maker may want to have cost removed from the trade study and also present the cost versus performance (trade study score), where clear trade-offs can be shown between cost and performance. Also, many decision-makers may look at this process from another perspective. When we were doing work with senior military decision-makers, they wanted the following question answered:

If I give you the ranked alternatives, can you give me the weights that imply such a ranking?

TABLE 6.23. Utilities for Three Outcomes

	$u(C)$	$u(P)$	$u(D)$
MD1	1.0	0.4	0
MD2	1.0	0.48	0

We developed a tool, termed "inverse decision aiding," that did exactly that (White et al., 1983). Such an approach fits a more inductive decision model and how many of us think—we know what we want, and we want to verify that it makes sense in terms of our considerations (attributes). Such an approach proved to be relevant behaviorally to decision-makers (White et al., 1984; Carlson and Scherer, 2006).

Finally, a similar process to the above trade study method can be extended to decisions under uncertainty. In such a case, we have alternatives with probabilistic outcomes, and outcomes have associated (multiple) attributes. Obviously, there is considerably more information to be assessed, and the value functions are replaced by utility functions.

Now That We've Ranked .... We've walked you through the main steps of a systems analysis. What's left is still important and necessary: iteration and the management of the process.

EXERCISES

6.1 Gibson once found himself, as a university administrator, in a situation that seems to have involved voting paradoxes. His financial VP called him one day during a budget planning period and said, "Jack, I have received your recommendations for faculty raises and they are within the guidelines I gave you. Now I want you to prepare a short list in rank order, of about 20 faculty names who are deserving of an additional $500 increment if funds are available. Then when I find out how much money I have left, I'll go down your list as far as I can. I have to proceed this way because I may have less than 24 hours within which to make a final decision."

At the time, he did not know about the Arrow paradox, but instinctively he didn't like that approach. Given your knowledge of the paradox, how would you have advised Gibson to proceed?

6.2 Two medical doctors (MD1 and MD2) must decide whether to treat a patient (T) or wait (W). Their utilities for three outcomes in Table 6.23 may be assumed independent of the strategy and are, where C = cure, P = paralysis, and D = death.

The conditional probabilities of the outcomes are in Table 6.24:

TABLE 6.24. Conditional Probabilities of the Outcomes

$P(C/T) = 0.5$	$P(P/T) = 0.2$	$P(D/T) = 0.3$
$P(C/W) = 0.2$	$P(P/W) = 0.6$	$P(D/W) = 0.2$

TABLE 6.25. Probability of Gaining Certain Market Shares and Respective Profits

Share of Market	President's Assessed Probability of Gaining This Share	Annual Profit ($ million)	
		Expand Facility	Build New Plant
45%	1/8	99	55
50%	1/2	110	110
55%	3/8	143	165

Assume that each M.D. desires to maximize utility. From this, calculate each M.D.'s optimal strategy. Draw a decision tree for this situation.

6.3 Consider the situation of Gamma Corporation (GC), which has to decide whether or not to build a new plant or expand the old one. The expected profits for GC will depend on the market share it expects. The president assesses the probability of his firm's maintaining its present 50% market share as 1/2, and he assesses the probabilities of 45% and 55% shares as 1/8 and 3/8, respectively. The profits are shown in Table 6.25:

Find the president's optimal strategy based on maximizing his company's economic return. Do you feel that the differences of the expected values convey the true qualitative difference between the probable economic effects of the two decisions?

6.4 Commercial Lending Corporation (CLC) is saddled with the problem of extending $150,000 credit to a new PC manufacturer. CLC classifies typical companies into three categories: poor risk, average risk, and good risk; 55% are average risks, and 15% are good risks. If CLC decides to extend credit, the expected profit for this size loan from a poor risk is $20,000, from an average risk $13,000, and from a good risk $27,000. If CLC does not make the loan, it is assumed that the PC manufacturer will turn to another lending institution.

(a) What is the Bayes' action, based on the above information?

(b) How much money would CLC be willing to pay for perfect information? Suppose CLC has the ability to hire an outside credit investigation team. CLC's experience with this team is shown in Table 6.26.

(c) The credit team's assistance is available for the price of $2600. What is the optimal expected loss if the credit investigation team's data are used? Does it

TABLE 6.26. CLC's Experience with Credit Investigation Team

Credit Team Evaluation	Actual Credit Rating Percent		
	Poor	Average	Good
Poor	50	30	20
Average	30	50	20
Good	20	20	60

TABLE 6.27. Payoff Table

	Table Values in $ mil.		
	Two-Year Maturation	Three-Year Maturation	Four-Year Maturation
a1 = buy land	$ 2.5	$ 0.5	($ 1.5)
a2 = don't buy	($ 0.1)	($ 0.1)	($ 0.1)

pay to utilize the credit investigation team? Determine the optimal strategy for CLC, given that the credit investigation team gives a poor evaluation, an average evaluation, or a good evaluation.

6.5 A land speculator is trying to decide whether or not to buy a certain parcel of property in a distant city. He knows that a regional shopping center will be built in this particular community in five years (property will need to be purchased by year 4). As all land speculators do, he operates with borrowed money (leverage). This causes large carrying costs if he should decide to buy the site. Commercial development is not tremendously profitable at this time in this community; in fact, the only major commercial development anticipated in the community in the near future is the regional shopping center.

The developer can obtain a one-year renewable note @ 12.5% (i.e., he can borrow the principal and only pay the interest and renew indefinitely as long as he makes the annual interest payment on the principal). If the shopping center goes through in two years, the speculator will net $2.5 million. If it takes three years, he will make $0.5 million ($2.5 million minus carrying costs). If it takes four years, he will lose $1.5 million. The price of the land is $16 million. Whether or not he buys the land, he will spend about $0.1 million of investigation and preparation (e.g., lawyers, architects, site developers, landscape architect, etc.). His decision is whether or not to buy the land. Table 6.27 shows the payoff table.

The speculator is certain that the shopping center will be built on this parcel by year 5. The speculator feels that the change of maturation in two years has a probability of 0.1, in three years 0.5, and in four years 0.4.

(a) Draw a decision tree for the speculator's situation and find his optimal strategy, assuming he is risk neutral.

(b) Now suppose that the speculator has been approached by a local developer who wishes to act as his associate. The local associate, due to his special knowledge and continuous availability to local planning agencies and outside organizations, can speed up the approval process, thereby enhancing an earlier approval date. The associate is not always successful in his forecasts and living up to them. His "track record" is shown in Table 6.28. The values in the table are based on his past performance in similar situations. He charges a fee of $250,000.

Draw a decision tree for the speculator in this situation. Calculate the optimal strategy for the speculator if the local associate gives a two-year forecast, a three-year forecast, a four-year forecast.

TABLE 6.28. The Associate's "Track Record"

	Actual Maturation		
Local Associate Says that Maturation Is	Two Years	Three Years	Four Years
Two Years (A)	0.67	0.19	0.11
Three Years (B)	0.22	0.61	0.19
Four Years (C)	0.11	0.20	0.70

TABLE 6.29. The Second Local Realtor's Estimates

	Actual Maturation		
Second Local Assessment	Two Years	Three Years	Four Years
2 Years (A)	0.68	0.22	0.10
3 Years (B)	0.17	0.56	0.22
4 Years (C)	0.15	0.22	0.68

(c) Now suppose another local realtor says he will give his opinion to the speculator after the first associate for no fee. The speculator agrees to this, because he feels free information is beneficial. The speculator assumes his estimates will be close to those given by the first associate and will be almost a simple "perturbation" of the first associate's performance. The second local realtor's estimates are shown in Table 6.29.

Calculate the optimal strategy for the speculator, based on the above data for a two-year forecast, a three-year forecast, and a four-year forecast. Comment on your results and what is probably in the mind of the speculator. What do you think the speculator will think about Bayesian Decision Analysis?

6.6 Formulate the issue of purchasing a new automobile as a decision tree. Include functional as well as technological issues. Establish your own value curve and calculate the optimum solution for you based on an EMV point of view, as well as your optimum value solution.

6.7 [team assignment] Review the BRAC study (available on-line; see http://www. defenselink.mil/brac/). Given the discussions in Section 6.12, create a list of questions and concerns regarding the ranking phase of BRAC.

CASE STUDY: TRAINING CENTER LOCATION

Our client company, Intelligent Systems Incorporated (ISC), offers high-end, leading-edge IT consulting services. They have approximately 5000 employees, are headquartered in the NOVA area, work predominantly with the federal government and large government contractors, and generate $1.7 billion per year in sales (of services). Employees are scattered at client sites throughout the United States. They have decided to build a training center and have hired us to evaluate candidate sites. An internal board has preselected 12 candidate sites, for various business and fiscal reasons, and they want our analysts to evaluate the 12 sites and make a recommendation.

Approximately 5% of the workforce is in intensive, off-site training at any one time by their internal training staff. Many of the training sessions are two or more weeks in duration, and the goal of the company is to have a location that will be desirable to the employees. Since the training is intensive, they also want to provide a wide range of activities (scheduled, formal, and informal opportunities) for the employees while in training in order to maintain employee morale and educational objectives (i.e., not have the employees burn out during training). Therefore, they want us to select the best location from an employee perspective.

Prepare a 20-minute briefing of your recommendation for our Senior Partner, Martin Landsdowne.

The cities under consideration are

1. San Diego, CA
2. Boston, MA
3. Olympia, WA
4. Chicago, IL
5. Santa Fe, NM
6. Colorado Springs, CO
7. West Palm Beach, FL
8. San Antonio, TX
9. Baltimore, MD
10. Salt Lake City, UT
11. Atlanta, GA
12. Charlotte, NC

CASE STUDY: CORPORATE HEADQUARTERS LOCATION

A young, small, high-technology business, with approximately 300 mostly technical employees, is relocating its corporate headquarters for various reasons. They have narrowed the decision down to 10 possible locations for business reasons; that is, all 10 locations meet the business goals. They want to select, therefore, the best environment for attracting and retaining employees. Corporate analysts have determined the selection criteria for use (below):

- Weather
- Crime
- Housing
- Education
- Economy
- Health
- Quality of life
- Transportation

The selected cities are:

1. Athens, GA
2. Asheville, NC
3. Charlottesville, VA
4. Decatur, AL
5. Florence, SC
6. Fort Walton Beach, FL
7. Gainesville, FL
8. Greenville, NC
9. Myrtle Beach, SC
10. Parkersburg–Marietta, GA

What is your recommendation? Why?

CASE STUDY: BUSINESS SCHOOL SELECTION

Your employer has agreed, as a condition of hiring you, that they will "fund" your MBA education after one year of employment. They will let you go, full salary, for two years to obtain the degree (after working one full year)—tuition payment is your responsibility. You will owe the company four years of employment after finishing school. You must select one school from a list of their 20 pre-approved MBA programs (schools); however, you must select the school now (so they can begin paperwork and financial arrangements) and it's your responsibility to get accepted.

What is your selection?

1. Harvard University (MA)
2. Stanford University (CA)
3. University of Pennsylvania (Wharton)
4. Massachusetts Institute of Technology (Sloan)
5. Northwestern University (Kellogg) (IL)

 6. University of Chicago
 7. Columbia University (NY)
 8. University of California—Berkeley (Haas)
 9. Dartmouth College (Tuck) (NH)
10. University of California—Los Angeles (Anderson)
11. Duke University (Fuqua) (NC)
12. University of Michigan—Ann Arbor (Ross)
13. New York University (Stern)
14. University of Virginia (Darden)
15. Yale University (CT)
16. Carnegie Mellon University (Tepper) (PA)
17. Cornell University (Johnson) (NY)
18. Emory University (Goizueta) (GA)
19. University of Texas—Austin (McCombs)
20. University of North Carolina—Chapel Hill (Kenan–Flagler)

NOTES

1. However, the role of intuition is not clearly understood; see Khatri and Alvin (2000).
2. However, there has been some claim of a decline in the number of decision analysis related publications [see Keefer et al. (2004, pp. 4–22)], while others claim that the maturing of the field has led to the movement and increase in publications in application domains [see Hämäläinen1 (2004), pp. 26–31].
3. Technical problem in this example is that mean values are not preserved by a strictly increasing transformation (i.e., System 2 is an increasing transformation of System 1); however, a linear transformation (e.g., multiplying System 1 values by 20) does preserve mean values.
4. The Expected Value of Perfect Information (EVPI); see Clemen and Reilly.
5. For an interesting discussion on people's interpretation of probabilities, see Chapter 4 in Behn and Vaupel (1982).
6. Obviously, we need to be careful in accepting manufacturer data.
7. See French (1988) for a detailed treatise.
8. See Buede (2000) for sample assessment techniques.

Chapter 7

Iteration and Transition

7.1 ITERATION

We have now arrived at the point at which it is appropriate to discuss "iteration," the final step in the *study* phase of systems analysis (SA). Following iteration, the system team should be ready to move into the *action* phase of the program. Presumably, the team has iterated within each of the major phases and now we have completed the first total pass through. Because we have discussed iteration previously and because the concept itself is simple, we need merely remind the reader of the major points.

Why Iterate? Moving rapidly through the complete system study with the intent to iterate is designed to provide a complete overview of the problem, including the data needed to fill in gaps and to complete the understanding of the problem. Not least important is the need to recognize possible gaps in the skills of members of the systems team at an early stage, so that new team members with the needed skills can be added.

What Is the Time Scale for Each Iteration? We have emphasized that the first few iterations should be done rapidly. But what does "rapidly" mean? Bureaucratically inclined individuals think in terms of months and years so that to them "rapidly" might mean six months or so. We reject that notion. We're talking about a few days for the first complete pass through of the SA, certainly less than a single

How to Do Systems Analysis. By John E. Gibson, William T. Scherer, and William F. Gibson
Copyright © 2007 John Wiley & Sons, Inc.

work week. The first several steps of the system study should be completed in a single session lasting perhaps a few hours. Then in one or two more days the first iteration can be finished and committed to paper. Almost inevitably, this first draft will have more holes in it than Swiss cheese, but now the team will have an understanding of the overall problem and what has to be done next. Now individuals on the team can take on personal assignments and all can work individually, but in parallel.

The second iteration will take more time, possibly two or three weeks because of the time needed to assemble necessary data and to fill in other blanks. The second iteration should carry along a number of alternative solution candidates, possibly as many as a dozen or more and certainly a half dozen at least. A session with the client is desirable in this period.

Beginning with the third iteration, the number of alternatives can be reduced to a half dozen or even fewer, but never less than three. These remaining few candidates should be carefully evaluated, using the client's criteria of course, and presented to the client. Inevitably, the SA team will have a preferred solution, but the client must make the choice. The team should guard against unduly influencing this decision and certainly must be very careful to present the pluses and minuses for each candidate in an objective manner.

How Many Iterations? Information has a cost. In each iteration, we gain more information about the problem and its solution, but we are paying for this information with time and money. It should be possible to estimate the probable cost of another iteration and the marginal value of the improvement we can make to our advice to the client. When the cost of another iteration appears to outweigh the probable benefit, stop iterating.

It is interesting that many of the formal methodologies mentioned in Chapter 1 allow for iteration in theory, often represented by lines with arrows, but don't really address the issue directly or they actually make it difficult to perform. Much of this could be a result of the environment they are designed for—for example, government procurement and its associated regulations that often stymie true iteration. Most methods, however, do allow or at least mention iteration at each stage (or step or phase) of their process, and this iteration is of significant value.

Editorial Comments on the Concept of "Iteration." We find a strong aversion to the concept of iteration in almost everyone who thinks about it a bit.[1] Almost everything about it seems contrary to nature. The idea of doing a complete iteration, including a slide show for the boss, in the first few days of a long project can be expected to raise the hackles of team members. Meeting with the client this early may also be disturbing. Perfectionists strongly resist turning loose their ideas after only a few days' work. In our diverse careers, we think we have heard about every conceivable objection to the concept, but we are not persuaded that the very real difficulties, including the need to confess one's ignorance on the details of the topic, overcome the advantages to be gained.

7.2   SEGMENT AND FOCUS

After the first or second iteration, the general issue generally becomes clear enough to segment the issue into its essential parts. Segmentation is a dangerous tool because we do not want the team to break into subgroups that concern themselves exclusively with only one segment of the problem. Rather, segmentation is a means of addressing the client's needs in the transition scenario. Many segmentation dimensions are possible. One common and very powerful segmentation divides the solution into short-, intermediate-, and long-term solutions. In the short term, capital improvements are impossible. Take the Sky High Baggage problem for example. In the short term, we might recommend that just a few critical airports be focused upon and retraining be employed to improve the execution of current procedures. In the intermediate term, changes in methods and procedures can be implemented. New types of tags could be printed, the work gangs could be restructured and retrained, procedures could be rearranged, and so on. Only in the long term could major changes in physical structures be contemplated.

Focusing refers to the special attention that should be given to the essential elements of a systems problem. There is never enough time and other resources to investigate every element of the problem fully. Thus, it is necessary that those (few) essential elements be identified first and attended to, then if time permits, less vital topics can be considered. Naturally, the judgment as to essentiality must be made from the client's perspective.

7.3   THE TRANSITION SCENARIO

The bridge between the study phase of the SA (almost complete now after several iterations) and the implementation phase is called the *Transition Scenario*. The Transition Scenario is an essential part of the final report to the client, because it tells the client how to get from where she is (i.e., the "Descriptive Scenario") to where she wants to be (i.e., the "Normative Scenario," sometimes called the "Preferred Future").

The main elements of the transition scenario are as follows:

1. A *Gantt chart* listing all major project steps, with major mileposts defined.
2. Delineations of constraints, critical incidents, resources required, relationships with affected groups, risk assessments, and so on. *Interaction matrices* are effective in clarifying interactions (more on this in Section 7.5).
3. Cost of failure to stay on schedule (for assessing contractor penalties, etc.)
4. Responsibilities of major actors.
5. Sign-offs required of major cooperating groups.

The Transition Scenario can be thought of as a checklist to be followed in moving into action, or for the client to follow should the systems study team not be involved in managing the installation phase. Even if the delivery of the final re-port is in fact the end of our involvement, we must demonstrate our "action ori-entation" by including a complete and definitive Transition Scenario section in our report.

7.4   THE GANTT CHART

The Gantt chart is among the simplest and most effective graphic devices for exerting management control of a project and for illustrating the interconnections between the various activities within it. Thus, it is a surprise how often it is resisted or ignored, especially in working with students. William Gantt was one of a small group of

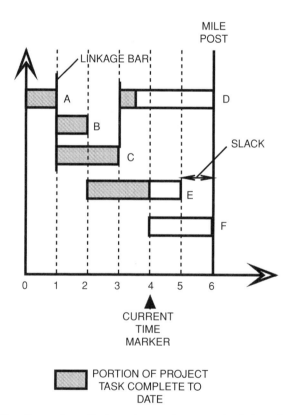

FIGURE 7.1   The Gantt chart. Project element bars are shaded to show the portion complete to the present. Present time is indicated by the "Current Time Marker." A solid vertical bar links the end of project element A with the start of elements B and C, indicating a linkage. Element A must finish before B and C can begin. Note that element E appears to have slack time before the milepost at month 6, and element D has fallen behind schedule.

pioneers who gathered around Frederick W. Taylor at the turn of the century to develop the principles of Taylor's "Scientific Management," including time and motion study, job shop scheduling, and factory operations in general. Figure 7.1 shows a simple example.

The bars shown in Figure 7.1 represent the schedule for initiation and termination of the various program elements as a function of time. Note that linkages between elements can easily be shown. For example, the solid vertical bar at month 1 indicates that element A must be complete before elements B and C can begin. The solid vertical milepost line at month 6 means that all the elements in the first six months must be complete before funding for the second half will be released. We can see that a one-month slack period has been scheduled in element E. Thus, project element E can run as much as a month behind schedule and we would still meet the month 6 milepost. The Gantt chart can also be used to detect the need to allocate extra resources to speed up a particular element that has fallen behind schedule.

The "Current Time Marker" is at month 4 in Figure 7.1, and we can see that there is a problem in project element D which is about two weeks behind schedule. Thus, extra resources should be allocated to it to permit recovery. We can't tell by examining this snapshot just where the program fell behind. We do know that element B was not the culprit, but either A or C might have failed to end on time. Possibly it was element C, but the manager might have recognized that to recover a day in element C would be more expensive than to recover a day during element D and therefore a decision was made to wait until element D was underway before allocating overtime.

Numerous software packages implement Gantt charts, with the ubiquitous Microsoft Project™ leading the charge. Packages such as AEC's FastTrack Schedule™ allow for valuable features, such as sensitivity analysis, critical path analysis, cost optimization, and visualization, to name a few [see Kerzner (2001) for an excellent and comprehensive review of the field].

7.5 INTERACTION MATRICES

We noted in a previous chapter that an Objectives Tree can aid greatly in clarifying and organizing the goals of a project. But it does not illustrate in a systemic manner the interrelations between Goals, Activities, Constraints, Resources, and so on. Thus, an interaction analysis provides another opportunity to reorganize or redefine the goals if the need is revealed by the interaction analysis. The concept of "House of Quality" from the Quality Function Deployment (QFD) and Total Quality Management (TQM) literature, for example, is fundamentally based on interaction matrices (including self- or cross-interaction matrices) [see, for example, Besterfield et al. (2003)]. Use of interaction matrices in this fashion predates the popular quality literature; for example, Sage (1977) illustrates the same concept. The fundamental importance of interaction matrices is also a fundamental concept in systems engineering—*traceability*. A network of interaction matrices and the associated traceability is a critical concept in any systems engineering methodology—the ability to trace the entire system from goals to requirements to functions to specifications to architectures to components, and so on [see Sage (1992)]. Here, we motivate the importance of the foundation of these concepts—interaction matrices.

There is still another reason for the importance of the interaction matrix. A systems team has a tendency to fragment itself if subtasks are assigned to subgroups within the team. Each subtask group will tend, if allowed, to pursue its subgoal to the exclusion of other considerations. Thus, certain subtasks may be studied well beyond the needed detail, while articulation with other groups may be ignored. This tendency to fragment and specialize has occurred in all system studies directed, participated in, or observed by the authors. This includes studies covering a wide range of topics and participated in by members of almost every identifiable profession.

It seems to be a general cultural trait for professionals to concentrate on specifics and to ignore interrelations. Yet, in a general systems study, interrelations are the central concern. One can usually find experts with a deep and intimate knowledge of any specific area one cares to name, but just as a group of expert musicians cannot create great music without coordination and direction, knowledgeable specialists alone cannot provide a well-balanced systems study. *Defining, understanding, and controlling the interactions among the elements within the study and with outside stakeholders and agencies defines the essence of SA.*

A properly conducted systems study concentrates on goals and interactions. Specific topics should be developed in detail sufficient only to permit the goals, interactions, constraints, and the like, to be delineated clearly. The Polaris System development provides an illustration of the centrality of interactions, or "interfaces" (Sapolsky,1972):

> Early in his tenure as Technical Director (of the Polaris system development), Admiral L. Smith began to focus his attention and that of his staff on the system interfaces rather than on the details of particular subsystems . . . . A focus on subsystem inter-relationships prevented the central staff from being buried in technical minutiae as the pace of the development effort accelerated.

Here is another way of emphasizing the central importance of interactions among the elements of a system. We know from the mathematics of stability theory that it is possible for components, which behave perfectly when separate, to become violently unstable when allowed to interact as a system. Perhaps this isn't too surprising; we see the evidence all about us in modern complex civilization. What may be more surprising is that choosing properly the interconnections and the interactions between unstable or unsatisfactory components, without otherwise changing them, can lead to stable and effective performance of the overall system.

The Self-Interaction Matrix. To chart the interactions between pairs of objects of the same class, we employ the self-interaction matrix. The value of such a chart may become apparent only if there are many elements in the set, because many analysts flatter themselves that they can handle the interactions of a half dozen elements or so in their head. Nevertheless, to simplify the illustration, our first example will be a set containing only a few objects.

TABLE 7.1. Major Subsystems of the Manned Mars Vehicle

1. Propulsion	4. Extra-vehicular exploration
2. Life support	5. Communications
3. Navigation	6. Sensing and recording

Suppose we are analyzing the practicality of a TV link between a manned-Mars space mission vehicle and the Earth. Table 7.1 gives one possible breakdown of the major subsystems of the vehicle.

It will be understood that there is no single, correct and objective classification of subsystems. Any classification system is for the convenience of the user, but at the same time, it does some violence to the integrity of the objects classified. This is not to say that the classification is arbitrary. One attempts to respect the natural divisions and to maintain order. It is to say, however, that after division into subsystems, an accurate accounting of the interactions becomes vital. In Figure 7.2, we chart the interactions of the communication subsystem, which is of particular interest in this study, with the other vehicle subsystems.

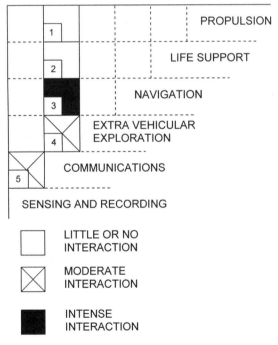

FIGURE 7.2 An interaction matrix for five of the main subsystems of a space vehicle. We show three interaction intensities in this matrix. Analysts seem to have little trouble with three levels. One advantage of using only two levels, even though a significant amount of detail is lost by this reduction, is the ability one gains thereby to utilize Boolean algebra in the computer production of complex interaction charts containing hundreds of interactions.

TABLE 7.2. Interactions Narrative for Communications and Other Major Subsystems in Manned Mars Mission

Interaction No.	Name	Intensity	Comment
1	Propulsion/ communication	Low	Energy demand of TV system will not be a significant portion of total demand
2	Life support/ communication	Low	Good design of life support system requires independence from other systems
3	Navigation/ communication	High	Must have accurate fix on earth to point antenna correctly
4	Extra-vehicular exploration/ communication	Medium	Need a porthole for TV camera
5	Sensing and recording/ communication	Medium	Need convenient way to dump data into communication system

Typically, either two or three intensity levels will be found most convenient in our interaction charts. A two-level index is convenient for Boolean algebraic manipulations by computer when charting hundreds of separate interactions in a depth analysis of a complete system. On the other hand, three levels provide significantly more discrimination than two and yet do not seem to provide special difficulty for the rater. Higher numbers of levels are possible of course, but do not seem to be widely used, probably because raters may perceive difficulty in making more granular distinctions.

Furthermore, we should point out that intensity levels are to some extent subjective and relative, rather than completely objective and fixed. In one sense, each object in the entire physical universe is related to and influences every other object. Yet for all practical purposes, almost all of these interactions are insignificant and irrelevant. When a system team begins its analysis, it will often find that it tends to weight all interactions at one extreme or the other. That is, almost all interactions will be considered either highly significant or completely insignificant. Only after some discussion will a common acceptable measure emerge. Team members may have to force themselves to pick measures that discriminate.[2]

Unlike the objectives tree, the interaction matrix does not prove to be self-explanatory. One must provide a short narrative, perhaps only a phrase, or a sentence or two, explaining why the raters chose a given intensity grade for each specific interaction. Thus, the narrative phrases provided in Table 7.2 are an integral part of Figure 7.2. In the table, we chart only those five interactions of the communication subsystem and the other five subsystems. A complete interaction matrix would chart all 15 pairwise interactions.[3]

Cross-Interaction Matrices. In the above example, we charted the physical impact of one subsystem on another. We may also chart the pairwise interactions between each of the elements of all of the conceptual sets of a system planning activity. At

TABLE 7.3. The Twelve Conceptual Sets Used in System Analysis

Objectives	Activities
Alterables	Constraints
Needs	Agencies
Measures of, or indicators for, each of the above	

least 12 conceptual sets whose interactions are of concern in a system planning effort have been recognized in the literature. These 12 are given in Table 7.3.

The cross-interactions, pair-by-pair, of the elements of any two sets of system planning concepts may be charted in exactly the same way as pairwise interactions within any one set of concepts may be handled. That much should be obvious. But what may not be obvious is that, given transitivity, many of the cross-interaction matrices can be generated automatically. It is only necessary that each element in every concept set have at least a single interaction link with any other element in one other set.

Let's illustrate this with a simple example. In Figure 7.3, we have defined three concept sets—Objectives, Activities, and Constraints. This example system has three objectives, four activities, and two constraints. Self-interactions within each of these sets can be established by explicit evaluation. A simple two-value scale has been used in the figure to portray the cross interactions between individual activities and objectives, for a reason that will be obvious in a moment.

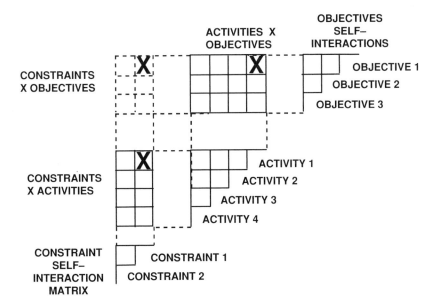

FIGURE 7.3 If the [Constraint] × [Activities] matrix and the [Activities] × [Objectives] matrix are as given, then the [Constraint] × [Objectives] matrix may be imputed by the use of Boolean algebra, assuming transitivity and a binary rating scale.

From the figure, we can see that Activity 1 will aid in achieving Objective 1. The [(Constraint) × (Activity)] cross-interaction matrix has also been established and we note that Constraint 1 affects Activity 1. Because of these two linkings, it is clear that Constraint 1 acting through Activity 1 influences Objective 1. If this were not so, the relationships would be said to be intransitive and a logical analysis of the system would be impossible.

Thus, it seems clear that an implied cross-interaction matrix [(Constraint) × (Objective)] exists and we can compute its values. In a system study with many conceptual sets, each of which contains many elements, it is of considerable practical importance that many of the cross-interaction matrices can be produced automatically by a computer routine. But it appears to the interested observer that still more important than computational convenience is the additional insight this process provides. The fact that Constraint 1 influences the achievement of Objective 1 may be surprising news to the analysts. Perhaps they were previously unaware of this or they may even have concluded just the opposite. Hence, we get *traceability*, one of the key concepts of systems engineering.

Measurement Indices for Concept Sets. It is essential that quantitative measures be established for each of the various concepts employed in system planning. It is difficult to see how to achieve an objective for which there is no measure. At the least, it means that the objective is vague and ill-defined. It probably also means that honest and possibly intense differences of opinion could arise as to whether the objective has been achieved. Perhaps the reader finds these two preceding remarks so obvious as to be soporific, but experience proves otherwise.

7.6   THE DELTA CHART

Network planning methods such as PERT and CPM have been in common use for many years. These charts are useful in organizing the sequence of activities to be carried out in completing a complex project. There are many versions of delta charts, and we'll illustrate one example here. However, all these methods suffer certain deficiencies when used in planning system studies (Warfield and Hill, 1971).

- Typical network methods such as PERT, while adequate for depicting and controlling a deterministic sequence of well-defined activities, may not conveniently allow the flexibility required for planning studies.
- Such methods have a limited and possibly confusing vocabulary, which may constrain thinking.
- Most network methods do not conveniently allow for alternatives, decisions, and logic. Thus, they may promote a tendency to plan for only a single, most likely approach.

The DELTA method is designed to correct these deficiencies. The basic DELTA chart uses the five symbols shown in Figure 7.4. An additional feature of the DELTA chart

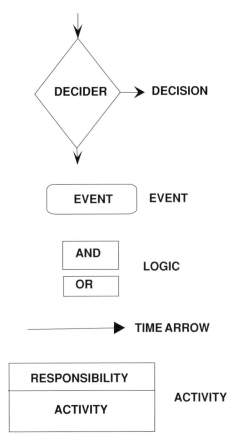

FIGURE 7.4 The five basic DELTA chart symbols. DELTA is an acronym for "Decision," "Event," "Logic," "Time" arrow, and "Activity."

is a precise syntax to aid in distinguishing "Events" from "Activities." The syntax to be used for defining an *Event* is a noun or object, followed by a verb or action phrase, followed by qualifiers. Table 7.4 gives several examples.

The syntax used to define an *Activity* is a verb followed by an object followed by constraints or qualifiers. Table 7.5 gives examples.

One will recall the syntax for *Objectives* as the infinitive form of a verb, followed by the object, followed by qualifiers. We give examples in Table 7.6 for the sake of completeness.

TABLE 7.4. The Syntax Used for Expressing "Events"

Object + Action Phrase + Qualifiers		
rats	killed	in city
seeds	planted	in garden

TABLE 7.5. Syntax Used to Define "Activities"

Action Verb	+ Object	+ Qualifiers
kill	rats	in city
plant	seeds	in garden

TABLE 7.6. The Syntax Used to Define "Objectives"

"To" Action Verb	+ Object	+ Qualifiers
to kill	rats	in city
to plant	seeds	in garden

Warfield and Hill discuss more complex forms of the five basic elements of the DELTA symbols, and they also add additional auxiliary elements, but the basic form of the DELTA chart discussed here is sufficient for our purposes. Rather than such theoretical complexities, let us give an example.

In Chapter 3, we discussed how we developed an Objectives Tree during a conference that was held to discuss how to obtain funding for an Urban Rat Control Project. Following that meeting, one of the authors constructed the DELTA chart shown in Figure 7.5 to explain to our systems team how we might go about the job. Notice that each of the activities is assigned an owner. In examining this chart some years later, we would fault it for not being sufficiently "action-oriented." It seems that the be-all and end-all of this project, if the DELTA chart is a proper representation, is to write a report to the sponsor. Consider what a similar chart to Figure 7.5 might look like for a proposed study on the containment of the Avian Flu in a region such as a Standard Metropolitan Statistical Area (SMSA).

For example, what happens if present methods are found to be cost-effective? The chart tells us that a report will be written, but it doesn't say that rat control will take place. Perhaps, to be charitable, the federal funding agency to which the proposal for funding was to be directed had insisted that it would not fund operating programs that used well-known, standard procedures. Thus, the likelihood of this study finding current techniques to be completely satisfactory is very low indeed.

7.7   THE AUDIT TRAIL

The concept of an *audit trail* is adopted from an equivalent concept in accounting. It is also a fundamental discipline in scientific research, as represented by the dated and signed laboratory notebook.[4] Just as it is a requirement for a business enterprise to keep track of its funds and to be able to demonstrate how these funds are acquired and disbursed, it is also necessary that a system team be able to demonstrate how it has gone about the process of gathering data, analyzing the problem, and reaching its recommendations. The reason for this necessity is the same in both the financial

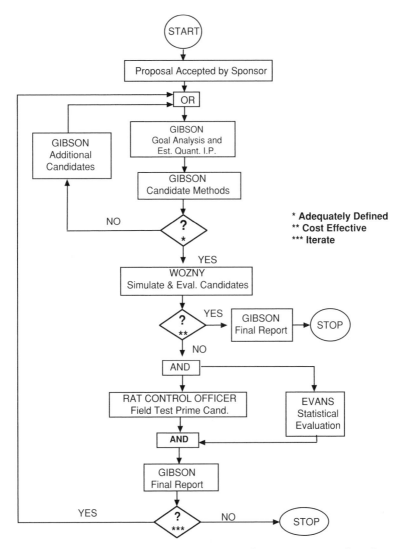

FIGURE 7.5 A DELTA chart for the Urban Rat Control Project mentioned in Chapter 3, the objective tree for which is given in Figure 3.1.

and the technical cases. An organization must be able to demonstrate that it has gone about its business in a legal, objective, unbiased fashion.

The final report of a system team must stand alone. Thus, this report must contain all of the material that would be needed to reconstruct the system analysis, including all original data sheets, stakeholder interviews, and so on. That is, *the final report must contain a complete audit trail.*

We were aware of a university that was analyzing its solid waste disposal problem. Pressure came from the state government for all state agencies to perform such a study and to reduce the weight and bulk of waste produced. The tipping fee at the local landfill used by the university was due to rise, and the landfill may be closed in the near future. As an element of the Descriptive Scenario, the system team weighted and classified several samples of the solid waste stream. Overall, the solid waste study was conducted at a cost of about four man-years of effort.

The university is made up of many constituencies, and those constituencies that felt that the report did not treat them sufficiently kindly had an opportunity to discredit it because the report failed to include the original waste survey data sheets and a complete description of how spot checks of the waste stream were extrapolated to obtain an overall waste stream estimate. Unfortunately, with respect to its conclusions and recommendations, the report gave the impression of *"We system analysts are the experts; take our word for it."* But this is precisely what various interested groups were not willing to do.

Based on the waste estimates, budgets would be impacted, personnel would be reassigned, and accomplishment of state goals might be brought into question. Thus jobs might be at stake. It was easy to discredit the study in question because the complete audit trail was absent. The study team recommendations were rejected and the study had to be repeated.

A complete audit trail is also essential in managerial decision-making. Here is an example from one of the author's experiences. As part of administrative responsibilities in a nongovernmental enterprise some years ago, the director of the main computer center of our enterprise and his operation reported to one of the authors. When it came time to upgrade our mainframe, we considered bids from three competitors. There were pluses and minuses for each machine of course, and finally the technical evaluation committee made its recommendation. Naturally, one had to weigh more than simple technical matters such as MIPS and storage capacity. Also, one had to factor in such matters as the ability of the vendor to train our operators, the response of the vendor to outages, availability and completeness of operators' manuals and other documentation, the availability and quality of operating systems, and the like.

All of these nonhardware issues tipped the scales against the machine that offered the most pure computing power, toward a machine that presented the maximum all-round advantages. But several of our research scientists were unhappy about this choice, and a group of them went to the president of our organization and accused the author of being in the pocket of the chosen vendor. While the president never lost confidence in the author, we can assure you that his life was considerably eased in the following few days because he was able to produce a complete audit trail of the evaluation and decision process.

No manager, whether in the private sector or public, is exempt from audit and review. Thus, we urge establishment of a complete audit trail of the procurement process as simply a matter of good business management practice.

7.8   COST OF FAILURE TO STAY ON SCHEDULE

One of the attributes of the PERT/CPM method of project management is the ability to assess and to control costs. We will discuss PERT/CPM in the next chapter. Here, however, we are looking for a broader and possibly less precise measure of the cost of falling off schedule. At this point in the process, we aren't doing the detailed installation engineering of the project. We are merely finishing up the final report. But, consistent with our determination to provide the client with an action-oriented report, we want the client to have sufficient information to be able to write a contract covering the system design and installation that will get the job done properly.

The Gantt chart can be used to make the required assessment. At the same time that we collect estimates of the time required for each project element, we can obtain approximate cost estimates, both for the total cost of each element and the incremental cost of removing a day from the project element. Obviously, the penalty assessed for late completion must be greater than the cost of reducing one or more days from the project. The reasoning for this statement is simple. Suppose the contractor has fallen behind the mutually agreed-upon schedule. If it is cheaper for the contractor to pay the penalty for late completion than it would be to attempt to complete on time by paying overtime, and so on, then one must assume the contractor will prefer to be late. All of this is fairly obvious and is covered in detail in texts and courses on project management. The next two topics are possibly even more important but are not as often given any attention.

7.9 RESPONSIBILITIES OF MAJOR ACTORS

As we move into the action phase, the number of people and the kinds of expertise required undergoes a rapid expansion. The time required to pass through the state of confusion often associated with initiation of a new project can often be reduced if the system planning team has given thought to the assignment of project element responsibility. After all, the SA team has spent weeks, perhaps months, living with the problem, and its advice should be valuable to the individuals appointed to carry out the action phase.

7.10 SIGN-OFFS BY COOPERATING GROUPS

Seldom, if ever, is the action team completely self-contained and self-supporting. Almost always it will be expected to seek support from independent groups with the resources needed. However, these resources will no doubt be committed to achieving other goals, unless redirected toward our project. It is contrary to good management principles for any manager voluntarily to surrender his or her resources to another manager. Yet this is exactly what some project leaders seem to expect. To "be a good neighbor" is not good management. "Good neighborliness" falls under the meta-value of equity, while good management falls under the equal meta-value of efficiency. The naïve project manager may make informal contact with a peer and be assured, just as informally, that of course he can expect cooperation "when the time comes."

However, when the "time" actually comes, the peer may be out for lunch. The way to handle this potential time bomb is for the overall project manager and/or his or her element managers to seek formal, written sign-offs from all important coordinate groups in advance. The formal sign-off process heads off incipient problems in advance and, furthermore, alerts the coordinate groups to exactly what is required and when it is to be delivered. This permits the coordinate group managers to make arrangements in advance. Moreover, the formal process provides an audit trail should problems arise in the future.[5]

We don't want to overemphasize what may be a minor point, but we have seen several projects fail to meet their deadlines due to failure to handle precisely this issue. We might note also that this issue is tension-producing for a different reason. The typical project manager is highly goal-oriented and usually exhibits a highly developed need for control. Peer cooperation on an informal, voluntary basis is not normal within such a highly structured state and will be a source of tension and concern. Get it down on paper in advance and signed off by all parties.

EXERCISES

7.1 Describe in one sentence the concept of "iteration" as used in this text. What is the point of this step?

7.2 Suppose we accept the concept of iteration for the sake of argument. Give a "stopping rule." That is, how many times does one iterate?

7.3 What impact does iteration have on previous steps in the systems methodology? Does it influence how we go about the other phases of SA? If so, in what way?

7.4 Granted that in some problems, iteration may be effective. Obviously, however, there are more problems, probably a vast majority for which iteration is not effective—a waste of time and money. Define these two classes of problems.

7.5 Select a case from Chapters 1–6 that you prepared and perform an additional, complete iteration (hopefully, some time has passed since you did the case). Analyze and reflect on the impact of this subsequent iteration.

NOTES

1. Even many beginning systems students cannot force themselves to iterate on their system cases!

2. One simple example of the tendency to fail to discriminate occurs in faculty members of a department advertising to fill new positions. It is not uncommon for raters to reject all candidates as unqualified to join their august selves.

3. Software does exist to assist for large problems; see, for example, UCINET for Windows (Version 6), which was designed for investigating social networks analysis.

4. The invention of the telephone is the best example of this. See Gorman, M., Mehalik, M., et al. (1993).

5. See INCOSE Guide to Systems Engineering Body of Knowledge, http://www.incose.org/practice/guidetosebodyofknow.aspx, or any of the systems engineering reference documents cited in Chapter 1, for typical documents required in formal systems engineering efforts.

Chapter **8**

Management of the Systems Team

8.1 INTRODUCTION

There are two different aspects of project management. The first of these, managing the systems team itself, will be covered in this chapter. Managing the systems team in an effective manner is an ongoing part of the study phase of the project and is always necessary. The second application for project management skills, and the more usual definition of the term, is the action phase of the project, after the go-ahead has been received. Implementation of the systems study requires a more complete and elaborate version of project management, because implementation is a more complex and expensive task than the study phase and a wider variety of personnel, professional skills, and organizations are usually involved. On the other hand, many system studies never reach the implementation phase, so this second form of project management is not always needed. Chapter 9 addresses this issue.

8.2 PERSONAL STYLE IN AN INTERDISCIPLINARY TEAM

The personal operating style and psychological profile of the typical engineer differs somewhat from that of the scientist and diverges rather dramatically from the profile of the typical social scientist or arts major. This may lead to unnecessary conflict if it is not understood and accounted for. C. G. Jung divides human personalities into 16 different types, depending on their preferences among four "functions" and four

How to Do Systems Analysis. By John E. Gibson, William T. Scherer, and William F. Gibson
Copyright © 2007 John Wiley & Sons, Inc.

"attitudes." The four functions are paired as follows:

Sensing (S)/Intuition (N)   and   Thinking (T)/Feeling (F)

The four attitudes are paired as follows:

Extroversion (E)/Introversion (I)   and   Judgment (J)/Perception (P)

According to Jung, all individuals operate at balance points between the extremes of each of the four pairs. The ideal personality is perfectly balanced between each of the extremes. Many engineers tend toward strong ISTJ extremes, even though this is a relatively rare combination in the total population. Let's go on now, at the risk of gross oversimplification, to draw some probable tendencies of the ISTJ personality in action.

The ISTJ personality stereotype probably

- has a low tolerance for ambiguity;
- is highly goal-directed;
- needs to crystallize the problem, define it precisely, set goals, design timetables, pick mileposts, assemble data, build models, and get answers;
- prefers a hierarchic work situation.

The need for low ambiguity seems to be for the Jungian part of, or a consequence of, the attitude of *judging*. That is, the ISTJ personality is not content to understand or perceive a situation or condition, but rather feels forced to judge, rank, or grade the situation. Thus, holding several possibilities in mind without expressing a preference is difficult for the ISTJ personality. This also induces the ISTJ to act to achieve goals and further reduce ambiguity. Working in a nonhierarchic, peer relationship is difficult for the ISTJ because relationships seem so ambiguous.

We remember once in a managerial situation where several months had been spent reducing the several hundred possible action options our group had into a reduced set for resource allocation. We brought the group together and said something like the following:

> "As you folks know, we've been working with you to establish those items on where we agree we should put our resources for the coming year. We started with several hundred suggestions and quickly reduced these down to about two dozen. Now, after much discussion and agonizing with you, we have reduced the list to the three top priority items for new initiatives for the coming year. They are...."

We were really quite proud of what we felt was a successful effort at participative resource allocation for the group. But, one of the best of our people, and a strong ISTJer, wasn't at all impressed. He said,

> "Damn it, why can't you make up your mind what it is you want us to do?"

And he wasn't kidding. To the ISTJer, it seems correct to take one thing at a time and finish it before going on to the next. It is distasteful to have to balance several items simultaneously. One can see the dangers in such perfectionism. We can get even more specific about how the ISTJ stereotype operates by talking in terms we have used in discussing SA. The confirmed ISTJer

- is a "bottom-upper";
- is a natural "in-scoper";
- is a "bean-counting" detail person;
- is a "little-picture" person.

When faced with frustration of these needs, the extreme ISTJ type

- may blame "incompetent" higher administration and/or the client/sponsor;
- may become withdrawn and/or irritable;
- will probably become more demanding, more scrupulous, querulous with subordinates and superiors;
- may begin to exhibit paranoia (i.e., "the whole world is plotting against me to make me fail in this project");
- may begin placing ultimatums on sponsor and bosses: "If you don't give me everything I want (need) to finish this project on time, (I'll quit) (I'll report you to higher authority) (I won't be responsible)."

This composite picture of the attitudes and personality functions we have built up here applies to the extreme ISTJ type. All in all, the ISTJ type appears not to be a natural team player and is likely to have difficulty with the broad-scope approach to systems analysis.

Not only does the ISTJ have difficulty with peer interactions, he or she is likely to have problems with other elements normal to working in teams. For example, the ISTJ personality doesn't like

- to write interim reports and mileposts;
- meetings;
- progress reports of any kind;
- interruptions;
- iterating.

The ISTJ is a linear mind, takes things in order, and is a perfectionist. Thus, the idea of a once-over-lightly, first-cut iteration sets ISTJ teeth on edge. Of course, all other extreme personality types have difficulties, some much more serious than those assigned to the ISTJ mind. We emphasize the difficulties the ISTJ personality type may encounter because so many of us ISTJs are attracted to engineering. Whatever the extreme personality elements in one's make-up, they are debilitating and possibly, in the extreme, incapacitating. We all must work at centering ourselves. We need to achieve the happy medium by working to get our heads into psychic balance.

The strongly ISTJ type is difficult to work with, both as a boss and subordinate, but he or she is tolerated because of his or her ability to get the job done. The story of Jay Forrester and the development of the "Whirlwind" computer is an excellent case in point (Redmond and Smith, 1981; Gibson, 1981a).

The ISTJ type gets the job done if humanly possible, but at perhaps excessive psychic cost to him or herself, subordinates, and the organization. The strongly ISTJ type needs to think carefully about the responsibility of leadership and to make every effort to build a better psychic balance, for his own comfort and that of those around him.

The ISTJ mind must learn to balance itself with the complementary attitudes without losing the productive aspects produced by its natural set. This will be a recurring struggle if the ISTJ type moves up through management to take on larger and broader responsibilities. At each new level of responsibility, the ISTJ type will have to struggle to reach a new psychological synthesis. And when this task becomes all-consuming, the ISTJ person must question whether the game is worth the candle.

8.3 "OUT-SCOPING" AND "IN-SCOPING" IN A SYSTEM STUDY

"In-scoping" and "out-scoping" are barbarous terms, but they describe the alternating sequence of phases in a well-organized system study. We have spoken previously of "generalizing the question" as an important early step in goal development. This is an example of an out-scoping phase. One encourages wide-sweeping speculation, and critical analysis is postponed. "Brainstorming" or "brainwriting" to develop an initial list of possible alternative solution scenarios are other out-scoping activities. On the other hand, in-scoping focuses on an analytic examination of the possibilities; one measures, calculates, weighs, and winnows.

Most professionals tend to feel more comfortable with either the more broad, speculative out-scoping activity or the more detailed, analytic, in-scoping process, but not with both. Humanists and social scientists are often attracted toward out-scoping activities, whereas statisticians, accountants, engineers, and so forth, are more likely to enjoy in-scoping. The out-scoping mind is often bored with detail and impatient with specific difficulties. The out-scoper is interested in the philosophy of approach, the general concept, intriguing anomalies, and unexpected interconnections.

The in-scoping mind, on the other hand, avoids value speculations, because it sees nothing to relate to them. It finds it difficult to suspend judgment and criticism. It enjoys getting to the bottom of things, laying bare the ultimate bedrock, specific concepts by rigorously peeling off the frills and ornamentalities. The out-scoping mind resists closure and premature decision for fear of neglecting a long-shot winner. The in-scoping mind has a low tolerance for ambiguity and needs to make choices.

If one has chosen one's profession because one's personal style seems adapted to its methodology, one has had one's natural proclivities enhanced by professional training. Thus one's tendency to "out-scope" or "in-scope" has been reinforced by extended education and practice. Very few professions have been successful in sustaining the tension required to contain both centralism and peripheralism, synthesis and analysis, action and reflection, practicality and artistry, within themselves simultaneously. Yet that is what we propose with the system method. That there will be tensions within a properly constituted system team, let there be no doubt.

8.4 BUILDING THE SYSTEMS TEAM

The team leader has a well-defined role to play, as do the other members. Contrary to naïve opinion, one should not seek the most popular or well-liked person for the team leader, nor should the person interested in popularity expect to gain it as a team leader. Studies of small group interaction processes make it clear that, while the effective leader of a goal-oriented team can expect to gain the respect of fellow team members, he or she must not expect popularity. Team members expect the team leader to be fair, calm, well-prepared, and goal-oriented. It is important to members not to be upset psychically by the leader. The leader is expected to listen to reason and to refrain from pursuing his or her pet solution. It is important to the team members that the leader not play favorites, not waste time, and move forward expeditiously toward the agreed-upon goal.

Not all individuals can work effectively as members of a team. Team play requires emotional maturity and practice.[1] Some individuals seem to have personalities that require them to deal only with superiors or subordinates. They are unable to deal effectively with peers on a cooperative basis. Experience indicates that attempts by the leader to deal with such personality deficiencies will not bring about a change. A rule of thumb for the team manager is that people are the way they are, because they *want* to be the way they are. At least for the short term, deal with what you see, not with what you would like to see. Unless an excessively individualistic team member expresses a desire to coperate and follows this up by appropriate action, the team leader is well-advised to replace the uncooperative individual.

The Team Must Have a Leader. The engineering mind may find this a trivial truism, but it is not. There is a strong body of sociological theory which advocates the "leaderless group." The research scientist, particularly the social scientist, will find the need for a leader difficult to accept. The value structure of the scientist is one of individualism, and thus to accept a leader may seem to be sacrificing one's scientific integrity (Gibson, 1981b).

The leaderless group mode can work under a particular set of circumstances, which coincidentally happen to be the circumstances under which sociologists find it easy to do their testing (i.e., transient groups such as students in a classroom and soldiers in a replacement depot), but which do not correspond to most real-world situations. This is regrettable because, in its proper sphere, leaderless groups such as groups of college students and casual groups in other nonhierarchic situations can be very productive. However, to attempt to create a small, protected enclave with an absence of hierarchy, within a larger, hierarchally organized enterprise, tends to promote (a) group tension and indecision and (b) a failure to drive toward and meet externally applied goals.

The Team Must Have a Goal. Those individuals who cannot accept the team's goal must be removed from the team. It is not unusual to find team members who ignore the team's goals in order to pursue private professional goals. This sometimes takes the form of an individual offering to go away and "write a paper" on one aspect of the team project. Unwillingness to work with the team is unacceptable in a team member. Another error is to permit the individual who does accept a team assignment to do more work on the specialized subject than can be justified by the needs of the project. Both these deviations must be resisted.

The Team Must Use a Common Methodology. It is essential that the team members accept a common language and an agreed-upon method of approach. While some system methodologies are better or more complete than others, most are essentially equivalent. Nevertheless, one methodology must be chosen and adhered to if group communication and progress toward the project goal are to be maintained.

The Team Must Use Subject-Area Specialists. Two errors concerning the matter of subject-area knowledge are common among systems analysts, potential clients, and stakeholders: these are the twin errors of deficiency and excess. The error of deficiency claims or assumes that no subject-area specialists are needed by a systems team, because system types are successors to the Renaissance or Universal man. This error claims or assumes that system types are brighter, better trained, and work harder than the rest of humankind; therefore, they are capable of doing the work of specialists. Such role confusion arrogance is common among systems analysts.

The error of excess is made by arguing that a successful systems team is made up simply by gathering representatives of each specialty needed, and if, as the study goes on, a new area of ignorance is discovered, another specialist can be added to the team. This error is common among analysts who lack a full understanding of the systems process.

Subject area knowledge is *necessary*, but not *sufficient*, for a successful systems study. It is true that an accomplished generalist can learn a great deal about a new area in a relatively short time by concentrated effort. And, for many of the ancillary concerns of a system study, this may be sufficient. But for certain key issues, in-depth knowledge will be needed. Usually, however, it is not possible to pinpoint these key issues in advance. Thus, it is an error to begin the analysis in depth across a broad front. The RTTV case illustrated this error. The system methodology is designed to bring the team to a proper understanding of the key issues relatively rapidly. Then, and only then, should the in-depth study of the key issues commence.

The Team Must Keep On Schedule. It is essential that interim mileposts, often set by the team, and the final deadline, usually set by the client, be met. The systems process is designed to bring the team quickly and efficiently to a definition of the key issues and to a confrontation with its own ignorance concerning the deeper substance of those key issues. This is the moment of crisis, and the weak team will feel it necessary to learn more about these critical elements of the problem even if deadlines are missed.

A losing football team would like to have a fifth quarter to overturn the score in a closely fought contest, and a losing systems team would like to have an extension of the deadline. This is a doctrine that is very difficult for a dedicated specialist to accept. It apparently places the specialist in the embarrassing position of giving assent to incomplete work if the deadline approaches before he finishes his study. If the specialist is unable to resolve this inner conflict, he or she must be invited to leave the team to prevent damage to the team's effort and/or the specialist's psyche.

The Team Must Pull Together. Perhaps this is merely a general restatement of the specific requirements listed above. We can think of examples of teams which pulled together and even more examples in which the team allowed itself to be pulled apart. We're not persuaded, however, that a recitation of these anecdotes would be useful here. To pull together means that the individual must think of how his success or failure will affect the team; it means helping and cooperating with fellow team members. It means holding one's ego in check.

8.5 TIPS ON MANAGING THE TEAM

Let us assume now that the team has been built and analysis is underway. How does one manage the effort so as to facilitate reaching the agreed-upon goals? Here are some specific suggestions:[2]

Hold The Team Together. Do not let the team disintegrate into a collection of individuals reporting to the team leader. Hold weekly, or even daily, team meetings. Ask each member to circulate a one-page summary of personal effort each week. Require that each member identify current effort with an approved task that appears on the project Gantt chart. Do not permit members to pursue professional hobbies on the team budget.

The Weekly Progress Report will be a source of great contention. Individuals may argue that they didn't make much progress in a given week and thus shouldn't have to write a report. This is wrong. They should have to declare this lack of progress to fellow team members. Others will argue that progress doesn't come in weekly chunks and that they feel constrained by reporting requirements. That is true, but irrelevant.

Others will argue that to write a weekly report and to attend progress meetings take away too much time from real work. The answer is that anyone who takes more than 15 minutes to write a one-page summary of his or her effort is such a slow writer that he or she shouldn't be on the team. And if team members feel that a one-hour progress meeting cuts into working time, tell them you'll schedule it at a brown-bag lunch once a week (Hawken, 1987).

Number each task and ask the team members in their weekly report to report on effort and progress in terms of the numbered task. Number the tasks consecutively throughout the entire project. Make sure that an outsider, a project officer from the sponsor for example, can follow a specific task through from beginning to end during the entire project by reading items with the same identification number in successive progress reports.

Alternate In-Scoping and Out-Scoping. Out-scoping especially must be a communal effort. Some in-scoping can be permitted on a solitary basis. Specialists will resist out-scoping, but it is especially important for exactly these persons. Engineers don't like meetings that don't have an agenda. They like short, crisp, business-like meetings rather than those that seem to be formless and wandering. But group out-scoping is important.

Interact with the Client. Specialists resist early client interaction, because specialists have a great need for control. The specialist wants to know the answer before he dares expose himself to interaction with the client, but this is wrong. The client should be involved with the team at an early point in working on goals and on success measures. In addition, in a corporate environment, your client usually has superiors to whom he must report. Keeping him informed from the early stages, and allowing him to "fly air cover," will allow the project team to proceed with a minimum amount of outside interference.

In public systems especially, it is disastrous to drop on the citizens a fully formed and frozen solution. One must seek to engage in a community dialogue even if an unfortunate by-product appears to be to invite controversy and contention. Too many major public projects have been stalled after construction has begun, by failure to consider at an early point all potential contending parties and to respond properly to their concerns.

8.6   FUNCTIONAL OR PROJECT MANAGEMENT?

A system team is often assembled initially to tackle a large new project. After the successful completion of the project, the question is whether the team should be held together to tackle new projects or its members should be assigned to separate duties. This question does not arise, of course, if the team consists of outside consultants brought into the organization for a specific job. In other situations as well, the question is not open for discussion. Furthermore, it is apparent from a review of system engineering literature that some authors advocate one approach and others favor another, so apparently there is no universally accepted answer to this question.

Naturally, managers of systems analysis groups think their problems are unique, but an objective look at the situation will reveal similarities to managing any group of creative professionals. Computer groups, electronics groups, accountants, research groups, and so forth, will argue, almost without exception, that they will better be able to serve the total organization if they are kept together and allowed to work for a boss who is one of themselves and thus understands their unique problems. Although this is true, the concomitant disadvantage is that there may be a lessening of pressure to serve the goals of the organization. Here is a relevant example from the past that serves as a good lesson.

> The shift at Bell Labs shows up most sharply in what has been happening lately to its team of systems engineers. Since 1955, these engineers—about 15% of the Labs' 7,500 man graduate technical staff—have worked largely as a single company-wide force of planners within the Labs and with Western [Electric]. Up to last year, their job has stressed long-range objectives in pulling together highly specialized new technology into new systems....
>
> During 1970, however, short-range planning to put existing technology to use, which has taken second place through the years, became top priority. The single systems engineering force was split up to serve in each of the main areas at the Labs.... "You need deep specialization when you have time to be creative," explains J. A. (Jack) Morton, Vice President for electronics technology, "but you need close coupling when either technology or the social system changes rapidly." [*Business Week*, 1971]

Doubtless, Mr. Morton's statement is correct, as far as it goes. But social change is no recent phenomenon. There seems to have been more to this reorganization than *Business Week* discovered. John Brook's book, *Telephone*, may have more completely revealed the background for this change (Brooks, 1976).

As Brooks relates, in 1955, AT&T committed itself to the installation of an electronic switching system (ESS), and in 1956, F. R. Kappel, newly elected President, announced a completion target date of 1959 for this project and predicted a development cost of $4.5 million. In fact, it was 1969, 10 years late, before ESS was in widespread use, and the total development cost was over $500 million. There was a widespread feeling at AT&T that the Systems Group at Bell Labs dropped the ball by failing to take sufficient interest in the practical difficulties of manufacturing, installing, and maintaining ESS. Once the Systems Group at the Labs had proved ESS in principle, they lost interest in it in favor of other blue-sky, non-goal-oriented work, it was claimed. As a consequence perhaps, the group, possibly the first systems group ever organized at so high a corporate level, was broken up.

The organization does not exist to serve the needs of a group of specialists. On the contrary, specialists are employed to help the organization meet its goals. Because of the difficult problem of harnessing a myriad of groups to meet performance requirements on time and within budget in a company or institution organized along functional lines, "organization-by-project" has been developed. Each project leader has as his goal successful accomplishment of a major project of the organization. In a project organization, system types and other specialists are assigned to project groups, and there is no system group as such.

Because this is not a book on management theory, we will not develop these ideas any further. Suffice it to say that, on the surface at least, there appears to be nothing unique about a group of system analysts. They should fit into the structure of the organization, whatever its form, functional or project-oriented, just as any other specialists would.

8.7   HOW TO MAKE AN EFFECTIVE ORAL PRESENTATION

Engineers and scientists all too often display a disdain for the essential elements of an effective oral presentation. Carelessness, lack of preparation, mumbling delivery, clumsy or unreadable graphics, repetitious, rambling, and overlong monologues ... these and other faults are more common than clear, crisp, well-prepared efforts. Very little, if any, time and effort are devoted in the typical university curriculum to developing the skills requisite for effective oral presentations, and it is clear that fear and ignorance of these skills breed contempt for them. Yet why this continues to be so, given that employers are unanimous in their testimony as to their importance, is difficult to say.

A dramatic example of the power of a poor oral presentation to hurt an organization was the effect produced by the Ralston Purina Company in the 1970s. Ralston invited about 100 stock market analysts to a conference at which its present status and future prospects were reviewed. Business was good, but the presentations were so bad and Ralston's reluctance to share information in an open and effective manner became so marked that the analysts turned against the company.

> "The sell-off [that followed in the next few days] had nothing to do with sound analytical evaluation," says one analyst, "It was caused purely by analysts' pique with the company for not telling us what we need[ed] to know." [*Business Week*, 1979]

Following the conference, analysts made "sell" recommendations to their clients, and in the next few days, Ralston lost over $100 million in the value of its shares. This is unusual, of course, although a similar example apparently occurred with Westinghouse Electric in 1973. Most of us aren't in a position to cost our organization $100 million with one poor oral presentation, it is true, but this is a clear example of the importance of a briefing well done. Many, or most, other examples of this nature don't make the light of day via public exposure. We were involved in observing a systems group at a major aircraft manufacturer, and a lead systems analyst was presenting the business case to the CEO and others for a major retrofit of the fleet costing in the hundreds of millions of dollars. Having observed the efforts of the analyst over several weeks, we were convinced of the method and numbers; however, the presentation was so poor that the CEO walked out and the excellent analyst's days with the company were short.

Rarely, if ever, do employers complain that their newly hired engineers lack needed analytic and scientific knowledge. Even if the new hires have not developed complete knowledge of a given engineering or mathematical science, their employers feel they can get it on their own. But employers *unanimously* complain that their young people cannot write an effective report or make an effective oral presentation.

There seems, in fact, to exist a perverse, inverse bias concerning this matter on the part of some university faculty members. That is, some academic engineers and scientists suspect, and will even say aloud, that a skillful, professional oral presentation indicates a lack of scientific depth and knowledge in the presenter! A more counterproductive attitude to inculcate in one's students would be difficult to find.

On the counter side of this argument, one needs to go no further than study the various presentations made by Steve Jobs, the Chairman and CEO of Apple Computer.

From the point of time when he returned to Apple (in 1996) after the acquisition of Next Computers, Jobs focused the communications to securities analysts and systems developers (at events such as WWDC). While the firm's products were very popular, Jobs' ability to communicate drove the stock from a low of 8 to 345 (before stock splits) in 8 years! Even without the splits, the 10-fold increase is in large part attributable to Jobs' ability to create a vision and communicate it.

Here are some specific suggestions on how to improve your oral presentations:

Rehearsals Are Necessary. This seems obvious, perhaps, but almost never are oral presentations properly rehearsed. To sit at one's desk and look over slides is not a rehearsal. To write out and memorize one's speech or to commit it in outline to 3 × 5 cards is not a rehearsal. A rehearsal means a complete presentation before a critical audience, followed by a critique.

A number of objections will be raised to the idea of a rehearsal. The slides won't be ready in time; a proper audience can't be found; it's personally demeaning; and so on.[3] But these are indictments of the state of preparation. The real reason for opposition to a rehearsal seems to be the embarrassment of the presenter and his/her wish not to be thought of as an actor. No further indicator is needed of a forthcoming inadequate presentation than a refusal to rehearse.

Visual Aids Are Strongly Advised. In addition to the ubiquitous Microsoft PowerPoint™ or Keynote™ presentation, a flip chart, overhead projector, white boards, or slide projector may also be valuable. The particular form one chooses should be based on the size of the audience, the nature of the meeting, and the type of information to be presented. The flip chart is still valuable for working meetings with small audiences, perhaps up to 20 people, in the intimacy that is generated with the audience. The overhead projector has only one advantage over computer projection and several disadvantages, the main advantage being able to write on the charts. Many new computer tools do allow for creative graphics with a cost of flexibility. Also, many hardware/software products allow for saving material written on a standard white board to the computer, while others use a computer white board which directly writes to the computer. Tablet personal computers equipped with sensitive screens are becoming viable and may have an increasing role to play in presentations.

Three basic drawbacks often encourage us to move away from the computer and/or overhead projector and toward the old-fashioned flip chart when possible. First, one is tempted to draw the shades and dim the lights when using the overhead projector. This may produce a drowsy, inattentive attitude in the audience. Also, using the computer/overhead projector may break one's eye contact with the audience. Third, the computer/overhead projector requires power, and sometimes plugs aren't available and/or the bulb may burn out. It is common sense to reduce uncontrollable variables to a minimum. For large audiences and for canned presentations, a computer must be used. Multiple projectors, "synched" music, and narrative for the prepared portion should be considered for very important presentations. We often see presenters, however, going overboard and losing the message in an overwhelming multimedia display of computer power.

There is an almost universal tendency to overload a chart with too much information. A paragraph of narrative is certainly too much. A complete sentence is probably too much. A few phrases or catch words are ideal. The idea is to support, underline, and reinforce the speaker's words, not to supply a complete text. Here is a good rule of thumb. *Not more than three bullet points per slide.* And absolutely no uninformative or irrelevant graphics cluttering charts.

Color is good, and an occasional cartoon or joke is not bad in a long presentation. But humor is for experts. You are a sincere, well-prepared, knowledgeable person, but you aren't a comedian. Thus, contrary to some advice, we suggest you minimize the humorous interludes.

It is generally advisable to give your audience copies of your slides. Hold back the chart with the punch line, if you wish, but even if you provide the complete set in advance, your audience will follow your presentation if it is well-presented. Rarely use the white/chalk board; the rate of information transfer is too slow, and one must break all eye contact with the audience. Never omit visual aids; one must be an accomplished actor/orator to carry a presentation with no aids; and remember, even actors need costumes, make-up, scenery, and props.

Time Your Presentation Carefully. If you have been given a half-hour, prepare a 20-minute presentation to permit introductions at the beginning and then a question session at the close. Announce the length of your presentation at the beginning and stick to it. This reduces uncertainty in the audience and encourages them to let you proceed uninterrupted. It is difficult to hold the audience's attention for more than 40 uninterrupted minutes; 20 minutes is much more reasonable. Always be prepared, however, to adjust the presentation for a sudden change in the time allotted. This should never be accomplished by talking faster—something we still see weekly. Rarely is the occasion, be it a client briefing, a professional meeting, or a conference, that we finish with our original, planned time. Organize your presentation in a hierarchical fashion. Thus, if you have only one minute of your allotted 30 minutes remaining, you can use only the single top slide in the hierarchy (the executive summary—more on this later). Given the time you are allotted, select the appropriate level of the hierarchy, realizing that at the very most you can do one chart per minute. Such a hierarchical organization is very easy in a tool like PowerPoint^{TM}.

Introduce The Team. Give your name and the names of your team members. Wear name tags with large letters, and, of course, your team will be in appropriate dress. Get the full name of each participant as well as his or her complete title. Pass out business cards if you have them. If the client has brought a number of people to the conference, pass around a sign-up sheet. Have a team member collect the list, and check to make sure you can identify everyone by name and title. We have made more than one presentation at which the real honcho was concealed in the back row somewhere, while an assistant did the talking.

Start With a Descriptive Scenario. It's hard to explain why one should begin the presentation with a short descriptive scenario. After all, why should one have to describe his own company to the client? But the point seems to be that you can relieve some of your client's tension by showing that you understand the problem setting.

Let us try to bring this point into focus with an example. Our church was considering an expansion of its worship space. As a member of the building committee, we interviewed five architects who had expressed an interest in the project. All the five presentations began with a slide show of recent commissions, but only one team went on to talk about our project. We did not take part in the deliberation that followed the presentations, thus we did not influence the choice. The team that discussed our church's project and showed sketches of some possibilities was selected over the other teams. We were not particularly impressed with this team's experience, but it was clear from the discussion that followed that the remainder of the building committee was particularly influenced by this "descriptive scenario."

In a 20-minute presentation, one cannot take more than two or three minutes for this description, so pack some hard facts and critical issues into several carefully prepared opening sentences. Newspaper writers learned long ago that their lead sentence must carry a heavy load. The same is true for your oral presentation. Make that first chart and your opening sentence or two carry a strong message. Give the key element of your problem, and hint at its resolution in your opening. Here are some suggestions for a few of the cases we discuss in this text:

The Real-Time TV Link with the Manned Mars Mission. Show first flip chart: a cartoon of a saber-toothed tiger crouched on a rock above a mounted knight in shining armor. Legend: "Ten Days to Tiger."
Presenter says:

> "The manned Mars mission scheduled for March 20XX will be the most difficult technical challenge ever faced by mankind. What are the costs, and what are the benefits of a real-time TV link for this mission? Should the NSA make the investment of our nation's resources that will be required to bring this TV link up? We know we can do it if the decision is 'go,' but let's look at the potential costs and payoffs before we charge ahead."

Urban Rat Control. Show cartoon of large rat threatening tiny family:

> "Rats will cost every family in Urban City at least $200 and perhaps as much as $2,000 in this decade. Rats carry 35 known diseases and make our town a dangerous place in which to live and work. How can we stop this menace without wrecking our city budget?"

Sky High Airline Baggage Problem. Show chart with average ticket price, total ticket revenue, cost of lost baggage per passenger, and total cost:

> "Sky High spent about $20 million on baggage handling last year, and half of that was wasted in lost baggage claims. Ten million is more than 10% of our total profit last year,

and this hemorrhage has got to stop before it leads to stockholder unrest and loss of passengers to our competition."

Discourage Questions During Presentation. To handle questions and at the same time maintain the pace and thrust of your presentation is very difficult for all but the most experienced. Don't try it. Even if you announce that questions should be held until later, you may get interruptions. Upper-level executives are accustomed to controlling the meetings in which they are involved, and to sit quietly through your presentation is likely to appear to them to be surrendering control to you. They will be tempted to break in "to clarify a point" or to "ask a crucial question." Moreover, chief executives are restless. They have a great need to get to the bottom line fast. Questions from junior staff people often reveal your inside opposition. Be careful.

We suggest that, if an interruption occurs, you compliment the questioner on the perceptiveness of the question, mention that the point will be covered in a moment, and hand the questioner a 3×5 card to write the question out to be answered later, if it is not properly covered in the presentation. Point out that you can save everyone's time now by moving right along, and do so. If that doesn't work, you have probably lost control anyway, perhaps due to audience hostility or perhaps due to your general ineptness, so just do your best.

Never Apologize. One of the most common errors made by beginners is to apologize for the inadequacy of their report. There seems to be in many of us an almost irresistible urge to tell our listeners that we could do better if we had more time or money. Perhaps the speaker views this as a form of modesty, and in Great Britain it might be taken as such. In the United States, however, it is clear that such disclaimers are taken as a sign of uncertainty and weakness. Stop dealing in promises and excuses, and deal in facts. You have worked hard and know a great deal of value to the client. You are there to explain to the client how, together, you are going to meet this interesting, meaningful challenge. Be positive.

A Pleasant, Confident Attitude Is the Secret. Nervousness or a stumbling, halting delivery tend to raise serious doubts of your knowledge and ability. However, an overly strong, aggressive style tends to raise counter-aggressive tendencies in your audience. Even if you can control this aggression during your presentation, it will pop out during the question session to hurt you. An excessively strong style invokes an adversary attitude in the audience, which is bad. You must seek to convey the fact that you have internalized the client's problem and that you are working together on it.

An Executive Summary of a report is all that can typically be presented in 20 or 30 minutes. Again, do *not* attempt to go through your whole written report by talking fast.

- Give a short description of the problem setting, and compliment the client on something in this section.
- Next briefly describe your approach to the problem. Define the goals agreed upon and the index of performance agreed on. Mention the possible solution options. All of the above should take about half your time.

- Next, discuss the few most likely solution options, and then give your final recommendation.
- Spend some time on explaining the final choice and buttressing your recommendation. Show why it best meets the client's goals and that it is the best according to the client's index of performance.
- Stop and ask for questions.

The first slide, though, should give the bottom-line recommendation, and the rest of the presentation should motivate or justify the recommendation. Why? In many meetings, the only thing anybody will remember is the bottom line—so put it up front to motivate and captivate the interest of the audience. Also, many of the audience, and typically the most senior attendees, will not stay for the entire presentation, and you don't want them to leave without the important message. We recall many meetings where the Partner, General, or COO was called from the meeting.

The Question Period Is the Most Difficult Part to Handle. You are most likely to lose control at this point. Do not let a junior member of the client's staff monopolize the session with technical details. He may feel resentment that an outsider was called in to solve his problem, or he may be showing off in front of his boss. Be polite, pleasant, and responsive but *brief* with such questioners. If they persist, suggest that you and your colleagues will remain after the meeting to address these very important but rather detailed questions. Swing back to the boss, and answer his or her questions in more detail.

When you have finished with your (relatively short) answer, do *not* take a second question from the same person. Do *not* ask if your answer is satisfactory. Remember that the Q&A is not the place to give detailed responses to minutiae.

Be wary of attempts to split the team. It is probably best for the presenter to handle all questions or else have one individual skilled at ad-libbing the handling of all questions. Individual team members, if present, should restrain themselves to short responses concerning facts, and *then only if* asked to supply them by the presenter. Do *not* pass the floor around among the team members. It is difficult for the client to become accustomed to different styles, and it is almost impossible to prevent the session from becoming an open discussion. Do *not* sit down during the question period. Do *not* have the rest of the team at the front of the room during the question period.

As soon as the questions slack off, adjourn the meeting with thanks to all for coming. Each team member should then approach a member of the audience and engage that individual in discussion. The team leader should seek out the client for private impressions.

Never Contradict. No team member should present a conclusion that differs from the team conclusion or throw doubt on the team conclusion in an answer to a question. If a team member holds a contrary position, he or she should not attend the oral presentation.

Never let a questioner see that you think the question is stupid. *Never* respond by saying that the answer was covered previously. This is especially difficult when the client makes a comment or asks a question which reveals that he missed the whole point of the presentation. Of course, no one ever says that a question is stupid in so many words. The usual way of conveying this is by elaborately returning to the visual aids and displaying a chart that specifically gives the answer.

If you must go back to the charts to show the answer, apologize for fouling up that part of the presentation. (There are exceptions to everything, even to "no apologies." Of course this isn't really an exception because it is apparent that you aren't sincere; you are trying to save face for the client.)

Take Notes. While the presenter is talking, other team members can note reactions of the client. Note-taking on all questions and responses is critical for future reference. Furthermore, it is sometimes difficult for team members to maintain an attitude of attention during presentation of material they have heard before or while questions are being answered in areas outside their own specialty. However, such inattention has a bad effect on the client, thus note-taking keeps idle team members looking busy. Every word of comment or criticism by the client should be noted down.

Never Interrupt the Client. Wait till the client has finished before attempting to redirect the discussion.

Never Argue with the Client. This sounds obvious, but it is surprising how often eager young analysts (and some of us older, arrogant types as well) break this rule.

Every Team Member Should Be Ready to Present. We recall one time when, as a young analyst, we pulled an all-nighter getting results for a client briefing the next morning. A team of four went to the meeting with a Navy Captain and his staff, with our senior member prepared to brief. As the presenter began, the Navy Captain pointed to the young analyst and asked him to present. Unfortunately, the young analyst had developed the results but had not reviewed nor seen the briefing. A rough client meeting ensued.

Have Back-Up Material. Assume the possibility of computer failure, a disk failure, a bad CD, or other possibilities. We can recall a presentation to be made in Monte Carlo to the Board of Directors of a client. The junior analyst checked his baggage, and, yes, the bag went to Montreal rather than Monte Carlo. This was before the time of personal computers (1977), and the presentation used a carrousel of slides. The lack of duplicates almost caused the premature demise of the analyst! Also, if a team is presenting and not traveling together, everyone should have copies. It's embarrassing to have the team drive in two cars from two locations, and have the only team arrive be the group without the briefing materials. This mistake again comes from the school of experience.

Never Contradict the Client. This above all!

Debrief Your Team immediately following the meeting if it is a low-key conference, or after a decompression period if it is an important milepost and everyone is physically exhausted. Notes taken by each team member will be very important at this debriefing session.

A Written Response to all important questions asked should be prepared. Send the edited response to the client with thanks for his or her participation. Mention your readiness to provide any further responses needed to move the project along.

8.8   HOW TO WRITE A REPORT[4]

The Executive Summary (ES) Is the Only Thing Your Client Will Read.   You might be lucky (or unlucky) enough to get a client who will read your whole report, but don't count on it. Staff people may read the whole thing, but you must put everything of importance in the Executive Summary. The ES is <u>not</u> an introduction. It must <u>not</u> say, *"If you read this report, you will learn the answers to all of these important questions."* The ES is self-contained. It must stand alone and give all of the important facts and recommendations. Generally speaking, the ES should be about five percent as long as the report that follows it.

Key Report to Original Request (or Request for Proposal [RFP]).   A planning document produced as a final report is only the first step in bringing the proposed system into physical realization, but it is by the quality of this report that the system group is most often judged. The report should be keyed, if possible, to the request that originated the study. This may seem like obvious advice, but experience teaches that it is not.

When it comes time to write the final report, the study group will have progressed far beyond even a well-constructed request for proposal (RFP) or initial problem statement in its understanding of the problem. Thus the temptation will be very great to write the report from this more sophisticated and integrated point of view. Furthermore, many RFPs are poorly constructed, thus increasing the temptation to ignore them.

Nevertheless, if the RFP has section headings and if specific items of work are listed, use exactly these headings in the final report. The young analyst is inclined to expect the client to modify his approach, to conform to the one that the analyst has adopted. Try to keep in mind the Golden Rule.[5]

If a formal RFP does not exist, the final report can be organized around the steps in the systems study. In this situation, it may seem unnecessary to expend much effort in the final report on "Goal Development," but experience indicates its value. If the presentation moves directly to the proposed solution without placing it in context, the client is less likely to accept it.

Remember the Repeated Injunctions Concerning the Descriptive Scenario.   Do not assume that the client is fully familiar with the situation. Start with a descriptive scenario. This does not mean, of course, that the report should be a chronological account of the team's efforts. Quite the contrary, as we have seen in our discussion of goal orientation in the introduction to the system method.

Segment the Report and Its Recommendations and Focus on the Important Issues. You aren't writing history. You were hired to save time for busy people. Put original data, reports of meetings, background information, and so on, in appendices.

Take an Action Orientation. An important element in the report is its action orientation. That is, it is not sufficient to propose an optimum solution to the client's problem in the normative sense. One must provide a *Transition Scenario* describing how to achieve the normative situation. Here are some of the elements of the transition scenario:

> ***Suggested Phasing.*** Many large-scale systems can conveniently be designed, constructed, and brought on stream in distinct phases or increments. These phases should be delineated, and specific mileposts should be identified. A PERT or DELTA chart is indicated here.

> ***Suggested Management.*** An organization chart should be provided for the action phase. Clearly show the relationship of the proposed action organization to the client. Make every effort to eliminate ambiguities between the proposed action management team and the client, as well as between the management team and proposed subcontractors.

> ***Time and Cost Budgets.*** A Gantt chart showing the duration of major activities and the interrelations among them is suggested here. In addition, a cost estimate for each major activity should be inserted to the right of the Gantt chart. These costs can be broken down quite easily into four or five major subcategories.

> ***Suggested Sensors.*** Specific indicators and sensors of progress along with interim success points must be defined for the action phase. This is especially difficult and uniquely critical when progress and success must be defined in terms of societal attitudes and actions, rather than in terms of a physical or structural goal.

Project Pay-Off. The specific accomplishments and rewards for completing the plan must be identified along with the costs. Compute for the client the cost-effectiveness of your proposal.

The oral and written final reports must give evidence that the systems planning group has internalized the problem of the sponsor. Think of it in this way. The sponsor has a difficult problem. He has tried to solve it himself and failed, or he realized initially that the problem is too complex for him. Thus, he called in the system team. If the systems team stands off and says, "Well, yes, you certainly do have a problem there," the sponsor will be alienated. Rather, the attitude to be engendered can be expressed as follows: "Yes, *we* do have a challenge here, and here is how we suggest *we* could meet it!"

The Audit Trail. Check to make sure that original data sheets, all interim calculations that lead to final results and to recommendations, and so on, are included in appendices. Don't let gaps in procedure cause otherwise solid recommendations to be lost. Don't let those opposed to your efforts gain an unreasonable advantage.

NOTES

1. Ability to work in a team is weighed heavily by employers.

2. For a good practical resource on this issue see Harrington-Mackin (1994). For a systemic approach to individual thinking, team building, and learning organizations see Senge (1994).

3. We know that one of the authors was insulted as a young professional when his boss insisted on having a rehearsal of an important client presentation he was to make. Nevertheless, the boss insisted and the author learned a lot from the criticisms that followed.

4. Obviously, there are specific report formats required in certain deliverables, and these comments are general guidelines.

5. The sponsor has the gold, so he makes the rules.

Chapter **9**

Project Management

9.1 INTRODUCTION

In Chapter 8, we discussed how to organize and manage the systems team so as to complete a systems analysis on time and within budget. Suppose now that the final reports, oral and written, have been delivered and the project has received initial approval to get underway. The next step in the process of system analysis is to organize and manage successful completion of the actual project. Thus, in this chapter, we will take up the techniques of project management (PM). The system analysis team is not always asked to follow-on its planning with actual installation management. But, whether it is or not, management of the project installation is an important topic for us. We have remarked that the final report of the systems analysis phase must take an "action orientation." That is, the analysis team must adopt the attitude that it will manage the actual installation. There appears to be no better way of imposing the discipline necessary for doing the analysis phase properly than to assume you will have to take responsibility for carrying your theoretical ideas out in practice.

In this text, we have advocated the alternate use of the "top-down" style of analysis and the "bottom-up" approach. Furthermore, it has been suggested that "top-down" should be the first step. We have the opportunity right now of illustrating these two approaches, in how we organize this chapter. Simply to be contrary, suppose we were to take the bottom-up approach to start. The bottom-up approach is the approach one might take to this subject if one didn't know better, or if one had to impress a naïve client that one understands the topic. In the case before us, one would probably

How to Do Systems Analysis. By John E. Gibson, William T. Scherer, and William F. Gibson
Copyright © 2007 John Wiley & Sons, Inc.

TABLE 9.1. Chapter Headings in 12 Project Management Texts

Topics Directly Related to PM		Topics Indirectly Related	
PERT/CPM	11	Decision-Making	6
Role of Project Engineer	10	System Design Consideration	6
Project Planning	10	Communication	5
Cost Estimation and Control	10	Problem-Solving	4
Organizing the Project	7	Evaluate and Rank Alternatives	4
Organize Project Team	5	Delegation and Integration	3
Implementation	5	Production and Quality Control	3
Legal Aspects	5	Computer Usage in PM	3
Life-Cycle Costing	5	Technology Forecasting	3
Project Monitoring	5	Reliability and Maintenance	2
Resource Management	4		
Project Termination	2		

start by drawing several books on PM from the library and comparing their Tables of Contents.

We did this. We examined 12 standard PM texts and found 23 different topics listed as chapter headings. The most popular topic, PERT/CPM, was covered in 11 of the texts, and the count of the other topics was reduced smoothly down to only two inclusions. There was no subgroup of topics that all texts included. Three topics were included 10 times, six were included five times, four three times, and so forth. It appears to us, therefore, that we must conclude that the border of the project management territory is vague, and the bottom-up approach doesn't help much to define it.

When we examined the 23 candidate topics still more closely, things got more mushy. All of the topics are interesting and cover useful knowledge, but many of them, it seemed to us, are only vaguely related to project management. We counted 12 of the topics as directly related to PM, 10 as only distantly related, and one ("proposal preparation") as directly related but rather specialized, and therefore not counted in Table 9.1. In the table, these topics are listed in two major categories, along with the number of citations for each topic. This bottom-up approach of counting entries in the standard textbooks doesn't help to organize the topic because there isn't general agreement on what constitutes the field.

Is there some other, more convenient and "natural" way in which these topics might be grouped? A chronological approach is popular. In that ordering, authors introduce topics as they might arise if one were actually managing a project. But we have seen in an early chapter of this text that this approach is often unwieldy. The chronological approach is clumsy and repetitive. In contrast, our approach attempts to organize Project Management from an overall top-down, conceptual approach. Five headings are given in Table 9.2 that seem to capture the topics listed in Table 9.1. One might call this a functional organization of the material.

TABLE 9.2. Possible Five-Heading Organization of Project Management and Example Topics

Major Headings	Topics Included
Project Planning	Life-Cycle Planning Goals and Objectives Critical Tasks and Mileposts Etc.
Project Scheduling	Define Specific Activities PERT/CPM Gantt Charts Etc.
Project Control	Cost Estimation Cost Control Etc.
Resource Allocation	Requirements Planning Time vs. Resources Constraints Etc.
Project Management	Proposal Writing Quality Control Reliability & Maintainability Legal and Contracts PM Computer Software Project Termination Etc.

Project scheduling, project control, and resource allocation constitute the technical core of P.M., and one needs an entire text to cover them properly.

9.2 PROJECT MANAGEMENT VERSUS PROCESS MANAGEMENT

The adjective "project" that modifies "management" needs a little clarification. For example, how many kinds of "management" are there? Perhaps hundreds? Does every kind of different activity in the world of work deserve a different kind of management? Our answer is, "No." In the general sense, there are only two kinds of management: process management and project management. Either kind can be applied to any job. However, the only reason that this categorization makes any sense is that certain jobs go better with one style of management and other tasks go better with the other.

Process-style management is more appropriate in those jobs that can be represented by a continuous flow process. If the workers are asked to do essentially the same tasks on different lot numbers, if the work flows through the shop on a continuous basis, process management is effective. Any assembly line operation is a flow process; in

TABLE 9.3. Comparison of Process Management and Project Management

Process Management	Project Management
Continuous flow of tasks	Discrete set of tasks
	Limited time and resources
Examples	Examples
Sorting mail	Construction projects
Run hardware store	Open new store
Manage computer center	Design new device
Airline baggage handling	Fight a war
Assembly line work	
High Interpersonal Management Style	High task orientation
Help make "happy campers" of workers	
Extrinsic rewards at work	Intrinsic rewards from work
Fellowship	Sense of craftsmanship
Achievement awards	Get job done (right)
Personal recognition	Reach goal with team
Etc.	Beat opponents
Management focus on	Management focus on
Throughput efficiency	Time schedule
Time and motion study	Organize tasks
Follow rules	Order tasks
Quality circles	Interim mileposts

fact any repetitive job is a flow process. Office work, retail trade, professional work, and so on, are all process style tasks.

The process-style manager is a high interpersonal relationship individual; he or she encourages workers to feel good about themselves and each other and takes an interest in them as people. The process-style manager understands that many of the values a worker finds in the process workplace are extrinsic. That is, rewards are gathered not merely from doing the job well, but also from fellowship on the job, achievement awards, personal recognition, and so on.

The effective process-style manager looks for operational efficiencies in the modern equivalent of time and motion studies. If the work to be done amounts to an infinite pile at the input, the process manager shouldn't focus on getting to the end of the pile. He or she must focus on throughput efficiency, and on keeping the workforce more or less contented. Quality circles can work well, if managed properly, in a process-type environment.[1] The process-style manager works through people to get the job done.

The project-style manager also works through people but in an entirely different way. The project manager is more job- or task-focused than people-focused. In the ideal, the project manager can be highly interpersonally related, but fundamentally, and primarily, he or she must be highly task-oriented; see Table 9.3 for a comparison of process and project management. Table 9.4 compares the way a process-style management meeting is conducted with a project-style meeting.

TABLE 9.4. Meeting Style of Process Managers and Project Managers: How to Tell Process Management from Project Management by Observing the Style in which Meetings Are Conducted[a]

Process-Style Meeting	Project-Style Meeting
Attendees are casual, good fellowship reigns, schmoozing	Manager is on-time
Manager may be late	Agenda is distributed (or was sent out in advance)
Manager is relaxed, casual, friendly	Manager is crisp, in-charge
No special agenda is evident	Discussion is organized, directed at agenda item, extraneous discussion is discouraged
Talk is on random topics (or at least on topics that visitor finds hard to place in categories)	Attendees are expected to keep quiet and take notes, answer questions and contribute to item under discussion
Meeting runs over time and/or seems to peter out	Attendees are called on to report progress and to mention any difficulties with assignments, etc.
	Manager seems eager to get through agenda and to "get back to work"
	Tasks are assigned with deadlines

[a]Quite obviously the "project-style" meeting isn't as much fun. Attendees will feel "under the gun," and will be glad to get out of the pressure cooker and back to their job or office.

The way one manages often depends on one's personal style, but in the abstract this should not be so. W. F. Whyte provides a strong validation of this point in his book *Men at Work* (Whyte, 1961). Whyte cites a study of the style of Sears' managers, done by Sears in 1949. Two types of management had evolved, seemingly by chance. One style, very close to the Hersey–Blanchard (H–B) D-Mode (see below) was found to be most effective. The other style, essentially the H–B T-Mode, was less effective. It was established then that the two styles reflected the personalities of the managers. Most telling, when a T-Mode manager was transferred to a D-Mode store, he soon began to move it backward into the T-Mode. Fortunately, the VP of Personnel at Sears discovered this situation and over time was able to correct it for the most part. *One of the important lessons of this chapter is that one should adopt a management style that is appropriate for the work environment.* There are several classifications of management style. McGregor's Theory X and Theory Y have now been around for about 50 years and have served a useful purpose, but we find the newer, Hersey–Blanchard four-mode theory much more powerful and useful.

9.3 THE HERSEY–BLANCHARD FOUR-MODE THEORY

Hersey and Blanchard have developed a theory of management style that breaks away from the static bimodality of Theory X and Theory Y to produce a four-mode theory of management style based on the social maturity of the group to be managed (Hersey and Blanchard, 1982). This dynamic four-mode theory seems to us to have a solid psychological base in that it focuses on the interpersonal context of the managerial situation. Furthermore, it can be used to provide a framework for an analysis of the less contextual and therefore more primitive Theories X and Y. The H–B theory accepts the dynamic nature of the interaction between worker and manager. In addition, the H–B theory can be employed by the worker to analyze his or her manager and to "manage" their mutual interactions. *That is, the worker can manage the manager* for the overall good of both, as well as that of the organization. Most valuable of all to the manager is the predictive ability of the H–B approach. Properly employed, it serves as a guide and feedback tool for improving managerial and worker effectiveness.

Starting with the mode appropriate for the lowest level of worker maturity, the four modes of Hersey and Blanchard are labeled "TELL," "SELL," "PARTICIPATE," and "DELEGATE." The "TELL" mode ("T-mode") of management is a strongly hierarchic, directive style directly comparable to the Theory X style advocated by Taylor. It is highly task-oriented and low in interpersonal relationship. It is the style used in the basic training of military troops and is common in heavy industry in the United States, even today. It is said to be necessary when workers are not mature and cannot be relied on to cooperate with management for the benefit of both. Psychologically, it assumes that the worker is childlike and does not know what is in his own long-term best interest.

Given the social conditions in the nation and the state of the factories of America at the turn of the twentieth century, one can see the applicability of this method. Many factory workers were immigrants who did not know English and who were unused to the discipline and organization necessary in the factory. They were farm lads from the hinterland or from Europe and completely without industrial training. Even expert workers were often trained in the guild system that featured individual craft skills rather than the more organized approach needed in the modern factory.

The next, more advanced mode is called "SELL" ("S-mode"). Here, the manager takes time to explain why a particular approach has been chosen. The mode is still hierarchic, task-oriented, and not fully based on the informed consent of the worker. It is the style used in leading more skilled military troops and in many modern blue-collar task groups. It is higher in interpersonal intensity but is not opposed to Theory X, and indeed it is an advanced form of the method. One can visualize Taylor stopping to explain to a bright and willing worker just why they are going to do something. The manager who practices the sell technique is moving toward seeking the informed consent of the worker. Psychologically, managers in this mode see the worker as an advanced adolescent who generally can be relied upon to understand what is good for him but is not yet ready for full adult responsibility and complete independence.

"PARTICIPATE" ("P-mode") is the third mode of management and may be compared to Theory Y. Here, the worker is viewed as mature and willing to give informed consent. Furthermore, the worker is viewed as having his own good ideas that can be incorporated in the management plan once all of the goals and constraints are made clear to him. In fact, it is the goal in this mode to elicit tactical suggestions from the workers rather than imposing directions from above. One likes to think that

TABLE 9.5. Characteristics of the Hersey–Blanchard Four-Mode Theory

Mode Name	Interpersonal Relationship	Task Orientation	Appropriate Worker Maturity Level	Brief Name
Tell	Low	High	Lowest	T-Mode
Sell	High	High	Moderate	S-Mode
Participate	High	Low	Mature	P-Mode
Delegate	Low	Low	Highest	D-Mode

white collar workers and professionals are in this mode. As a matter of fact, many factory workers have long been ready for this mode as well, as the success of such methods as the Scanlon plan and Quality Circles demonstrate. Psychologically, one thinks here of the worker as a young adult, fully responsible and ready to participate in the decision process insofar as his training and experience will permit. The P-Mode is lower in directive task orientation than the T-Mode but retains the high interpersonal flavor of the S-Mode.

Finally, we arrive at "DELEGATE" ("D-mode"), the most mature mode of management. Here, one assumes fully self-actualized workers, ready and able to organize themselves to handle their own responsibilities. This is similar to, but not the same as, the concept psychologists call the "leaderless group" mode of management. In the delegate mode, the manager and those in his work group have arrived at a common understanding of the general goals of the organization and then the manager leaves the team to handle the tactical and organizational details as well as the daily operations to accomplish the goals. Management acts as a resource and a consultant rather than a task leader. In the delegate mode, one views the worker as a motivated and mature adult with whom one is transacting business. Table 9.5 gives the characteristics of each mode.

Figure 9.1 gives the H–B matrix and the trajectory of management style that depends on the maturity level of the worker. Each quadrant is uniquely defined by the combination of intensity of interpersonal relationship between the worker and the manager and the intensity of task orientation.

Suppose you are the leader of a group that is operating well in the T-mode. What do you do to move into the S-mode? Start by supervising tasks less closely by revealing more of the overall plan and delegating a little freedom. Do <u>not</u> increase your intensity of interpersonal relations before this delegation is successful. Thus, on the H–B trajectory shown in Figure 9.1, we start at a point in the middle of the T-mode and move off the trajectory to the left. Do not make a large change, but rather one that is small but noticeable. When this is successful, move up the trajectory by increasing your interpersonal relationship. Become more interested and supportive of your people's personal mental state. Be a little less formal and more friendly, but cautious. Sometimes the manager that reverses these two steps becomes viewed as a "soft touch" by the workers, according to Hersey and Blanchard.

Let's try another example. Suppose the group is operating well in the P-mode and then additional delegation is successful. Hersey and Blanchard suggest that this be rewarded by the manager withdrawing somewhat by reducing his or her relational

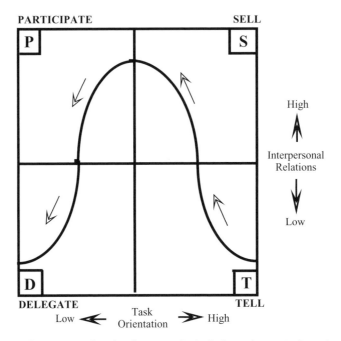

FIGURE 9.1 The Hersey–Blanchard matrix. The bell-shaped curve is the trajectory along which the mature manager moves his management style in response to, and to cause, increased socioemotional maturity level of the workers. It is this appreciation of environmental context that makes the H–B approach unique. [From: Hersey and Blanchard (1982).]

effort. Won't this be viewed as punishment, as it would be in the S-mode? Not if the workers are truly mature. They will be happy in the P-mode, but their self-actualization will be increased by leaving them more on their own.

Almost all humans seem to resist change automatically, and the manager can expect such resistance in his or her efforts to move forward along the H–B trajectory. On the other hand, this same resistance may be useful through peer pressure in resisting the back-sliding of an individual. Not all workers in a group are uniform in their maturity level, and not all will react similarly to the managerial stimulus. The manager must expect that a year or more may be required to move a group from one quadrant to the next. Some individuals and groups may never move all the way along the trajectory to the D-Mode.

Workers are not alone in resisting change. Some traditional middle-level managers resist the implications they see in the H–B modes. Reactionary managers sometimes find it difficult to give up the "control" they believe is essential to their management style. Sometimes middle-level managers argue that the higher H–B modes, "Participate" and "Delegate," seem to be giving away the store. (We have heard it put even more colorfully, namely "putting the inmates in charge of the asylum.") This is not so. Hersey and Blanchard are not suggesting that the goals and objectives are to be put up for discussion. Rather, the point is to obtain worker input to the process of how to go about achieving management's goals.

Of course, any theory is an abstraction and this H–B theory is no exception, yet it does provide a powerful illuminating effect. The manager attempts to move his people along a maturity curve as rapidly as possible because one believes that mature transactions among adults are superior to other games people play. Naturally, not all individuals will arrive simultaneously at the same maturity level. Furthermore, the manager himself must be mature if he or she is to work with various groups at differing levels of maturity. One must be alert to temporary slips in maturity. For example, unusual pressure on the job or family problems are often met by a downward migration in maturity level. Because the Hersey–Blanchard theory focuses on the social maturity of those managed, it provides an indicator to the manager of the appropriate approach to a management situation and a check on the proper application through the response of the group. This guide and feedback effect is not present in Theories X, Y, or Z.

9.4 RELATION OF MANAGEMENT STYLE TO PROJECT MANAGEMENT

The personal style of engineers often tends to be one of high task orientation and a low interpersonal relationship. Notice from the H–B theory how this might get one off on the wrong foot with a new project team. If an engineer follows typical style in managing the first project meeting, he will be right in the middle of the T-Mode, that is, the most primitive and least effective management style. It will signal to the new project team that the manager intends to treat team members as less than adult, and they may respond accordingly.

At the same time, for technical people, one must maintain a moderately high task orientation in order to maintain their respect. To move immediately to the P-Mode or the D-Mode with an untried new group of project team members is risky. Thus, we recommend that a new project leader adopt a position on the border between the S-Mode and the P-Mode. This means taking a high interpersonal relationship. Smile a lot and get on a first-name basis with your people. Don't stand on ceremony and don't be too formal. At the same time, take a strong task orientation. Make sure everyone understands that cost and time deadlines are important and must be met. Don't sit back and wait for suggestions.

Conduct your project meetings in an open and friendly, but business-like, way. Have an agenda and stick to it. Keep the meetings on a time schedule, just as you expect your people to keep themselves on time. You are a group of colleagues. You respect one another, but you are at the project meeting for a purpose. The focus is first on the task and only then on interpersonal relations, not vice versa. You are all busy people with other pressing matters to attend to and thus are not at the project meeting to share fellowship or for socializing. You are there to get through the agenda and to get back to work.

Your respect for your people means that you will act in a quiet and mature manner, no loud jokes and horsing around, and it also means that you will assume that your people are doing their best. So you won't get angry and lose your temper when the schedule starts to slip. You will ask for and respect explanations for slippage and you will request suggestions from the individual responsible as to the best way to correct the problem. Your people should see you as someone who supports them and is ready to help when needed. You ask for and respect ideas and suggestions. At the same time, you take seriously the schedule and the budget and, above all, the performance specifications of the project. Don't forget to smile.

The manager who calls a meeting and who doesn't stay in control wastes time. Objectively speaking, a few minutes of "wasted time" might not seem all that important. After all, if you are the boss, in effect you have bought the time of the attendees, so if you don't care about the cost of the meeting, why should the team members? There is, however, a more important psychological problem in running an inefficient meeting that is not generally understood.

Team members <u>do</u> care about wasting time in a meeting and they care deeply, because you are doing more than using their time. In calling a meeting, you have stepped out of the usual adult–adult role of the manager and moved, perhaps without understanding it, into a parent–child (teacher–pupil) mode. You have reverted to the most primitive mode of management, one that you would probably never use consciously. You are no longer merely telling your people <u>what</u> to do, which is bad enough, you are telling them <u>how</u> to do it, and worse, you are sitting there to see that they perform exactly as you have directed. You may think that you are running a business meeting, but your body language is saying:

"Sit up straight, children, and pay close attention. This is very important."

Thus, an inefficiently run project meeting is a breach of good manners and an expensive waste of time. It is unmannerly because you have assumed a role of social superiority, and it is inefficient because it permits only one individual at a time, whoever is speaking, to operate at full potential. Everyone else is more or less idle and yet under social coercion. Thus, simultaneously, meetings offend against equity and efficiency. That's why people don't like badly run meetings.

9.5   PRELIMINARY PROJECT PLANNING

The first step in PM is preparation of a careful project plan. This plan should be based on the preceding system analysis and the final report of the systems study. That is the source, for example, of the goals statement for the project. But now the project plan must be carried to greater detail. In addition to overall goals, intermediate objectives and specific intermediate mileposts must be established.

Table 9.6 gives a checklist of steps to be taken in preliminary PM.

Not only are objective project goals to be included, but also some process objectives must be considered. For example, space is very scarce and expensive in Manhattan. Thus, the erectors of major buildings on the island cannot set aside space near the construction site to assemble and store all of the construction materials that will be needed during the two- to three-year construction process. Material will have to be

TABLE 9.6. Suggested Major Steps to Take in Developing a Project Plan

Project Management Checklist

1. **Outline** the major phases of the whole project in tabular and Gantt chart form.
2. Begin to **identify specific tasks** at several levels of detail. Aim at capturing the broad scope first, you can break out detailed tasks later if necessary.
3. **Establish task sequence**. Estimate rough time durations for each task and establish their dependency relations. That is, certain tasks are "predecessors" to "successor" tasks in that they must be completed before the successor tasks can begin.
4. **Define mileposts**. Mileposts are important interim objectives. They must be objectively observable. Set more mileposts rather than fewer. Achieving a short-term milepost is a good motivator, and missing one gives an early indication of a deficiency.
5. **Assign resources**. Identify specific individuals responsible for each task and check for balance in resource allocation.
6. **Estimate costs** for each task, as well as for general and administrative costs. Don't forget overhead and other hidden costs.
7. **Review and revise** plan and identify the critical path. Make sure the plan is realistic, and neither overly optimistic nor pessimistic. Carefully iterate on the budget.
8. **Obtain approval** of plan. Start with a self-review and then obtain key team member sign-offs. Obtain ancillary group sign-offs. Now is the time to surface doubts and concerns. Submit to senior management for review and approval.
9. **Implement** the plan. Take the mileposts seriously and do continuous, unobtrusive checking. Catching deficiencies early costs less. Don't forget to smile.

assembled at a remote site, possibly in another state, and moved to the construction site just a few hours before it is needed. Planning for this specific problem would come under the category of process goals.

Unless the project of which you have just been appointed manager is very small and quite similar to projects that you have managed in the past, you will need technical support in the form of software. There are several well-known PM software packages available, including the ubiquitous Microsoft Project™.

9.6 DEALING WITH CONFLICT IN PROJECT MANAGEMENT

PM produces certain conflicts *by definition*. They are supposed to be there! The problem is not how to eliminate them, but rather how to *manage* them. Project management is inherently wasteful of resources because so many activities that could be most efficiently handled in a centralized fashion are carried out separately on separate projects. This must be, but duplication of functions must be held to a reasonable minimum. Thus, no project will be allowed to handle all functions with project staff. Some functions will have to be done by ancillary groups. The project manager must identify those activities and seek out the leader of the ancillary group for assistance.

Ancillary group support is not to be casually sought. The project manager should set up a formal appointment with his counterpart and carefully review his needs. The most likely response to the request for assistance is "no." How can it be otherwise?

You are asking for a significant chunk of your counterpart's resources. If he gives them without a whimper, he must have surplus resources. That's bad. So there is the conflict.

The following is one way to resolve this conflict. Start with agreeing that you understand the reason for the initial reluctance of your peer to surrender resources. But point out that this conflict will have to be resolved by your mutual bosses if it can't be solved at your level. Either this will persuade your counterpart or it won't. In either case, write a polite, friendly letter to him stating the outcome and give a copy to your boss and your counterpart's boss. Do not get emotionally involved. Remain friends. You can see why these outside resource needs have to be identified well in advance so that these negotiations, which take time, can be resolved without recriminations.

9.7 LIFE-CYCLE PLANNING AND DESIGN

Another issue is the matter of life-cycle planning. The project manager must consider the project over its entire life cycle, including its termination, removal, and replacement [see Blanchard and Fabrycky (2006) for a complete discussion of the "ilities," including reliability, usability, survivability, and so on]. The issue of life-cycle planning should be addressed in the preliminary design phase in at least the following five specific respects:

1. Design for maintainability
2. Design for modular upgrade and replacement
3. Design for capacity expansion
4. Design for termination and replacement
5. Design for sustainabilty

In current practice, life-cycle planning is perhaps the least well done of all the steps in PM. Sometimes, life-cycle design is omitted entirely in a deliberate attempt to reduce the first cost of the project. Often, however, life-cycle design is overlooked through ignorance on the part of the project manager. Because of its importance, we will discuss the matter in detail in the next section. We will take each of the five points above and give examples of life-cycle design in each of three application areas: first in software project design, then electronics, and finally in a mechanical and/or construction project. Some are examples of good design practice, but others are horror stories.

9.7.1 Design for Maintainability

1. Structured programming is an excellent example of design for maintainability in software PM. We pointed out in an earlier chapter that the initial cost of coding of a piece of software is minuscule compared to its total life-cycle costs. Many

extraordinarily large pieces of code that were written 40 or even 50 years ago are still currently used in production. For example, some of the earliest FORTRAN code for essential calculations in nuclear reactor design, written in the 1950s, is still in use. What is more, many design specifications are written to conform to this old and inefficient code. In other words, a particular design specification for a commercial nuclear reactor may in part be defined in terms of a particular result obtained from running a specific FORTRAN program. In fact, while much of the scandalous increase in cost of commercial nuclear reactor construction must be assigned to inept and incompetent federal regulation, some of it is due to the continuing use of old spaghetti FORTRAN design code.

Very early COBOL code is still in wide use in payroll and other business applications. This early code was not designed from the top down and was not structured. Thus, it is extraordinarily costly in both time and money to modify the code when necessary.

2. The design of the original IBM Personal Computer is an example of excellent design for maintainability. Many other early models of electronic components are equally excellent from this point of view. Early models of RCA television sets come to mind. However, follow-on designs are often reengineered to optimize for minimum first cost to the purchaser and an unfortunate by-product is that maintainability is sacrificed.

3. American automobiles prior to World War II were designed with maintainability and repairability in mind, but over the past 30 years this feature has been totally ignored. In a conversation along these lines with a former student who had risen to a high management position in an American auto firm, he admitted our concern was valid, but he said:

"You insist on acting naïve! If I am a design engineer for an American auto producer, I get no brownie points for maintainability; that's the dealers' problem. But, if I can redesign a part to cut off a tenth of a second in final assembly, I'll get promoted. And of course, this often results in reduced maintainability."

9.7.2 Design for Modular Upgrade and Replacement

1. Often the same design spirit that produces excellent maintainability will result in good design for modular upgrade and replacement. This is certainly true in software production. Modularity and structure in design permits addition of new features to the package without complete redesign. This is valuable for the final user, it goes without saying. But it is equally valuable, if not more valuable, to the producer. "Wordstar," the well-known (in the 1980s) word processing package, migrated successfully from a CP/M environment to a DOS environment because of limited modularity in its design, but then it lost its leadership to "WordPerfect" because of the cost of adding new features. One long-delayed upgrade, Wordstar 4.0, was purchased from an outside vendor, in part because of the difficulty experienced in-house in rewriting spaghetti code. WordPerfect subsequently lost its share to MS Word.

2. The original IBM PC was an excellent example of designing for modular upgrade and replacement. The resident chip memory could be expanded by a factor of 10 to 100. The CPU cycle rate could be increased. The original full-height floppy disk drives could be replaced by two half-height drives and a hard disk drive with as much as 30 megabytes of storage or more. Graphics cards could be installed, and on and on.

Some might argue that it is true that the IBM "open-architecture" design does indeed do all of the things mentioned, and even more, this design philosophy has resulted in Dell, Gateway, Compaq, and H-P taking business away from IBM. Such an argument would be fallacious. It is true that IBM has lost PC market share, but this was due to the lack of an alert market strategy on IBM's part, rather than the fault of modular design. In reality, the open architecture helped IBM gain its share in the first place.

3. Passenger and military aircraft should be designed for modular upgrade and replacement. The Boeing Corporation knows this, and some of its aircraft are in the second or third retrofit. More powerful engines, stretch bodies, and so forth, are common. The B-52 bomber is over 50 years old and has been upgraded and retro-fit many times in its unusually long life. The same is true of the C-130s, and the iconic Boeing 747 has undergone at least eight variations in its 36-year lifespan.

9.7.3 Design for Capacity Expansion

1. Lack of attention to the need for possible capacity expansion is an indicator of incompetence in systems programmers. A university computer center, the administration of which one of the authors was once forced to assume after it had been mismanaged for several years, had a number of such animals on its support staff. One payroll program was particularly notorious. As just one example, the payroll program limited the amount of money that could be deducted annually for the United Way to $999.99. Fortunately for the United Way, but unfortunately for the computer center, our President was a very generous individual and he wished to deduct from his salary and donate several thousand dollars.

Other examples abound, such as databases that limit the number of fields, or the number of entries, for example, and so forth. Rather than forcing himself to play God by rigidly allocating the number of cells for specific items, a programmer using a more modern approach would employ dynamic reallocation.

2. It was generally agreed that the Betamax format for recording VCR tapes was technically superior to the VHS format. Furthermore, Betamax was first into the marketplace, an apparently unbeatable combination. But the consumer wanted longer recording times than Betamax could or would provide. Thus, VHS became the clear market leader.

3. Building architecture is possibly the field in which an "anti-modular" project design approach is most rampant. Many architects are more interested in making a "personal design statement" with their buildings than they are in serving the needs of the client. Examples are endless, but one that comes immediately to mind because of

the rapidly growing crisis it has produced is Dulles Airport, which serves Washington, D.C. The Dulles terminal building has been given adulatory attention since it was first opened, and as a sculptural monument it no doubt deserves praise. It is only as a functional airport terminal that it is a flaming disaster. The extraordinary dysfunctionality of the Dulles terminal is evident in every aspect of its operation, from baggage handling, to passenger ticketing, to ground transportation, to loading and unloading. After years of low usage, the flight arrival/departure schedule at Dulles had entered a rapid growth phase in the early to mid-1990s when it became a United hub, and the anti-modularity of the terminal has rapidly become insupportable. Probably the most cost-effective solution would be to convert the present terminal into a museum and go across the field and start over with a totally new terminal.

9.7.4 Design for Termination and Replacement

1. It might seem that designers of stand-alone software packages need not be concerned with this element of life-cycle planning. Not true. The year 1987 saw IBM challenged in its mainframe and mid-range computer lines by DEC. DEC had integrated its entire line so that all of its machines could talk to each other. This ability was not present in the IBM lines, which featured as many as seven totally incompatible operating systems. IBM then announced that its self-created chaos would be reduced to three mutually incompatible systems in the near future. But by then, DEC had broken into a business segment formerly dominated by IBM.

But what has this to do with the issue at hand? Just this. When a business wanted to upgrade its computer to get more memory and speed, a DEC machine was available that ran all of the programs used on the old terminated machine. Not so with IBM. Given that the cost of software now exceeds the cost of hardware, this is a serious issue.

2. Standard electronic hardware interfaces permit convenient replacement of obsolete black boxes and should be insisted upon. Military aircraft electronics is a particularly important example of this issue.

3. Commercial nuclear reactors provide a gruesome example of the incredible cost that may be incurred by failing to provide for retirement and replacement in project planning. In fact, this single issue was more than sufficient to cancel the commercial feasibility of nuclear power in the United States for the remainder of the twentieth century and perhaps beyond. This crippling wasn't accomplished by politics or by eco-maniacs. This fatality was inflicted by the nuclear power community on itself.

9.7.5 Design for Sustainability

1. Electronic components, such as televisions, are an excellent example of this concept. In the near future in the United States, and currently in many European countries, electronic devices can be returned to the original manufacturer at the end of their "normal" life [for an editorial on this topic, see Goosey (2004)]. The manufacturer is then

responsible for disposal and, better yet, reuse of the materials. If the components can truly be recycled, as opposed to down-cycled, significant environmental and economic benefits are possible.

2. Total life-cycle costs must be considered, and this includes any future costs that may be incurred, such as clean-up of a manufacturing or usage site and/or proper disposal of materials. Such life-cycle costs also include the impact costs incurred during manufacture, such as pollutants produced and their impacts, whether it be the immediate economic impacts or the difficult-to-quantify short- and long-term environmental impacts [see McDonough and Braungart (2000); also see Gorman et al. (2000)].

3. DesignTex, Inc., is an example of design for the environment and the entire life-cycle cost [see Mehalik et al. (1996)]. Its goal was to produce a fabric product for which the manufacturing process resulted in minimal (preferably, no) waste, including by-products, and was completely biodegradable. They were able to make significant progress toward their goals, greatly reducing environmental impacts. It is likely that in the near future such designs will not be at the discretion of the manufacturer but mandated.

Sustainability issues are currently difficult to quantify, especially in dollars, and are likely a difficult sell to organizations. Corporate boards, for example, may be reluctant to incur additional costs and difficulties to improve a nonrequired and/or nonmeasured sustainability concept unless mandated by legislation. It would be foolish, however, to ignore these issues even if not currently regulated. Critical to good design is consideration for the future, and sustainability is on the horizon. It's interesting that sustainability considerations practically incorporate all of the previous four design aspects.

9.8   PERT/CPM PROGRAM PLANNING METHOD: AN EXAMPLE

PERT is a graphical computerized program planning technique that assembles the time estimates required to complete each project subtask and the dependencies of each task on other tasks, into a complete time-ordered organization chart for the overall project. PERT was developed by Booz, Allen & Hamilton, a management consulting firm, under contract to, and directed by, the Polaris Special Projects Office of the U.S. Navy in late 1957 and early 1958. CPM is a similar technique developed independently and concurrently by the DuPont Corporation. For a rather complete historical description of the development of PERT, early opposition to its use in the Polaris project, and a revisionist interpretation of PERT's contribution to the success of Polaris, see Sapolsky (1972). Our goal here is not to cover the concepts and tools of project management but to put them in the context of a systems analysis. For a complete treatment of the tools and the associated trade-offs in project management, we refer the reader to Klastorin (2003).

The completed PERT chart informs the analyst of the expected project completion time and those subtasks upon whose timely completion the project depends. The PERT

TABLE 9.7. Definitions of Three Estimates of "Time to Complete a Project"

t_p = pessimistic estimate
t_o = optimistic estimate
t_a = average estimate

chart aids in scheduling necessary overtime, ordering of materials, and organizing the overall effort. A computer program is often used to produce the complete chart showing all links and total time for completion. Like several other early systems analysis techniques, PERT and CPM have gained a coterie of fanatical believers and considerable special terminology and mystique. As with other system analysis tools, a major benefit of PERT/CPM is *not* the final computer-produced chart, but simply the fact that the analyst has been forced to go through, in some detail, a complete description of the project. This discipline is possibly PERT/CPM's greatest contribution.

Nevertheless, there are some interesting insights that can develop from a PERT/CPM analysis that could come as a surprise to the novice. We can best demonstrate the method and such insight by giving a concrete example. While similar examples are common in the literature, this specific one is given in a General Electric report (General Electric, 1964).

Suppose a particular R&D project requires eight different tasks for successful completion. The project manager will be asked to estimate the length of time required for each activity and its cost. Experience indicates that managers are reluctant to give a single time estimate for an activity, because so many variables are involved. Furthermore, if forced to give only one time estimate for an activity, the prudent manager will build in slack to protect himself. Thus, with secret and uncontrolled slack hidden in many places, an adversarial situation has been created. The time estimation task is made simpler, psychologically at least, by requesting that three time estimates be given. These times are defined in Table 9.7.

Charles Clark of the original Booz, Allen and Hamilton team noted that when many estimates of the same project are obtained, the distribution of the estimates often approaches a Beta statistical distribution function.[2] Based on this empiric observation of the Beta distribution, the expected time for the activity can be calculated as follows:

$$t_e = [t_p + 4t_a + t_o]/6 \qquad (9.1)$$

With this normal expected time will be associated a normal expected cost. In addition, one can estimate a "crash" cost and time. This would present an all-out effort and a minimum time. A cost slope can then be calculated as shown in Equation 9.2:

$$\text{Cost slope} = \frac{t_{\text{normal}} - t_{\text{crash}} \text{ (days)}}{c_{\text{crash}} - c_{\text{normal}} \text{ (dollars)}} \qquad (9.2)$$

TABLE 9.8. Time and Cost Estimates for the Example Project[a]

Activity	Normal		Crash		Cost Slope ($/day)
	Time (days)	Cost ($)	Time (days)	Cost ($)	
(0, 1)	4	210	3	280	70
(0, 2)	8	400	6	560	80
(1, 2)	6	500	4	600	50
(1, 4)	9	540	7	600	30
(2, 3)	4	500	1	1100	200
(2, 4)	5	150	4	240	90
(3, 5)	3	150	3	150	[b]
(4, 5)	7	600	6	750	150
Totals		3050		4280	

[a]This table does not contain activity linkage information sufficient to enable the construction of Figure 9.2. Each of the numbered nodes is an event, and the event does not occur until all activities terminating into it are complete. The cost-slope is calculated from data in other columns using Eq. (9.2).
[b]Activity (3, 5) cannot be expedited.

Next, the manager must define the linkages between the activities by stating which activities must be complete before others can begin. Table 9.8 gives the estimates for our example project, and Figure 9.2 illustrates the linkages. Usually, the analyst need not produce the PERT/CPM map manually. While manual construction is not difficult in this example, because it has only a few activities, manual construction rapidly becomes complex when the number of activities grows into the hundreds. We can use the data given in Table 9.8 to compute the earliest event time at each node under a normal schedule. Because activity (0,1) requires four days, it is apparent that event 1 can occur four days after the project is initiated. Thus a "4" is placed in the box near node 1 in Figure 9.3.

The earliest event time (EET) for each node is shown in a box by the node, and the latest occurrence time (LOT) is shown in an oval by each node. The necessary condition for an activity to be on the critical path is EET = LOT at the nodes at its

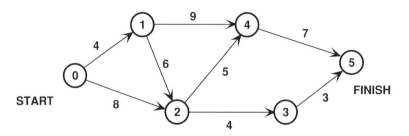

FIGURE 9.2 The PERT network for our example. Five nodes and eight activities make up this project.

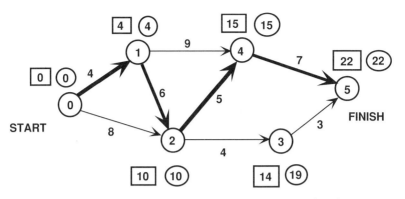

FIGURE 9.3 The PERT network showing the critical path.

ends. The sufficient condition for an activity to be on the critical path is that the time of the activity must be equal to the difference in node times at the beginning and end.

Next, we will go backwards through the network calculating the latest permissible occurrence of each activity completion if the project is to finish on time. The LOT will be shown in an oval at each node. Obviously the latest permissible occurrence of activities (4, 5) and (3, 5) is day 22. Thus "22" is shown in the oval at node 5. Activity (4, 5) takes seven days. Thus, for the project to be complete on time, the activities terminating at node 4 must be complete at day 15. The latest permissible occurrence of the event terminating on node 3 is day 19, if the project is to be completed on time. The LOT at Node 2 is not 15, but 10. Why?

The <u>critical path</u> through the network is that set of activities, any of which is delayed, will delay the completion of the project. For a node to lie on the critical path, it is necessary but not sufficient that EET equals LOT. If, in addition, the time for an activity equals the difference in the node times at its beginning and its end, it is sufficient for the activity to be on the critical path. Nodes 0, 1, 2, 4, and 5 are candidates for the critical path, because they satisfy the necessary condition. Although activity (1, 4) lies between nodes that satisfy the necessary condition, it is not an element in the critical path, because its duration does not equal the time difference between the nodes. The critical path is shown in Figure 9.3. Although there is a single critical path through this network, multiple critical paths are possible in general. Those activities not on the critical path are said to have slack time or "float." The activity (0, 2) has two days of float, because even if it took 10 days to complete rather than its scheduled eight days, event 2 would still take place on time.

The concept of the critical path is one of the major claims to power of the PERT/CPM process. The critical path identifies those specific activities that must be accelerated if the overall project must be completed early. To accelerate those activities not on the critical path would be to waste money.

While we know that to reduce the total project time by one day it is necessary to reduce the duration of an activity on the critical path by one, the choice of which activity to reduce is not arbitrary. Table 9.9 shows the cost slope of the activities on the critical path.

TABLE 9.9. Cost Slope for Critical Path Elements[a]

Critical Path Element	Cost Slope ($/day)
(0,1)	70
(1,2)	50
(2,4)	90
(4,5)	150

[a]Data for this table were extracted from Table 9.8

It is apparent that activity (1, 2) can be expedited at minimum cost. Up to two days may be removed from the project duration by expediting activity (1, 2). At that point, activity (0, 2) becomes an alternate critical path, and reducing the duration of (1, 2), even if possible, would not affect project duration. Further examination of the new 20-day project will show that activity (1, 4) has also become part of the critical path. Table 9.10 gives all of the critical paths on the 20-day project and the associated cost slopes.

To reduce the project below a 20-day duration requires that the same number of days be removed from each critical path. By this point, the reader should be well aware of why a computerized bookkeeping process for CPM planning would be a real aid. In path 1, a day can be cut from activity (1, 4) at an additional cost of $30. In paths 2 and 3, the best alternative is to cut one day from activity (2, 4) at a cost of $90. Thus, a 19-day schedule can be achieved at a total premium of $120. Is this better than expediting activity (0, 1) in paths 1 and 2 at a cost of $70 and activity (0, 2) in path 3 at a cost of $80? Since that alternative would cost $150, the answer is yes. But is this the best that can be done?

We will now demonstrate an alternative that illustrates perhaps the most important feature of PERT/CPM analysis. Suppose activities (0, 1) at $70/day and (2, 4) at $90/day were both reduced by one day. This represents a total incremental cost of $160, and it does remove a one-day duration from all three critical paths. But, at the same time, activity (1, 2) can also be allocated one day of slack, saving $50. Thus, the overall incremental cost of this alternative is not $160, but rather $110. This is the best alternative.

The concept of allocating slack while at the same time reducing project duration is a startling and nonobvious idea. Perhaps, as we study the diagram further, the logic becomes more apparent. Activity (0,1) is on critical paths 1 and 2 while activity (2,4) is on paths 2 and 3. Thus, paths 1 and 3 have been reduced by one day, and path 2 has been reduced by two days, making it noncritical. Therefore, if we can find an activity

TABLE 9.10. Critical Paths and Cost Slopes for 20-Day Project[a]

Path 1	Cost Slope ($/day)	Path 2	Cost Slope ($/day)	Path 3	Cost Slope ($/day)
(0, 1)	70	(0, 1)	70	(0, 2)	80
(1, 4)	30	(2, 4)	90	(2, 4)	90
(4, 5)	150	(4, 5)	150	(4, 5)	150

[a]Activity (1, 2) for path 2 not shown because it is already at its crash limit.

on path 2 which is not on either paths 1 or 3, we can allocate a day of slack to that activity without interfering with paths 1 or 3 and bringing path 2 back up to critical. That activity is (1, 2). Considerably more involved trade-off possibilities may occur in more complex networks, one can appreciate. Thus, a computer program that tests all conceivable combinations is almost essential for practical application of PERT/CPM. We will leave to the reader the development of the most economical 18-day schedule and the optimum 17-day schedule in this example See Klastorin (2003) for many more examples and illustrations of issues with PERT networks.

One general point remains to be made explicit. Why bother trimming days off the normal schedule? If trimming is desirable, exactly how much is optimum? As each day is trimmed off our example project, direct costs mount. Thus, it is apparent that such action is justified only if other, indirect cost savings more than counterbalance the increase in direct costs. Often either the indirect costs or direct costs predominate, and the project manager thus finds the minimum total cost for the project occurs at the minimum or maximum time, respectively. However, upon occasion, a partial acceleration is the best solution.

9.9   QUALITY CONTROL IN SYSTEMS PROJECTS

Many systems analysis projects exhibit no evidence of a specific quality control (QC) effort. In fact, many think tanks such as SRI have been criticized over the years for a complete lack of objective quality control on their output (Dickson, 1972). No doubt this lack grows out of SRI's origin at Stanford University. University research is totally without objective quality control because to impose QC is confused with academic freedom. The two issues are totally separate, but nevertheless confusion exists. Academic research is, in principle, totally open and subject only to the criticism of one's academic peers. But, sponsored research, especially applied research and development such as that done by SRI, is not open. It is a product, bought and owned by the client. In fact, the Stanford faculty insisted on the separation of SRI from Stanford University because of this obvious fact. However, when SRI broke free, it carried with it much academic baggage in the form of partially understood academic values. No specific criticism of SRI is intended here. The criticism is more general. It applies essentially to all think tanks with academic origins. Research organizations such as ADL and Battelle, on the other hand, which have an industrial origin, ordinarily accept their responsibility for the quality of their product.

In the early 1990s, in a reorganization of the Software Engineering Institute (SEI) located at Carnegie-Mellon, an effective QC operation was belatedly installed. It might serve as a model for other research organizations. Separate research *projects* have been gathered together in *programs*. While projects are expected to have short lives in general, perhaps one to three years, programs are of more general import and are expected to have longer periods of existence, perhaps 5–10 years. Neither the individual project managers nor their more senior leaders, the program managers, however, have responsibility for QC at SEI. That function is carried out by a small group of senior scientists, who report directly to the Institute Director. The QC board is charged with the responsibility of ensuring the validity and responsiveness of the reports produced on each project. The QC Board checks to see that required progress reports are produced on time and that the direction of research is consistent with the funding agreement with the sponsor. The Board also reviews all reports, prior to publication and/or delivery to the sponsor, for quality and accuracy.

Of course, the SEI has become famous for its Capability Maturity Models (CMM), which originally focused on software and then began working on systems engineering [SECMM (Systems Engineering CMM)], and now have integrated systems, along with software and other models, into the CMMI (CMM Integrated). The overall goal of these process models and appraisal methods is to improve and measure that ability of an organization to develop quality systems. A fundamental principal idea of this comes from TQM and the idea of sustainable processes that allow for continuous improvement. They are not without controversy with regard to their actual improvements in the "quality" of organizations and their products [see, for example, Cattaneo et al. (2001)]. Regardless, they play an important and critical role in all kinds of acquisition, especially with Federal and State governments. We refer the reader to numerous resources on these models for details (see http://www.sei.cmu.edu/cmmi/general/general.html).

By analogy to the SEI QC process, we recommend that all reports and oral presentations of a systems analysis team be reviewed by an internal QC Board prior to release to the client. This QC Board might consist of top management in a small system house, or of other Program Directors in a medium-size organization. In a larger enterprise, the QC Board might be made up of permanent senior staff, as at SEI. The QC Board, however constituted, should check for the following:

- Is the initial project plan consistent with the directions of the client?
- Will the proposed work effort, if properly carried out, result in a solution to the client's problem?
- Are process reports to the client informative, correct, well-balanced, and timely?
- Are oral presentations client-oriented? How is the Q&A handled?
- Are reports professionally organized? Is the Executive Summary complete? Is the body of the report well done? Are all statements justified and all data referenced? Is the audit trail complete? Are the results worth the price the client has paid?
- Based on our performance on this contract, is the client likely to fund follow-on and/or repeat assignments with our organization?

From a commercial point of view, the final bullet carries the message.

CASE STUDY: PROJECT MANAGEMENT

Our company has the choice of one of three projects (#1, #2, or #3; see Figure 9.4). Each project has multiple tasks, and some have requirements for two tasks to be completed before moving on to the next task. Project #1, for example, requires that Tasks A and B be complete before moving on to Task D. If Task A took 5 days and

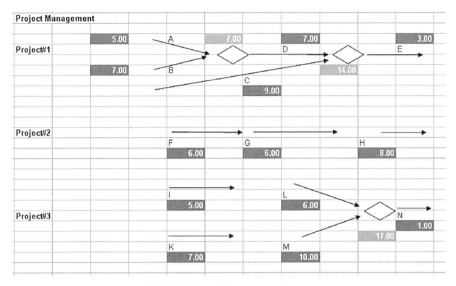

FIGURE 9.4 The three projects.

Task B took 7 days (their most likely values), then we could start Task D on the eighth day. Gray blocks show the most likely times for each task.

The completion time for each task is stochastic and is described by a triangular density function [defined by the minimum (a), most likely (b), and maximum (c) times to completion (see Table 9.11); note that the mean of a triangular density is $(a + b + c)/3$].

TABLE 9.11. Task Parameters

Task	Minimum Time to Complete	Most Likely Time to Complete	Maximum Time to Complete
A	0	5	10
B	3	7	9
C	4	9	15
D	2	7	14
E	1	3	5
F	5	6	7
G	5	6	6
H	4	8	8
I	4.5	5	5.5
K	6.3	7	7.7
L	5.4	6	6.6
M	7	10	13
N	.9	1	1.1

Profit for each of the projects is determined by the completion time in the following manner. If the project is completed in 20 days, then the profit is $1 million. For every day delivered less than 20 days, there is a $50,000 additional bonus (e.g., 1.5 days early gives a profit of $1.075 million). For every day over, there is loss of $300,000; for example, 1 day late (over 20 days) results in a profit of $700,000.

Only one project can be selected, and we are required to undertake a project. Which of the three projects should we select?

NOTES

1. Quality Circles, considered by many a fad, fell out of favor in the 1980s and were replaced by other TQM principles. Variants of quality circles are still used in many industries. See Macy and Strang (2001).
2. Alternatively, one could use a triangular distribution. See Haimes (1998) for examples and details, and see the case study at the end of this chapter.

Chapter **10**

The 10 Golden Rules of Systems Analysis

10.1 INTRODUCTION

We take it as an axiom that System Analysis (SA) is a practical and an applied activity. We can study mathematics for its intrinsic truth and beauty. But we don't do that in SA. It is fair to say that Operations Research/Management Science (OR/MS) and its close relative SA exist <u>to solve real problems for real clients</u>. No argument to this point. Originally, OR existed to bring mathematics to bear on real problems. We must remember this mathematical core, and without this core of mathematics, SA would have been delayed in its trek into the university world. Nevertheless, if only the mathematics of SA is emphasized, divorced from the client's real-world problem, we lose the whole point. The tools of SA are important, but they are not the product. The product is produced by using the tools of SA for solving real-world problems in the service of real clients. An essential complement to the tools and a component of SA is systems thinking (see Churchman, 1979).

To engage systems thinking, we believe that the analyst needs to see the world with new eyes—that of a "systems perspective." Much of the present literature in the area of systems analysis and systems engineering is very good; however, many sources fail to convey the *art* of systems problem-solving (systems analysis) by focusing instead on either operations research methods (mathematical models such as linear programming) or formal Systems Engineering. Numerous excellent books (examples: Blanchard and Fabrycky, 2006; Blanchard, 2004; Buede, 2000; Dallenbach, 1994; Eisner, 1997; Martin, 1997; Reilly, 1993; Sage and Armstrong, 2000; and Sage, 1992) and handbooks describe the processes of systems engineering, including systems engineering handbooks developed by NASA, DOD, Boeing, and so on (see reference list). Currently, there is also considerable discussion on the concept of system-of-systems (S.O.S.), that is, systems that are of significant complexity and order that they may require methodologies beyond the classic systems methodologies that are all basically derivatives of MIL-499B, a classic systems engineering military standard, which was never actually adopted. The emphasis of this book, however, is not on these formal processes of systems engineering so eloquently described in the referenced books, but on the systems thinking and the associated thought processes.

Fundamentally, we see two worlds typical in systems engineering and analysis—both are necessary:

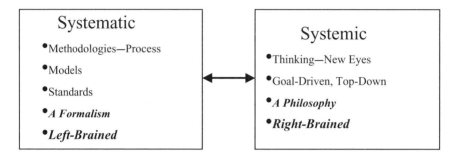

By systemic, we mean affecting the entire system or holistic.[1] By systematic, we mean a formal step-by-step process (in the most direct form, computer code is an example). An analogy could be made to the left-brain (logical; often engineers) and right-brain (artistic) thinkers. Here, we focus on problem definition and rules we have observed from practice, which is in our opinion a very difficult part of the systems process and an often neglected (or failed) part in practice.

It is important to note that we refer to a very general notion of SA, practiced in wide-ranging domains including health care, finance, policy analysis, transportation, nonprofits, and, of course, all government levels and defense industries.

Thus, we present 10 Golden Rules for Systems Analysts.

10.2   RULE 1: THERE ALWAYS IS A CLIENT

In a sense, we suppose that the first rule is warning you that it is easy to get subjective—that is, to begin fooling yourself. You begin to carve the system problem to fit your tools and to suit yourself, rather than confronting nasty reality. Abraham Maslow, one of the towering figures in American psychology, denigrates some scientists' fixation with the tools of their work (Maslow, 1969). He argues that "technique fixation" is a case of arrested psychological development. Scientific maturity requires problem-focusing, not tool-focusing.

We need a client focus to provide a reality check, to prevent ourselves from becoming subjective and taking the easy way out and also because it is the most efficient and cost-effective way of accomplishing system project goals.

Example. An analyst we were working with on an FFRDC (Federally Funded Research and Development Center) simulation modeling project said "I don't have a client, only a sponsor." In this case, the model is doomed—nobody is interested in the project or the analyst doesn't know whom it is—either way, the project is doomed to inconsequentiality without client input (see Rules 2 and 3).

10.3 RULE 2: YOUR CLIENT DOES NOT UNDERSTAND HIS OWN PROBLEM

Of all the guidelines, this one is perhaps the most difficult for the novice systems analyst to accept. The other rules are interesting perhaps, and some are fairly obvious on the surface, but this one apparently contradicts common sense. But we have heard veteran consultants put it even more strongly. A very successful practitioner once said to us on this subject:

> *"The client always lies. Sometimes he does it deliberately and sometimes apparently inadvertently, but you must never trust the client."*

Now that is what we call strong language. Let's try to see what this accomplished professional was trying to say. Why would a client deliberately lie? In the first place, we have to be clear about what we mean by <u>client</u>. Sometimes a single individual plays all of the roles involved in system analysis, but more often than not there exists some role differentiation. That is, there are a number of personalities involved in the problem solution, and the analyst must attempt to keep their roles clear. We will define and discuss these various roles in detail in Rule #10. For now, we will say that the person with whom you interact is the client, although he or she may not be the decision-maker.

Here is a simple and common example in which the client might deliberately lie. A problem exists: Perhaps an airline is having trouble with its baggage handling system, or perhaps a particular subsystem in a future space mission appears to be behind schedule, or maybe one group within a federal agency wants to let a contract for a particular design study out for bid while another group within the same agency opposes the idea.

Suppose now that a fairly high-level manager in the client organization learns about the problem and brings in an outside organization, of which you are a part, as a systems consultant to suggest a solution. Your boss maybe talks with the high-level manager, but you don't. Then your boss calls you in and asks you to go over and talk to the individual that the high-level manager of the client organization appoints as liaison. Is this unusual? No, we suggest that it is almost universal. We think you will agree that you are going to get a version of the problem that the liaison individual wants you to have. To you, the liaison individual is "the client." He or she is the only person in the whole organization you know.

Suppose that "client" is part of the problem and knows it. Is this unusual? Again, "no." It would only be human nature for that client to attempt to cover up his mistakes, out of fear for his job, from embarrassment, or out of misplaced pride. It would not be at all unusual for the client to lie deliberately and if you take the lie as the truth, you are in trouble.

The client lies accidentally or unconsciously even more often. In fact, one might say that the case of accidental or unconscious lying represents the totality of the remaining situations after deliberate lying is subtracted. This may be overstating the case, but it conveys the principle. We are dealing here with human nature, and there are always exceptions to these rules. It would be naïve of you to think that we can give you scientific certainty.

Think about the situation this way. There exists a problem in the mind of the client, and a system analyst is summoned. Obviously, the client has made an error in reality or in perception. Something is wrong. If the client knew what it was, he would fix it without seeking the analyst's advice. Thus, wouldn't it be dangerous for the analyst to accept the problem definition from someone who has admitted he/she is in error?

The physician listens to the patient recite his symptoms. But she does not accept the patient's diagnosis of the illness. The physician doesn't let the patient decide which are important symptoms and which are trivial. The physician doesn't rely solely on the patient's story, but rather goes on to gather data, take measurements, and order tests. The system analyst should be in a similar professional relationship with the client.

Finally, we note that this is a self-healing counsel. Suppose the analyst takes our advice and assumes that the initial understanding of the problem conveyed by the client is incorrect. Then if the analyst goes on to define the problem as the first step in the system analysis and it turns out that the initial problem statement was satisfactory, no harm is done. On the other hand, if the initial client statement is accepted and turns out to be wrong, the analyst has a failure on his hands.

Example. A consumer client approached us about developing a staffing simulation model in order to optimize the size and allocation of the staff at their chain of retail stores. A quick SA determined that the problem was not staffing but instead store layout and that a simulation model was premature.

10.4 RULE 3: THE ORIGINAL PROBLEM STATEMENT IS TOO SPECIFIC: YOU MUST GENERALIZE THE PROBLEM TO GIVE IT CONTEXTUAL INTEGRITY

You might think this rule is a subset of Rule 2. It is in one sense, but it also is meant to imply something more. Suppose a system analyst starts discussions with a client with full knowledge that the client doesn't understand the problem initially. Through these discussions, the analyst and the client arrive at a mutual understanding of the client's problem. It is that problem which is too specific. The analyst must generalize the client's problem first to arrive at a better understanding of the client's needs, but also to ensure that the problem context will be dealt with properly.

One of the primary ways in which system analysis differs from engineering analysis is the way in which the problem context is handled. One of the basic rules in engineering design is to abstract the problem from its context, in order to do a careful engineering study of the specific issue in isolation. This concept works for a certain class of problem, and indeed the concept of "partitioning" exceeds the realm of conventional engineering design practice. Take the word "interface," for example. The concept of an interface comes from the partitioning process in engineering design. When the engineering designer abstracts his problem from its context, he or she is left with a few, carefully defined "interfaces" or connections between the object to be designed and the rest of the world. There is undeniable strength and power in this engineering approach to design, but not all of physical reality submits to it.

The engineer seeks to optimize the parameters of objects under design in order to meet performance specifications, sometimes called the index of performance, about which we write in Rule 4. The process of engineering design takes a well-defined problem and subdivides it into components to be optimized. This may be termed a bottom-up approach. The bottom-up approach starts with the specific and works up to the general. It is effective and efficient if the problem is well-defined and the method of solution is familiar. It is not as effective in uncharted problem areas and with problems that must be defined by interactions with the client as one proceeds. There, a top-down approach is recommended. This, of course, is the area in which system analysis is practiced.

"Generalize the problem" is all well and good as academic advice, but in practice how do you do it? If you start generalizing with the client, she will likely suspect you of avoiding the problem. Furthermore, it looks expensive to the client if the analyst immediately begins to extend the problem beyond the boundaries of interest. Finally, where do you stop generalizing and start solving? After all, everything affects everything else in the end.

Naturally, there are limits to how far one can generalize. To generalize too far will broaden the topic to the point that it will be difficult to solve it in the time and with the money available. One also runs the risk of alienating the client by appearing to generalize excessively. The client will often be tightly focused on a very specific crisis. If the system analyst takes a relaxed and broad view of the client's problem, the client may object strongly. One must admit furthermore that, in the past, some system analysts have used this generalization dictum to expand the problem beyond all recognition. This usually results in a failure to provide a satisfactory solution on time and within budget. As a result, one often hears arguments against funding another study to produce another report. However:

> A system study that begs the question and has as its major recommendation another study more costly in time and money than the first is a failure. Answer the client's real question on time and within budget.

This is easy to say in theory, but it is difficult to do in practice. The notion of generalizing the question in order to lend it contextual integrity and to define it properly was considered quite bizarre when it was introduced (Gibson, 1973, 1977). It is diametrically opposed to the usual engineering bottom-up approach to problems which consists of subdividing the overall problem into easily solved elements. Yet it is clear that the top-down approach is rather a standard procedure in non-Western societies. Japanese businessmen, for example, insist on examining the contextual integrity of proposed agreements with American firms, much to the annoyance of American managers anxious to "close the deal."

Example. A large consumer products chain wanted us to mange a trade-study involving selecting an Enterprise Resource Planning (ERP) system. An initial client meeting clearly indicated that no goals were established for the ERP—the scope of the problem was much larger, and the need for an ERP not yet established.

10.5   RULE 4: THE CLIENT DOES NOT UNDERSTAND THE CONCEPT OF THE INDEX OF PERFORMANCE

Let's make sure we understand the index of performance concept ourselves before we move on to discuss our duty to inform the client about it. There is embedded here a very strong hidden assumption, about which many system analysts choose not to inform themselves. The concept of optimization is a bedrock axiom from which SA derives its shape and texture, but which is counterintuitive to almost all of human experience. We systems types go about optimizing things. We maximize profit, or mean time between failures, or minimize cost, or installation time, or whatever.

This is not the way in which the world works. Almost no one optimizes anything in real life. In real life, we try to behave so as to avoid major risks. We seek merely to better things incrementally. Discrete incrementalism is the way the world works—discrete in the sense of very tiny steps from the *status quo*. Using a hill-climbing metaphor, the discrete incrementalist climbs a hill with a bucket over his head. He can see only the slope of the hill within the immediate vicinity of his feet. Obviously the discrete incrementalist, if he or she persists in taking tiny steps in the correct direction, will find the nearest local maximum and stick there. If there is a better hill somewhere else in the parameter space, the discrete incrementalist will never find it.

The performance index (IP) is the tool used for measuring the progress the system is making toward the optimum. We have argued that to optimize a system is a radical idea and contrary to most of the folk wisdom of humankind. Nevertheless, optimization is a new and galvanic idea. Previously, people merely accepted the way things were.

Picture Frederick W. Taylor in a Bethlehem, Pennsylvania, machine shop around the turn of the century. Taylor was a bright young lad of inquiring mind and his father was a friend of the owner of the shop. Taylor was a product of the middle class and parental design had him aimed for Harvard, but he would have none of that. He preferred to work with his hands. Taylor immediately began to question current foundry and machine shop practice, but he received no satisfactory answers. He was told by the grizzled master mechanics to keep his mouth shut and to do as he was told. The way they did things was the way they had always been done.

This was the old apprentice system and Taylor would have none of it. Taylor was making himself into a systems engineer. He asked optimization questions:

"What is the best speed at which to run this lathe?"
"What is the best rate at which to load pig iron onto rail cars?"
"What is the best-sized shovel to use for moving sand, or coal, or ore?"

The conventional answer was to do it the way it had always been done or, at most, to make a small change and note the effect. Taylor, on the other hand, sought the optimum by careful experimentation. The measure of improvement he used was straightforward—productivity. He knew that as he increased machine tool speed, for example, tool wear and breakage would increase but he also knew, contrary to conventional wisdom of the time, that this wasn't the point.

Taylor could see a simple optimization hill in one parameter. He could plot productivity versus tool speed and observe that the slope increases to a certain point and then decreases. Above the optimum speed, the cost of excess tool breakage and wear and part spoilage exceeds the value of the extra production gained. This seems like a perfectly simple idea to us today, hardly worth pointing to as the start of a new science.

But, back then, a mechanic was expected to buy his own tools, so his implicit criterion was to save his tools, not to increase production! Here we have a basic controversy. What is the correct optimization criterion? We had it then in one of the first systems studies and it has continued ever since.

Taylor and the shop owner wanted to increase productivity in order to increase profits. The machinists wanted to minimize their out-of-pocket costs for tools, and furthermore they wanted to "preserve the work." The workers knew if the day came that no more work was available, they would be laid off. Note how deeply discrete incrementalism penetrates. To slow down <u>will</u> preserve the work, on <u>this</u> contract. In the long run, of course, the policy is destructive to job security.

One can't count on shop managers to understand what is going on either, as Taylor found throughout his career. Managers have an implicit picture of a well-run shop. It is clean, neat, and orderly. People work quietly and steadily. No running and shouting, no workers sitting idle, no tools breaking and no emergencies. Just smooth, steady production. The implicit IP of these managers is a shop that is easy to manage, not one that maximizes productivity. But Taylor's shops weren't always like that. His index was productivity, and the shops he managed didn't always look well-ordered.

What we have been trying to portray here in this small, isolated anecdote are a few of the differences between the systems approach and discrete incrementalism. We have already noted several facts. First, in the systems approach there must be a distinct, quantifiable measure of performance. In Taylor's shop practice, it was productivity. Second, we saw a refusal by various stakeholders to accept the proposed index of performance. Third, we saw that often the acceptance of the index of performance may require changes in the conventional way of doing things. In shops managed by Taylor, workers did not have to supply their own tools. On the other hand, they did not have the right to go about their jobs in the way they felt best. They did it Taylor's way or they were fired.

Now we are grappling with the fourth rule. As a system analyst, you are in the business of optimization. First, you obtain from the client the goals of the system. This may sound easy enough, but it is perhaps your most difficult task. Then, you obtain from the client an agreement on the measure of performance. No longer can the criterion be left implicit. It must be explicit and measurable. The client usually thinks he understands the goal of the system; that is, he thinks he knows what he wants, although the second rule says he doesn't. The client usually does not think he understands the concept of the index of performance, and in this the fourth rule says he is correct.

We system types understand that one must quantify the IP so that we can rank order the effect produced by each trial solution or "scenario," and thus be able to recommend the optimum to the client. This wasn't necessary in the good old days of discrete incrementalism. Then, the decision-maker needed merely say that a given change would likely produce an improvement over the *status quo*. Political science has never felt the need unfailingly to connect a means of measurement and a quantitative index to every policy recommendation.

Take the legal profession as an example. Is there any evidence available of the effect of jail sentence length on subsequent behavior of criminals? Would a lawyer or judge think to request such evidence? No, of course not. So we regularly incarcerate individuals at an annual cost *per capita* of more than the annual tuition at Harvard, without really knowing or even caring about the marginal impact on behavior? Yes.

All in all, optimization and its measuring stick, the index of performance, provide major conceptual barriers between the system analyst and the client. In addition to the conceptual barrier, there remains the problem of making meaningful measurements.

Critics of SA, such as Hoos for example, make much of the fact that indices chosen are not always directly linked to real objectives (Hoos, 1972). Rather, criteria are sometimes used because they are easy to observe. This is a valid objection. Hamilton et al. (1969) give an example of this fallacy. In a systems study of the recreation potential of the Delaware River basin, the systems team felt it wise to include an index of the purity of the river water. A perfectly acceptable part of a reasonable performance criterion, one would have to agree. The team found that sewage engineers often use the percent of dissolved oxygen (DO) in water as representative of its condition. Thus, the team used the DO content in the Delaware River as the index for recreational potential of the basin. Hamilton argues, and one would tend to agree, that this simplistic criterion hardly represents adequately the overall recreation potential of the entire basin.

On the other hand, this should not be turned into a contest. The systems analyst should not say to the policymaker, "I can measure anything you pick as your goal." This simply isn't true. The analyst and the policymaker should agree in advance on a criterion that is both meaningful and measurable.

Example. A call center that we were consulting for was focused on measuring performance of its call representatives by a measure RPC (right party connect). Again, a quick goal definition exercise and early iteration SA showed that RPC was not related to their main objective—making a profit.

10.6 RULE 5: YOU ARE THE ANALYST, NOT THE DECISION-MAKER

There seems to be a fairly standard cycle of emotions through which system analysts put themselves as they deal with an assignment. The first is fear. It seems only natural for a normal person to approach a system problem with nervousness and fear. After all, the client organization is often well known and thought to be competent, and the specific individual client(s) is/are well-paid and experienced people. If they are having trouble, maybe the analyst won't be able to help either.

As the first meeting progresses, the issue often looks more and more complex. Sometimes, it is apparent from the very first that the client has an axe to grind or has a desired answer in mind. But confusion generally reigns. After the client meeting, the system team talks things over and various ideas emerge. Seldom, if ever, is there agreement at this point as to the real problem. If an apparent, well-defined problem emerges too quickly, analysts should suspect that it is not the real problem. See the Second Rule.

Gradually though, sometimes after much effort, the issue does clarify itself in the minds of the analysts. Now different emotions often take hold; they are arrogance and disdain. How could the client be so stupid as to get himself in this scrape? If he had only done thus-and-so, or avoided such-and-such, this mess would never have happened. And "thus-and-so" or "such-and-such" usually are perfectly standard prescriptions of good management techniques or good engineering design or even just common sense. Notice the implication here that the analyst will *not* have to use advanced or esoteric techniques to solve the typical client's problem.

If an inexperienced analyst is permitted to make the next client presentation, it is almost inevitable that he or she will let the client see this developing disdainful attitude and feelings will get hurt. The client will be hurt by the attitude of disdain, the SA enterprise will be hurt when it is disengaged, and the young analyst will be hurt when he or she is demoted.

It seems almost impossible for the young analyst to overcome this personality deficiency except through experience. It really is evidence of the young analyst's insecurity working itself out of course, but the client won't pay for that. It seems to be totally unconscious and even if the young analyst is warned about it in advance, he can't seem to stop trying to make mincemeat of the client. Thus:

> The analyst must take care of the client. The analyst isn't there to get the client fired. Save the client's job.

The third psychological stage in the maturation of the system analyst, following fear and then arrogance, is one in which the analyst begins to identify so closely with the client's problem that the analyst decides what must be done and begins to play an advocacy role. Identification with the client or the patient is not at all rare in the healing professions, and there is no reason to be surprised when it happens to us. One of the reasons why SA should be practiced in a team setting is to help cancel out this individual analyst bias and subjectivity. Remember, you are not the decision-maker. It is not your place to decide what to do.

By the same principle, as the system analyst, you must <u>internalize</u> the problem. You must be ready to lead the charge, to take the first test flight or test dive. You must follow through by producing a complete transition scenario as part of the final report. And this transition scenario must be prepared with all of the care you would take if your career rested on the success of the project. You must take care of the client.

Example. An analysis case used by the authors with students illustrates this concept very clearly. Students are asked to perform an analysis on a new Wal-Mart store being built in their town. If a student has a preconceived notion of Wal-Mart (such as "I hate/love Wal-Mart"), then they are incapable of performing an objective analysis.

10.7 RULE 6: MEET THE TIME DEADLINE AND THE COST BUDGET

Sometimes we think that people who are attracted to systems analysis are afraid to face reality. Many students can't wait to get to practice their profession. Education majors want to teach, MBAs and commerce students want to make money, engineers want to build things, and computer scientists want to write computer software, but systems students seem only to want more time and money to do another study.

We don't want to solve the client's real problem; we want to tinker some more. Our focus all too often is not a problem to be solved and a better world for the solution. Our focus is the final report. See the Fifth Rule. Unfortunately, the final report often doesn't reveal the truth, it just explains why we did such an inadequate job thus far in the study and why we need more time and money to do a better job in the proposed follow-on analysis.

One of the reasons that some clients go into hysterics if we tell them we are "generalizing" their problem and taking a "top-down approach" is that they suspect this is a trick to avoid facing hard reality. They conclude that we won't finish the study on time and intend to ask for more time and money.

Generalizing the problem isn't a way of avoiding reality, it is a way of coming to grips with it. We must answer the client's real question, on time and within budget. This presents difficulties of course. Think about it this way. The problem probably is ill-defined or the system analyst wouldn't have been hired in the first place. If the problem were well-defined, the client would have solved it himself or handed it to a specialist for solution. The analyst's first task is properly to define the problem, a job the client probably has muffed. So why shouldn't problem definition alone be worth something? It is really. This is the most difficult systems task. After the problem has been defined properly, the issue space narrows and sharper, more straightforward analytic tools become available.

A system study is never really finished. There is always more to do, more scenarios to be produced, more data to be collected, more things to look into, and so on. But the analyst who asks for more time and money to follow up on these will be giving the impression of incompleteness, unless he or she is very careful. We recommend that the decision-maker always refuses to provide more time and money, except under the following carefully defined situations.

As part of the system study, one must always provide a sensitivity analysis and a critical incident analysis. A <u>sensitivity analysis</u> is an examination of the effect on the solution, as system parameters are varied about their assumed set points. Typically, one finds that small variations in most of the system parameters do not affect the outcome significantly. In fact, the analyst should deliberately search for and recommend such "robust" solutions. However, on occasion, it is necessary to recommend to the client a solution containing certain parameters that do have a major impact on the IP. If this is the case, the analyst should recommend to the client a more careful evaluation of these (few and specific) sensitive parameters.

A <u>critical incident analysis</u> is also part of the validation step in a well-conducted SA. The recommended solution for any problem contains many assumptions—for example, the set points of the various system parameters. The SA also contains assumptions concerning the problem environment. The critical incident analysis should contain an evaluation of the effect of any major "off-center" incidents in the problem environment. For example, most urban mass transit studies in the past 20 years assume federal cost-sharing of construction. A change in the percent of this cost sharing would certainly be a critical incident. This whole area is now becoming more prominent and is coming to be called Risk Assessment and Risk Management.

The final report should discuss the major critical incidents ranked by the intensity of the impact. Intensity is the product of the cost of the impact and the probability of its occurrence. If the intensity of one or two of these critical incidents looms very large, the analyst should recommend an additional effort to tie down these estimates more firmly. Of course, if many of the critical incidents have a major potential impact, or if there is a high sensitivity of the outcome to many parameters, the solution is very fragile and should only be recommended in those terms.

So, if we recommend that more time and money be spent, we must be extremely careful to focus very tightly on the way the extra resources will be used <u>and</u> the expected value of the resulting information. This focusing is essential if the analysis is to have credibility with the client.

Example. The concept of ignoring critical incidents, often missed in sensitivity analysis, is typical in many SA activities. Consider the loss of the space shuttle Columbia: Sensitivity analysis was beyond the scope of the foam impact analysis models. However, consideration of a critical incident of a piece outside the scope of the model was warranted, but not considered.

10.8 RULE 7: TAKE A GOAL-CENTERED APPROACH TO THE PROBLEM, NOT A TECHNOLOGY-CENTERED OR CHRONOLOGICAL APPROACH

Obviously, the proper place to start solving a systems problem is at the beginning, right? Wrong. The correct place to start is at the end. We call the step-by-step approach of problem-solving "the chronological approach" because in it we ask, "What happens first?" and we analyze that step. Then we ask, "What happens second?" and so on. We suppose one could say that this is discrete incrementalism applied to the solution process. The chronological approach seems so logical and straightforward that it might be called part of the folk wisdom of humankind. One might also note in passing that if the system approach to problem-solving simply were a collection of folk wisdom, it would not be novel or worth talking about. The problems with the chronological approach are two in the main. The first problem is that it requires the exploration of many blind alleys.

The goal-centered approach appears to be wasting time at the beginning, and it frustrates its practitioners by preventing the release of tension and anxiety to get going. You remember as a kid getting ready to make a family trip in the car. Mom and Dad were trying to remember if they had packed everything and you were jumping around saying, "Let's go! Let's go!" Engineers are like that. They want to start producing computer code without flow charting, and they want to start designing before they understand the problem.

> "Let's doodle around here on the board a bit, just to get the juices flowing."
> "Let's just run a few rough calculations to see what we've got here. Just some back-of-the-envelope calculations, O.K.?"

Not O.K. These early scribblings have a way of committing the group prematurely. Usually, early ideas are conventional solutions and they unconsciously freeze out unconventional solutions. The options field gets narrowed without anyone really knowing it. Note that we are making a strong claim here. We are going further than saying merely that a follow-up to trial-and-error technical suggestions is a waste of time and money. We are saying:

> The technological approach tends to produce an artificially narrow options field and may result in exclusion of superior solutions.

That is the second problem with the chronological approach.

We might want to ask the following question here. Why does conventional wisdom suggest the incremental approach, if it is so apparent that it won't work? We think the answer is contained in the phrase in a preceding paragraph, "Choices keep presenting themselves and without something to go on . . . ." Folk wisdom tells us how the human tribe has handled similar problems previously, so we do have "something to go on." But trial and error is simply too expensive when we confront a new problem, in which we have nothing previous from which to proceed.

Example.   In designing a Traffic Management Center (TMC), our clients took a starting position of a computer platform choice. Considerable effort was needed to get them to first consider the goals and measures and then consider alternatives.

10.9   RULE 8: NONUSERS MUST BE CONSIDERED IN THE ANALYSIS AND IN THE FINAL RECOMMENDATIONS

"Beggar thy neighbor" is not a satisfactory system design philosophy. Of course, so boldly put, no one would agree that this is part of her design value system, but by intention or not, it is a design value often used. On the other hand, one would suppose that it is not part of a normal system design requirement to leave the nonuser <u>better</u> off than before, but we will see that this is sometimes precisely the demand.

Let's start with an easy one. How do you feel about graveyards? Many modern middle-class agnostics in America feel that graveyard ostentationism is quite tasteless, and even nominal believers grow uncomfortable at the huge sums of money sometimes spent on necrology in past eras, and even today in some areas. So let's say you are a city planner with a responsibility for urban freeway location. You are aware of the tendency to ram freeways downtown through poor and rundown neighborhoods. Highway planners don't want to discriminate racially; it's just a matter of economics and property values.

But, suppose you have another option. What do you think about running the freeway through cemeteries? Naturally, the graves would be relocated, and so on. Would there be any major objections do you think? Freeway planners in Baltimore and other American cities found to their surprise that the outcry was loud and continuous. Could this have been anticipated had these planners not been so egocentric? Yes, we think so. They could have found out, perhaps by asking the people themselves, or by consulting anthropologists or sociologists.

What's the point of all this? To make our readers uncomfortable? Perhaps. But our conscious purpose is to suggest that:

> The system analyst should respect the value system of non-users and not project his/her value system on others.

Please don't try to decide for the citizens matters over which they should have a say. Don't do public system planning in private. See the Tenth Rule.

Now we'll turn to the other side of the matter. We have to recognize that nonusers are sometimes unreasonable. Many anti-nuclear power protesters are unreasonable, although it must be said that the pro-nuclear fraternity brought the problem on itself. There is no reason why nuclear power plants can't be designed and operated to be among the safest man-made objects in the universe. That they have not been so designed and operated is due to the ignorance and carelessness of the Nuclear Regulatory Commission and utility executives, as well as the original designers. We engineering professors also must bear part of the burden and shame as well. We failed in our obligation of training young nuclear engineers in their public duty and we failed to call attention to potential problems before they became real ones. Our failure is all the more serious, because we have been given tenure so that we could speak out without fear on such matters.

So damage not the nonuser, but let's try to be reasonable, O.K. guys?

Example. The Snail Darter and its impediment on the Tennessee Valley Authority is well-known and a classic, if not extreme, example of a non-user. Another example involves a grocery store in Washington, D.C., that added an oppressive security system to stop theft. Neighborhood residents, who were not considered, were offended and picketed the store, resulting in a shutdown.

10.10   RULE 9: THE UNIVERSAL COMPUTER MODEL IS A FANTASY

You can't get out of a computer model any more than you put into it. This doesn't mean, however, that you can't learn some surprising things from a computer model. We have here the same situation as we have with any mathematical relationship. By definition, all of the results or "solutions" of a mathematical relationship are implied by the relationship itself. But, that doesn't mean you know all of the solutions when you write the mathematical equation. The same is true of a computer model, which, after all, is simply an electronic way of writing equations. What does the mathematics care, whether you write it in ink on paper or write it with electrons in a computer? But it surprises us how few observers recognize this rather obvious fact about computer models.

Of course, the computer can plot very rapidly the solution trajectory for any desired parameter settings and any input and initial conditions. And therein lies its power. But this power is deceiving. It persuades the uninitiated that the computer is a very bright machine indeed. They imagine that one can ask the "giant brain" questions on any subject and get answers, which is nonsense. One can query the "giant brain" only on a very limited set of predetermined and preprogrammed matters and over a very limited range of prestored data values.

The curse of dimensionality is always present in large computer models. What is a reasonable level of detail for the computer to handle for one geographic cell is difficult for 100 cells, and it may be almost impossible for 10,000 cells. The system modeler is usually attracted to the generalized sweep of the model, but she should remember that the client will test the model by specific, individual questions. To provide one more level of detail does not merely add a few more lines of code it won't merely double the size of the program, it may increase its size by a factor of 1,000 or more.

Example. Typical of this quandary is the development of military simulations. It is often the goal to develop the all-encompassing computer-based simulation system; however, repeated attempts have shown that an integrated system of multiple simulation types (hardware and software), humans in the loop, and actual hardware is necessary.

10.11   RULE 10: THE ROLE OF DECISION-MAKER IN PUBLIC SYSTEMS IS OFTEN A CONFUSED ONE

We have referred informally to several roles played by individuals and groups in system analysis. We have mentioned the analyst and his team, the client, and the sponsor. But there are others involved, such as the stakeholders, promoters, opponents, initiators, and advisors, and some authors even mention ghosts. The Tenth Rule says that individuals confuse their roles, thus complicating life for the analyst. This role confusion extends to the analyst himself and the Fifth Rule addresses that point. The Rule explicitly mentions public SA, but corporate and military SA also suffer from this problem.

Let's see if we can define the major role types involved in a typical SA. It is true that role titles are sometimes used interchangeably. Yet each has a slightly different meaning, and so one loses precision and introduces ambiguity by failing to maintain the inherent distinctions.

- The Analyst, or "systems analyst," is the professional who aids those involved with a problem to order the alternatives and decide on a course of action. The analyst should be neutral and objective and should have no stake in the outcome. Yet this counsel of perfection sucks the life and juice from reality. The analyst cannot surmount his own value system and would thus be best advised to declare it to himself and the client when it seems to intrude.

- The Client is a person or group with whom the analyst interacts during goal definition. The client usually receives the final report and sometimes pays the bill. In all probability, the client is affected by the outcome and is thus a stakeholder. The client may also be empowered to choose from among the options offered by the analyst and is thus the decision-maker, but not always. A distinction between client and decision-maker occurs if the analyst is told to deal with the client but the client is not empowered to make the final decision concerning goals and options.

- Stakeholders are all those affected by the system. They may be users or non-users. They need not be clients or decision-makers. Stakeholders may be major or minor, and the ways in which they interact with a large-scale system are myriad.

- The Sponsor pays the bill. The sponsor is usually the decision-maker and may or may not be the client. The sponsor is usually a stakeholder.

- The Decision-Maker chooses from among the options. Thus, the decision-maker must choose the particular index of performance.

One of the most common problems in SA, we find, is figuring out who is whom. Quite often, even before the contract is awarded perhaps, the analyst may be asked to give an initial presentation to a room full of people, under tight time constraints. It isn't always easy to find the sponsor or the decision-makers. We *have* observed that they don't usually sit at the front of the room and they usually don't ask questions. Thus, we suggest you don't get too involved with the vocal critic in the front row, to the point of neglecting others more diffident. However, someone who interrupts your presentation or cuts you off (sob!) is probably revealing his or her power status.

There are almost always ghost actors and hidden agendas. This has been true in all of the system studies which we have been associated with during our careers.

Example. Recent construction of a parking complex at our University brought this issue out—the new garage involved the city, the county, University officials, VDOT (Virginia Department of Transportation), citizens, employees, business owners, and so on, and at many of the decision points it was not clear what group was in what role, resulting in legal challenges, protests, and so on (Rule 8 also came into play: A gravesite was discovered on the parking complex location).

In our experiences, these rules have been invaluable as guidelines for the practice of systems analysis and the teaching of students in systems engineering. We believe that an outstanding systems engineering process, without keeping in mind these rules, is at risk.

Thus, it is done.

NOTES

1. A wide reaching term, designating views in which the individual elements of a system are determined by their relations to all other elements of that system. Being highly relational, holistic theories do not see the sum of the parts as adding up to the whole. In addition to the individual parts of a system, there are "emergent," or "arising," properties that add to or transform the individual parts. As such, holistic theories claim that no element of a system can exist apart from the system in which it is a part. Holistic theories can be found in philosophical, religious, social, or scientific doctrines (*source*: Public Broadcasting Service).

References

CHAPTER 1

Anonymous (1972). East–west think-tank bovn. *Science*, Oct. 13; see also www.iiasa.ac.at/.

Anonymous (1975). Lawrence Klein and his forecasting machine. *Fortune*, March, p. 152ff.

Anonymous (2005a). After the fall: Soaring house prices have given a huge boost to the world economy. What happens when they drop? *The Economist*, June 16.

Anonymous (2005b). Little caution in Virginia. *Washington Post*, March 13, p. B06.

Birkenhead, E. (1962). *The Professor and the Prime Minister*, Houghton Mifflin, Boston.

Black, H. S. (1934). Stabilized feedback amplifiers. *Bell Syst. Tech.*, June.

Blanchard, B. (2004). *Systems Engineering Management*, Wiley, Hoboken, NJ.

Blanchard, B., and Fabrycky, W. J. (1998). *Systems Engineering and Analysis*, Prentice-Hall, Englewood Cliffs, NJ.

Bode, H. W. (1945). *Network Analysis and Feedback Amplifier Design*, Van Nostrand, New York.

Brewer, G. D. (1973). *Politicians, Bureaucrats and the Consultant*, Basic Books, New York.

Brown, D., and Scherer, W. (2000). A survey of systems engineering programs. *IEEE SMC Trans.*, May, pp. 204–212.

Copley, F. B. (1923). *Frederick W. Taylor, Father of Scientific Management*, 2 volumes, Harper, New York.

Daellenbach, H. (1994). *Systems and Decision Making: A Management Science Approach*, Wiley, New York.

Dickson, P. (1971). *Think Tanks*, Ballantine Books, New York.

How to Do Systems Analysis. By John E. Gibson, William T. Scherer, and William F. Gibson
Copyright © 2007 John Wiley & Sons, Inc.

Ellul, J. (1964, 1973). *The Technological Society*, A. A. Knopf, New York; original French in 1954.

Flood, R., and Carson, E. (1993). *Dealing with Complexity*, 2nd edition, Plenum Press, New York.

Gibson, J. E. (1977). *Designing the New City*, Wiley, New York, p. 4.

Goode, H. H., and Machol, R. E. (1957). *System Engineering*, McGraw-Hill, New York.

Haefele, E. T. (Ed.). (1969). *Transport and National Goals*, Brookings Institute, Washington, D.C. See especially R. Weisskopf, The Colombian experience, 1950–62, pp. 122–176; and E. F. Haefele, Transport planning and national goals, pp. 177–193.

Hall, A. D. (1962). *A Methodology for Systems Engineering*, Van Nostrand, Princeton, NJ.

Harrod, R. F. (1951). *The Life of John Maynard Keynes*, St. Martin Press, London.

He, W., and Schachter, J. P. (2003). *Internal Migration of the Older Population: 1995–2000*, CENSR-10, United States Census 2000, August.

Herbert, G. R. (1968). High-speed ground transportation—a research challenge. *Proc. IEEE*, Vol. 56, No. 4, pp. 487–492.

Hoos, I. R. (1972). *Systems Analysis in Public Policy*, University of California Press, Berkeley, CA.

Honour, E. (1998). INCOSE: History of the International Council on Systems Engineering. *Syst. Eng.*, Vol. 1, No. 1, pp. 4–13.

James, H. M., Nichols, N. B., and Phillips, R. S. (1947). *Theory of Servomechanisms*, McGraw-Hill, New York.

Klein, L. R. (1950). *Economic Fluctuations in the U.S., 1921–1941*, North Holland, Amsterdam.

Klein, L. R., and Goldberger, A. S. (1955). *An Economic Model of the U.S., 1929–1952*, North Holland, Amsterdam.

Koestler, A. (1971). *The Ghost in the Machine*, Gateway Edition, Henry Regnery Co., Chicago, 1971, Chapter 3.

Leontief, W. W. (1941). *The Structure of the American Economy, 1919–1939*, Oxford University Press, New York.

Maslow, A. M. (1969). *The Psychology of Science*, Regnery, Chicago.

McGregor, D. (1960). *The Human Side of Enterprise*, McGraw-Hill, New York.

Morse, P. M. (1970). The history and development of operations research. In *The Challenge to Systems Analysis*, G. J. Kelleher (Ed.), Wiley, New York, Chapter 3.

Rechtin, E., and Maier, M. (1997). *The Art of Systems Architecting*, CRC Press, New York.

Sage, A. P. (1992). *Systems Engineering*, Wiley, New York.

Sage, A., and Armstrong, J. (2000). *Introduction to Systems Engineering*, Wiley, New York.

Smith, B. L. R. (1966). *The RAND Corporation*, Harvard University Press, Cambridge, MA.

Stiglitz, J. E. (1966). *The Collected Scientific Works of P. A. Samuelson*, MIT Press, Cambridge, MA.

Stockfisch, J. A. (1970). The genesis of systems analysis with the bureaucracy. In *The Challenge to Systems Analysis*, G. J. Kelleher (Ed.), Wiley, New York, Chapter 2.

Stockwell, J. (2005). Red-light cameras stop rolling in N. Va.: Police lament the end of photo surveillance. *Washington Post*, Sunday, July 3, p. C03.

Szanton, P. L. (1972). Systems problems in the city. *Operational Research*, Vol. 20, pp. 465–473.

Taylor, F. W. (1911). *Shop Management*, McGraw-Hill, New York.

Teil, H., Bork, J. C. G., and Kloek, T. (1965). *Operations Research and Quantitative Economics*, McGraw-Hill, New York.

Tominson, R., and Kiss, I. (Eds.). (1984). *Rethinking the Process of Operational Research & Systems Analysis*, Pergamon Press, Oxford.

U.S. Department of Commerce (1967). Research and Development for high speed ground transportation. *Clearinghouse for Federal Scientific and Technical Information,* PB 1739, March 11.

U.S. Department of Commerce (1974). *Survey of Current Business*, Vol. 54, No. 2, February.

White, D. J. (1985). *Operational Research*, Wiley, New York.

CHAPTER 2

Anonymous (2004). The seed of Apple's innovation. *Business Week Online*, Oct. 12.

Business Week, Sept. 1. 1975, p. 37ff.

Chestnut, H. (1965). *System Engineering Tools*, Wiley, New York.

Dewey, J. (1933). *How We Think*, Heath, Boston.

Galbraith, J. K. (1967). *The New Industrial State*, Houghton Mifflin, Boston.

Gibson, J. E., Rekasius, Z. V., McVey, E. S., and Sridhar, R. (1961). A set of standard specifications for linear automatic control systems. *Trans. A.I.E.E.*, Vol. 80, Pt. II, pp. 65–78.

Hall, A. D. (1962). *A Methodology for Systems Engineering*, Van Nostrand, Princeton.

Hughes, T. (1998). *Rescuing Prometheus*, First Vintage Books, New York, Chapter V.

Jervis, R. (1997). *System Effects: Complexity in Political and Social Life*, Princeton University Press, Princeton, NJ.

Ludvissen, K. (1972). The big bust. *Motor Trend*, pp. 71–75, 94, 99, Jan.

McDonald, J. (2004). Road pricing in practice and theory. *Rev. Network Models*, Vol. 3, Issue 4, p. 347–355.

Michael, D. N. (1972). On the social psychology of organizational resistance to long-range social planning. *IEEE Trans. Syst., Man Cyberne.*, Vol. SMC-2, No. 5, pp. 578–584.

Plutarch (no date). *Lives*, Modern Library, New York.

Polya, L. G. (1957). *How to Solve It*, Doubleday-Anchor Books, Garden City.

Rothblatt, D. N. (1971). Rational planning reexamined. *J. Am. Inst. Planners*, Vol. 37, pp. 26–37.

Sapolsky, H. M. (1972). *The Polaris System Development*, Harvard, Cambridge, MA, p. 142.

Wall Street Journal, Oct. 31, 1967, p. 1, col. 6; Nov. 1, 1967, p. 2, col. 3; Dec. 24, 1970, p. 2, col. 3.

CHAPTER 3

Banfield, E. C. (1968). Why governments cannot solve the urban problem. *DAEDALUS*, Vol. 97, No. 4, pp. 1231–1241.

Beckert, Beverly A. (1986). CAD/CAM on campus. *Computer Aided Engineering*, Vol. 37, No. 1.

Fitch, L. C. (1968). Eight goals for an urbanizing America. *DAEDALUS*, Vol. 97, No. 4, pp. 1141–1164.

Geschka, H., Schaude, G. R., and Schlicksupp (1973). Modern techniques for solving problems. *Chem. Eng.*, Vol. 80, No. 18, pp. 91–97.

Gibson, J. E. (1973). Why design a new city? *IEEE Trans. Syst. Man Cybern.*, Vol. SMC-3, pp. 1–10.

Gibson, J. E. (1977). *Designing the New City*, Wiley, New York, p. 46.

Horwitch, M. (1982). *Clipped Wings, The American SST Conflict*, MIT Press, Cambridge, MA, pp. 215, 409.

Rawlinson, J. G. (1981). *Creative Thinking and Brainstorming*, Wiley, New York.

Robbins, S. P. (1988). *Essentials of Organizational Behavior*, 2nd edition, Prentice-Hall, Englewood Cliffs, NJ, p. 8.

Rokeach, M. (1973). *The Nature of Human Values*, Free Press, New York, 1973.

Stevens, C. H. (1990). *Cotechnology for the Global 90s.* Management in the 1990s Working Paper 89-074, Sloan School of Management, MIT, Cambridge, MA 02139. Cited by John D. C. Little, *Operations Research in Industry*, 1990 Morse Lecture, ORSA/TIMS Joint National Meeting, Philadelphia, October 29, 1990.

Warfield, J. N. (1973a). Intent structures. In *An Assault on Complexity*, Battelle Monograph No. 3, Columbus, OH, 1973.

Warfield, J. N. (1973b). On arranging elements of a hierarchy in graphic form. *IEEE Trans. Syst. Man Cybern.*, Vol. SMC-3, pp. 121–132.

Williams, R. M. *American Society*, 2nd edition, Knopf, New York, 1960.

CHAPTER 4

Anonymous (1987). Naval Secretary questioned U.S. Persian Gulf policies. *Washington Post*, p. A30, Sept. 6.

Argyris, C. (1982). *Reasoning, Learning, and Action*, Jossey-Bass, San Francisco.

AT&T (1971). *Engineering Economy*, 3rd edition, McGraw-Hill, New York; first edition, 1952.

Au, T., and Au, T. P. (1983) *Engineering Economics for Capital Investment Analysis*, Allyn and Bacon, Boston, Chapter 8.

Barlett, M. L. (1987). *US Marines in Lebanon*, 1982–1984, GPO.

Biderman, A. D. (1967). Social indicators and goals. In: *Social Indicators*, R. A. Bauer (Ed.), M.I.T. Press, Cambridge, MA, p. 87.

Blanchard, B. S., and Fabrycky, W. J. (2006). *Systems Engineering and Analysis*, 4th edition, Prentice-Hall, Upper Saddle River, NJ.

Bowman, M. (2003). *Applied Economic Analysis for Technologists, Engineers, and Managers*, Prentice Hall, Upper Saddle River, NJ, Chapter 7.

Bussey, L. E. (1978). *The Economic Analysis of Industrial Projects*, Prentice-Hall, Englewood Cliffs, NJ.

Churchman, C. W. (1979). *The Systems Approach and Its Enemies*, Basic Books, New York.

DeGroot, M. (1970). *Optimal Statistical Decisions*, McGraw Hill, New York.

de Neufville, R., and Stafford, J. H. (1971). *Systems Analysis for Engineers and Managers*, McGraw-Hill, New York, p. 176.

Fisher, I. (1930). *The Theory of Interest*, Kelley and Millman, New York.

French, D. (1981). *Forbes*, February 16, p. 38.

Haimes, Y. (1998). *Risk Modeling, Assessment, and Management*, Wiley, New York.

Heyes, A., and Liston-Heyes, C. (2005). Economies of scope and scale in green advocacy. *Public Choice*, Vol. 124, Nos 3–4, pp. 423–436.

Kerzner, H. (2001). Project *Management: A Systems Approach to Planning, Scheduling, and Control*, Wiley, New York.

Lorie, J. H., and Savage, L. J. (1955). Three problems in rationing capital, *Business*, Vol. 28, No. 4, pp. 229–239.

NIMBY, NOPE, LULU, and BANANA: A warning to independent power (not in my back yard, not on planet earth, locally undesirable land use, build absolutely nothing anywhere near anything), Maize, K. P., and McCaughey, J. (1992). *Public Utilities Fortnightly*, Vol. 130, No. 3, Aug. 1. p. 19(3).

Martinez, J. (1998). Residents Wary of Study that Says Sixth Runway at Denver Airport will Reduce Noise. *The Denver Post*, March 6, p. B-01.

Paulos, J. (1988). *Innumeracy*, Hill and Wang, New York.

Peters, R. A. (1979). *ROI: Practical Theory and Applications*, AMACOM, a Division of American Management Associations, New York.

Quade, E. S. (1975). *Analysis for Public Decisions*, Elsevier, New York, p. 250.

Remer, D., Stokdyk, S., and Van Driel, M. (1973). Survey of project evaluation techniques currently used in industry, *Int. J. Prod. Econ.*, Vol. 32, pp. 103–115.

Schwartz, S., and Vertinsky, I. (1977). Multi-attribute investment decisions: A study of R and D project selection. *Management Sci.*, Vol. 24, No. 3, pp. 285–303.

Sheib, M. (1981). Reagan's nuclear reactions, *Newsweek*, Jan. 12, pp. 62–64.

Spivak, C., and Bice, D. (2000). *Milwaukee J. Sentinel*, July 16.

Warfield, J. (1976). *Societal Systems: Planning, Policy, and Complexity*, Wiley, New York (also 1989, Intersystems Publishing).

Whitmore, C. W. (2005). Noise pollution assessment of the Morgantown Municipal Airport: An evaluation of the present airport and the proposed expansion. MA Thesis, Department of Geography & Geology, University of West Virginia, p. 5.

Wohl, M. (1979). Common misunderstandings about the internal rate of return and net present value economic analysis methods. *Transport. Res. Rec.*, Vol. 731, pp. 1–19.

Wohl, M. (1981). New ranking procedure and set of decision rules for method of internal rate of return. *Transport. Res. Rec.*, Vol. 828, pp. 3–5.

CHAPTER 5

Adams, J. (1986). *The Care & Feeding of Ideas: A Guide to Encouraging Creativity*, Addison-Wesley, New York.

Anonymous (1971). Chesapeake Bay. *Science*, Vol. 172, May 21, pp. 825–830.

Babcock, D. L. (1972). Assumptions in Forrester's Urban Dynamics Model and their implications. In K. Chen (Ed.), *Urban Dynamics Extensions and Reflections*, San Francisco Press, San Francisco, pp. 57–70.

Barkhi, R., Jacob, V. S., and Pirkul, H. (2004). The influence of communication mode and incentive structure on GDSS process and outcomes. *Decision Support Syst.*, Vol. 37, No. 2, pp. 287–305.

Boulding, K. (1985). *The World as a Total System*, Sage Publications, Beverly Hills, CA.

Bransford, J., and Stein, B. (1984). *The Ideal Problem Solver: A Guide for Improving Thinking, Learning, and Creativity*, Freeman & Company, New York.

Bui, T. X., and Jarke, M. (1986). Communications design for co-op: A group decision support system. *ACM Trans. Inf. Syst.*, Vol. 4, No. 2, pp. 81–103.

Chen, K. (Ed.). (1972). *Urban Dynamics Extensions and Reflections,* San Francisco Press, San Francisco, pp. 15–42.

Cougar, D. (1995). *Creative Problem Solving for Opportunity Finding*, Boyd & Fraser, New York.

de Bono, E. (1970). *Lateral Thinking: Creativity Step by Step*, Harper & Row, New York.

Desanctis, G., and Gallupe, R. B. (1987). A foundation for the study of group decision support systems. *Manage. Sci.*, Vol, 33, No. 5, pp. 589–609.

Detroit Transportation and Land Use Study (TALUS) (1969). *Growth, Change and a Choice for 1990*, 3 Vols., August.

Dewey, J. (1933). *How we Think*, Heath, Boston.

Evans, J. (1991). *Creative Thinking in the Decision and Management Sciences*, South-Western, Dallas.

Flax, S. The ten toughest bosses in America. *FORTUNE*, Aug. 6, pp. 18–23.

Forrester, J. W. *Industrial Dynamics*, MIT Press, Cambridge, MA.

Forrester, J. W. (1969a). *Urban Dynamics*, MIT Press, Cambridge, MA.

Forrester, J. W. (1969b) Rebuttal to review by J. F. Kain, *FORTUNE*, Dec., pp. 191–192.

Forrester, J. W. (1970). System analysis as a tool for urban planning. *IEEE Trans. Syst. Man Cyber.*, Vol. SMC-6, No. 4, pp. 258–265.

Forrester, J. W. (1971a). *World Dynamics*, Wright-Allen, Cambridge, MA.

Forrester, J. W. (1971b). Counterintuitive behavior of social systems. *Technol. Rev.*, Vol. 73, No. 3, pp. 52–66.

Froehle, T. C., Mullen, C., Pappas, V., Tracy, M., and Chait, J. (1999). Using group decision support systems to brainstorm and evaluate prospective consultation interventions. *Consulting Psychol. J. Pract. Res*, Vol. 51, No. 3, pp. 181–190.

Gardner, M. (1978). *aha!*, Scientific American, Inc., New York.

Geschka, H. (1983). Creativity techniques in product planning and development: A view from West Germany. *R & D Manage.*, Vol. 13, No. 4, pp. 169–183.

Geschka, H., Schaude, G. R., and Schlicksupp, H. (1973). Modern techniques for solving problems. *Chem. Eng.*, Vol. 80. No. 18, pp. 91–97.

Gibson, J. E. (1972). A philosophy for urban simulations. *IEEE Trans. Syst. Man Cybern.*, Vol. SMC-2, No. 2, pp. 129–139; also Chen, K. (Ed.) (1972). *Urban Dynamics Extensions and Reflections*, San Francisco Press, San Francisco, pp. 15–42.

Gray, J., Pessel, D., and Varaiya, P. A critique of Forrester's model of an urban area. In *Urban Dynamics Extensions and Reflections*, Chen, K. (Ed.), San Francisco Press, San Francisco, pp. 43–56.

Grove A. S. (1984). How to make confrontation work for you, *FORTUNE*, July 23, p. 73ff.

Hamilton, H. R., Goldstone, S. E., Milliman J. W., Pugh, A. L., III, Roberts, E. B., and Zellner, A. (1969). *Systems Simulation for Regional Analysis: An Application to River Basin Planning*, MIT Press, Cambridge, MA.

Harrington-Mackin, D. (1994). *The Team Building Toolkit*, American Management Association, New York.

Hoos, I. (1984). *Systems Analysis in Public Policy: A Critique*, revised edition, University of California Press, Berkeley, CA.

Kain, J. F. (1969). A computer version of how a city works. *Fortune*, Nov., pp. 241–242.

Keepin, B., and Wynne, B. (1984). Technical analysis of IIASA energy scenarios. *Nature*, Vol. 312, Dec.20/27, pp. 691–695.

Lumsdaine, E., and Lumsdaine, M. (1995). *Creative Problem Solving: Thinking Skills for a Changing World*, McGraw-Hill, New York.

Matsatsinis, N. F., and Samaras, A. (2001). MCDA and preference disaggregation in group decision support systems. *Eur. J. Op. Res.*, Vol. 130, No. 2, pp. 414–429.

Polya, L. G. (1957). *How to Solve It*, Doubleday-Anchor Books, Garden City, NY, p. 5.

Pugh, S. (1991). *Total Design: Integrated Methods for Successful Product Engineering*, Addison-Wesley, New York.

Seitz, R. (1986). The melting of 'nuclear winter.' *Wall Street Journal*, Nov. 5; and *The National Interest*, Fall.

Senge, P. M. (1990). The *Fifth Discipline: The Art & Practice of The Learning Organization*, Doubleday, New York; and several follow-up books.

Sheather, G. D. (1969). North and Central Great Lakes Region; A general systems theory analysis. In *Research Report No. 7*, Athens Center of Ekistics, Athens.

Sterman, J. D. (2000). *Business Dynamics: Systems Thinking and Modeling for a Complex World*, McGraw-Hill, New York.

Wack, P. (1985a). Scenarios: Uncharted waters ahead. *Harvard Business Review*, Sept.–Oct., pp. 73–89.

Wack, P. (1985b). Scenarios: shooting the rapids. *Harvard Business Review*, Nov.–Dec., pp. 139–150.

Wallas, G. (1962). In *A Source Book for Creative Thinking*, Parnes, S. J., and Harding, H. F. (Eds.), Scribners, New York.

Warfield, J. (1980). *The Options Field/Options Profile Method*, Internal Report, Center for Interactive Management, School of Engineering and Applied Science, University of Virginia.

Zwicky, F., and Wilson A. G. (Eds.). (1967). *New Methods of Thought and Procedure*, Springer, Berlin.

Zwicky, F. (1969). *Discovery, Invention, Research*, Macmillan, New York.

CHAPTER 6

Arrow, K. J. (1950). A difficulty in the concept of social welfare. *J. Political Econ.*, Vol. 58, pp. 328–346.

Arrow, K. J. (1963). *Social Choice and Individual Values*, 2nd edition, Yale, New Haven.

Behn, R., and Vaupel, J., (1982). *Quick Analysis for Busy Decision Makers*, Basic Books, New York.

Bell, D. E., and Farquhar, P. H. (1986). Perspectives of utility theory. *Op. Res.*, Vol. 34, No. 1, pp. 179–183.

Boorstin, D. (1974). *The Americans, The Democratic Experience*, Random House, New York, pp. 195–198.

Buede, D. (2000). *The Engineering Design of Systems*, Wiley, New York, Chapter 13.

Carlson, M., and Scherer, W. (2006). A case study in SISMAUT using BRAC 2005 military value analysis. *SIEDS 2006*, University of Virginia.

Clarke, T. E. (1974). Decision-making in technologically based organizations: A literature survey of present practice. *IEEE Trans. Eng. Management*, Vol. EM-21, No. 1, pp. 9–23.

Clemen, R., and Kelly, T. (2001). *Making Hard Decisions*, Duxbury, Pacific Grove, CA, Chapter 15.

Clemen, R., and Reilly, T. (2001). *Making Hard Decisions with DecisonTools®*, Duxbury, Pacific Grove, CA, Chapter 12.

Durant, W., and Durant, A. (1967). *The Story of Civilization*, Vol. X, Simon and Schuster, New York, p. 884ff.

Farrell, C. (2001). Boeing and the New Corporate Nomads; the behemoths are getting more mobile. That's one reason cities must work harder to attract and nurture homegrown entrepreneurs. *Business Week Online*, March 30.

Fishburn, P. C. (1970). *Utility Theory for Decision Makers*, Wiley, New York.

Fishburn, P. C. (1974). Paradoxes in voting. *Am. Politi. Sci. Rev.*, Vol. 68, pp. 537–546.

Fishburn, P. C. (1982). Nontransitive measurable utility. *J. Math. Psych.*, Vol. 26, pp. 31–67.

Fishburn P. C. (1983). Transitive measurable utility. *J. Econ. Theory*, Vol. 31, pp. 293–317.

French, (1988). *Decision Theory: An Introduction to the Mathematics of Rationality*, Elis Horwood Limited, Chichester, England.

Gee, E. A., and Tyler, C. (1976). *Managing Innovation*, Wiley, New York.

Gibson, J. E. (1977). *Designing the New City*, Wiley, New York, pp. 228–244.

Gibson, J. E. (1989). *Modern Management*, Prentice-Hall, Englewood Cliffs. NJ, p. 67ff.

Ginsberg, A. S., and Offensend, F. L. (1968). An application of decision theory to a medical diagnosis-treatment problem. *IEEE Trans. SSC*, Vol. SSC-4, No. 3, pp. 355–362.

Hämäläinenl, R. P. (2004). Reversing the perspective on the applications of decision analysis. *Decision Analysis*, Vol. 1, Issue 1, pp. 26–31.

Howard, R. A. (1976). Risk preferences. In *Readings in Decision Analysis*, 2nd edition, SRI, Palo Alto, CA, Chapter 21.

Keefer, D., Kirkwood, C., and Corner, J. (2004). Perspective on decision analysis applications, 1990–2000. *Decision Analysis*, 1.1, March, p4–22.

Keeney, R., and Raiffa, H. (1976). *Decisions with Multiple Objectives*, Wiley, New York, Chapter. 4.

Khatri, N., and Alvin, H. (2000). The role of intuition in strategic decision making. *Hum. Relat.*, Vol. 53, No. 1, pp. 57–86.

Moore, J. R., Jr., and Baker, N. R. (1969). Computational analysis of scoring models for R and D project selection. *Management Sci.*, Vol. 16, No. 4, pp. B212–B232.

Pauker, S. G. (1976). Coronary artery surgery: The use of opinion analysis. *Ann. Intern. Med.*, Vol. 85, No. 1, pp. 8–18.

Pessemier, E. A., and Baker, N. R. (1971). Project and program decisions in research and development. *R & D Management*, Vol. 2, No. 1, pp. 3–14.

Raiffa, H. (1968). *Decision Analysis*, Addison-Wesley, Reading, MA.

Saaty, T. (2003). Decision-making with the AHP: Why is the principal eigenvector necessary. *Eur. J. Op. Res.*, Vol. 145, No. 1, pp. 85–91.

Saaty, T. (1980). *The Analytic Hierarchy Process: Planning Setting Priorities, Resource Allocation*, McGraw-Hill, New York.

Saaty, T., and Vargas, L. (2000). *Fundamentals of Decision-Making and Priority Theory with the Analytic Hierarchy Process*, Analytic Hierarchy Process Series, Vol. 6.

Sage, A. P. (1977). *Methodology of Large-Scale Systems*, McGraw-Hill, New York, Chapter 7.

Sage, A. (1992). *Systems Engineering*, Wiley, New York, Chapter 7.

Shewhart, W. A. (1931). *Control of Quality of Manufactured Product.* Reprinted by SME, Economic.

Simon, H. (1978). Rational decision-making in business organizations. *Economic Sci.* pp. 343–371 (Nobel Prize Memorial Lecture, Dec. 8, 1978).

Smith, J., and Winkler, R. (2006). The optimizer's curse: Skepticism and postdecision surprise in decision analysis. *Management Sci. 52.3*, March, pp. 311–322.

Von Neumann, J., and Morgenstern, O. (1964). *Theory of Games and Economic Behavior*, Wiley, New York.

Von Winterfeldt, D., and Edwards, W. (1975). Error in Decision Analysis, etc. ONR, ARPA Rpt. 001597, Grant N0014-67-A-0269-0034, NR 197-021, April.

Wald, A. (1947). *Sequential Analysis*, Wiley, New York.

Wallenius, E., Wallenius J., and Zionts S. (2000). A study of high-level managerial decision processes, with implications for MCDM research. *Eur. J. Op. Res.*, Vol. 120, No. 3, pp. 496–510.

White, C. C., Dozono, S., and Scherer, W. T. (1983). An interactive procedure for aiding multiattribute alternative selection. *OMEGA*, Vol. 11, No. 2, pp. 212–214.

White, C. C., Sage, A. P., Dozono, S., and Scherer, W. T. (1984). Performance evaluation of a decision support system. *Large Scale Syst.* Vol. 6, 1984, pp. 39–48.

CHAPTER 7

Besterfield, D., Besterfield-Micha, C., Besterfield, G., and Besterfield-Sacre, M. (2003). *Total Quality Mangement*, Prentice-Hall, Upper Saddle River, NJ, pp. 322–342.

Gorman, M., Mehalik, M., Carlson, B., and Oblon, M. (1993). "Alexander Graham Bell, Elisha Gray and the speaking telegraph: A cognitive comparison. *History of Technology*, Vol. 15, 1–56.

Kerzner, H. (2001). *Project Management: A Systemic Approach to Planning, Scheduling, and Controlling*, Wiley, New York.

Sage, A. (1977). *Methodology for Large-Scale Systems*, McGraw-Hill, New York.

Sage, A. (1992). *Systems Engineering*, Wiley, New York.

Sapolsky, H. M. (1972). *The Polaris Systems Development*, Harvard, University Press, Cambridge, MA, pp. 145–146.

Warfield J. N. and Hill, J. D. (1971). The DELTA chart: A method for R&D project portrayal. *IEEE Trans. Eng. Management*, Vol. E-18, No. 4, pp. 132–139.

CHAPTER 8

Brooks, J. (1976). *Telephone* Harper & Row, New York, pp. 278, 279, 288–295. *Business Week*, Jan. 23, p. 39, 1971. *Business Week* Jan. 15. pp. 82, 83 (1979).

Gibson, J. E. (1981). *Managing Research and Development*, Wiley, New York, Chapter 5.

Harrington-Mackin, D. (1994). *The Team Building Toolkit*, American Management Association, New York, 1994. Senge, P. (1994). *The Fifth Discipline Fieldbook: The Art and Practice of Learning Organizations*, Doubleday, New York.

Hawken, P. (1987). *Growing a Business*, Simon & Schuster, New York: pp. 224–226.

Redmond K. C. and Smith, T. M. (1977). Lesson from Project Whirlwind. *IEEE Spectrum*, Vol. 14, No. 10, pp. 50–59, Gibson, J. E. *Managing Research and Development*, Section 2.6, "Three ISTJ Case Histories," Wiley, New York, 1981a pp. 24–31.

CHAPTER 9

Blanchard, B. S. and Fabrycky, W. J. (2006). *Systems Engineering and Analysis*, 4th edition, Prentice-Hall, Upper Saddle River, NJ.

General Electric (1964). "GE-200 Series," CPM Program, G.E. Computer Department, Nov.

Haimes, Y. (1998). *Risk Modeling, Assessment, and Management*, Wiley, New York.

Klastorin, T. (2003). *Project Management: Tools and Tradeoffs*, Wiley, Hoboken, NJ.

Goosey, M. (2004). [Edtorial]. End-of life electronics legislation—an industry perspective *Circuit World*, 30/2, p. 41–45.

Gorman, M., Mehalik, M., and Werhane, P. 2000. *Ethical and Environmental Challenges to Engineering*, Prentice-Hall, Upper Saddle Riven, NJ.

Hersey, P. and Blanchard, K. (1982). *Management of Organizational Behavior*, 4th edition, Prentice-Hall, Englewood Cliffs, NJ.

McDonough, W., and Braungart, M., (1998). The NEXT Industrial Revolution. *The Atlantic Monthly*, Vol. 282, No. 4, pp. 82–92.

Macy, M. W. and Strang D. (2001). In Search of excellence: Fads, success stories, and adaptive emulation, *Am. J. Social*, Vol. 107, pp. 147–182.

Mehalik, M. M., Gorman, M., and Werhane, P. (1996). "Design Tex, Inc (a)," *Darden Case Collection*, Darden School of Graduate Business Administration, University of Virginia, Charlottesville, V. A.

Sapolsky, H. M. (1972). *The Polaris Systems Development*, Harvard, University Press, Cambridge, MA.

Whyte, W. F. (1961). *Men at Work*, Dorsey Press, Homewood; IL, pp. 88–92.

CHAPTER 10

Blanchard, B. (2004). *Systems Engineering Management*, Wiley, New York.

Blanchard, B. S., and Fabrycky, W. J. (2006). *System Engineering and Analysis,* 4th edition, Prentice-Hall, Upper Saddle River, N. J.

Buede, D. (2000). *The Engineering Design of Systems: Models and Methods*, Wiley, New York.

Churchman, C. W. (1979). *The Systems Approach*, Laurel Press, New Yrok.

Daellenbach, H. (1994). *Systems and Decision Making: A Management Science Approach*, Wiley, New York.

Eisner, H. (1997). *Essentials of Project and Systems Engineering Management*, Wiley, New York.

Gibson, J. E. (1973). Why design a new city? *IEEE Trans. Syst. Man Cybern.*, Vol. SMC-3, pp. 1–10.

Gibson, J. E. (1977). *Designing the New City*, Wiley, New York.

Hoos, I. R. (1972). *Analysis in Public Policy*, University of California Press, Berkeley, CA.

Hamilton, H. R. Goldstone, S. E., Milliman, J. W. Pugh, A. L., III. Roberts, E. B., and Zellner, A. (1969). *Systems Simulation for Regional Analysis: An Application to River Basin Planning*, MIT Press, Cambridge, MA.

Martin, J. (1997). *Systems Engineering Guidelbook: A Process for Developing Systems and Products*, CRC Press, New York.

Maslow, A. M. (1969). The *Psychology of Science*, Henry Regnery, Chicago.

Reilly, N. (1993). *Successful Systems Engineering for Engineers and Managers*, Van Nostrand Reinhold, New York.

Sage, A., and Armstrong, J. (2000). *Introduction to Systems Engineering*, Wiley, New York.

Sage, A. P. (1992). *Systems Engineering*, Wiley New York.

Index

How to Do Systems Analysis. By John E. Gibson, William T. Scherer, and William F. Gibson
Copyright © 2007 John Wiley & Sons, Inc.